HIGHER EDUCATION ADMISSIONS PRACTICES

An International Perspective

EDITED BY

MARÍA ELENA OLIVERI

Educational Testing Service, Princeton

CATHY WENDLER

Educational Testing Service, Princeton

CAMBRIDGE UNIVERSITY PRESS

CAMBRIDGE
UNIVERSITY PRESS

University Printing House, Cambridge CB2 8BS, United Kingdom

One Liberty Plaza, 20th Floor, New York, NY 10006, USA

477 Williamstown Road, Port Melbourne, VIC 3207, Australia

314–321, 3rd Floor, Plot 3, Splendor Forum, Jasola District Centre, New Delhi – 110025, India

79 Anson Road, #06–04/06, Singapore 079906

Cambridge University Press is part of the University of Cambridge.

It furthers the University's mission by disseminating knowledge in the pursuit of education, learning, and research at the highest international levels of excellence.

www.cambridge.org
Information on this title: www.cambridge.org/9781108472265
DOI: 10.1017/9781108559607

First published 2020

Printed in the United Kingdom by TJ International Ltd, Padstow Cornwall

A catalogue record for this publication is available from the British Library.

ISBN 978-1-108-47226-5 Hardback

Contents

Figures

Tables

Contributors

Avi Allalouf is the Director of Scoring & Equating at the National Institute for Testing and Evaluation (Israel). His primary areas of research include test adaptation, differential item functioning, test scoring and equating, essay rating, quality control, and testing and society. He leads the certificate program in psychometrics and teaches at the Academic College of Tel-Aviv–Yaffo. He has served as co-editor of the *International Journal of Testing*.

Hans-Joachim Althaus has been the Director of the TestDaF-Institut (Germany) since its foundation in October 2000. He is also the CEO of the Society for Academic Study Preparation and Test Development (g.a. s.t.). He has been a researcher at the University of Tuebingen (Germany) and at the University of Wrocław (Poland). He acts as an adviser to many committees at a number of institutions concerned with language, cultural, and educational policy.

Becky Bobek is the Director of Learning, Assessment, & Navigation Experiences Research at ACT, Inc. (United States), supporting the scientific understanding of conditions and processes that influence people's education and work experiences. Her research focuses on education and career transitions, informed choices, and influences on education, career exploration, decision-making, and planning.

Cynthia Bourne is a doctoral candidate in the University of British Columbia Okanagan School of Education (Canada), as well as Manager of Learning Resources and Supports at the university. She has published in the areas of global service-learning and design thinking and has supervised five global experiences for teacher candidates in both East (Tanzania) and West (Ghana) Africa.

Jeremy Burrus is the Senior Director of the Center for Social, Emotional, and Academic Learning at ACT, Inc. (United States). He has written more than 40 journal articles, book chapters, research reports, and books. His main research interests are in developing innovative assessments of social and emotional skills.

Yoav Cohen has undertaken research in assessment, cognitive psychology, and computerized vision. He served as the CEO of the National Institute for Testing and Evaluation (Israel) and is a founding member of the Israeli Psychometric Association. His primary areas of research and development in assessment include computerized adaptive testing, test calibration and equating, essay rating, and automated essay scoring.

Thomas Eckes is the Head of the Psychometrics and Language Testing Research Department, TestDaF-Institut, University of Bochum (Germany). His research focuses on psychometric modeling of language competencies, rater effects in large-scale assessments, the development and validation of web-based language placement tests, standard-setting methods, and multivariate data analysis. He is on the editorial boards of the journals *Language Testing* and *Assessing Writing.*

Norbert Elliot is a Research Professor at the University of South Florida and Professor Emeritus of English at the New Jersey Institute of Technology (United States). A specialist in writing assessment, with publications in theory, history, and methodologies, he is most recently co-editor of *Writing Assessment, Social Justice, and the Advancement of Opportunity* (2018).

Naomi Gafni is the Director of Research and Development at the National Institute for Testing and Evaluation (Israel). Her research focuses on equating, differential item functioning, guessing, IRT parameter estimation, fairness in selection, assessment of non-cognitive attributes, and test trans-adaptation. She also teaches educational and psychological measurement at various universities in Israel.

Kurt F. Geisinger is the Director of the Buros Center for Testing and the Meierhenry Distinguished University Professor at the University of Nebraska (United States). He serves as President of the International Test Commission and is President-elect of Division 5 of the American Psychological Association. He has edited or co-edited more than 12 books and is the editor for *Applied Measurement in Education.*

Naziema Jappie is the Director of the Centre for Educational Testing for Access and Placement at the University of Cape Town (South Africa). She has held executive positions in student affairs and has served on many committees in the higher education sector. Her research and publication interests include assessments, student retention, and social justice leadership in higher education.

Mladen Koljatic retired after four decades as full professor at the Escuela de Administración, Pontificia Universidad Católica de Chile (Chile). He is currently the Vice-Chancellor of Academic Affairs at Universidad Católica Silva Henríquez in Santiago. His recent scholarly work focuses on college admissions testing, business ethics education, and social responsibility.

Nathan Kuncel is the Marvin D. Dunnette Distinguished Professor at the University of Minnesota (United States). His award-winning research has appeared in *Science*, *Psychological Bulletin* and the *Review of Educational Research*, among others. Nathan has written for the *Wall Street Journal* and *Harvard Business Review*. He is a Fellow of the American Psychological Association and the Association for Psychological Science.

Per-Erik Lyrén is an assistant professor of educational measurement in the Department of Applied Educational Science at Umeå University (Sweden). His research interests include admissions testing, score reporting, validity, test-takers' perspectives on testing, and instruments for patient-reported outcomes.

Stephanie McKeown is the Chief Institutional Research Officer at the University of British Columbia (Canada). Her background is in measurement, evaluation, and research methodology. Her research is concerned with understanding how patterns of student behavior, perceptions of their educational experiences, and institutional structures are related to educational access and persistence, social and personal development, and academic achievement.

Rob R. Meijer is a professor in the Department of Psychometrics and Statistics, Faculty of Behavioral and Social Sciences, University of Groningen (the Netherlands). His research focuses on applied psychometrics, educational and personnel selection, and decision-making through tests.

Michalis P. Michaelides is an assistant professor at the Department of Psychology at the University of Cyprus (Cyprus), teaching research methods and applied statistics. He has published over 50 articles, book chapters, and technical reports in the areas of educational assessment, psychometrics, and educational psychology.

Rochelle Michel is the Executive Director of the Independent School Entrance Exam at the Educational Records Bureau (ERB) (United States). Prior to joining ERB, she was Director of Research for higher education admissions within the Academic to Career Research Center at Educational Testing Service, where she managed the research agenda for the GRE® Program.

Robert J. Mislevy is the Frederic M. Lord Chair in Measurement and Statistics at Educational Testing Service and Professor Emeritus at the University of Maryland (United States). His research applies developments in statistics, technology, and cognitive science to practical problems in educational assessment. His work includes a multiple-imputation approach to integrate sampling and psychometric models in large-scale assessments; an evidence-centered framework for assessment design; development of simulation-based assessment with the Cisco Networking Academy; and a book on the sociocognitive foundations of educational measurement.

A. Susan M. Niessen is an assistant professor in the Department of Psychometrics and Statistics, Faculty of Behavioral and Social Sciences, at the University of Groningen (the Netherlands). She has published in the areas of admission testing, predictive validity, applicant perceptions, faking on self-report instruments, and test bias.

Ryan O'Connor is a Lead Measurement and Learning Specialist in the Assessment Design and Development Division at ACT, Inc. (United States), providing strategic vision for the evaluation of student learning on multiple dimensions. He has worked on several large-scale national and international testing programs, including *The Cognitive Abilities Test* (CogAT) and the *Programme for International Student Assessment* (PISA).

Ibrahim Oanda is the Senior Program Officer and head of the Training, Grants and Fellowship program at the Council for the Development of Social Science Research in Africa (CODESRIA). His research interests include inequalities and knowledge production in African higher education, and he has published journal articles and book chapters on these topics. He was also co-author on a book on privatization of higher education in Africa.

María Elena Oliveri is a research scientist in the Center for Academic-to-Career Readiness at Educational Testing Service (United States). She is an Associate Editor for the *International Journal of Testing*. She has published in the areas of higher education and graduate education, validity, fairness, international large-scale assessments, and innovative assessment design for populations from culturally and linguistically diverse backgrounds.

Elena C. Papanastasiou is the Associate Dean at the University of Nicosia (Cyprus), and has expertise in measurement and quantitative methods. In 2018, she became a Fellow of the Association of Educational Assessment–Europe. She also serves as a General Assembly representative in the International Educational Association, where she was elected to the Standing Committee of the organization in 2014.

Duy Ngoc Pham is an associate psychometrician at Educational Testing Service (United States). His background is in higher education and educational measurement. He has published and presented at regional and national conferences in the areas of student success, university admissions, and learning assessments.

Martha F. Pitts is the Executive Director for Higher Education at the College Board (United States) where she works with higher education leaders around the world on strategic initiatives and partnerships related to admission and enrollment. She led work with higher education on SAT® redesign and use, and also leads access and international initiatives. She previously served as Assistant Vice President for Enrollment Management and Director of Admission at University of Oregon.

Simone Pollard is an experienced professional with recruitment and admissions expertise in the K–12, undergraduate, and graduate school arenas. She has led recruitment and admissions teams at institutions in the United States. Formerly, she was the Senior Director of Business Development for the GRE® Program at Educational Testing Service.

Rosemary Reshetar is the Executive Director for Psychometrics at the College Board (United States) where she plays a critical role in overseeing psychometric work to support state and district clients and major testing programs including Advanced Placement®, SAT®, PSAT/ NMSQT®, and College Level Examination Program®. Her expertise is in developing and implementing psychometrics and assessment design solutions to support the quality and validity of assessment scores.

Hong Cong Sai is the Deputy Director of the Department of Education Quality Management, Ministry of Educational and Training (Vietnam), where he manages the Test Development and Quality Evaluation division of the department. He is also a lecturer at Vietnam National University, Hanoi. His background is in educational measurement.

Leah Sanford is an experienced director, facilitator, faculty member, and consultant in Canada whose goal is to see diversity, equity, inclusion, and anti-racism practices embedded into every community and organizational sphere. Her career, research, and publication areas, and education all lie in the fields of diversity and inclusion, equitable and social-justice driven practices, and anti-racism.

Mónica Silva is an associate researcher at the Escuela de Administración, Pontificia Universidad Católica de Chile (Chile). She and her colleague Mladen Koljatic have collaborated in several projects on business ethics education and social responsibility and have coauthored a number of local and international publications related to fairness in testing and university admissions in Chile.

Kristin Stoeffler is the Senior Learning Solutions Designer at ACTNext/ACT (United States). She is the architect of the Cross-Cutting Capabilities of the ACT Holistic Framework®. Her focus is on the design and development of twenty-first-century skill constructs, assessments, and learning solutions. Her work extends from developing classroom prototypes to leading the assessment design for PISA 2021 Innovative Domain – Creative Thinking.

Hak Ping Tam is an associate professor at the National Taiwan Normal University (Taiwan). His areas of expertise include research methodology, applied statistics, assessment in mathematics, and developing modern curriculum of mathematics via an inquiry approach. Currently, he is interested in developing approaches to automatic scoring of constructed response items.

Khue Tran is a graduate student in industrial/organizational psychology at the University of Minnesota (United States). Her research interests encompass topics related to individual differences, personality, cognitive ability, and creativity, especially in the context of selection and assessment.

Jackson Traplin is an undergraduate student in his fourth year of an Indigenous studies major at the University of British Columbia (Canada). Jackson is currently involved in a province-wide research study on the topics of Indigenous student access, mobility, and persistence in the British Columbia postsecondary school transfer system while he completes his degree.

Adrienne Vedan is Okanagan and Shuswap and a member of the Okanagan Indian Band. She is Director of Aboriginal Programs and Services at the Okanagan campus of the University of British Columbia (Canada). Adrienne has led several research studies examining the effectiveness of programs and services in support of Indigenous students on campus and how to improve and develop them further.

Matthias von Davier is Distinguished Research Scientist at the National Board of Medical Examiners (United States). Previously, he was Senior Research Director and Co-director of the Center for Global Assessment at Educational Testing Service. He is the recipient of a number of awards and honors from professional organizations. He was editor-in-chief of the *British Journal of Mathematical and Statistical Psychology* and is currently editor of *Psychometrika*. He is also co-editor of the book series *Methodology of Educational Measurement and Assessment*.

Jason Way is a senior research psychologist in the Center for Social, Emotional, and Academic Learning at ACT, Inc. (United States). His research focuses on the social and emotional skills relevant to success in educational and work contexts. At ACT, he worked on the development of the Behavioral Skills Framework and is the lead scientist for research on social and emotional skills at work.

Cathy Wendler is the Senior Strategic Advisor in the Psychometrics, Statistics, and Data Sciences Division at Educational Testing Service (United States). She has published in the areas of higher education and graduate education, validity, large-scale testing programs, English language learners, constructed-response scoring, and gender differences. She is an associate editor for *Applied Measurement in Education* and her publications include *The Path Forward: The Future of Graduate Education in the United States* (2010).

Kevin M. Williams is a managing research scientist in the Academic to Career Research Center at Educational Testing Service (United States). He has published several influential journal articles examining assessment and validity topics in the areas of personality psychology, educational psychology, clinical psychology, industrial/organizational psychology, and forensic psychology.

Christina Wikström is an associate professor in educational measurement at the Department of Applied Educational Science, Umeå University (Sweden). Her research focuses on selection to higher education and the validity of instruments used for selection purposes.

Magnus Wikström is a professor of economics at the Department of Economics, Umeå School of Business, Economics, and Statistics, Umeå University (Sweden). His research interests lie in the areas of public economics and the economics of education, where he has studied a large number of issues including school competition, childcare, and higher education.

Shu Han (Charlene) Zhang is a doctoral student in industrial and organizational psychology at the University of Minnesota (United States). Her work focuses on selection and training, with active research in personality, biodata, situational judgment tests, research methodology, and student and work criteria.

Rebecca Zwick is Distinguished Presidential Appointee at Educational Testing Service and Professor Emerita at the University of California, Santa Barbara (United States). Her areas of specialization are educational measurement and statistics, test validity and fairness, and college admissions. Her publications include *Who Gets In? Strategies for Fair and Effective College Admissions* (2017).

Series Editor's Foreword

In the last several decades, globalization has influenced the lives of all people. Business and education, as well as scientific disciplines, have all experienced the need to understand and work with people whose political, social, cultural, and linguistic origins are often very different. This has been true of psychology, education, and other social science disciplines. These developments also have important implications for the development and use of measures of human individual differences. Business and educational institutions using tests and institutions interested in certifying or accrediting test users have all experienced the challenges and opportunities generated by increased globalization.

Recognizing the need for the education of psychometricians and users of tests, Jean Cardinet spearheaded the formation of the International Test Commission (ITC) in the late 1960s and early 1970s. It was formally established in 1978. Current members include scholars and institutions from most of the European and North American countries as well as some countries in the Middle and Far East, Africa, and South America.

The major goals of the ITC are the exchange of information among members and furthering cooperation on problems related to the construction, distribution, and use of psychological measures and diagnostic tools. To accomplish these goals, the ITC has initiated a number of educational activities. The ITC has also developed and published guidelines on quality control in scoring; test analysis and reporting of test scores; adapting tests for use in various linguistic and cultural contexts; test use in general; and computer-based and internet-delivered testing; as well as a test-taker's guide to technology-based testing. The ITC publishes a journal, *International Journal of Testing*. This peer-reviewed journal seeks to publish papers of interest to a cross-disciplinary international audience in the area of testing and measurement. In 2016, the ITC led the effort to produce the *International Handbook of Testing and Assessment*.

In 2013, the ITC proposed to Cambridge University Press a series of books on issues related to the development and use of tests. The goal of the series is to advance theory, research, and practice in the areas of international testing and assessment in psychology, education, counseling, organizational behavior, human resource management, and related disciplines. This series seeks to explore topics in more depth than was possible in the *Handbook* or in any single volume. The series will explore the national and cultural idiosyncrasies of test use and how they affect the psychometric quality of assessments and the decisions made on the basis of those measures. As such, we hope the series will contribute to the quality of measurement, but that it will also facilitate the work of professionals who must use practices or measures with which they may be unfamiliar or adapt familiar measures to a local context. We have asked both ITC members and other scholars familiar with a topic and who are also familiar with the global situation related to various topics to be the editors and contributors to individual volumes.

We are especially pleased to see this series develop and are confident that the books in the series will contribute to the effectiveness of testing and assessment throughout the world. Certainly, this volume on the evaluation of students' capability to succeed in their undergraduate or postsecondary educational pursuits is timely. Increasing diversity, access, and equality of higher educational opportunities are global challenges. There is a recognition that there are different models of the higher education admissions process (e.g., meritocracy, open access, holistic) and authors in this volume explore the implications of these models for the admissions process in various parts of the world. Several chapters describe the competencies evaluated and the manner in which information from various assessments is combined/used in making admissions decisions. We hope that this sharing of different approaches will aid students and professionals in understanding admissions processes in areas of the world in which they are likely to be unfamiliar.

We hope to publish a book at least biennially and encourage scholars who might be interested in developing a book proposal that addresses assessment in an international context to talk with the series editor, the ITC President, or other ITC leaders.

Neal Schmitt

Foreword

I agreed to write the foreword for this volume about a year before the chapters composing the book actually came to pass. Then, when the editors sent me the drafts of the 19 chapters, I questioned my sanity when I had said "Yes" to reading 19 chapters in order to write just a few pages. However, I found the chapters terribly interesting, and day after day I looked forward to reading a few more chapters – an involvement I usually only experience when nearing the end of an absorbing novel. One of the primary goals of the International Test Commission is to share testing practices across borders so that we can all learn from each other. In the case of this volume, we can evaluate the admissions policies and practices of other countries in the context of our own country's cultures, practices, and Zeitgeist. We can hope to consider what works for others, why it works, and decide if such changes would help us improve.

In many, if not most, parts of the world, college attendance constitutes a life-changing experience. A relatively small proportion of those who might be eligible to attend college can do so, and in many cases it is the advantaged few rather than those who are in greatest need who are accepted. To say that admissions decisions are high-stakes is probably a considerable understatement. The basis for admissions decisions is frequently that of meritocracy. That is, those who are most able to succeed in college are admitted and those that are less likely to do so are placed on waiting lists or rejected outright. One could question whether minor differences in test scores or grade point averages are meaningful in highly competitive situations. After a number of court cases in the United States, where merit versus diversity (primarily gender, racial, and ethnic) of the class occurred, Lerner (1977) suggested a model whereby a threshold defining acceptance decisions is employed and decisions above that threshold are made randomly. Readers of this volume will learn that such approaches have been used in other countries when the percentage of students admitted to college is low, given the extremely limited resources of the country as well as financial issues for applicants. The alternative in some countries is to make the relatively inexpensive or free public colleges and universities available to the most able students. Private institutions may accept those who do not meet the high standards but who still seek advanced education. Unfortunately, such institutions are often considerably more expensive and many of the students seeking such education are among those least able to afford it.

Ultimately, two issues are most important in college admissions where meritocratic principles are invoked: validity and fairness. Validity refers to the notion that the information used to make admissions decisions that identifies those applicants as most able are indeed most likely to succeed in college and, perhaps, later in the workforce. Fairness generally refers to the effect of admissions decisions on pre-existing groups and whether some under-represented groups might be disadvantaged by the approach taken to ensure the best possible entering class. Many ways of determining fairness have been developed in the psychometric literature, however, and ultimately some combination of psychometric procedures, legal rulings, and common sense are needed to determine if approaches are truly fair for all groups. This principle is especially clear when there is a history of differential treatment for racial, ethnic, gender, religious, disability, or other groups (Bowen & Bok, 1998; Zwick, 2006).

There are many ways that higher education differs around the world. At one point in the United States there were many institutions of higher education that selected only students of a given racial, ethnic, gender, or religious group (Bowen & Bok, 1998). While many of these institutions have become more diverse in the United States, such institutions continue to exist throughout the world. Another way in which higher education differs around the world relates to whether students' entry into higher education leads to a general, typically liberal arts and sciences education, or whether it begins with professional education. Americans may be surprised to learn that in many parts of the world a student goes to medical or law school as an undergraduate, straight from secondary school. In the United States, students must seek admission to a professional post-tertiary institution – a graduate or professional school – after first being admitted to and receiving a bachelor's degree from a college or university. Still another way university education has changed is the huge influx of foreign students, especially from less-developed countries, to study in the universities in countries that have more well-established universities.

Countries, and even higher education institutions within countries, differ by the kinds of information that they use in making admissions decisions. Nevertheless, almost all universities around the world use indices of the success of one's previous secondary education. In the United States, one's high school grade point average is most commonly used; other countries (and indeed some institutions within the United States) use analogous indices, such as a secondary-level certificate that confirms the student has passed particular coursework. Chapters in this volume not only address the types of information countries employ in making admissions decisions, but there are also chapters devoted to many of the types of measures employed. One of the most fundamental factors that some countries consider is test data. Such tests may be developed and administered by a national government, by independent testing companies, or locally by individual universities. Most tests that are used in admissions are academic in nature, such as measures of general developed abilities, analogous to adult measures of scholastic aptitude or intelligence, or achievement tests of the subjects studied in secondary education. Determining the actual use and nature of such measures is dependent upon the local cultures, philosophical positions within the educational sphere, governmental determinations, politics, and validity considerations. Some measures may be non-cognitive in nature, whether based upon conventional personality dimensions, measures of so-called twenty-first-century skills (e.g., teamwork), situational judgment measures, or work-related attributes as might be provided by letters or ratings by references (Camara, 2005). Chapters in this volume address these types of measures as well as models where a variety of admissions factors may be combined. As mentioned above, fairness should be a consideration in the types of measures used, as part of the overall determination of the validity of the admissions decisions.

Given the diversity of languages in some countries, and the increase in international students entering foreign institutions, measures of language competence in the language of instruction are increasingly valuable to determine if potential students have the language skills needed to succeed (Oakland, 2016). Similarly, while accepting students for a general liberal arts program may use general types of academic and/or non-cognitive measures, acceptance into specific professional programs (e.g., medical school) may be considerably more specific (Camara, Packman, & Wiley, 2013).

One conclusion of many of the chapters in this volume is that the amount of empirical research on the information used in making admissions decisions is lacking in many countries. I believe that the diversity of student bodies is incredibly important to the student experience and using valid and fair measures is one of the time-tested methods for achieving diversity. Therefore, there is an ongoing need for research pertaining to the fairness of the many types of tests and non-test indices of admissions data. We also often need to study our admissions measures against broader criteria than college grades, such as success subsequent to the university and providing a variety of skills that make for a successful class of students (e.g., artistic abilities of various types, athletic prowess, as well as those with advanced intellects). Ultimately, most universities need to see balance in their accepted classes. Validation and fairness research needs to be ongoing and an ever-changing activity.

We must remember that the characteristics that may make a student successful in one program may not be true in another. Success in the sciences and the humanities often differs somewhat, for example. Similarly, characteristics that engender success in universities in one country may differ in another country. Moreover, the work in a given program at one point of time is also likely to change. These determinations are simply not static and there are numerous factors that could change.

I would like to make two final points before inviting you to enjoy this volume. First, we need to concentrate far more on getting students to succeed in college and to graduate, rather than just to be admitted. We have a considerable need for better diagnostic and placement measures that will help universities and their students plan their individual paths through the university, which may require remedial instruction in some areas. Likewise, requiring students to take courses covering material that they have already learned is a waste of resources for both students and institutions. Finally, we need to recall that the very best colleges and universities are not those whose students have the highest entrance measures, but the schools that graduate students with the best skills. Certainly, there is overlap between these two, yet the very best universities are those that lead students to transform themselves into successful lifelong learners having the work and citizenship skills that they need to succeed throughout their lifetimes.

Kurt F. Geisinger

REFERENCES

Bowen, W. G., & Bok, D. (1998). *The shape of the river: Long-term consequences of considering race in college and university admissions*. Princeton, NJ: Princeton University Press.

Camara, W. J. (2005). Broadening predictors of college success. In W. J. Camara & E. W. Kimmel (Eds.). *Choosing students: Higher education admissions tools for the 21st Century* (pp. 81–105). Mahwah, NJ: Erlbaum.

Camara, W. J. Packman, S., & Wiley, A. (2013). College, graduate, and professional school admissions testing. In K. F. Geisinger (Ed.). *APA handbook of testing and assessment in psychology* (Vol. 3, pp. 297–318). Washington, DC: American Psychological Association.

Lerner, B. (1977). Equal protection and external screening. In Davis, De Funis, and Bakke (EDs.). *Educational testing and the law: Proceedings of the 1977 ETS invitational conference*. Princeton, NJ: Educational Testing Service.

Oakland, T. (2016). Testing and assessment of immigrants and second-language learners. In F. T. L. Leong, D. Bartram, F. M. Cheung, K. F. Geisinger, & D. Iliescu (Eds.). *The ITC international handbook of testing and assessment* (pp. 318–332). New York: Oxford University Press.

Zwick, R. (2006). Higher education admissions testing. In R. L. Brennan (Ed.). *Educational measurement* (4th ed.) (pp. 647–679). Westport, CT: ACE/Praeger.

Acknowledgments

We are very grateful to many individuals who supported this book through their expertise, commitment, and advice from its very beginning to final editing.

First, we are deeply indebted to René Lawless for her unwavering support, competence, and full commitment to this project along all of its phases. Her skills kept us on track as well as helped maintain order during the entire process.

We also express sincere gratitude to Alina von Davier for encouragement and support in developing the initial stages of the proposal and to a number of colleagues from Educational Testing Service (ETS) who provided feedback, insight, and suggestions.

We are thankful to the International Test Commission for sponsoring this book and to Neal Schmitt for endorsing it.

We thank Mike Patane and Dawn King from ETS, and David Repetto and Emily Watton from Cambridge University Press, for all their contract-related support.

We thank all authors for their commitment to writing, revising, and getting their chapter ready for publication. Their voices, expertise in the field, and knowledge of higher education admissions are what make this book unique. Collectively their voices elucidate different ways to understand admissions practices from a multinational perspective.

Finally, we thank the reviewers of individual chapters: Mark Ashwill, Nathan Bell, Michal Beller, Brent Bridgeman, Wayne Camara, James Carlson, Filio Constantinou, Thomas Eckes, Sam Fongwa, Anthony Green, Thomas Heilke, David Klieger, Nathan Kuncel, Iasonas Lamprianou, Per-Erik Lyren, Rob Meijer, Gerald Melican, Rochelle Michel, Robert Mislevy, Susan Niessen, John Norris, Ibrahim Oanda, Björn Öckert, Elena Papanastasiou, Thanos Patelis, Duy Ngoc Pham, Richard Phelps, Donald Powers, Rosemary Reshetar, David Rutkowski, Daniel Sifuna, David Slomp, Sebastiaan Steenman, Saran Stewart, Jörgen Tholin,

Jason Way, and Rebecca Zwick. We are grateful to Kim Fryer from ETS for organizing the copy-editing process for all chapters.

ETS staff time for work on this book was supported by the company. However, the opinions and recommendations expressed here are those of the editors and authors and not necessarily those of ETS.

PART I

Global Challenges and Common Admissions Models

María Elena Oliveri

The chapters in this part provide an overview and critical discussion of college-level higher education admissions practices from around the world. This discussion illustrates common goals, concerns, and challenges related to: broadening higher education admissions criteria to diverse populations; improving student preparation to meet labor market demands; and preparing students to complete increasingly more advanced courses, all from an international perspective. They address questions such as: How should merit be defined and measured? To what extent should background factors be measured? How are multiple criteria such as previous classwork, grades, test scores, personal experience, and recommendations used in admissions decisions? How can higher education institutions include students from multiple populations such as students from ethnically, socioeconomically, or culturally and linguistically diverse backgrounds?

This multinational lens elucidates the different types of constraints higher education institutions face in relation to meeting economic, political, and societal needs related to fairness, equity, and opportunity to learn. Thus, the authors' examples provide useful illustrations of lessons learned that can be applied to institutions in other countries that share similar higher education goals or that may want to examine alternative approaches to the current admissions practices models they use.

The various higher education admissions models (merit-based, open access, character-based, and cross-cultural) and practices higher education institutions and countries use to address the goals of increasing access, diversity, predictive validity, and/or capacity building are also described. The authors also discuss the following types of model-related questions: What are the goals of the model? What are its challenges and drawbacks related to retention, graduation, and providing access to diverse populations? The authors also identify differences across elements that comprise the various higher education models ranging from the types of materials requested for admissions reviews (e.g., cognitive or language standardized test scores, secondary school transcripts, teacher recommendations, personal statements) to the kinds of instruments used to inform admissions decisions (e.g., cognitive and noncognitive measures). The models also differ in how they guide decisions regarding which students to admit – from more students in an eligibility-based admissions model to fewer students in a selection-based model.

Beyond the higher education admissions models, the authors discuss the kinds of external challenges higher education institutions face, which are often motivated by national goals for political, economic, or social reasons. These national-level issues need to be considered and interpreted with institutional goals and the admissions models higher education institutions use. For example, governments might incentivize applicants to apply for particular fields to increase the number of graduates in particular areas of study or might encourage high school graduates to pursue higher education studies to reduce the rate of youth unemployment. Along the same lines, diversity issues are considered in relation to fairness and equity perspectives that sometimes have historical implications. For instance, higher education institutions may need to diversify their applicant pool to increase the number of students of a particular gender or ethnic background if they are under-represented in fields of study or increase the number of seats provided to students of color.

Additionally, the chapters discuss the challenges involved in considering admissions processes such as: What are optimal ways of providing access to higher education to diverse populations? What educational paths are effective in completing higher education studies and meeting labor market and educational demands? What are the limitations of using data from international surveys of achievement to interpret students' aspirations to attend college and obtain a higher education degree? The chapters in this section discuss the above-mentioned issues in greater depth.

Michel and Pollard provide an overview of what is meant by higher education admissions processes. They define much of the basic terminology used throughout this volume. They provide the reader with the appropriate context to discuss higher education models and better understand the complexities higher education institutions face in diversifying their student body and identifying which measures to use and how.

The chapter by von Davier and Tam uses data from the Program for International Student Assessment to discuss differences in students' college aspirations. They explain that because countries differ in the kinds of requirements for particular occupations, there are differences across countries that need to be acknowledged when using data from international surveys to make informed, meaningful, and valid cross-national comparisons. For instance, particular occupations in different countries might require different degrees and certification levels that render the process of comparing degrees across countries complex at best and impossible at worst.

The remaining chapters in this part describe various models or approaches that may be used as part of the admissions process. Common goals include identifying admissions processes that are fair and transparent, determining what the admissions process should do, and what fair selection really means. Establishing these processes has philosophical and practical implications that need to be considered together in an effort both to identify optimal approaches to minimize the unintended effects of higher education admissions processes and to optimize the intended effects for individuals, higher education institutions, and society.

Wikström and Wikström take an in-depth look at a merit-based admissions model that focuses on academic achievement as admissions-relevant criteria. The authors discuss the ways in which institutions determine who should or should not be admitted. They also provide examples about the application of such a model for admitting candidates and discuss the challenges related to the implementation of this practice, consequences to students who are not selected or admitted, and the costs and benefits of this approach. Moreover, the authors discuss the tensions that emerge among stakeholders (e.g., institutions, faculty, and professionals in various fields of study) relative to defining what merit is, how to measure it, and the types of materials and instruments that are included in admissions decisions.

The chapter by Williams and Wendler describes an open-access model, designed to provide access to students of diverse backgrounds or for those who are disadvantaged or underprivileged. The authors describe the benefits, drawbacks, and challenges of using the model. For instance, they discuss that graduating from community colleges with associate degrees may provide benefits related to open admissions policies, flexibility in course scheduling, and lower tuitions. However, it may also present challenges related to the number of jobs available with the types of qualifications obtained in these colleges.

Niessen and Meijer describe character-based models and the reasons for the use of character-based measures, including the challenges and opportunities associated with their use. These models are gaining ground in Europe and elsewhere because they are viewed as useful alternatives to the use of high school grades and/or standardized test scores as these traditional approaches sometimes are considered unfair when they are the sole admissions criterion. The noncognitive measures are thought to be relevant in predicting outcomes beyond academic achievement and are viewed as adding incremental validity above traditional criteria for predicting academic achievement and helping better to differentiate among homogeneous student groups beyond the use of cognitive test scores. The authors also point to challenges of the measures, such as faking and coaching, which could pose a threat to the use of these measures for improving fair access to higher education institutions.

The final chapter, by McKeown, Vedan, Traplin, Sanford, and Bourne, describes admissions models that emphasize the readiness to work collaboratively in nations around the world as part of the college experience. The authors address questions such as: Which criteria do institutions consider for applicant selection? What experiences do they provide to admitted students to promote multiculturalism or global competencies? How do institutions use such experiences to promote the teaching and learning of academic and noncognitive constructs (e.g., collaboration, negotiation, and global citizenry)? What benefits do international students bring to the university such as helping to diversify the student body? And how do institutions enhance participation in higher education and increased success of traditionally under-represented populations, especially for students from Indigenous groups? The authors describe institutions' use of equity-related policies to lessen and ultimately remove obstacles to higher education access based on personal or social circumstances and support students in achieving their academic goals.

CHAPTER I

An Overview of Higher Education Admissions Processes

Rochelle Michel and Simone Pollard

Pursuing higher education is an important milestone for individuals around the world – whether the individual is the first in their family to pursue higher education or it is a family tradition. Education can play a major role in shaping and defining one's future as it provides opportunity and access to a wide variety of careers. Social mobility and social capital can result from increased education – particularly obtaining education above typical levels for a given society or culture. For first-generation seekers of higher education or individuals in developing countries, education can be a leading factor in elevating social and economic statuses. The achievement of obtaining a baccalaureate degree helps graduates establish a career and build the foundation from which career advancement and additional educational pursuits evolve.

Admissions processes for entry into higher education vary by world region, country, or institution, and this variation can span all stages of the admissions process, from materials requested for review to how admissions decisions are made. Additionally, the level at which admissions decisions are made is also varied depending on whether admissions decisions are made centrally – for instance, at the government level – or locally, at the institution level. These variations may be due to different admissions philosophies in use and how these philosophies influence the establishment of guidelines for the manner in which applicants are considered eligible for higher education and admitted, versus selected for admission.

This chapter will focus on a discussion of admissions philosophies that guide how admissions processes are viewed and, therefore, implemented and measured in various world regions. Additionally, other considerations and factors that influence these admissions philosophies will be discussed to highlight how they connect the education sector to other sectors and relate to societal indicators. Some of the countries highlighted in this chapter and their respective admissions models will be further explored throughout the book.

1.1   Terminology and Definitions

There are a variety of terms associated with higher education admissions processes, and these terms may be defined differently in various countries and educational systems. The terms mentioned in this section are defined below and this definition should be associated with the respective term throughout this chapter to convey a common understanding of the intention and points being made.

Higher education is the level of study beyond the secondary level. Higher education includes community colleges, trade schools, colleges, universities, and other tertiary levels of education. It also includes programs of study at the associate, bachelor's/baccalaureate, master's, and doctoral levels. In this chapter, the phrase admissions process is used to describe the process by which an applicant is evaluated for admission to an institution of higher education. The admissions process may include several steps and rely on the review of materials submitted by an applicant applying for or seeking admission. Given the international focus of this chapter, it is also important to clarify who we define as international students. In this context, international students are individuals who are residents of a different country or region from where they are applying, studying, or intending to study.

In addition to the aforementioned terms, the admissions models and practices will be framed in terms of eligibility- and selection-based admissions models. Eligibility-based admissions models are ones in which prospective students are evaluated with respect to some published standard to determine eligibility. Selection-based admissions models are those in which prospective students are evaluated with respect to the pool of applicants for entry into the higher education institution and selected from that pool. The next section contains a discussion of the eligibility- and selection-based admissions models.

1.2   Admissions Philosophies (or Guiding Principles)

As Perfetto (1999) has noted, the admissions process should reflect the mission of a particular institution, as well as resources and constraints. While Perfetto's statement was in the context of higher education admissions within the United States, a similar position should be taken in the context of international entities that are responsible for making decisions about their admissions practices (i.e., mission driven and considering their context and resources). Clearly, classifying admissions practices can be challenging. In this chapter, we situate admissions models in the context of eligibility-based and selection-based admissions philosophies.

1.2.1 *Eligibility-Based Admissions Models*

Eligibility-based admissions models are some of the more transparent admissions models, since they establish a clear set of criteria for admission that are made available to the public, including interested applicants. In a true eligibility-based admissions model, anyone who meets the eligibility criteria set forth by the institution will be admitted to the institution. The decision-making process is clear: Those who meet the criteria are admitted and those who do not meet the criteria are not admitted. Entitlement and open-access models are examples of eligibility-based admissions models (Perfetto, 1999). In an entitlement model, higher education is seen as a right and in open-access models higher education is seen as a natural next step after secondary education. For example, some types of higher education institutions, by their very nature (e.g., community colleges within the United States) share similar practices and may have minimal admissions requirements, using more of an eligibility-based admissions model (for a discussion of open-access admissions models, see Williams and Wendler, in this volume).

However, as we will see in this and subsequent chapters, although an individual may be eligible, meeting the eligibility requirements is not always a guarantee for admission. In some admissions processes, eligibility is a first step in the process. Every institution responsible for making higher education admissions decisions has a set of criteria that indicate whether an individual is eligible for entry into the higher education institution. In many contexts, evaluating an applicant's eligibility may be the extent of the admissions process and the difference between practices may just be the specific eligibility requirements used to make the admission decision.

1.2.2 *Selection-Based Admissions Models*

In a variety of instances, applicants who meet minimum eligibility guidelines are not guaranteed admission to the higher education institution. The pool of eligible applicants is moved forward to a subsequent competitive evaluation process. Any admissions process that results in denying admission to eligible applicants is enacting some form of selection-based decision-making. If the rejection of eligible applicants is possible, a process must be put in place to determine who among the larger group of eligible applicants will or will not be admitted into the institution.

Perfetto (1999) presented three categories of selection-based admissions models that take into consideration an applicant's demonstrated performance prior to entering higher education as an indication of their potential to succeed, the benefit that higher education will provide the applicant, and how higher education promotes the greater good and development of society. The educational entity's philosophy will drive the admissions requirements and required admissions materials that inform the decisions made in both eligibility- and selection-based admissions models.

1.2.3   *Admissions Requirements and Admissions Materials*

Admissions requirements refer to the materials that an applicant must submit so that their application can be evaluated and a decision made about whether they will be admitted into the higher education institution. The level at which these decisions are made, and the materials reviewed differ depending on the context and whether an eligibility- or selection-based admissions model is used. In some contexts, the admissions process is centralized at the country level and institutions follow the procedures outlined at the national level (see Papanastasiou and Michaelides, in this volume, for an example in the context of Cyprus). In some other contexts, the admissions process is decentralized, and individual institutions are able to develop their own admissions practices (e.g., higher education institutions in the United States). The degree of centralization influences the use of an eligibility- or selection-based admissions model.

Whether or not a higher education institution is part of a centralized or decentralized system, the decision-making body determines the materials that they require to evaluate an application for admission to the institution or intended field of study. These materials can include standardized test scores, transcripts of secondary-level courses taken and the corresponding grades, recommendations from secondary teachers, writing samples, and personal statements (e.g., applicants' responses to specific questions or prompts). Additionally, institutions may require or recommend that applicants interview with a representative of the institution as part of the admissions process.

In several countries, a major or course of study must be declared at the time of admission (e.g., Japan, the Netherlands, New Zealand, South Korea, Spain, and the United Kingdom) and maintained throughout a student's time at the institution (National Association for College

Admission Counseling, 2018). For certain areas of study, there may be requirements for courses that an applicant should have taken prior to beginning studies at the university level. These requirements are often referred to as prerequisites. For instance, applicants interested in studying engineering, science, medicine, law, the arts, or music may need to fulfill prerequisite coursework prior to being officially admitted into the higher education institution. In countries where there is a national curriculum, prerequisite knowledge may be assumed once the student has received their certificate. Higher education institutions offering courses of study in these specialized areas with limited openings use a selection-based model to make admissions decisions. In other instances, for less-specialized courses of study, meeting a specific level on their certificate may meet the eligibility requirement for an institution (e.g., France, the United Kingdom).

Admissions requirements may vary depending on the nationality of the prospective student or country in which the applicant attended secondary school. That is, if the applicant is applying to an institution in another region or country from his or her own, the admissions requirements for this applicant may request or require additional or different materials from the international applicant than from a domestic applicant. This difference in requirements for applicants aspiring to study at an institution in another region or country may be to account for the differences in educational systems between the applicant's country and the country where they hope to study. Examples of additional materials could be language proficiency test scores in the language of instruction in the region to which the applicant is applying or a credential evaluation to compare an applicant's academic accomplishments to the standards within the region or country in which the applicant aspires to study.

A number of institutions in Europe and elsewhere deliver courses in English. In these cases, if English is not their native language, applicants may have to provide verification of English proficiency by submitting results from an English proficiency test (e.g., TOEFL iBT®, IELTS). The request is made to verify that an applicant's English-language skills are at the level necessary to complete the desired degree program. Similarly, applicants intending to study in a country where the language of instruction at the university is different from theirs may also have to provide evidence of proficiency in that language (see Eckes and Althaus, in this volume, for a discussion of different language proficiency tests used in admissions).

The test scores an applicant submits are often from a standardized test such as the Swedish SweSAT, the Israeli Psychometric Entrance Test (PET), and the US SAT®, and ACT®. Test scores may also come from national examinations that secondary school students take within a particular country. For instance, the National College Entrance Examination, also known as the Gaokao, is delivered in China annually and is the entrance examination for the majority of institutions of higher education in China. Test-takers' Gaokao scores determine the type of institution, by selectivity, to which they will be granted admission. That is, the students with the highest scores in the examination are generally granted admission to the most selective institutions while those with lower scores are admitted to less-selective institutions. For international applicants to Chinese institutions, applicants are required to meet several requirements established by the government (e.g., no criminal record), in addition to the institution's application. If the program they wish to pursue is administered in Chinese, they must also submit test scores to demonstrate Chinese-language proficiency (Chen & Kesten, 2017; China's University and College Admission System, 2018).

In Europe, admissions requirements for universities will differ depending on whether the applicant is from within the European Union (EU) or from outside the EU. And there may be differing requirements depending on whether the institution is public or private, or focused on applied sciences or other specializations. For instance, in France, the Grandes Écoles are public or private institutions that have their own admissions process unique to preparing individuals to study within that system of prestigious institutions and these requirements differ from requirements of other French institutions (Frys & Staat, 2016). Additionally, international students aspiring to study in France follow an admissions process where they identify up to three schools where they wish to be considered for admissions and their application is presented to their first choice initially for consideration. The application is presented to the second and third choices if admission is not granted at the former choice (National Association for College Admission Counseling, 2018).

In the United States, applicants must submit many of the materials mentioned above and may participate in an interview (if an interview is a requirement of the application process). This is typically the case regardless of the institution's status as public or private. Applicants from outside the United States must also submit language-assessment scores to demonstrate English language proficiency (see Zwick, 2017, for a description of admissions practices used in the United States).

Part II of this volume provides descriptions of specific admissions practices, admissions requirements, and their underlying philosophy and challenges for a number of countries and regions around the world.

1.3 Importance of Admissions in Reflecting the Goals of Higher Education

Admissions requirements for higher education are communicated in several ways, including by an institution's or program's promotional materials or website, through government-provided materials, or through institutional representatives. Admissions requirements provide applicants with guidance on the information they must submit as part of the admissions process or the eligibility requirements for gaining admission. The list of required materials also provides applicants with insight into the various elements of the review process, on what the focus will be during the review of an individual's application, as well as whether an eligibility- or selection-based admissions model is being used for making admissions decisions. What may be unclear to applicants and vary from institution to institution and from country to country is the importance that each component of the application has on the admissions decision and how the information is used when selection-based admissions models are used. Institutions may determine this weight based on many factors including institutional policy, institutional mission, culture, government rules and regulations, or admissions goals. It will be important for the applicant to understand whether an eligibility-based or selection-based admissions model is being used for making an admissions decision.

The National Association for College Admission Counseling (NACAC) conducted a study of colleges and universities in the United States to better understand their admissions practices. Based on the *2017 state of college admissions* report by NACAC (Clinedinst, & Koranteng, 2017), the top application components considered in the admissions decision were course grades, overall secondary school grade point average, admissions test scores, and strength of the secondary school curriculum. These materials identified as top application components are often used as indicators of an applicant's preparedness for study at the tertiary level. Some countries weight grades and/or test scores to make their admissions decisions (see Allalouf, Cohen, & Gafni and Lyrén & Wikström, in this volume, for examples). Within the United States and elsewhere, there are ongoing debates about the weight that these materials should have in the admissions process (Zwick, 2017) or whether admissions test scores should even be required for admissions (Buckley, Letukas, & Wildavsky, 2018). While there is also an ongoing debate about the value of using secondary school grade point average and admissions test scores in the admissions process, there is continued discussion about the need for more emphasis on the more qualitative aspects of the application materials. Clinedinst and Koranteng (2017) found that among the next most important factors were the essay, an applicant's demonstrated interest, counselor and teacher recommendations, extracurricular activities, and class rank. The next most important group of materials is often used to obtain additional qualitative information about applicants beyond their academic preparedness. Measures of applicants' social and emotional learning skills (e.g., teamwork, creativity, planning and organization, ethics and integrity, resilience) have also been identified as important components for considering an applicant's admission to the higher education institution. This is particularly true in circumstances where selection-based models are used and character is a key component for consideration (see Perfetto, 1999, for a discussion of character-based consideration in selection-based admissions models). In addition, Niessen and Meijer (in this volume) provide an in-depth discussion of the use of character-based criteria in the United States and Europe.

In the United States, many institutions will communicate to applicants that they use a holistic admissions approach, which may be defined as a process where all materials are reviewed and considered before making an admissions decision. Essentially, this means that admissions decisions are not made from reviewing one or just a couple of components of the application. Each element of an applicant's file is reviewed prior to making an admissions decision. By contrast, in China, an applicant's score on the Gaokao essentially determines the institution to which an applicant will be granted admission. In this context, the example from the United States in relation to that from China provides an illustration of a selection-based versus eligibility-based admissions model, respectively.

Despite the differences institutions may place on the weight or importance of materials submitted in the application process, it is critical that reviewers of admission files are clear on the admissions goals for each cycle and that these goals are communicated to all faculty and staff involved in the admissions process. It is also critical that the student recruitment process is developed to support the achievement of these goals. In selection-based admissions models, the application pool from which the selection of students is being made needs to be sufficiently rich to allow for the identification and selection of students to enable the institution to meet its admissions goals. Application reviewers should be explicit about the goals for each admissions cycle and then measure their progress against these goals throughout the cycle. Mid-cycle measurement allows the admissions committee not only to track progress but also to make adjustments, as necessary, to achieve the stated goals.

Many institutions place an emphasis on diversity and therefore implement strategies and tactics that enable them to diversify their applicant pool and thus their incoming class or cohort. Diversity and the diversification efforts will have a specific meaning depending on the institution, country, or region. For instance, some institutions may focus on gender diversity for programs that can be dominated by one gender – diversifying education programs to include more men or engineering programs to include more women. Other institutions may focus on diversity in terms of religion, nationality, region, race, or ethnic group. An admissions policy cannot be evaluated in a vacuum – it must be judged with reference to the mission of the institution and, more broadly, the ideas of the society at large. What is the purpose of higher education, and who should be eligible to receive one? Wikström and Wikström and Lyrén and Wikström (in this volume) provide insights from the Swedish system and their consideration of students from nontraditional backgrounds and older students, while Pham and Sai (in this volume) identify communities of individuals within Vietnam who are given special consideration in the admissions process, including children of veterans, minority groups, and those who live in remote or mountainous areas. Zwick (2017) identifies five broad goals that can be achieved through universities' admissions policies, including fulfilling their institutional needs, rewarding past performance, identifying and nurturing the most talented students, expanding college access and promoting social mobility, and maximizing the benefit to society. Regardless of an institution's admissions policies, admissions goals should be developed to encompass all important elements, including diversity, and then be clearly articulated and measured.

1.4 Measuring the Effectiveness of Admissions

It is important to measure the effectiveness of the admissions process, regardless of whether an institution or system is using an eligibility-based or selection-based philosophy for making admissions decisions. Given the impact that educational opportunities can have on an individual's social and economic status, institutions have a responsibility to measure the effectiveness of the admissions process, their institution's success in meeting their admissions goals, and if the admissions process is aligned with their overall mission. While there is a need to conduct these types of efficacy studies, this is not an easy task. The institution needs to evaluate the relationship between the pieces of information that were used to make admissions decisions and the success outcomes deemed important to the institution or program. To this end, it is common practice for higher education institutions to evaluate the relationship between the grade point average (GPA) from the previous level of education (i.e., secondary school GPA) and standardized test scores with students' first-year GPA at the higher education institution. These data are the easiest components to use in typical studies due to their quantitative nature, and first-year grade point average is also one of the earliest indicators of success and is not difficult to obtain. However, institutions are generally more interested in longer-term outcomes, as in the United States, where there is interest in whether students graduate from college or university within four to six years of beginning full-time study (see Reshetar and Pitts, in this volume, for a discussion of academic-based examinations used in higher education admissions).

However, two things are clear: There is a need for transparency in how admissions decisions are made and there is limited published research demonstrating the effectiveness of higher education admissions practices. Those using an eligibility-based admissions model have clearer and more explicit information about applicants than those institutions applying a more selection-based model that requires a diverse set of admissions materials. Universities should have a clear set of goals and objectives for the admissions process that are aligned with the admissions requirements. There has been a growing call for more high-quality research evidence to make better use of tools available to those responsible for reviewing application files (Buckley, Letukas, & Wildavsky, 2018; Niessen & Meijer, in this volume). As noted by Zwick (2017), publishing research on the effects of admissions policies is one way to achieve transparency in the admissions process and will also allow the public to hold educational institutions accountable for their decision-making processes.

1.5   Other Important Considerations

Admissions processes, whether based on eligibility or selectivity, can be influenced by external factors such as demographic shifts, politics, or economic indicators. For instance, the demographics of a country or presence of disadvantaged or underserved groups can lead institutions, or the government, to establish affirmative-action programs or other initiatives that are focused on addressing "the multi-faceted issue of equity" (Helms, 2008, p. 29). These programs or initiatives could include outreach efforts to encourage members of disadvantaged groups to pursue higher education. It could also result in alternative admissions practices that consider criteria used to project the future, including potential societal impact the applicant might make (Perfetto, 1999). In Norway, applicants are awarded additional points for demographic factors in the centrally administered admissions process (Helms, 2008).

Shifting demographics also make it necessary for those involved in the admissions process, and the process itself, to adapt to the shifts (Perfetto, 1999). Similarly, fluctuations in the size of the age group that typically pursues higher education may influence the competitiveness of admissions for available positions, regardless of admissions philosophy, assuming that there is a finite number of available positions within the country or at the institution. Essentially, competition for available positions may increase if the generation currently pursuing higher education is larger than the previous generation, as is the case with the millennial generation (Catalyst, 2018; Fry, 2018).

Political considerations related to the labor market may also influence higher education admissions and its processes. A government may choose to incentivize studying in particular fields (e.g., medicine) to address labor shortages within the country. Addressing this shortage could be part of the national agenda and encouraging study in the field(s) supports this aspect of the agenda. Furthermore, a government might mandate that all secondary education leavers continue their studies by pursuing higher education as a way to control youth unemployment rates (Helms, 2008). The connection between politics and higher education can be utilized to support national agendas by implementing policy within the education sector to achieve specific national goals.

The socioeconomic landscape in a country may also influence the characteristics of the individuals and the number who pursue higher education. For example, a secondary school leaver from a lower socioeconomic background or from a background without sufficient disposable income may not be able to pursue higher education, regardless of whether the institution charges tuition fees (Kelly & Shale, 2004). That is, prospective applicants may not be able to afford the opportunity cost of pursuing higher education and, instead, may need to work to support themselves and their family. Conversely, someone from a higher socioeconomic group might be able to afford the opportunity cost of pursuing higher education in this same system because of the financial resources available to them and because of their socioeconomic status.

In countries like the United States, where higher education is not free, those who pursue higher education must be able to pay for or finance their education, and this financial cost can be a barrier to many. The financial cost of pursuing higher education may also influence interest in higher education, specifically at the most selective institutions, as prospective students ponder their situation in relation to what it will take financially to pursue higher education (Kornicker, 2018).

Emerging economies may also consider the historical context under which educational systems were developed, such as whether the education framework and system of a former colonial power is appropriate for the current time. The historical system and accompanying practices may not be aligned with current national strategies, goals, priorities, or culture, and, therefore, adjustments to the system may be warranted to adapt it to one that is more reflective and appropriate for the current society and its people (Helms, 2008).

1.6   Summary

This chapter provides an overview of higher education admissions processes, using eligibility- and selection-based admissions models to frame higher education admissions practices. These philosophies help to contextualize an institution's or educational system's admissions requirements and the admissions materials that are requested of applicants. Connecting philosophies with the admissions requirements and admissions materials helps to connect the goals of higher education to the admissions process used within the system. While this chapter highlighted some examples of the admissions models used in a variety of countries, additional and more focused country-specific practices are discussed in subsequent chapters.

REFERENCES

Buckley, J., Letukas, L., & Wildavsky, B. (2018). *Measuring success: Testing, grades, and the future of college admissions*. Baltimore, MD: Johns Hopkins University Press.

Catalyst (2018). *Quick tale: Generations in the workplace*. Retrieved from www .catalyst.org/knowledge/generations-demographic-trends-population-and-workforce.

Chen, Y., & Kesten, O. (2017). Chinese college admissions and school choice reforms: A theoretical analysis. *Journal of Political Economy, 125*, 99–139. https://doi.org/10.1086/689773.

China's University and College Admission System. (2018). *Admission requirements*. Retrieved from www.cucas.edu.cn/feature/index/2832/2832.

Clinedinst, M., & Koranteng, A.-M. (2017). *2017 state of college admissions*. Retrieved from www.nacacnet.org/globalassets/documents/publications/ research/soca17final.pdf.

Fry, R. (2018). *Millennials are the largest generation in the U.S. labor force.* Retrieved from www.pewresearch.org/fact-tank/2018/04/11/millennials-largest-generation-us-labor-force/.

Frys, L., & Staat, C. (2016). *MiP country profile 23: University admission practices – France.* Retrieved from www.matching-in-practice.eu/wp-content/uploads/2016/10/MiP_-Profile_No.23.pdf.

Helms, R. M. (2008). *University admission worldwide* (Education Working Paper Series No. 15). Washington, DC: International Bank of Reconstruction and Development/The World Bank.

Kelly, W., & Shale, D. (2004). *Does the rising cost of tuition affect the socioeconomic status of students entering university?* Paper presented at the Association for Institutional Research Forum, Boston, MA. Retrieved from https://files.eric.ed.gov/fulltext/ED491010.pdf.

Kornicker, C. (2018). *Impacts of lower socioeconomic status on college admission.* Retrieved from https://publicpolicy.wharton.upenn.edu/live/news/2302-impacts-of-lower-socioeconomic-status-on-college.

National Association for College Admission Counseling (2018). *Guide to international university admission.* Arlington, VA: NACAC. Retrieved from www.nacacnet.org/globalassets/documents/publications/international-initiatives/2018-guide-to-international-university-admission.

Perfetto, G. (1999). *Toward a taxonomy of the admissions decision-making process.* New York: The College Board.

Zwick, R. (2017). *Who gets in? Strategies for fair and effective college admissions.* Cambridge, MA: Harvard University Press.

CHAPTER 2

Comparing College Aspirations across PISA Countries: Are *17* Percent Oranges Less than *75* Percent Apples?

Matthias von Davier and Hak Ping Tam

In August 2017, the Organisation for Economic Co-operation and Development (OECD) tweeted a message about a chapter in a report on the 2015 round of the Programme for International Student Assessment (PISA) around students' well-being. This tweet stated that, across countries participating in the PISA assessment, 44 percent of all 15-year-old students expect to complete a college or university degree after finishing secondary school. Figure 2.1 provides information on the tweet as well as the linked 2017 OECD publication that provides further information. The table presenting the data that formed the basis of the tweet is Figure III.6.1: 'Percentage of students expecting to complete each education level' (see Organisation for Economic Co-operation and Development, 2017, p. 105).

This chapter examines the data underlying this tweet as an example of claims made using systems-level data by organizations funding international assessments. Every three years, the OECD produces a comprehensive database on skills and background data of 15-year-old students from a large number of countries using the PISA data collection. This chapter focuses on whether educational aspirations, assessed in the background questionnaire as students' expected highest level of education, can be compared in the way implied by the communication shown in Figure 2.1.

Very large differences between countries become apparent with respect to what percentage of 15-year-old students sampled in PISA expect to attend and finish college after secondary school. The table in the PISA report shows that roughly 75 percent of students in countries such as Colombia, the United States, and Qatar expect to obtain a college degree, while, at the other extreme, only 17 percent of 15-year-old students sampled for PISA in Germany, the Netherlands, and Russia expect to go to college after finishing secondary school. This expectation

Table 2.1 *Background Question ST111Q01TA on the expected highest degree*
of education

Which of the following do you expect to complete? (Please select one response.)
   <ISCED level 2> [USA: Less than high school]
   <ISCED level 3b or c> [USA: High school (high school diploma or GED)]
   <ISCED level 3a> [USA: Vocational or technical certificate (such as cosmetology or auto
   mechanics)]
   <ISCED level 4> [USA: Associates degree (2-year degree from a community college)]
   <ISCED level 5b> [USA: Bachelor's degree (4-year college degree)]
   <ISCED level 5a or 6> [USA: Master's degree or doctoral or professional degree such as
   medicine or law]

Note. Interestingly, the ISCED level 5B is described in Figure III.6.1 of the OECD
Report III as vocationally-/technically-oriented tertiary (ISCED 5B), whereas in the
United States the description is bachelor's degree (4-year college degree), which could
be considered a broader category that does not only include technical and vocational
degrees.

---

1. Twitter account: @OECDeduSkills.
2. Or page 2, sixth bullet point at: www.oecd.org/pisa/PISA-in-Focus-No-71-Are-students-happy.pdf
3. Or www.oecd.org/education/

Figure 2.1   Sources used in the Tweet by OECD's @OECDeduSkills feed on
college aspirations
Note. The original Tweet cannot be reproduced here because of potential copyright issues.

to go to college is determined by combining responses that represent a
college-level education based on answers to a question that asks about the
expected highest level of education. The question is reproduced in
Table 2.1, listing both the international education levels and the corresponding response category provided in the US version of the PISA
2015 background questionnaire.

The International Standard Classification of Education (ISCED) levels
(United Nations Educational, Scientific, and Cultural Organization, 2012)
are not given in the background questionnaires but translated into
country-specific equivalents of educational tracks. ISCED Levels 5a and
6 represent the equivalent of a degree obtained in an institution of tertiary
education, according to the ISCED 1997 description. While there is a

revision from 2011 that also includes levels for master's and doctoral degrees, the ISCED 1997 is still used and appears to be the basis for the PISA 2015 background questionnaire. The question is whether the 75 percent of students from Qatar, Colombia, and the United States on the one hand and the 17 percent of students in Germany, the Netherlands, and Russia on the other hand do indeed mean the same when they say they expect to go to college after graduating from compulsory schooling. In other words, does the concept of going to college after high school have the same implications as not going to college after high school in all countries participating in PISA. Some may say this seems like a vague question, but an example may clarify the issue: The traditional way of becoming a registered nurse in the United States involves college. Up to four years for a bachelor of science in nursing is said to provide the best opportunity in the job market. In Germany, a nurse is a professional who is trained in an apprenticeship program, which means working some days in a hospital or clinic, while attending a special school that is not considered a college on other days. The same is true for kindergarten teachers, who are also trained in an apprenticeship rather than a college-degree program, since the kindergarten is a separate institution outside of mandatory schooling in Germany. However, this job typically requires a degree in elementary education in the United States, maybe because kindergarten is considered part of elementary school. This means that there are important system-level differences in how people train for certain job categories. Some job categories require a college-level degree in certain countries, while they may be taught in integrated practice/school programs in other countries.

More broadly, is it possible to compare variables that depend on system-level differences of established educational and career tracks that may prepare students for similar careers in (very) dissimilar ways? As indicated above, different countries may use different educational pathways that may belong to different ISCED categories for the same job category. Economies may also differ in what they call their educational institutions. Therefore, the complexity of finding equivalent institutional training programs that provide comparable career preparation increases by using the same term for different educational pathways and using different terms for training programs that train for the same job. For example, what do we call schools that do not provide master's- and doctoral-level courses? What do we call schools that provide classes only in a narrow artistic or artisanal field? Even worse, the same or very similar training is provided by professors in higher education institutions (colleges) in some countries, while it is provided as part of the training in companies, governmental agencies, factories, restaurants, or studios by certified masters of trades (or similar titles that indicate high levels of experience and expertise) in other countries. As the examples above show, two different students with the same occupational goal (kindergarten teacher, nurse) may show up in the PISA data as expecting to go to college in one country, while expecting to have less than a college degree in another country. This has striking similarities with what Marsh (1994) described as the "jingle-jangle fallacy" when examining terminology used in psychology: The same psychological construct may be assessed with different tests, independently developed in different contexts and carry different names; but, while two tests may carry the same name or label, they may assess very different constructs.

Different educational institutions may have the same label (college, university), while one prepares students for careers in fundamental research in fields such as computer science and particle physics; others educate students in classes of general studies or train them to be a chef in the food industry. Without implying a hierarchy, some may value a college degree more if it has that name attached than a degree obtained through an apprenticeship, while both may take the same amount of time and lead to very similar careers. A chef who obtained a degree as an apprentice in a Zagat- or Michelin-rated restaurant may deliver service to customers that is on par with another chef who was trained at a culinary-arts college.

One issue with social science research is that ideas about what should be and how things are valued are not only influenced by objectively measurable standards of quality, but also by policy and political ideas (Duarte et al., 2015). It is important to understand preferences in favor of one over another model of higher education in terms of what Tetlock (1994) called "turnabout tests" – for example, "College is the one preferred system of higher education and everyone should have the chance to go to college!" vs. "Not everyone needs (or even is able) to go to college and providing alternative pathways for students with diverse preferences and skills gives broader opportunities to a variety of students with different skill sets."

2.1   How Can Differences Like This Occur?

To understand the complexities of cross-country comparisons better, let us examine practices in another domain: Specifically, looking at how different enrollment rates in the military service may influence students' perceptions regarding enrollment in institutions such as colleges or other forms of tertiary education. There are countries (Type A) in which military service is mandatory for females and males, and other countries (Type B) where it is mandatory only for males. In countries (Type C) without a formal military structure (e.g., Switzerland), service is optional, but governments may request their young citizens to train in a civic defense program. These differences in military service enrollment, just like students' educational pathways, also lead to very different base rates of who may expect to do military service after leaving school. In addition, depending on how the service is organized, there will be systematic differences in the age at which students start thinking about which educational pathway to pursue, which type of college to attend, and how it will be funded (e.g., partially funded by the military or an external organization).

Important for our discussion about rates of students expecting different educational trajectories is that very different expected proportions also emerge from differences in how military service is organized. Different percentages of students will expect to undertake military service before entering higher education in different countries. This can be explained with system-level differences (among these Types A, B, and C, as described above), rather than with different aspirations to participate in military service. The same holds true for aspirations to attend college. If we were unaware of these stark differences in how military service is organized in different countries, we may come to the false conclusions that, in countries of Type C, fewer students find military service suitable for them, or find themselves less suited for service, while in countries of Type A more than 75 percent express their expectation to undertake military service. This is of course a false conclusion, as the underlying mechanism that leads to these very different results is how military service is organized in the different countries.

2.2   More on Aspirations

Section 2.1 was intended to show that military service is one example where stakeholders may expect important differences between systems. Depending on whether service is mandatory or voluntary for one or all gender groups, one may expect that students between high school and higher education will be participating at very different rates across countries. However, the same holds true also for expectations to attend college, for the reasons described above. If we replace the ideas of (a) expecting to participate in military service with expecting to go to college, and (b) expecting to join civic defense training with expecting to enter a formal apprenticeship or job training outside college, it becomes apparent that we can also expect large differences in college attendance, if college was required for the majority of career tracks, or if college was inaccessible for large parts of the population due to current or historical racial or gender discrimination laws (e.g., see Jappie, in this volume, regarding South African higher education). Differences might also appear if there is an alternative to four-year colleges (e.g., less expensive and more accessible 2-year colleges [see, Williams & Wendler, in this volume, on the open admissions model], or trade schools or formal career training by means of apprenticeships or formal training programs outside of college.

Now let us look at some differences between countries that stand out in terms of how many students expect to go to college after finishing secondary school. In the United States, there is no formal tracking in secondary school. While there are different school types such as public, private, and faith-based schools, virtually all high schools offer classes for students up to the 12th grade. However, there is a problem with high school dropout rates that affects racial/ethnic groups differentially, and that leaves a substantial number of students without an opportunity to enter college after high school without jumping through additional hoops.

In the United States, there are different types of colleges. Without providing a complete typology of institutions of higher education, there are two- and four-year colleges and there are four-year colleges with and without graduate schools offering master's and doctoral degrees. Four-year colleges in the United States offer a wide variety of programs, some of which would not be considered college-level education but offered through apprenticeships or similar types of formal trainings in other countries, as outlined above. Thus, if one aspires to become a nurse or a kindergarten teacher in the United States, one would likely attend college even if other programs are available. In other countries, students may be trained in specialized schools or apprenticeship programs for the same type of job. In both cases, the programs may provide the same quality of education, but, in one case, the institutions may be referred to as colleges or universities and students may receive a degree, but not in others. The percentage of students sampled in PISA in the United States who expect to go to college after high school is roughly 75 percent (OECD, 2017).

Another system-level difference that leads to differences in college-level aspirations is that, in Germany, there is tracking at the secondary school level, and this tracking indeed is cause for some concern, as it starts rather early – until recently, often after the fourth grade. The different school types can be described (roughly) as low-level vocational (with nine or ten years of mandatory schooling), medium-level academic track (with ten years of mandatory schooling), and college-bound high school track (with 12 or 13 years of schooling).

A certificate of each of the school types provides students with the formal qualification to apply for positions with companies who offer apprenticeships or training programs. While a higher percentage of students from the college-preparatory schools aim at a college education, a substantial percentage of students even from this most challenging track will first enter an apprenticeship after high school. Alternatively, they may take on some other company-sponsored training. Later, they may enter college, or add a second, more challenging three-year training to earn a master-craftsman (electrician, carpenter, or car mechanic) degree that qualifies them to start their own business and run an apprenticeship program within this business. These are all activities that lead to well-established and well-regulated vocational careers outside of college. For masters and former apprentices who obtained a college-bound school degree before, there is the option to attend college.

Sometimes, college attendance is sponsored by the bank or the company who trained the apprentice. As an example, a substantial number of Chief Executive Officers and Senior Vice Presidents of car makers such as Mercedes and Audi went through formal education that started with an apprenticeship in that industry.[1] They may not have planned this career, may even have stated they did not want to go to college, but learned to become a trained worker, or master mechanic. Therefore, the percentage of students who will express that they will enter college after finishing high school can be expected to be much lower in countries that have pathways to educated professions outside of college.

Consequently, due to the system-level differences existing between countries, as illustrated in the examples above, the percentage of students expecting to go to college after finishing high school is not comparable across countries. The low percentage is due to other variables that need to be considered jointly. Consideration of multiple variables underlying college attendance is needed to make sense of the differences in percentages of youth sampled in PISA who expect to attend college after finishing high

---

[1] A closer inspection of Figure III.6.1 in the PISA report shows that there are countries in which certain ISCED levels are reported with 0 percent expected attendance (e.g., Czech Republic, France, Korea, USA). The absence of counts in these categories indicates that no student has expressed an expectation of gaining a degree associated with this ISCED level. This is an indicator that, while ISCED may provide a valid crosswalk of general types of education, the distribution of degrees and job types across these levels may have very different base rates across countries.

school. To reiterate, the college aspiration questions are not comparable across countries for the reasons outlined above.

2.3   Comparability, or Differential Question Functioning?

The PISA data described above are based on very different rates when it comes to the endorsement of college expectations after finishing high school. Germany and the United States do not differ vastly in terms of results on the PISA cognitive tests. Neither country belongs to the highest performers. Unlike Taiwan, Hong Kong, and other high-performing countries, the United States and Germany have a larger number of students who struggle academically. Nevertheless, they do have a percentage of high-performing students. PISA and other international comparative studies aim at providing reliable, valid, and comparable measures of academic potential, so how can it be that one country has 75 percent of students expecting to go to college while the other has a mere 17 percent who intend to go to college?

By definition, among the 75 percent who report college aspirations in the United States, at least 25 percent must be below median performance on the PISA results of that country, while it appears unlikely that of the 17 percent who expect to go to college in Germany are below median performance when it comes to PISA scores. Some insight can be gained from tables III.6.7. and III.6.8 in volume 3 of the *PISA 2015 results* (OECD, 2017), which provide a split of the results by low achievers (below level 2 in all three PISA domains in table III.6.7) and high achievers (above levels 5 or 6) with respect to their expectation of further education.

As indicated by OECD (2017), among the low achievers, 53.8 percent of students in the United States expect to go to college, while in Germany, less than 7.3 percent expect to go to college (at least 71.9 % + 16.7 % + 4.1 % = 92.7 % of the low achievers in Germany choose other ISCED levels and hence expect not to go to college). Among the high achievers, 91.9 percent of students in the United States expect a college education, while in Germany, 33.4 percent expect to go to college. Similarly, in Colombia, 64.5 percent of low-skilled students expect to go to college, while 98.3 percent of high-skilled students do. However, in Russia, only 6 percent of low-skilled students expect to attend college, while 28.8 percent of the high-skilled PISA students in Russia expect to attend college.

A comparison of subjective probability ratios within each country also shows a striking tendency. One should expect that many more high achievers want to go to college than low achievers. In Germany, the subjective probability of going to college is 4.57 times higher for high achievers compared with low achievers. The same ratio of high achievers to low achievers who expect to go to college is 4.8 in Russia, which equals 28.8 percent divided by 6 percent. As expected, about four times more high achievers believe they will attend college than low achievers in PISA in both Germany and Russia.

The same ratio for the United States shows that high achievers are only 1.71 times more likely to expect to go to college than low achievers. This value is 1.52 in Colombia. This means that low achievers are almost as likely to expect college attendance compared with high achievers in the United States and Colombia. Note that the high-skilled and low-skilled definitions are identical across countries, as these are based on internationally comparable PISA proficiency levels, which have the same definition and are based on the same international assessment in these countries. Hence, this discrepancy suggests one of two hypotheses. Either skills are less predictive of the same dependent variable of expecting a college degree in countries with overall high expectations of college attendance compared with countries with low expected percentages, or the dependent variable of expecting a college degree has a different meaning across countries.[2]

The question about the highest-expected education level can be, based on plausibility as well as empirical arguments, expected to be correlated with actual academic skill level as well as self-concept measures and other variables that are relevant predictors of educational and economic outcomes. Assuming there is a strong and positive relationship between expecting to go to college after mandatory school and academic skills, we would expect that respondents with low skills have a low probability of expecting to go to college, while highly skilled students have a high probability of expecting to go to college. Just for the sake of argument, one could assume that this is not the case for the skills measured in PISA, and they are unrelated, or only weakly related to what is needed in order to succeed in higher education. That would mean that skills as measured in PISA would not be a good predictor as to whether students would succeed in college. It is an additional question whether students would expect to go to college and how that relates to their actual academic skills. We will turn

---

[2] The argument that students were asked in terms of the ISCED-provided crosswalk of academic degrees does not help here, since the same career track (of, for example, becoming a nurse or a kindergarten teacher or a chef) is indeed regarded as a tertiary-education or college-level (ISCED 5 and 6) degree in some countries, while it is considered a trained job- or apprenticeship-based career in other countries.

to that question in the next section and examine whether this varies by country. That PISA scores and academic skills are unrelated is, of course, a highly artificial assumption, as empirical studies again and again show that broad measures of skills tend to form a positive manifold, and predicting academic performance based on broad cognitive skill measures is not only commonplace, but one of the reasons why they were developed. Examples of empirical research that relates PISA scores to academic outcomes (e.g., Fischbach et al., 2013) and research that shows strong prediction of performance indicators collected later in life, in one case more than ten years later (Knighton & Bussière, 2006; Albæk, 2018) can be found in the literature.

Therefore, if PISA scores can be assumed to be comparable across countries, and if, as research indicates, they are predictive of academic outcomes, this begs the question why the expectation of students with regard to obtaining a college degree appears to diverge so much across countries. In cognitive testing, if a question behaves very differently between populations of test-takers (gender, country, language groups) who were stratified into homogeneous skill groups, this question is labeled as exhibiting differential item functioning (DIF) (e.g., Dorans, 2017; von Davier, 2017; Barclay-McKeown & Oliveri, 2017). Again, while self-reports of individuals regarding their expected highest level of education is not a cognitive test item, a strong relation to skills measured in a manner that is internationally comparable should be expected. Therefore, we propose using the term DQF (differential question functioning) in order to clarify that a background question is studied with methods that are borrowed from DIF research, in which item-level performance is predicted based on estimates of ability. DQF, in this context, would be applied as a quantification of how much the prediction of the college-expectation variable based on PISA skills varies across groups. DQF (as does DIF) describes the extent to which a background question functions (i.e., is predicted by ability or skill measures) differently in different groups. Thus, the use of a variable that does relate differentially to underlying causes of behavior calls into question whether this variable can be compared and even averaged across countries (as done in the tweet shown in Figure 2.1). It also raises the question of whether such an average provides a meaningful summary of the targeted issue. If the question about college expectations would be scrutinized for differential associations with underlying potential causes (such as cognitive skills that make success in college more likely), we would most likely reach the conclusion that the question indeed exhibits DQF.

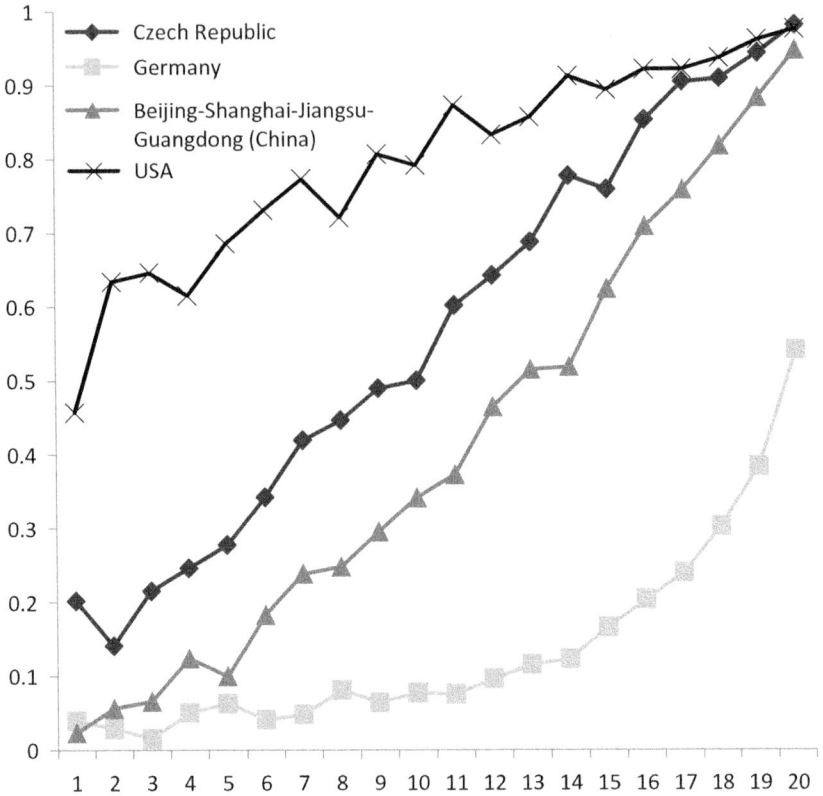

Figure 2.2   The probability of expecting to finish a college level education (ISCED levels 5 and 6) by PISA science proficiency
Note. Each country proficiency distribution was grouped into the same 20 international vigintiles.

The association between college aspiration and cognitive skills as exemplified by the PISA science score is depicted in Figure 2.2. The differences seen across countries show how the question is indeed differentially predicted by skills.

It is evident that students in the United States, even at the lowest level of science achievement, aim at a college-level education in the majority of cases. In the United States, even in the 0 percent to 5 percent and 5 percent to 10 percent groups that represent the 10 percent lowest-performing students in PISA, approximately 45 percent to 65 percent of students expect to complete a college-level education. In contrast, in Germany, only about 2 percent to 3 percent of the lowest-performing students report that they expect to finish college. However, when looking at the highest-performing students, the probability of expecting a college-level education is at about the same level in Germany for high performers as it was for the lowest performing students in the United States. The tendency to expect high educational attainment in the United States at a level that is not found in other countries has been the focus of several sociological studies (e.g., Schneider & Stevenson, 2000; Jerrim, 2014). However, we are not aware of any study that directly relates educational attainment expectations to cognitive skills that are measured in an internationally comparative way. Not only are college expectations exceptionally high in the United States (Jerrim, 2014), but research has shown that a large proportion of college graduates, who indeed complete a four-year college degree, are working in jobs that do not require that level of education. Pew Research Center (2016) reported that roughly 40 percent of respondents with a four-year bachelor's degree consider themselves overqualified for their current job, while Rose (2017) found, based on employment data only, that about 25 percent of employees with a four-year college degree work in jobs that do not require it.

Coming back to the association between skills and college aspirations, we contrast the somewhat extreme trajectories found in Germany and the United States with the graphs of two countries for which we find an almost linear trace of the question of college aspiration. In the Czech Republic and in the four provinces of China that participated in PISA, we find a strong linear relationship between the skills of students and the proportion of students who expect to finish college. Czech students, and even more so Chinese students, cover almost the full vertical range in Figure 2.2. The lowest-performing students in China almost surely (close to 0 percent) do not expect to attend college, while the highest performers almost certainly expect to attend college (almost 100 percent).

The same dependencies can also be seen for mathematics and reading. The correlations of college aspiration and skills do not vary much across these three core domains of PISA. This is true within countries. Across countries, as can be imagined, based on Figure 2.2, the correlation of college aspirations and proficiency varies greatly (see also Table 2.2). At the same time, the correlation of college aspirations and skills is among the lowest in the United States.

Table 2.2 *Correlations of college aspirations (expect to finish*
college degree) and proficiency in PISA mathematics, reading, and science
domains for four countries

PISA participant	Math	Reading	Science
B-S-J-G (China)	0.57	0.57	0.58
Czech Republic	0.52	0.54	0.49
Germany	0.34	0.33	0.37
USA	0.30	0.32	0.30

2.4   Potential Reasons for the Observed Differences

One reason for the results presented here are possible cultural differences between countries with respect to how students present themselves. Presenting themselves positively, for example, by aspiring to apparently higher goals is one way in which students may differ across countries. It is a well-researched finding that students in Asian countries show a so-called modesty effect when answering questions about self-concept topics (see e.g., Boucher, 2010). Moreover, it is an empirical finding that, particularly in North America, more extreme answers and, in particular, more positive choices are selected (He & van de Vijver, 2013; Khorramdel & von Davier, 2014).

Another reason could be that the expectation to attend college after finishing secondary school has little to do with the skills measured in PISA, which is targeted as measuring skills for participation in modern society (OECD, 2017). Therefore, whether someone expects to go to college could have little to do with how they perform on a skill measure such as PISA. This could be true in some countries, or all, or it could vary by country. The expectation to attend college could depend on other skills not measured in PISA, or on background variables such as socioeconomic status of parents or on whether parents attended college. However, PISA has been shown to predict academic outcomes and performance later in life (Albaek, 2018; Fischbach et al., 2013; Knighton & Bussière, 2006), and while these other variables may have some effect on whether someone expects to attend college, it is at least somewhat likely that academic outcomes are also related to academic aspirations, unless students are fundamentally unable to judge their skills (Kruger & Dunning, 1999).

Yet another reason (and the main reason discussed in this chapter) is that the differences in how college expectations relate to skills are due to system-level differences, in particular what types of career paths college attendance implies. As described earlier, attending college to earn a degree very likely means different things in different countries. For instance, in some countries, this umbrella term may describe studies that focus on an academic degree in mathematics, hard sciences (e.g., physics, chemistry, or biology), social sciences, or the arts. In other countries, it may be more broadly defined and include degrees that prepare students for certain professions that may not be described as hard science in the classical sense (e.g., nursing, or culinary arts). The solution is not to ask seemingly more specific questions, such as whether students intend to be a college professor. As more students attend colleges in some systems compared to others, there will be more job types and career paths prepared for in colleges. This means more college professors have jobs in teaching positions that would be done by teachers who would self-identify as artisans or master craftsmen in other countries. One potential solution appears to be to drill down into a sample of specific career tracks such as academic careers in STEM (science, technology, engineering, and mathematics), rather than social science, the arts, crafts, and other vocational occupations in order to find out in which country more students expect to become master's- or doctoral-level scientists, IT experts, economists, engineers, or doctors. Again, this is not meant to imply any value system, but, since college education in terms of career tracks covered is more broadly defined in some and more narrowly defined in other countries, a simple question about whether students expect to go to college is likely to produce results that are not comparable.

2.5   Conclusion

PISA samples 15-year-old students at the end of compulsory school. Thus, in many countries these students may attend schools that prepare them for careers outside of college. Such careers may have a well-established and long-standing status in these countries. However, differences in the rate of endorsement of the question of college aspiration may emerge due to differences such as the existence of: (a) alternative education and training paths outside of college; (b) school tracking; or (c) delayed college attendance (this may not be reported as it is not considered by students immediately after high school). Other reasons may include differential access to college by region, gender, race/ethnicity, or religion. While some reasons are well within the bounds of looking at these as societal considerations that may affect students' aspirations – such as gender- or race/ethnicity-based limitations – others, such as the existence of a well-established apprentice-ship and master-craftsperson systems outside of college tracks to jobs, are clearly not a limiting factor. Instead, the latter may offer additional, alternative pathways to a successful participation in modern economies. To compare the percentages of students who expect to go to college after finishing compulsory school is, therefore, indeed, somewhat like the proverbial comparison of apples and oranges. Along the same lines, an average of apples and oranges, or college-aspiration proportions across countries, as tweeted by OECD, makes little sense, as it averages quantities that have very different base rates just by means of how education and job-training structures differ across countries.

REFERENCES

Albæk, K. (2018). Skill-persistence and the impact of post-compulsory education on skills – evidence from a linked PISA-PIAAC data set. Paper presented at the Nordic PIAAC Expert Seminar, Stockholm, Sweden. Retrieved from http://folk.ntnu.no/mariahar/Workshop/2017/Papers/albaek.pdf.

Barclay-McKeown, S., & Oliveri, M. E. (2017). *Exploratory analysis of differential item functioning in the National Survey of Student Engagement and of its possible sources* (ETS RM-17-07). Princeton, NJ: Educational Testing Service. Retrieved from www.ets.org/Media/Research/pdf/RM-17-07.pdf.

Boucher, H. (2010). Understanding Western–East Asian differences and similarities in self-enhancement. *Social and Personality Psychology Compass, 4*, 304–317. https://doi.org/10.1111/j.1751-9004.2010.00266.x.

Dorans N. J. (2017) Contributions to the quantitative assessment of item, test and score fairness. In R. E. Bennett & von M. Davier (Eds.). *Advancing human assessment: The methodological, psychological and policy contributions of ETS*. (pp. 201–230). New York: Springer. https://doi.org/10.1007/978-3-319-58689-2_7.

Duarte, J. L., Crawford, J. T., Stern, C., Haidt, J., Jussim, L., & Tetlock, P. E. (2015). Political diversity will improve social psychological science 1. *Behavioral and Brain Sciences, 38*, E130. https://doi.org/10.1017/S0140525X14000430.

Fischbach, A., Keller, U., Preckel, F., & Brunner, M. (2013). PISA proficiency scores predict educational outcomes. *Learning and Individual Differences, 24*, 63–72. https://doi.org/10.1016/j.lindif.2012.10.012.

He, J., & van de Vijver, F. J. (2013). Methodological issues in cross-cultural studies in educational psychology. In G. A. D. Liem & A. B. I. Bernardo (Eds.). *Advancing cross-cultural perspectives on educational psychology: A festschrift for Dennis M. McInerney*. (pp. 39–55). Charlotte, NC: IAP Information Age Publishing.

Jerrim, J. (2014). The unrealistic educational expectations of high school pupils: Is America exceptional? *Sociological Quarterly, 55*, 196–231. https://doi.org/10.1111/tsq.12049.

Khorramdel, L., & von Davier, M. (2014). Measuring response styles across the Big Five: A multiscale extension of an approach using multinomial processing trees. *Multivariate Behavioral Research, 49*, 161–177. https://doi.org/ 10.1080/00273171.2013.866536.

Knighton, T., & Bussière, P. (2006). *Educational outcomes at age 19 associated with reading ability at age 15*. Ottawa: Statistics Canada.

Kruger, J., & Dunning, D. (1999). Unskilled and unaware of it: How difficulties in recognizing one's own incompetence lead to inflated self-assessments. *Journal of Personality and Social Psychology, 77*, 1121–1134. https://doi.org/ 10.1037/0022-3514.77.6.1121.

Marsh, H. (1994). Sport motivation orientations: Beware of jingle-jangle fallacies. *Journal of Sport & Exercise Psychology, 16*, 365–380. https://doi.org/10.1123/ jsep.16.4.365.

Organisation for Economic Co-operation and Development. (2017). *PISA 2015 results: Students' well-being* (Vol. 3). Paris: Organisation for Economic Co-operation and Development. www.oecd-ilibrary.org/education/pisa-2015- results-volume-iii_9789264273856-en.

Pew Research Center. (2016). The state of American jobs: How the shifting economic landscape is reshaping work and society and affecting the way people think about the skills and training they need to get ahead. Retrieved from http://assets.pewresearch.org/wp-content/uploads/sites/3/2016/10/ST_ 2016.10.06_Future-of-Work_FINAL4.pdf.

Rose, S. J. (2017). *How many workers with a bachelor's degree are overqualified for their jobs?* Washington, DC: Urban Institute Income and Benefits Policy Center.

Schneider, B. L., & Stevenson, D. (2000). *The ambitious generation: America's teenagers, motivated but directionless*. New Haven, CT: Yale University Press.

Tetlock, P. E. (1994). Political psychology or politicized psychology: Is the road to scientific hell paved with good moral intentions? *Political Psychology*, 509–529. https://doi.org/10.2307/3791569.

United Nations Educational, Scientific and Cultural Organization. (2012). International standard classification of education (ISCED) 2011. Retrieved from http://uis.unesco.org/en/topic/international-standard-classification-education- isced.

von Davier, M. (2017). CTT and No-DIF and ? = (Almost) Rasch Model. In M. Rosén, K. Y. Hansen, & U. Wolff (Eds.). *Cognitive abilities and educational outcomes*. (pp. 249–272). New York: Springer.

CHAPTER 3

Merit-Based Admissions in Higher Education

Christina Wikström and Magnus Wikström

In higher education admissions systems, different principles guide how students are selected when there is competition for study positions or when there is a limit on the number of students that can be admitted. The merit-based approach is very common in which the candidate with the best qualifications, or merits, is accepted. The way merit is defined and measured is, however, a complicated matter and reflects various views on validity and fairness. This chapter describes and discusses principles for the allocation of study positions, focusing on admissions practices where individuals are promoted or selected on the basis of their merits. Applications and challenges of such models, and the consequences for individuals, universities or colleges, and society at large are also discussed.

As discussed by Schofer and Meyer (2005), many educational systems have expanded over time, partly due to democratic and egalitarian mechanisms and partly due to the recognition that prosperity is dependent on an educated population and workforce. However, as higher education becomes increasingly important for many professions, there is likely to be an increase in students competing for admission to the most attractive higher education institutions. The selection process is often high stakes to all stakeholders, who may have different expectations regarding what the admissions process should do and what fair selection really means. For instance, institutions may be especially interested in admitting students possessing the best prerequisites to meet specific study programs' academic demands, while applicants may be interested in a transparent and fair admissions process. Future employers may have other expectations that are related to future job positions, such as the ability to perform well in academic studies (see Oliveri, Mislevy, & Elliot, in this volume). As discussed by Zwick (2017), the admissions system does not exist in a vacuum and, therefore, has to be evaluated in a larger context. Overall, the selection to higher education may ultimately be seen as a sorting mechanism for important positions that will shape future society. This belief determines how institution-level resources should be allocated to ensure that society derives the most value for these investments. However, how to define this value is a highly philosophical question, as will be discussed later in this chapter.

3.1 Fairness in Admissions

3.1.1 *Defining Fairness*

Fairness is a concept that can have different meanings – especially in admissions. Theoretical principles can guide this discussion and provide examples of their implementation in practice. Jacobs (2003) discusses the importance of linking theory with practice in the context of equality:

> It is my view that the theoretical and practical challenges of pursuing equality are closely inter-related and that neither the theoretical nor the practical challenges can be met without an eye toward the other. This means that is it unhelpful for philosophers to construct elaborate, abstract theories of egalitarian justice without some account of how to address the practical problems of realizing and implementing equality. Likewise, analysis of law and public policy cannot ignore recent sophisticated philosophical discussions around what is equality. (p. 3)

Most people would likely agree that fair access to higher education is important. However, this does not mean that everyone agrees on what this actually means, theoretically or in practice. What fair access means, and whether a system or an admissions instrument, such as a test or grade point average which is used in the system, is fair or not, varies across individuals and contexts (Zwick, 2017). The majority of the literature discussing fairness in admissions focuses on the selection instruments used in the admissions process, what they are, and what they are measuring (see American Educational Research Association, American Psychological Association, & National Council on Measurement in Education, 2014; Camilli, 2006; Dorans & Cook, 2016 for reviews and definitions of the concept of fairness in a measurement context).

In a practical context, one strategy is to view admissions instruments in light of two aspects of fairness – procedural and substantive – as suggested by Kane (2010). Procedural fairness is concerned with how applicants are treated and that the same rules are applied, and the same test or equivalent tests are given to everyone. Substantive fairness is concerned with how well a testing program functions, and, in particular, how it functions for different groups of test takers.

How instruments for selection are developed and administrated is of great importance from a fairness perspective. Issues relating to substantive fairness have implications for social ideology and lead to overall questions regarding who should be admitted and how systematic group differences detected in performance are viewed and handled.

3.1.2   Equality of Opportunity

In discussing fairness in admissions, there are also considerations beyond the practical aspects that have to be addressed. One important concept is that of equality of opportunity (EOP). An example of this concept comes from the British Admissions to Higher Education Steering Group (2004):

> [A] fair admissions system is one that provides equal opportunity for all individuals, regardless of background, to gain admission to a course suited to their ability and aspirations. Everyone agrees that applicants should be chosen on merit: the problem arises when we try to define it. Merit could mean admitting applicants with the highest examination marks, or it could mean taking a wider view about each applicant's achievement and potential. (p. 5)

The definitions of merit and EOP are important, especially since the terms are subject to a number of different interpretations. In relation to EOP, we distinguish between formal and substantive EOP, since they are useful in the discussion of fairness in admissions. When competing for a favorable position, such as a spot in a prestigious education program or a job position, many would agree that an open contest in which candidates are judged by the same criteria relevant to the position is appropriate. Here the candidate who is the most qualified would be selected. This is an example of formal EOP. It is sometimes known as the nondiscrimination principle, since it rejects criteria that are not relevant to the position at stake, such as ethnicity or gender (Roemer, 1998). While formal EOP implies that all individuals should be treated equally, it does not say anything about how to compensate for differences among people.

Substantive EOP, on the other hand, allows for compensatory measures. One way of characterizing substantive EOP is to view outcomes as a result of ability and ambition on the one hand, and circumstances on the other. Circumstances vary between individuals and are generally out of the individual's control. For example, individuals may be from rich or poor families. If being from a rich or poor family affects the possibility of gaining access to a prestigious education institution (all other things considered), actions compensating for the difference in family income may be taken, according to the substantive EOP ideal.

Fair equality of opportunity (FEO) was introduced by the late American philosopher John Rawls (1999) as a concept limiting the influence of circumstances on prospects later in life (see also Zwick, 2017). This concept specifies that if circumstances under which individuals are born are compensated for, the only factors determining success in the pursuit of social positions are native ability (or talent) and ambition. Under FEO, two persons with the same ability and ambition would have the same chance to gain access to a prestigious education program, even if they were born under different circumstances, such as being from a rich or poor family. Exactly what circumstances are to be accounted for are not precisely defined by Rawls. Nevertheless, this concept is useful here, since it contributes toward a classification of how far society should be willing to redistribute resources. For example, on the extreme end of the spectrum is *luck egalitarianism*, which limits differences as to how well off individuals are to only those choices that individuals can make, not to differences in unchosen circumstances (see Arneson, 2015 for a lengthier discussion of luck egalitarianism and related concepts).

3.2 Expectations and Principles for Resource Allocation

Before discussing merit-based admissions from an EOP perspective, we address the issue of theory versus practice in admissions. Theory consists of the principles that guide the admissions process, and practice refers to what is generally expected as a result of the admissions process. The principles below are all, to varying degrees, relevant to EOP. We first discuss expectations and, thereafter, the principles that can guide the admissions process.

3.2.1 Expectations

As previously indicated, there are cultural differences that reflect on admissions processes and the instruments used as part of the process. There may be similar overall goals, but expectations from different stakeholders are not always aligned. The Swedish system provides a good example of how complex and multifaceted expectations are (see Lyrén & Wikström, in this volume, for greater detail on admissions practices used in Sweden), and it is likely that admissions systems elsewhere are challenged with similar types of complexity.

In Swedish policy documents, the overall aims for higher education and the admissions system are expressed as the following:

> Higher education of high quality is crucial for securing future jobs and in the long term to strengthen Sweden's competitiveness, but also to give women and men increased security in the job market and increased power to shape their own lives. (Proposition 2017/18: 204, 2018, p. 7)

The same document (translated by the authors) states that:

> Access to higher education of high quality is an important prerequisite for giving young people choices, and, later in life giving women and men the opportunity for education and professional development and increased security in new and changing times. Proximity to higher education is also necessary for broadening recruitment and giving more people the chance to get an education. In Sweden, recruitment to higher education is skewed and this needs to be changed. (p. 9)

Such statements reveal different expectations – that universities need to provide society with excellence, but also need to broaden recruitment by admitting more students with nontraditional backgrounds, including older students. These aims are not necessarily contradictory, but one may hypothesize that universities will take into consideration that nontraditional students may require more support than students with a more traditional educational background. The ambition to broaden recruitment also challenges admissions policies, since these nontraditional students may be less likely to be able to compete with the higher grades presented by students from more traditional educational backgrounds.

There may also be a conflict between values and economic expectations. As described by Lyrén & Wikström (in this volume), there is a strong belief in lifelong learning and the opportunity to make changes throughout one's life. However, this duality raises a relevant question as to how to allocate resources: If the number of study positions is limited, is it wise to encourage older students or students who have several weaknesses in previous schooling to apply? The answer to this question depends on how fairness is interpreted and on the beliefs and interpretations of the fundamental principles that guide societal resource allocation.

3.2.2   Principles for Resource Allocation

There are a number of different principles that can guide admissions processes. Wolming (1999) argues that the application of utilitarian, egalitarian, and meritocratic principles are particularly relevant. Following Wolming, we describe these three principles next.

3.2.2.1 Meritocracy

The first principle is that of meritocracy. Meritocracy means that promotion in society or within a system is based on merit and when applicants, or potential recruits to a position or a higher education institution, are ranked ordered on the basis of a set of criteria or merits. This approach is often called merit-based selection, where there is a strong belief in objective measurement and the rank ordering of individuals based on such measurement. Merit-based selection is probably the most common selection principle in higher education and is also frequently used in workforce selection.

It should be noted that there is a strong connection between EOP and merit-based selection. Meritocracy can also be perceived as a type of reward system. As Amartaya Sen (2000) states:

> In fact, meritocracy is just an extension of a general system of rewarding merit, and elements of such a system clearly have been present in one form or another throughout human history. There are, it can be argued, at least two different ways of seeing merit and systems of rewarding it:
>
> 1. Incentives: Actions may be rewarded for the good they do, and a system of remunerating the activities that generate good consequences would, it is presumed, tend to produce a better society. The rationale of incentive structures may be more complex than this simple statement suggests, but the idea of merits in this instrumental perspective relates to the motivation of producing better results. In this view, actions are meritorious in a derivative and contingent way, depending on the good they do, and more particularly the good that can be brought about by rewarding them.
>
> 2. Action propriety: Actions may be judged by their propriety – not by their results – and they may be rewarded according to the quality of such actions, judged in a result-independent way. Much use has been made of this approach to merit, and parts of deontological ethics separate out right conduct – for praise and emulation – independent of the goodness of the consequences generated. (p. 8)

Seen from this perspective, we argue that meritocratic systems have two potential advantages – to provide: (a) a certain degree of fairness (in terms of formal EOP) and (b) a signal of what is a desirable consequence or action for a stakeholder.

Although the term meritocratic may describe a merit-awarding system, it is highly controversial. While some see it as another term for merit-based selection, others see it as a mechanism for maintaining class structure in society through the use of tests, particularly intelligence tests, or tests built on similar principles (see, for instance, Guinier, 2015; Lemann, 1999; Sacks, 2001).

The term meritocracy originated in the novel *The Rise of the Meritocracy*, published in 1958 by British sociologist Michael Young. The book describes a future society ruled by a merited elite, formed by promotion based on measures of intelligence and merit. The debate on the use of standardized aptitude tests (SATs) for high-stakes decisions and its consequences for society has been especially heated in the United States. Books such as *The Bell Curve: Intelligence and Class Structure in American Life*, by Richard J. Herrnstein and Charles Murray (1994), where systematic differences in group performance were aligned with ethnicity and race, and *The Mismeasure of Man*, by Stephen Jay Gould (1996), which argued that systematic differences in test performance have social and cultural explanations, have also contributed to this negative view of what meritocracy means and entails. From a European perspective, the criticism against negative consequences of high-stakes testing has mainly focused on its effects on educational quality and learning (see, for instance, Stobart, 2008), and not so much on the group consequences.

Merit-based selection practices are not new. Already in ancient China, tests were used in the recruitment of important positions in society. This test use spread to Europe and the rest of the world much later. From the eighteenth century on, as industry expanded and the need to recruit skilled workers became more urgent, selection based on the outcome from different types of tests spread (Stobart, 2008). The possibility of measuring individuals' abilities and skills resulted in an increasing interest in measurement and psychometrics. Testing was seen as an efficient way to place an individual on a scale. There was a belief in the possibilities and trustworthiness of using tests for making claims about a person's aptitude for a specific task or position.

As the educational sector expanded during the twentieth century, so did the development and use of standardized tests. Some of the most influential tests included the Stanford–Binet scale, which provided the foundation for the Army Alpha used in selection among military recruits, which then provided the basic foundation for the American first standardized admissions test, the Scholastic Aptitude Test (SAT®). The SAT then inspired the development of the Israeli Psychometric Entrance Test (PET), the Swedish SweSAT, the American ACT® Test and other tests used in the selection to higher education. See, for instance, Lemann (1999; 2004) for more detailed descriptions of the background of standardized testing and admissions testing in the United States, and Stobart (2008) for a more international perspective.

In summary, meritocracy is the principle that selection and promotion should be based on merit alone. What is meant by merit, its definition and operationalization, provides interesting questions, and the consequences that follow such definitions and choices are highly relevant from an egalitarian perspective.

3.2.2.2 *Egalitarianism*

As the name suggests, the principle of egalitarianism is based on the belief in equality – that all individuals should be treated equally and have the same quality of life. Theories on equal opportunity and what they mean, as described earlier, are directly related to egalitarianism. In a simplified sense, egalitarianism suggests that the world's aggregated assets should be equally shared. There are, however, many different interpretations of what egalitarianism really means in practice. These different interpretations reflect different political and religious beliefs, and ongoing debates on this issue continue in various fields such as philosophy, politics, history, law, and economics (Whaples, 2017).

A contemporary interpretation of egalitarianism has to do with equal distribution of rights and authorities and the pursuit of equality in civil society (Jacobs, 2003). Two different paths, relevant for discussing admissions practices, can be identified. One path, the pursuit of political equality, is more traditional and legally oriented as it reflects individual rights: All individuals should be treated equally and have the same rights (cf. formal EOP). A second path deals with social aspects and fundamental requirements for equality in society (cf. substantive EOP). Here, economic inequalities should be removed, and power decentralized and distributed among individuals (Jacobs, 2003). In this sense, egalitarianism does not just concern the current state of the world, but also the direction of future development (e.g., a more equal society than the current state).

There are different ways that the egalitarian principle can reflect on practice in admissions. One approach could be to distribute available study positions at an institution proportionally to the population. It could be carried out through a lottery or by a stratified sampling approach, by allocating available study positions according to students' backgrounds. Another approach could be to adjust for imbalances between admitted students of different gender, race/ethnicity or socioeconomic background when the admitted group is disproportionate to the group of applicants. In practice, this could be carried out by giving additional weight to required criteria for underrepresented groups or providing different paths in the selection process to different groups. Scholarship systems can also be a way to broaden recruitment which give able students from underrepresented groups more access to higher education, especially at institutions where private economic resources are important to obtain admission to higher education.

3.2.2.3   Utilitarianism

Utilitarianism is another principle relevant for higher education admissions that differs somewhat from the previous two principles. Utilitarianism is part of the consequentialist tradition, in which actions are valued by the consequences they have on society. Early utilitarians, such as John Stuart Mill, thought that society should maximize happiness or pleasure among the largest number of people. One way to clarify the implications of utilitarianism on distributive justice is through the concept of a social welfare function, a standard tool of welfare economics.

A social welfare function dictates how to rank order different social outcomes – for example, if individual A or individual B should be admitted into college. One often-used formulation of the social welfare function is the additive (the so-called Benthamite social welfare function), in which all individuals' utilities (here in the sense of well-being) are aggregated with equal weight. In the comparison of social outcomes, the best one is the one that maximizes welfare (the sum of individual utilities if the Benthamite social welfare function is applied). Maximizing welfare in this way does not rule out perfect equalization of utilities among individuals (outcome equality) or status quo situations.

The amount of equalization that maximizes welfare depends upon assumptions regarding what brings well-being and to whom, as well as the market and nonmarket environment prevailing in society. Modern welfare economists generally admit to a certain degree of redistribution. This follows from a built-in assumption that one additional dollar is of higher value to those with lesser wealth and, therefore, brings more well-being than to a person with more wealth.

The utilitarian approach to distributive justice has been criticized on several grounds. One source of criticism concerns what should be included in the definition of individual well-being and how to make comparisons across individuals. Another source of criticism follows from the lack of morality concerning how total welfare should be distributed. For example, there could be a policy that will hurt specific people, but where the total welfare is higher than the status quo (Sen, 1979).

Nevertheless, the utilitarian approach is of interest when discussing admissions policies. Since it is an outcome-oriented approach, it can be used for evaluating success of a particular admissions practice. One example is the age cap sometimes observed in admissions to certain professional fields, such as medicine. If a nondiscrimination approach such as the egalitarian principle is applied, age discrimination would not be allowed. Rank ordering candidates on the basis of some measure as is done with a meritocratic approach – for instance, using upper secondary GPA, may also not be allowed since it does not necessarily maximize social welfare even if the grades perfectly predict academic success. A utilitarian approach would take into consideration the benefits over candidates' entire career, with a focus on which student will be most useful to society after graduation.

The utilitarian perspective, being focused on consequences, is highly relevant when it comes to discussing a broader set of issues indirectly related to admissions. Such issues include how many students in particular fields society should allow to be educated, or whether expanding particular fields would be at the expense of the number of students in other fields. Since many educational systems rely on public funding, there is competition in terms of how resources are used in education.

3.3   Selection Principles in a Practical Context

As previously discussed, there are a number of principles that are relevant for understanding how admissions systems function, or should function, in practice. In most cases, there will be elements of several principles embedded in the admissions approach used by an institution and it can be important to understand how these are manifested and how they interact with each other.

3.3.1   *The Swedish Admissions System*

As an illustration of the complexity of applying various principles in practice, the Swedish admissions system serves as a good example. All three principles discussed in this chapter – meritocratic, egalitarian, and utilitarian – are part of the design of the Swedish system. These principles are reflected in the policy documents that were previously mentioned, that discuss expectations about excellence, broad recruitment, and lifelong learning. Whether or not the admissions design is optimal with regards to these expectations is, however, a different question, but that discussion requires much more elaboration than this chapter allows.

It should also be mentioned that the Swedish system stands out in two ways. First, admission to higher education is centrally administered.

Universities and other higher education institutions have some local authority when it comes to allocating study positions based on different selection instruments, but otherwise the process is centrally regulated. Second, selection is based on the upper secondary grade point average (GPA) and a standardized selection test, but not in combination, as is common in other countries. There are specific reasons for this.

In Swedish society, there is an overall belief in meritocracy, or merit-based promotion to positions in the job market as well as to study positions in higher education. Study positions are allocated on the basis of previous performance (school grades) or by measured abilities or skills (performance on the admissions test, the SweSAT). This is an interesting aspect that is worth further discussion.

There are two parallel traditions in Swedish education. One is characterized by a psychometric tradition and the other is characterized by a distrust in standardized measures and a belief in teacher assessment (Tveit, 2018; Wikström & Lind Pantzare, 2018). These traditions explain the design of the grading system in Swedish schools and the origin of the SweSAT, but, most of all, the existence of parallel measures has to do with a belief in providing alternatives and second chances to all individuals. This complicates the meritocratic principle underlying the Swedish admissions system. The belief in the importance of equal opportunities for all individuals reflects an egalitarian approach – as long as they do not violate the principle that the person with the highest merits should be first in line. In an ideal society, where all students are given equal opportunities to develop prerequisite skills and be provided with equal schooling, this would not be a problem. Unfortunately, this is not the case in Sweden nor, most probably, in any other country.

The focus on providing equal opportunities is visible throughout the school system since school law specifies that quality education should be available to all students, under the same conditions. To achieve this, an important strategy was to remove economic barriers by funding education from preschool to university with taxes, disallowing tuition fees and implementing compensatory measures to give extra support to schools where many students come from low socioeconomic backgrounds or have a non-Swedish origin.

The third principle, utilitarian, is less prominent in the Swedish higher education admissions system, depending on how utilitarianism is viewed. For example, the belief in lifelong learning and in promoting diversity can be viewed in different ways. In a positive sense, there are benefits for the student and to society, since diversity is expected to have a number of positive effects. But, in a negative sense, the money used to finance career changes late in life or for students who are more challenging to teach might be better spent elsewhere. The utilitarian principle is generally what guides changes in government policy, as it reflects beliefs of what is best for society using a longer-term perspective.

Even if one aim of Swedish education policy has been to achieve a society free from social structures, it has not been as successful as expected. From an international perspective, Swedish society has fairly low social segregation and good quality education, but the trend has been changing recently. The achievement gaps have increased as regards both students' social background and origin; equality in education has decreased (Organisation for Economic Co-operation and Development, 2015). This will inevitably affect higher education admissions and the student body in higher education. The question is then what to do about it, when equal opportunities cannot be guaranteed.

Implementing affirmative-action policies are the kinds of measures that may be thought of first. While such policies have been used at times, they tend to be controversial and many countries ban their use. Another alternative is to provide separate paths to higher education or to provide alternative instruments to measure prerequisite skills, since individuals may perform differently on different instruments. These differences can be explained by factors such as familiarity with particular content or contexts, or motivation and anxiety levels in relation to a particular instrument. However, this can be problematic in other respects. For instance, the separate paths may not really make a difference in terms of how students are rank ordered, or one instrument may be found to be more relevant than another.

When it comes to the Swedish system, both scenarios are problematic. First, in Sweden, affirmative action is not allowed. Second, the original idea behind separate paths to higher education was to give students with nontraditional backgrounds a second chance via the SweSAT. When first introduced, the SweSAT was only open to older students (25 years or older) with at least four years of work experience. This model is aligned with egalitarian aspirations since the intention was to make higher education more representative of the population. However, it also violated the meritocratic principle that all candidates should compete under the same conditions. To give some students an alternative that was not open to all students has been criticized for being unfair, and the introduction of the SweSAT for older applicants only led to strong criticism and pressure to revise the model.

In 1991, the path via the test was opened up for all students, meaning that students with upper secondary grades can also take the test and now compete in both admissions groups. In this case, students are selected on the basis of where they are ranked the highest. The results were not as intended because students with a traditional educational background, and especially students on the academic track, generally outperform students with a nontraditional background. An argument for the current model can, however, still be made in that different criteria work differently for different groups of students. For example, females tend to have higher grades, while males tend to have higher test scores. Thus, using both criteria contributes to a more balanced admissions practice. Furthermore, there are other arguments that continue to support the current model. These include a belief in a second chance and the ability to compete for attractive study positions if upper secondary school grades do not reflect applicants' true knowledge and skills, or if upper secondary school grades were assigned at a time when, or in a place where, the grading system was not comparable to grades currently used in Swedish education.

Moreover, the relevance of both grades and test scores as selection criteria in higher education is a familiar issue in the achievement vs. aptitude debate. The debate concerns what grades and tests are really measuring, and to what extent they are relevant for predicting academic success. In the United States, the debate has particularly focused on the two widely used admissions tests, the SAT and ACT. The SAT has been criticized for not being aligned with school curricula (see Zwick, 2004 for an overview of the issues; also Atkinson & Geiser, 2009 and Linn, 2009 for different positions on the issue). This is an area where there is a difference between Sweden and other countries with similar tests; expectations are that the SweSAT is not linked to the curriculum but, instead, measures more general knowledge and skills relevant for academic studies.

3.3.2 *Predicting Academic Success*

As described above, the debate on what the admissions instruments used in the selection process are measuring, and how this affects who is selected, is a key issue in the discussion of fair and relevant admissions. The discussion seems, however, often to focus primarily on one issue: their ability to predict academic success. This issue has dominated research on the instruments used in the admissions process, both in the United States (Zwick, 2002) and in Sweden (Lyrén, 2008; Wolming & Wikström, 2010).

Predictive validity is important, but the focus on this aspect represents a narrow view, as discussed by Zwick (2017), where measures of prediction are also connected with a number of methodological problems that are often overlooked. Important questions that need to be addressed include not only what the criterion for academic success really is, how it can be described and measured, but also the potential consequences of the chosen approach.

Academic success is a complex construct to measure, and construct underrepresentation of the instruments used in merit-based systems is a valid criticism. It is unlikely that academic success can be measured by a standardized test or even by school grades alone. There are probably many other things that explain why students do well in school, such as maturity, motivation, and industriousness (see Kuncel, Tran & Zhang, in this volume).

A recent literature review by York, Gibson and Rankin (2015) concluded that academic success is a combination of academic achievement, attainment of learning objectives, acquisition of desired skills and competencies, satisfaction, persistence, and post-college performance. They list methods that can be used for measuring this and conclude that it cannot be done solely by achievement tests, but should be comprised of a variety of instruments and methods. Some of the critics of the traditional selection tests – for instance, Sedlacek (2004) and Guinier (2015) – have suggested alternatives to traditional selection instruments. Guinier presents ideas of how *democratic merit* can be measured and used in the selection to higher education, while Sedlacek suggests a self-report instrument measuring noncognitive aspects that he claims are more relevant for predicting academic success. It may be the case that these could be relevant measures in an admissions context, but questions on how they would be viewed by the stakeholders in terms of fairness and relevance, whether the construct will be better represented this way and how sensitive such instruments are to group differences remain (see Kuncel, Tran, & Zhang, in this volume for a discussion of other relevant aspects, such as coaching or social desirability, seen with self-report instruments). The question is also, of course, whether the introduction of other types of instruments would improve selection in admissions with regard to the principles discussed in this chapter. If selection is made using a number of instruments in combination, will this be practicable, or economically defensible? The more complex the selection process, the more difficult it will be to validate.

3.4   Concluding Remarks

To summarize, there is, unfortunately, no simple answer as to how an admissions system should be designed. Views on fairness and relevance vary with culture and context, and all instruments used for selection have their strengths and weaknesses and are likely to work differently for different individuals. The key issue is, as always, to define what the result of the admissions system should be. What should be measured in the selection process must be determined first and then attention focused on the criteria used and its validity. In the absence of this, the discussion on the design of an admissions system is pointless.

What is also clear is that EOP is a prerequisite for fair admissions and fair assessment in a merit-based system. If students are not given EOP to obtain the required skills due to previous schooling, socioeconomic background, lack of information or financial constraints, comparisons of students will not be equal. This is something that falls outside the reach of higher education admissions but is a major challenge for educational systems and society.

REFERENCES

Admissions to Higher Education Steering Group. (2004). Fair admissions to higher education: Recommendations for good practice. Retrieved from http://dera.ioe.ac.uk/5284/1/finalreport.pdf.

American Educational Research Association, American Psychological Association, & National Council on Measurement in Education. (2014). *Standards for educational and psychological testing.* Washington, DC: American Educational Research Association.

Arneson, R. (2015). Equality of opportunity. In E. N. Zalta (Ed.), The Stanford encyclopedia of philosophy: Summer 2015 edition. Retrieved from https://plato.stanford.edu/archives/sum2015/entries/equal-opportunity.

Atkinson, R. C., & Geiser, S. (2009). *Reflections on a century of college admissions tests.* (Center for Studies in Higher Education Research & Occasional Paper Series, CSHE.4.09). https://doi.org/10.3102/0013189X09351981.

Camilli, G. (2006). Test fairness. In R. Brennan (Ed.), *Educational measurement* (4th ed.) (pp. 221–256). Lanham, MD: Rowman & Littlefield.

Dorans, N., & Cook, L. (2016). *Fairness in educational assessment and measurement.* New York: Routledge. https://doi.org/10.4324/9781315774527.

Gould, S. J. (1996). *The mismeasure of man.* New York: W. W. Norton & Company.

Guinier, L. (2015). *The tyranny of the meritocracy: Democratizing higher education in America.* Boston, MA: Beacon Press.

Herrnstein, R. J., & Murray, C. (1994). *The bell curve: Intelligence and class structure in American life.* New York: Free Press.

Jacobs, L. A. (2003). *Pursuing equal opportunities: The theory and practice of egalitarian justice.* Cambridge: Cambridge University Press. https://doi.org/10.1017/CBO9780511616556.

Kane, M. (2010). Validity and fairness. *Language Testing, 27,* 177–182. https://doi.org/10.1177/0265532209349467.

Lemann, N. (1999). *The big test: The secret history of the American meritocracy.* New York: Farrar, Straus & Giroux.

(2004). The history of admissions testing. In R. Zwick (Ed.), *Rethinking the SAT: The future of standardized testing in university admissions.* New York: RoutledgeFalmer.

Linn, R. L. (2009). Considerations for college admissions testing. *Educational Researcher, 38,* 677–679. https://doi.org/10.3102/0013189X09351982.

Lyrén, P.-E. (2008). Prediction of academic performance by means of the Swedish scholastic assessment test. *Scandinavian Journal of Educational Research, 52,* 565–581. https://doi.org/10.1080/00313830802497158.

Organisation for Economic Co-operation and Development. (2015). Improving schools in Sweden: An OECD perspective. Retrieved from www.oecd.org/edu/school/Improving-Schools-in-Sweden.pdf.

Proposition 2017/18: 204. (2018).Fler vägar till kunskap – en högskola för livslångt lärande. [More routes to knowledge – higher education for lifelong learning]. Retrieved from www.regeringen.se/rattsdokument/proposition/2018/03/201718204/.

Rawls, J. (1999). *A theory of justice* (Revised ed.). Cambridge, MA: Harvard University Press.

Roemer, J. E. (1998). *Equality of opportunity.* Cambridge, MA: Harvard University Press.

Sacks, P. (2001). *Standardized minds: The high price of America's testing culture and what we can do to change it.* New York: HarperCollins.

Schofer, E., & Meyer, J. W. (2005). The worldwide expansion of higher education in the twentieth century. *American Sociological Review, 70,* 898–920. https://doi.org/10.1177/000312240507000602.

Sedlacek, W. E. (2004). *Beyond the big test: Noncognitive assessment in higher education.* San Francisco, CA: Jossey-Bass.

Sen, A. (1979). Utilitarianism and welfarism. *Journal of Philosophy, 76,* 463–489. https://doi.org/10.2307/2025934.

(2000). Merit and justice. In K. J. Arrow, S. Bowles, & S. N. Durlauf (Eds.), *Meritocracy and economic inequality* (pp. 5–16). Princeton, NJ: Princeton University Press.

Stobart, G. (2009). *Testing times: The uses and abuses of assessment.* Hoboken: Taylor & Francis.

Tveit, S. (2018). (Trans)national trends and cultures of educational assessment: Reception and resistance of national testing in Norway and Sweden during the twentieth century. In C. Alarcon & M. Lawn (Eds.), *Assessment cultures:*

Historical perspectives. Berlin: Peter Lang. https://doi.org/10.3726/978-3-653-06867-2

Whaples, R. M. (2017). The economics of Pope Francis: An introduction. *The Independent Review: A Journal of Political Economy*, *21*, 325–345.

Wikström, C., & Lind Pantzare, A. (2018). Standard setting. In J.-A. Baird, T. Isaacs, & D. Opposs (Eds.), *Examination standards: How measures and meanings differ around the world*. London: UCL Institute of Education Press.

Wolming, S. (1999). Ett rättvist urval? [A fair selection?]. *Pedagogisk Forskning i Sverige*, *4*(3), 245–258.

Wolming, S., & Wikström, C. (2010). The concept of validity in theory and practice. *Assessment in Education: Principles, Policy & Practice*, *17*, 117–132.

York, T. T., Gibson, C., & Rankin, S. (2015). Defining and measuring academic success. *Practical Assessment, Research and Evaluation*, *20*(5).

Young, M. (1958). *The rise of the meritocracy, 1870–2033*. London: Thames & Hudson.

Zwick, R. (2002). *Fair game? The use of standardized admissions tests in higher education*. New York, NY: RoutledgeFalmer.

(2004). *Rethinking the SAT: The future of standardized testing in university admissions*. New York, NY: RoutledgeFalmer.

(2017). *Who gets in? Strategies for fair and effective college admissions*. Cambridge, MA: Harvard University Press.

CHAPTER 4

The Open Admissions Model: An Example from the United States

Kevin M. Williams and Cathy Wendler

When former President Obama announced his intention to increase the proportion of individuals completing college, he reinforced the need to increase opportunity for all students to participate in higher education in the United States as a national priority (Obama, 2009). Subsequently, a goal was set for 60 percent of the nation's adult population (ages 25 through 34) to have a 2-year associate or 4-year bachelor's degree by the year 2020 (US Department of Education, 2012). However, even with this goal, factors such as rising costs, reduction in the availability of financial aid, concerns with the return on investment, and selectivity of college admissions create barriers for all students but may be particularly problematic for those who come from underserved populations. This population includes those students from lower-income families, underserved racial/ethnic groups, and first-generation college attendees, all of whose enrollment rates continue to lag behind those of other student populations (Morley, 2003; Nagaoka, Roderick, & Coca, 2008). Since 2009, the proportion of Americans who are 25 years or older who have completed at least four years of college has barely increased, and the proportion enrolled in college each year has remained stable (US Census Bureau, 2017a; 2017b), suggesting continued room for improvement in achieving these goals.

Open admissions approaches in the United States serve as a mechanism to reduce barriers for students whose backgrounds are disadvantaged or underprivileged. Institutions with open admissions provide higher education opportunities to many types of students such as those who need or wish to reduce the costs of a more selective 4-year institution by completing basic requirements at a more affordable 2-year institution; students who are seeking vocational or technical education; students who may need

The opinions and recommendations expressed here are those of the authors and not necessarily those of Educational Testing Service.

further academic preparation before entering a more selective 4-year institution; and students who do not qualify for admissions to institutions having particular entrance requirements. In order to attract and better serve these students, these institutions often offer flexible scheduling such as online and evening courses or provide credit for past employment experience.

The remainder of this chapter discusses open admissions across four sections. First, we provide a working definition of the open admissions model in the United States, including its rationale, historical origins, and current practices. We then present a section discussing some of the benefits of the open admissions model, followed by a section describing some of its remaining challenges. We conclude with a section detailing some limitations of our review, future research directions, and final comments.

4.1   The Open Admissions Model

While this chapter focuses on the United States, it is acknowledged that other countries also use various open admissions approaches or something similar (Guri-Rosenblit, 2010). For example, in the late 1960s, the Open University was established in the United Kingdom, based on an open-access approach. This allowed part-time students, mostly from blue-collar backgrounds, to enroll for academic study. From their very beginning, Scottish universities admitted anyone who wished to study a particular subject (Guri-Rosenblit, 2010). In 2015, Germany established the Kiron Open Higher Education organization to help refugees avoid barriers that they often face regarding higher education (see https://kiron.ngo/). Students do not receive a degree through Kiron, but they receive course certificates which can help them transfer to a higher education institution. In Belgium, postsecondary enrollment is available for students with a qualifying secondary education diploma, although requirements may differ depending on whether they plan on studying in the Flemish-, French-, or German-speaking communities. In addition, special-entrance examinations developed by the Ministry of Education are required for a few specific programs (e.g., medicine, dentistry) or there are skills tests developed by each institution for programs in art and music. Finally, one of the goals of the Bologna Process (European Union, 2018) is to create more consistency in terms of access policies across universities whose countries are part of the European Union. Part II in this volume provides details on country-specific admissions practices, some of which are open admissions.

This chapter only focuses on nonprofit postsecondary institutions in the United States. For-profit institutions carry with them specific challenges, risks, and benefits and would require a separate chapter. Similarly, a detailed discussion of the differences between for-profit and nonprofit institutions is complex and beyond the scope of this chapter. Levy (2015) provides a more thorough comparison, including an orientation for readers outside the United States.

There are two basic implementation approaches used at open admissions institutions in the United States (Perfetto et al., 1999). The first, an *entitlement* approach, takes the perspective that higher education is a right and should be available to all individuals. This approach is based on progression through required prior experiences and is similar to approaches used in Europe where any student with a qualifying secondary-level diploma or certificate may enroll.

The second approach is *open access*, with the perspective that higher education is a natural progression following high school and should be available for any individual who is qualified. In this approach, the criteria for admissions are based on achieving predetermined minimums. Here, selection criteria may be traded: A higher level of academic performance may take the place of poor test scores, while higher test scores may take priority over poor academic performance.

For the purposes of this chapter, we discuss the open admissions model using the entitlement definition. The open admissions model has also been referred to as "open enrollment," "open door," "open access," or "non-selective." Some open admissions institutions may require additional information (e.g., standardized test scores) to determine placement into remedial courses, but there is no minimum score required for acceptance. Although admissions criteria could be characterized using a continuum, our focus is on institutions whose criteria are at the extreme (low) end of this continuum. Put differently, the admissions criteria of selective institutions (i.e., those that are not open admissions institutions) vary. For instance, some may require higher standardized test scores than others. In turn, we primarily use a dichotomy to compare open admissions institutions with all other institutions.

Open admissions institutions (e.g., community colleges) appear to be attractive options for international students, as their enrollment rate grew approximately 10 percent between 2004 and 2011 (Anayah & Kuk, 2015). However, international students require additional credentials (such as the requisite visa), but this goes beyond the scope of this chapter. Otherwise, these students are subjected to an essentially identical admissions process to that US citizens undergo.

An institution's acceptance rate is not synonymous with the type of admissions model that is used at the institution. Acceptance rates are not only a function of the institution's admissions criteria. They also reflect the size and nature of the respective applicant pool. For instance, the National Center for Education Statistics' (NCES) Integrated Postsecondary Education Data System provides information on the acceptance rates of US postsecondary institutions, including those with 100 percent acceptance rates, but explicitly states that it does not collect information on open admissions institutions (Ginder, Kelly-Reid, & Mann, 2018). Therefore, although 100 percent acceptance is used to define open admissions, 100 percent acceptance does not mean that the institution uses an open admissions approach.

4.2   A Brief History of Open Admissions in the United States

The Morrill Act of 1862 (also called the Land-Grant College Act) initiated the practice of open admissions in the United States and provided financial assistance for higher education institutions to teach agriculture and mechanical arts. The result of the Morrill Act was for land-grant institutions to become open to all residents of a state who had completed high school and created the foundation of an open-access policy (Lorenzo, 1993). The second Morrill Act, in 1890, reinforced open access to all students by withholding federal funds to colleges that withheld student admission to land-grant colleges based on race (unless the state provided a separate institution for minority students).

4.2.1   Open Admissions and 2-Year Institutions

If there is a single concept that defines 2-year institutions – referred to as "community colleges" in the United States – it is that of their open admissions policy (Shannon & Smith, 2006). In many ways, community colleges are unique: They hold a special place between secondary schools and 4-year colleges, they provide services to different types of students than those who attend a traditional 4-year college, and they are responsive to and motivated by vocational and economic needs. The role and scope of the community college system has been defined as "the only sector of higher education that can truly be called a *movement*, one in which the members are bound together and inspired by common goals . . . The open door [admissions] policy has been pursued with an intensity and dedication ... [and] community colleges have sought excellence in service to the many" (American Association of Community Colleges, 1998, p. 5). Drury (2003) presents a concise history of the development of the community college system and the social, political, and economic factors that influenced its development.

While community colleges have been historically the strongest proponent of the open admissions policy, the first community college was not established until 1901. Even then, few 2-year institutions existed in the early 1900s; by 1910, there were three public community colleges and by 1914 there were 14 public and 32 private community colleges (Drury, 2003).

4.2.2 Open Admissions and 4-Year Institutions

Open admissions approaches in 4-year colleges became more prominent in the 1960s and 1970s. Open admissions approaches were adopted by the University of California and the City University of New York (CUNY) during that time. The open admissions policy reflected the belief that *all* students, regardless of their background, should have an equal access to higher education. The changing demographics of the country, including the population of college-aged students, and the tenets of the civil rights movement also influenced the open-door policy of 4-year institutions.

One of the better-known examples of the benefits and challenges of open admissions is that of the approach instituted by CUNY. There was tremendous political pressure on CUNY in the 1960s in that the system no longer reflected the demographics of the New York City population. Moving to an open admissions policy was expected to provide more diversity on campuses. As a result, in 1970, CUNY implemented a new policy where any student who graduated from high school with at least an 80 average in academic courses or ranked within the top 50 percent of their class could enroll in one of the CUNY senior (4-year) colleges (Fullinwider, 1999). Graduates who did not meet these criteria were still guaranteed acceptance at a junior (community) college or a job-training program. The result of this change was that the number of students enrolling in a CUNY campus nearly doubled and the number of Black and Hispanic students enrolling nearly tripled.

Unfortunately, the open admissions policy also had its drawbacks. It was found that, on average, those students who enrolled as open admissions students had fewer academic credits and lower grade point averages than regular students. Subsequently, remedial courses were put into place to accommodate the open admissions students who fell below college-level preparation in mathematics and language skills. After five years, 58 percent of the open admissions students had left CUNY without a degree (Full-inwider, 1999).

In the mid-1970s, additional changes occurred at CUNY campuses. Tuition was instituted in 1975, due to the near bankruptcy of the CUNY system. Since many of the open admissions students came from families with smaller incomes, the introduction of tuition presented a new barrier. In addition, in 1976, admission was limited to students who graduated from high school with at least an average score of 80 in academic courses or ranked within the top 35 percent (revised from the earlier 50 percent) of their class. The result was that enrollment dropped dramatically (New York Times, 1976).

4.2.3   Current Open Admissions Practices

Currently, there are more than 1,100 community colleges in the United States (American Association of Community Colleges, 2018). More than half of all 2-year degree-granting institutions in the United States in the 2015–2016 academic year practiced open admissions (McFarland et al., 2017). Enrollment at 2-year institutions increased substantially over the past few decades (Camara & Westrick, 2017; McFarland et al., 2017). A recent survey from the National Association for College Admission Counseling indicated that 43 percent of enrolled freshmen were from less selective (more than 70 percent acceptance) institutions (Clinedinst, Koranteng, & Nicola, 2016). In the 4-year college system, there were 342 public and private nonprofit institutions with open admissions in 2014–2015 (Camara & Westrick, 2017).

Recent statistics describing the size and demographics of the community college student population reinforces their continued open-door policy mission. In fall 2015, 6.5 million undergraduate students attended 2-year degree-granting institutions (McFarland et al., 2017). For students who graduated from high school in spring 2015, about 25 percent of them enrolled in community college for the subsequent fall semester, compared to 44 percent who enrolled in a 4-year college. Across the 18- to 24-year-old student population, the proportion of students enrolled in community colleges in 2015 was roughly one-third (11 percent) of those enrolled in 4-year institutions (30 percent) and has remained relatively stable since 2000. Part-time students represent 61 percent of 2-year college students compared to 23 percent of 4-year students (McFarland et al., 2017), suggesting that community colleges may be the preferred option among individuals with other obligations (e.g., family, employment) (National Student Clearinghouse Research Center, 2017a).

Thus, community colleges continue to have a vital role in providing higher education opportunities for many students. Factors such as their open admissions policy, low tuition, and geographical locations make "them an important pathway to postsecondary education for many students, especially first-generation college students and those who are from low-income families" (Ma & Baum, 2016, p. 1).

4.3 Benefits of Open Admissions

4.3.1 Evaluating Open Admissions Institutions

Several goals have been outlined as part of the rationale for the open admissions model, such as increasing accessibility to all students, diversity, career possibilities, and economic stability. Relevant data available from various large agencies such as the US Department of Education (e.g., McFarland et al., 2017) and the US Department of Labor (e.g., Bureau of Labor Statistics, 2018) allow us to further evaluate these goals. Note that, in some cases, we conducted new analyses with these publicly available data. In addition, various proxies are used as part of the analyses since the required data were unavailable. For example, given the popularity of open admissions policies in 2-year institutions, these institutions are used as a more general estimate of the entire open admissions population. Similarly, because associate degrees are the most commonly conferred credential at 2-year institutions, these data are used as a proxy for degrees obtained from any open admissions institution.

4.3.2 Accessibility and Diversity

One of the primary goals for the open admissions model is to increase the overall size of the higher education population in the United States (Ingram & Morrissey, 2009). Comparisons between 2-year institutions and 4-year institutions who use a more selective admissions process (hence referred to as "selective institutions") provide a useful approach in evaluating this goal. For example, 2-year college enrollment increased by approximately 35 percent from 1985 to 2014 (Camara & Westrick, 2017; see also McFarland et al., 2017), while enrollment in selective institutions remained relatively stable over this same time period (Ma & Baum, 2016). Similarly, between the 2004–2005 and 2014–2015 academic years, the number of associate degrees conferred in the United States increased by nearly 46 percent compared to approximately 32 percent for bachelor's degrees (McFarland et al., 2017). Associate degrees are also among those with the highest growth projections and are expected to increase by 29 percent between the 2013–2014 and 2025–2026 academic years, compared to increases of 9 percent for bachelor's degrees (Hussar & Bailey, 2017).

Another important goal of open admissions is to increase the diversity of the postsecondary population (e.g., Clancy & Goastellec, 2007; Ma & Baum, 2016). Supporting this goal, community college enrollment represents 41 percent of all students but 56 percent of Native American, 52 percent of Hispanic, and 43 percent of Black students (American Association of Community Colleges, 2018). During the fall of 2015, the proportion of non-White students was greater in 2-year public institutions (49 percent) compared to 4-year public institutions (40 percent) (McFarland et al., 2017).[1] Among non-White students, the discrepancy between 2- and 4-year public institution enrollment was greatest for Hispanic students (24 percent versus 16 percent, respectively). In addition, as seen in Figure 4.1, in the 2014–2015 academic year the proportion of non-White students who received an associate degree (40 percent) was higher than those receiving a bachelor's degree (32 percent) (McFarland et al., 2017). As previously mentioned, the number of associate degrees conferred in the United States since the 2004–2005 academic year has increased substantially (approximately 46 percent), but this increase is particularly dramatic for members of several racial/ethnic groups. In particular, the number of associate degrees earned by Pacific Islander, Black, and Hispanic students increased by nearly 54 percent, 60 percent, and 130 percent, respectively, compared to approximately 24 percent for White non-Hispanic students (McFarland et al., 2017).

Beyond increasing racial and ethnic diversity, the open admissions model was designed to promote access to higher education to individuals who might face difficulties based on other demographic variables. For example, a higher percentage of students indicating they had one or more disabilities received an associate degree (8 percent) than received a bachelor's degree (4 percent) in 2015 (McFarland et al., 2017).

---

[1] All results pertaining to non-White individuals include persons who may have identified as White racially but as Hispanic ethnically.

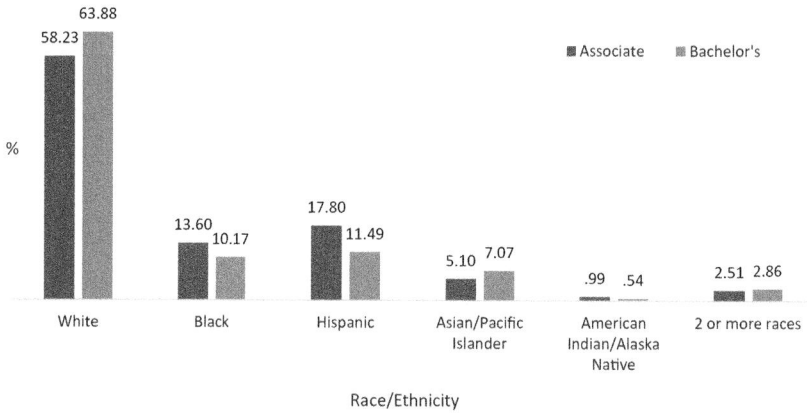

Figure 4.1   Race/ethnicity distribution of associate and bachelor's degree recipients
(2014–2015 academic year)
Note. Values represent new analyses conducted by authors, based on data presented in
McFarland et al. (2017, table 1). Values may not sum to 100 percent due to missing data.
N = 1,013,971 (associate) and 1,894,934 (bachelor's).

Two-year institutions also provide a desirable option for students with low socioeconomic status (SES), as reflected in the large proportion of low SES students who enroll in 2-year institutions relative to 4-year institutions (National Student Clearinghouse Research Center, 2017b; see also Ma & Baum, 2016). It is not surprising then, that although there is wide variation across 2-year institutions (Ma & Baum, 2016), 2-year colleges are less expensive than 4-year colleges. In the 2015–2016 calendar year, the average annual undergraduate tuition and fees at 2-year public institutions was less than half that of public 4-year institutions (McFarland et al., 2017). Similar trends were observed when comparing 2- and 4-year private nonprofit institutions, independent of students' residential situation (McFarland et al., 2017).

Similarly, enrollment trends during and after the Great Recession (2007–2013), a period of general global economic decline, suggest that community colleges are a primary option for individuals upon loss of employment (National Student Clearinghouse Research Center, 2017b). This group may include older individuals who have not been exposed to an academic setting for an extended period of time, and therefore may also struggle to gain admission to a higher education institution based on barriers such as ageism and less technological experience (Myles, 2017). NCES data demonstrate that the proportion of full-time students aged 25 years or older in United States public 2-year institutions (23 percent) is just over twice that of public 4-year institutions (11 percent) based on 2015 fall undergraduate enrollment (McFarland et al., 2017; see also Ma & Baum, 2016). This discrepancy is even greater for private nonprofit institutions, where 46 percent of students at 2-year institutions are aged 25 years or older compared to 14 percent of students at 4-year institutions (McFarland et al., 2017).

4.3.3   *Enhanced Career Pathways*

The overall number of students receiving an associate degree has increased over the past decade: approximately one million associate degrees were conferred during the 2014–2015 academic year, representing a 46 percent increase since 2004–2005 (McFarland et al., 2017). By comparison, the number of bachelor's degrees conferred over the same time frame increased by 32 percent (McFarland et al., 2017). If one of the goals in degree attainment is to enhance graduates' career pathway, what types of occupations do associate degree recipients engage in?

Overall, the vocational potential of associate degree earners appears to be weak relative to those with more advanced degrees, as there are fewer occupations that typically require only an associate degree compared to those that require a bachelor's degree or above. Individuals with an associate degree represented just over 9 percent of the workforce in 2017, the third smallest group (Bureau of Labor Statistics, 2018, table 1.11).[2]

Figure 4.2 displays our analysis of recently provided data on 819 occupations available in the United States in 2016. Results indicated that only 48 occupations (about 6 percent) typically target associate degree holders (see Bureau of Labor Statistics, 2018, table 1.12). Thus, associate degree recipients' occupational prospects may be limited, as they are underqualified for approximately one-third (about 34 percent) of all occupations and may be overqualified for approximately 60 percent of occupations (see Bureau of Labor Statistics, 2018, table 1.12). Furthermore, future vocational opportunities for associate degree holders do not appear to be optimistic: Of the 30 occupations projected to demonstrate the most growth between 2016 and 2026, only two require an associate degree (see Table 4.1 for specific examples; Bureau of Labor Statistics, 2018, tables 1.3 and 1.12).

---

[2] Note that only groups at the extreme ends of the educational attainment spectrum – those with less than a high-school degree and those with a doctoral or professional degree – represented lower percentages of the workforce.

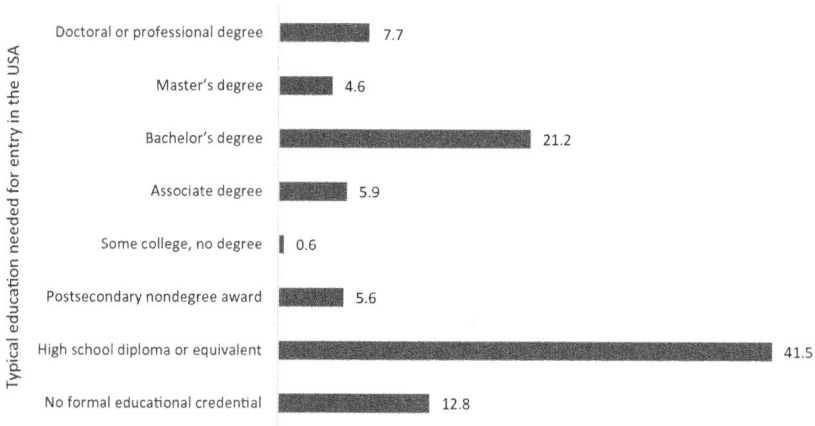

Figure 4.2   Percentage of occupations based on typical education needed for entry (2016)
Note. Values represent new analyses conducted by authors, based on data presented in Bureau of Labor Statistics 2018, table 1.12. Total number of occupations = 819.

Nonetheless, associate degree recipients significantly contribute to a specialized segment of the workforce, primarily in health-related fields (Bureau of Labor Statistics, 2018, table 1.11). These findings partially align with the most common fields of study among associate degree recipients (McFarland et al., 2017). Among students who graduated with an associate degree in the 2014–2015 academic year, health professions and related programs represented the second most popular field of study (20 percent). The most common fields of study were liberal arts and sciences, general studies, and humanities (approximately 37 percent), with business students (approximately 13 percent) also representing a notable percentage of associate degree recipients. No other field of study accounted for more than 5 percent of associate degrees. These values tend to be similar across racial and ethnic groups when examining science, technology, engineering, and mathematics (STEM) majors compared to all other combined majors.

4.3.4   Increased Economic Stability

As discussed earlier, community colleges may be a primary option for many individuals who wish to obtain a degree but cannot afford one. But do the costs associated with obtaining a degree from a 2-year institution produce a reasonable return on investment given the occupational

Table 4.1 *The 30 fastest growing occupations in the United States (2016–2026), cross-referenced by typical education requirement*

Occupation	Typical education needed for entry	Percentage increase of individuals employed, 2016–2026
Solar photovoltaic installers	High school diploma or equivalent	104.9
Wind turbine service technicians	Postsecondary non degree award	96.3
Home health aides	High school diploma or equivalent	47.3
Personal care aides	High school diploma or equivalent	38.6
Physician assistants	Master's degree	37.3
Nurse practitioners	Master's degree	36.1
Statisticians	Master's degree	33.8
Physical therapist assistants	Associate degree	31.0
Software developers, applications	Bachelor's degree	30.7
Mathematicians	Master's degree	29.7
Physical therapist aides	High school diploma or equivalent	29.4
Bicycle repairers	High school diploma or equivalent	29.3
Medical assistants	Postsecondary non degree award	29.0
Genetic counselors	Master's degree	29.0
Occupational therapy assistants	Associate degree	28.9
Information security analysts	Bachelor's degree	28.5
Physical therapists	Doctoral or professional degree	28.0
Operations research analysts	Bachelor's degree	27.4
Forest fire inspectors and prevention specialists	High school diploma or equivalent	26.6
Massage therapists	Postsecondary non degree award	26.3
Health specialties teachers, postsecondary	Doctoral or professional degree	25.9
Derrick operators, oil and gas	No formal educational credential	25.7
Roustabouts, oil and gas	No formal educational credential	24.8
Occupational therapy aides	High school diploma or equivalent	24.7
Phlebotomists	Postsecondary non degree award	24.5
Non-farm animal caretakers	High school diploma or equivalent	24.2
Rotary drill operators, oil and gas	No formal educational credential	24.2
Nursing instructors and teachers, postsecondary	Doctoral or professional degree	24.0
Occupational therapists	Master's degree	23.8
Service unit operators, oil, gas, and mining	No formal educational credential	23.4

Note. Values represent new analyses conducted by authors, based on data presented in Bureau of Labor Statistics, 2018, tables 1.3 and 1.12.

outlook? Data show that the median annual earnings of associate degree holders are greater than those with either no or only partial postsecondary credentials (Carnevale, Rose, & Cheah, 2011; McFarland et al., 2017; see also Ma & Baum, 2016). A recent analysis also indicates that the economic returns from an associate degree are positive, and completing an associate degree has been shown to increase yearly earnings, on average, of $4,640 to $7,160 per year compared to those who enter college but do not complete their course of study (Belfield & Bailey, 2017). In addition, students with an associate degree are less likely to be unemployed during downturns in employment (Carnevale, Cheah, & Strohl, 2011), although both salary and unemployment are dependent upon the particular field of study and occupation. Finally, individuals with technical- or occupation-based associate degrees can earn more in their first year following graduation than do many individuals with bachelor's degrees (Klor de Alva & Schneider, 2013).

However, in addition to income discrepancies across different majors, associate degree recipients exhibit the largest gender wage gap across all educational attainment groups. Our analyses indicated that the median annual earnings of female full-time, year-round workers aged 25–34 with associate degrees are about 74 percent of their male counterparts, compared to 91 percent for other education levels (see McFarland et al., 2017). While this discrepancy may be influenced by other factors, such as the particular field or occupation individuals engage in, these results suggest that, overall, open admissions institutions may yet have room to improve in some areas of vocational outcomes.

4.3.5 Further Academic Opportunities

As indicated earlier, one of the tenets of 2-year institutions is to prepare students for further academic opportunities. In particular, community colleges provide a viable pathway for individuals who aspire to complete their bachelor's but are looking for an affordable first two years of college, or for those who feel they need additional academic preparation before moving on to a 4-year institution. An updated analysis by NSC indicated that for students who began college at a 2-year public institution in 2010, nearly 32 percent transferred to a 4-year institution within 6 years (Shapiro et al., 2017).

However, the benefits of enrollment in a 2-year college as a means for completing a bachelor's degree may be mitigated by other factors, such as previous degree completion. Studies have shown that while most students transfer from the 2-year institution prior to completing their degree, the likelihood of obtaining a bachelor's degree within six years is higher if they earned an associate degree, because these students are in a better position to select schools with higher graduation rates and may transfer more credits to their bachelor's degree program, among other reasons (Kopko & Crosta, 2016).

Nevertheless, there appears to be an additional benefit beyond the baccalaureate. A recent report indicates that attendance at a 2-year institution may also benefit individuals who wish to obtain a master's, doctoral, or professional degree (National Student Clearinghouse Research Center, 2017c).[3] For example, for students who earned a master's degree in 2016–2017, nearly 20 percent entered higher education at a 2-year institution. Nearly 12 percent of master's degree students earned an associate degree before moving on to a 4-year institution, with even higher percentages for those who earned a master's degree in health and clinical sciences.

Time to completion of the degree, however, was long for those students who earned both an associate and master's; in general, nearly ten years separated the two completion dates. The shortest time between completion dates was seen for students in social sciences/psychology and science/engineering, with the longest time observed for students in education, health/clinical sciences, and business. The authors concluded that longer times between completion dates suggest that students may have earned their master's during part-time study or following periods of non-enrollment, particularly for fields with longer completion durations (National Student Clearinghouse Research Center, 2017c). Similar percentages were seen with students who received a doctorate or professional degree (National Student Clearinghouse Research Center, 2017c). The average length of time between the two degrees was 16 years for the doctorate and eight years for a professional degree.

These results suggest that the benefit of open admissions can be more far-reaching than just completing an associate or bachelor's degree. The opportunity to attend open admissions colleges may have contributed to the long-term education goal for many students who go on to obtain graduate-level degrees. This may present an opportunity for open admissions institutions to consider.

---

[3] "Doctorate" refers to students who received a research doctorate. "Professional" refers to degrees in law and medicine.

4.4 Challenges of Open Admissions

4.4.1 *Predictors of Performance*

The open admissions model has proven to be a boon for a significant segment of the population striving to improve their academic or occupational standing. However, some challenges and criticisms of this model remain. One of the more notable criticisms highlights the fundamental feature of the open admissions model – namely, its exclusion of various admissions criteria whose ability to predict postsecondary performance has been well established. Beyond the simple presence or absence of a high school credential, postsecondary performance (e.g., GPA, retention, completion) is strongly associated with high school performance (or aptitude), as assessed by either standardized (e.g., entrance examinations) or non-standardized (e.g., GPA) metrics (for a review, see Shaw, 2018). By ignoring these criteria, critical information regarding incoming students' potential college performance is unavailable.

As mentioned earlier, some open admissions institutions use these performance criteria to place students into remedial coursework. Unfortunately, this practice forms the basis of another criticism of the open admissions model: the ethical dilemma of admitting students who have a low probability of succeeding in higher education, along with the time and resources required to prepare these students. The segment of community college students who are arguably "not college ready" may be reflected by those enrolled in remedial coursework in areas such as English, reading, or mathematics. Estimates of the proportion of students enrolled in remedial community college courses vary, largely depending on how remediated students are defined. In some instances, these figures are as low as approximately 22 percent (National Center for Education Statistics, 2018) but have also been reported to be as high as approximately 75 percent to 80 percent (e.g., Scott-Clayton, 2012; Scott-Clayton & Stacey, 2015).

In many cases, these courses do not count toward a college degree, but must be completed nonetheless in order for the student to retain enrollment, reflecting an additional demand of time, finances, and resources for both the student and the institution (Jenkins & Boswell, 2002). In other cases, there may be insufficient open admissions institutions for specific demographic groups (e.g., individuals with learning disabilities) that may be disproportionally applying to these colleges (Hart et al., 2004). Critics of the open admissions system further contend that this policy may negatively impact the K–12 system, as these students may be unmotivated to achieve under the perception that they will be provided college access regardless of their high school performance (Scherer & Anson, 2014). Furthermore, it is argued that tactics and incentives used to graduate unqualified college students delegitimizes the resulting credential (Scherer & Anson, 2014). However, it should be noted that many of these latter arguments are rarely supported by objective data (see Doran, 2014).

4.4.2   Retention and Graduation

Perhaps the most common concern regarding open admissions institutions involves the lower retention and graduation rates among students at these institutions.[4] Retention rates are defined as the percentage of students who return to their institution the following fall. In 2015, the retention rate of first-time, full-time degree-seeking students from the previous year was 59 percent in open admissions 4-year institutions, compared to 96 percent for the most selective 4-year institutions (i.e., those who admitted less than 25 percent of applicants) (McFarland et al., 2017). These results are consistent when public and private nonprofit institutions are examined separately. Similar trends are noted when considering graduation rates. These rates are defined by the Student Right-to-Know Act (1990) as the percentage of students who complete their program within 150 percent of the expected completion time (e.g., 6 years for bachelor's degree students). Among bachelor's degree students, graduation rates decrease linearly as a function of their institution's acceptance rate. For instance, among degree students who entered their 4-year institution in 2009, roughly one-third of students from open admissions institutions had graduated by 2015, compared to 88 percent of students from the most selective institutions (McFarland et al., 2017).

Although 4-year institutions represent the majority of colleges in the United States (McFarland et al., 2017), only about 15 percent of public and private 4-year institutions used open admissions in the 2014–2015 academic year (Camara & Westrick, 2017). Factors such as retention (the proportion of first-year students who return to campus the next year) and graduation (proportion of students who receive a degree within 6 years) rates form nearly one-quarter (22.5 percent) of the measures used in the annual ranking of colleges produced by US News (Morse, Brooks, & Mason, 2017). The belief is that the rankings help students and their

---

[4] Since nearly 32 percent of community college students transfer to a 4-year institution within six years, lower retention and graduate rates are not synonymous with higher dropout rates.

families to determine to which college to apply. Thus, retention and graduation rates are important metrics to institutions. The use of retention and graduation rates as measures in college rankings may explain why relatively few 4-year institutions use open admissions. Therefore, advocating that 4-year US institutions adopt an open admissions policy seems unlikely, undesirable, and impractical.

4.4.3   *Financial and Additional Support*

Additional challenges remain for low SES students, another group that is a key demographic for open-access institutions. Although the annual cost of 2-year institutions is significantly lower than for 4-year institutions, fewer students are generally awarded financial aid at 2-year institutions (McFarland et al., 2017).

Open-access institutions are also lauded for providing a more flexible postsecondary experience for its students (e.g., National Student Clearinghouse Research Center, 2017b). One metric for describing an institution's flexibility is its ability to provide distance-education courses which may alleviate financial burdens associated with transportation and on-campus housing. However, empirical evidence supporting greater flexibility for 2-year institutions based on this criterion is mixed at best. Specifically, when comparing the proportion of students enrolled exclusively in distance-education courses in 2- and 4-year institutions in 2015, 2-year colleges boasted a greater proportion than 4-year among public institutions (12 percent versus 7 percent, respectively), but the opposite was reported for private nonprofit institutions (2 percent versus 14 percent, respectively) (McFarland et al., 2017). It is possible that many private nonprofit 2-year institutions lack the resources and technology necessary to accommodate students in this critical manner. Other nonacademic support mechanisms that may be particularly beneficial to open admissions students, such as childcare services and social programs, may also be lacking (Karp, 2016; Nelson, Froehner, & Gault, 2013). Overall, these criticisms pose considerable challenges for institutions and researchers to address.

4.5   Conclusions and Future Directions

Despite the widespread use of the open admissions model in the US community college system, there are many avenues for future research. Because much of the existing research relies on data from 2-year/community colleges or associate degree holders, not data from 4-year institutions or recipients of bachelor's degrees, the creation of databases that distinguish current and previous students from open admissions colleges versus other institutions (separated by 2- and 4-year status) are central to the future understanding of the full impact of open admissions.

4.5.1   Demographic and Noncognitive Factors

Within the open admissions population, several demographic groups who are often considered to be particularly prevalent in these institutions remain understudied, including immigrants, English language learners (ELLs), and individuals with disabilities. There also appear to be few studies of gender differences in the experiences and performance of open admissions students. Further research should investigate the unique challenges faced by postsecondary students from these and other groups (e.g., older students), and whether open admissions institutions are adequately addressing these challenges. For instance, studying open admissions institutions' efficacy in utilizing technology to facilitate student success could provide numerous implementational results.

Aside from demographic characteristics, there appears to be less research examining other skill sets of students in open admissions colleges. In higher education more generally, one burgeoning area of research involves identifying noncognitive constructs that contribute to performance (e.g., Heckman & Kautz, 2012). Also called soft skills or twenty-first-century skills, noncognitive constructs include various social/emotional skills or personality traits, including communication skills, motivation, conscientiousness (or "grit"), ethical or moral decision-making, leadership, vocational interests, teamwork, emotional intelligence, attitudes, and cross-cultural skills, among others (e.g., Cappelli, 2012; Klieger et al., 2015). As their name implies, noncognitive constructs are largely unrelated to other academic- or workplace-relevant cognitive or technical skills such as traditional definitions of cognitive ability, mathematical skills, or problem-solving ability that standardized cognitive tests are designed to measure (e.g., Klieger et al., 2015). Furthermore, another appealing feature of noncognitive constructs is that they may be improved through training, possibly more easily than cognitive skills (e.g., Aguinis & Kraiger, 2009; Melby-Lervåg, Redick, & Hulme, 2016; see review by Martin-Raugh, Williams, & Lentini, 2020). An impressive body of reviews and meta-analyses demonstrates that noncognitive constructs predict academic and workplace success to a similar degree as cognitive or technical skills, and may do so independently (e.g., Roberts et al., 2014; Schwager et al., 2014;

Schmidt & Hunter, 1998). However, these studies have not examined these claims within the open-access population specifically or in comparison to students from more selective institutions. The reader might also refer to chapters in this volume by Niessen and Meijer and Kuncel, Tran, and Zhang, which provide more detail on the benefits and advantages of such tests as part of college admissions.

4.5.2   Pre- and Post-College Pathways of Open Admissions Students

There are many criticisms of the open-access model that remain largely devoid of empirical support. For instance, the notion that students who plan to attend open-access institutions tend to underachieve in high school is largely speculative (e.g., Scherer & Anson, 2014), but could be explored scientifically. Furthermore, even if an association is reported, the direction of this relationship is debatable. The notion that students who are already struggling may be more likely to select less-selective schools would appear to be as plausible as the suggestion that students' decisions to attend an open admissions institution would lead to decreased motivation to perform well in high school. It has also been implied that the quality of education delivered in open-access institutions is poorer than that in more-selective institutions (e.g., Scherer & Anson, 2014); but, again, empirical support for such claims is needed.

More research examining the academic pathways of open admissions students would be welcomed. This includes a more thorough investigation into the factors high school students consider when selecting an open admissions college. Research has established that many students at 2-year institutions use this experience as an entry point for 4-year or more selective institutions (Shapiro et al., 2017) or even graduate education (National Student Clearinghouse Research Center, 2017c). Regardless, factors that contribute to open admissions students failing to complete their degree, as well as the factors that facilitate successful transition between institutions, could be enlightening to the academic community.

As we have discussed, some evidence suggests that the occupational and economic prospects of associate degree holders appear to be limited (see Table 4.1). In addition to academic pathways, vocational opportunities are another critical route that follow experience at open admission institutions. Although the relationship between greater socioeconomic outcomes and higher educational levels is well established, these results generally do not separate associate degree holders into their own category, let alone students at open admissions colleges (Bureau of Labor Statistics, 2018).

Furthermore, the educational and socioeconomic impact of educational attainment typically extends across generations, as children of parents with lower educational attainment often experience poorer educational outcomes themselves (e.g., McFarland et al., 2017). Again however, this evidence is primarily presented in the context of degree conferment rather than the institution's level of selectivity.

Future research could also examine whether potential employers hold any biases against students from open-access institutions or the institutions themselves. Existing evidence that indicates these students perform more poorly academically than cohorts from more selective colleges could be expanded to include outcomes beyond retention or graduation, such as performance in the workplace, obtaining additional academic degrees or credentials, etc. Various existing studies offer suggestions for studying the relative quality of open-access education. For instance, comparisons involving faculty members' rank and salary between 2- and 4-year institutions have been reported (e.g., McFarland et al., 2017), but other criteria such as experience, performance ratings, or accolades could help to advance this research.

Overall, studies such as these could be used to further describe the open-admissions student population, the factors students consider when selecting an open admissions institution, unique challenges these students face during their postsecondary career, and the overall social and economic impact of open admissions policy along with possible approaches for addressing these challenges.

4.5.3   Moving Forward

Open admissions institutions will likely continue to serve a large proportion of students in the United States. The philosophy underlying open admissions will continue to benefit various populations such as adult learners, racial/ethnic minority groups, lower-income individuals, and first-generation college students. However, challenges remain in facilitating these students' success both within the educational context and beyond. These challenges may be experienced prior to, during, and following open admissions students' postsecondary education. In order to promote success during and following their academic tenure, other information must be gathered and disseminated, including the following.

• The factors influencing students' decision to attend open admissions institutions. Understanding the full span of reasons as to why students enroll in open admissions institutions would provide guidance to institutions in developing and administering support programs and other resources that may facilitate students' success.

- The types of support needed by open admissions students. Providing adequate support – financial, academic, and personal – to open admissions students is critical as they navigate their college experience. This support may be disproportionately required or different from support needed by students who choose to attend selective institutions.
- Future academic and vocational pathways. While many open admissions students attending a 2-year institution continue academically, many others stop following their associate degree. For these students, vocational opportunities, both current and future, are limited. Having a fuller picture of the reasons open admissions students choose not to continue could lead to helping such students decide whether their time spent at a 2-year institution should be viewed as only the first step toward additional academic or occupational training.

The result of the research described above will provide a better understanding of students' personal needs, academic aspirations, and vocational goals, and, ultimately, could help open admission institutions ultimately fulfill their mission of making college accessible for all students.

REFERENCES

Aguinis, H., & Kraiger, K. (2009). Benefits of training and development for individuals and teams, organizations, and society. *Annual Review of Psychology*, *60*, 451–474. https://doi.org/10.1146/annurev.psych.60.110707.163505.

American Association of Community Colleges. (2018). *Fast facts*. Washington, DC: AACC. Retrieved from www.aacc.nche.edu/wp-content/uploads/2018/04/2018-Fast-Facts.pdf.

(1998). (Commission on the Future of the Community Colleges). *Building communities: A vision for a new century*. Washington, DC: AACC.

Anayah, B., & Kuk, L. (2015). The growth of international student enrollment at community colleges and implications. *Community College Journal of Research and Practice*, *39*, 1099–1110. https://doi.org/10.1080/10668926.2014.934409.

Belfield, C., & Bailey, T. (2017). *The labor market returns to sub-baccalaureate college: A review*. New York, NY: Center for Analysis of Postsecondary Education and Employment.

Bureau of Labor Statistics. (2018). Employment projections. Retrieved from www.bls.gov/emp/tables.htm.

Camara, W. J., & Westrick, P. (2017). *USA: Perspectives on admissions and admissions testing*. Iowa City, IA: ACT.

Cappelli, P. (2012). *Why good people can't get jobs: The skills gap and what companies can do about it.* Philadelphia, PA: Wharton Digital Press.

Carnevale, A. P., Cheah, B., & Strohl, J. (2011). *Hard times, unemployment, majors and earnings: Not all college degrees are created equal.* Washington, DC: Georgetown University Center on Education and the Workforces.

Carnevale, A. P., Rose, S. J., & Cheah, B. (2011). *The college payoff: Education, occupations, lifetime earnings.* Washington, DC: Georgetown University Center on Education and the Workforce.

Clancy, P., & Goastellec, G. (2007). Exploring access and equity in higher education: Policy and performance in a comparative perspective. *Higher Education Quarterly, 61,* 136–154. https://doi.org/10.1111/j.1468-2273.2007.00343.x.

Clinedinst, M. E., Koranteng, A., & Nicola, T. (2016). *2015 State of college admissions.* Washington, DC: National Association of Collegiate Admissions Counselors.

Doran, E. (2014). [Review of the book *Community colleges and the access effect: Why open admissions suppresses achievement,* by J. L. Scherer & M. L. Anson]. *Community College Enterprise, 20,* 85–87.

Drury, R. L. (2003). Community colleges in America: A historical perspective. *Inquiry, 8*(1).

European Union. (2018). *The EU in support of the Bologna process.* Luxembourg: Publications Office of the European Union.

Fullinwider, R. K. (1999). Open admissions and remedial education at CUNY. *Philosophy & Public Policy Quarterly. 19*(1), 7–13.

Ginder, S. A., Kelly-Reid, J. E., & Mann, F. B. (2018). *2017–18 Integrated Postsecondary Education Data System (IPEDS) methodology report (NCES 2018-195).* Washington, DC: US Department of Education, National Center for Education Statistics.

Guri-Rosenblit, S. (2010). Access and equity in higher education: Historical and cultural contexts. In H. Eggins (Ed.). *Access and equity: Comparative perspectives,* 9–34. Rotterdam: Sense Publishers.

Hart, D., Mele-McCarthy, J., Pasternack, R. H., Zimbrich, K., & Parker, D. R. (2004). Community college: A pathway to success for youth with learning, cognitive, and intellectual disabilities in secondary settings. *Education and Training in Developmental Disabilities, 39,* 54–66.

Heckman, J. J., & Kautz, T. (2012). Hard evidence on soft skills. *Labour Economics, 19,* 451–464. https://doi.org/10.1016/j.labeco.2012.05.014.

Hussar, W. J., & Bailey, T. M. (2017). *Projections of education statistics to 2025 (NCES 2017-019).* Washington, DC: National Center for Education Statistics, US Department of Education.

Ingram, W. G., & Morrissey, S. E. (2009). Ethical dimensions of the open door admissions policy. *New Directions for Community Colleges, 148,* 31–38. https://doi.org/10.1002/cc.384.

Jenkins, D., & Boswell, K. (2002). *State policies on community college remedial education: Findings from a national survey.* Denver, CO: Center for Community College Policy, Education Commission of the States.

Karp, M. M. (2016). A holistic conception of nonacademic support: How four mechanisms combine to encourage positive student outcomes in the community college. *New Directions for Community College, 2016* (175), 33–44. https://doi.org/10.1002/cc.20210.

Klieger, D., Ezzo, C., Bochenek, J., & Cline, F. (2015). The predictive validity of noncognitive skills for graduate and professional student success: Some initial findings. Paper presented at the Validity and Fairness Issues in Assessing Higher Education Students Symposium, Annual Meeting of the American Educational Research Association, Chicago, IL.

Klor de Alva, J., & Schneider, M. (2013). *What's the value of an associate's degree? The return on investment for graduates and taxpayers.* Washington, DC: Nexus Research and Policy Center and American Institutes for Research. Retrieved from www.air.org/sites/default/files/Value_of_an_Associate_Degree_10.13.pdf.

Kopko, E. M., & Crosta, P. M. (2016). Should community college students earn an associate degree before transferring to a 4-year institution? *Research in Higher Education, 57*, 190–222. https://doi.org/10.1007/s11162-015-9383.

Levy, D. (2015). For-profit versus nonprofit private higher education. *International Higher Education, 54*, 12–13.

Lorenzo, A. L. (1993). The mission and functions of the community college: An overview. In G. A. Baker, III (Ed.). *A Handbook on community college in America.* Westport, CT: Greenwood Press.

Ma, J., & Baum, S. (2016). *Trends in community colleges: Enrollment, prices, student debt, and completion.* New York, NY: The College Board.

McFarland, J., Hussar, B., de Brey, C., Snyder, T., Wang, X., Wilkinson-Flicker, S., & Hinz, S. (2017). *The condition of education 2017 (NCES 2017-144).* Washington, DC: US Department of Education, National Center for Education Statistics. Retrieved from https://nces.ed.gov/pubsearch/pubsinfo.asp?pubid=2017144.

Martin-Raugh, M. P., Williams, K. M., & Lentini, J. E. (2020). The malleability of workplace-relevant noncognitive constructs: Empirical evidence from 92 meta-analyses and reviews. Manuscript in preparation.

Melby-Lervåg, M., Redick, T. S., & Hulme, C. (2016). Working memory training does not improve performance on measures of intelligence or other measures of "far transfer": Evidence from a meta-analytic review. *Perspectives on Psychological Science, 11*, 512–534. https://doi.org/10.1177/1745691616635612.

Morley, K. M. (2003). Fitting in by race/ethnicity: The social and academic integration of diverse students at a large predominantly white university. *Journal of College Student Retention: Research, Theory & Practice. 5*, 147–174. https://doi.org/10.2190/K1KF-RTLW-1DPW-T4CC.

Morse, R., Brooks, E., & Mason, M. (2017). How U.S. News Calculated the 2019 Best Colleges Rankings. *U.S. News & World Report.* Retrieved from www.usnews.com/education/best-colleges/articles/how-us-news-calculated-the-rankings.

Myles, N. N. (2017). The face of an intergenerational community in higher education. *Journal of Research, Assessment, and Practice in Higher Education, 2*, 42–46.

Nagaoka, J., Roderick, M., & Coca, V. (2008). *Barriers to college attainment: Lessons from Chicago*. Washington, DC: The Center for American Progress.

National Center for Education Statistics. (2018). Beginning college students in 2011–12, followed through 2014 (BPS2014). Retrieved from https://nces .ed.gov/datalab/powerstats/pdf/bps2014_subject.pdf.

National Student Clearinghouse Research Center. (2017a). Current term enrollment – Fall 2017. Retrieved from https://nscresearchcenter.org/current-term-enrollment-estimates-fall-2017/.

(2017b). The role of community colleges in postsecondary success: Community colleges outcomes report. Retrieved from https://studentclearinghouse .info/onestop/wp-content/uploads/Comm-Colleges-Outcomes-Report.pdf.

(2017c). Snapshot report: The role of community colleges in postsecondary success. Retrieved from https://nscresearchcenter.org/snapshotreport-from-community-college-to-graduate-and-professional-degrees30/.

Nelson, B., Froehner, M., & Gault, B. (2013). *College students with children are common and face many challenges in completing higher education* (Briefing Paper IWPR# C404). Washington, DC: Institute for Women's Policy Research.

New York Times. (1976, December 4). Retreat from learning. *New York Times*. Retrieved from www.nytimes.com/1976/12/04/archives/retreat-from-learning.html.

Obama, B. H. (2009). *State of the union address*. Presented to the United States Congress, Washington, DC. Retrieved from http://stateoftheunionaddress .org/2009-barack-obama.

Perfetto, G., Escandón, M., Graff, S., Rigol, G. W., & Schmidt, A. E. (1999). *Towards a taxonomy of the admission decision-making process*. New York, NY: College Entrance Examination Board.

Roberts, B. W., Lejuez, C., Krueger, R. F., Richards, J. M., & Hill, P. L. (2014). What is conscientiousness and how can it be assessed? *Developmental Psychology, 50*, 1315–1330. https://doi.org/10.1037/a0031109.

Scherer, J. L., & Anson, M. L. (2014). *Community colleges and the access effect: Why open admissions suppresses achievement*. New York, NY: Palgrave Macmillan. https://doi.org/10.1057/9781137331007.

Schmidt, F. L., & Hunter, J. E. (1998). The validity and utility of selection methods in personnel psychology: Practical and theoretical implications of 85 years of research findings. *Psychological Bulletin, 124*, 262–274. https:// doi.org/10.1037/0033-2909.124.2.262.

Schwager, I. T. L., Hülsheger, U. R., Lang, J. W. B., Bridgeman, B., Klieger, D. M., & Wendler, C. (2014). Supervisor ratings of students' academic potential as predictors of citizenship and counterproductive behavior. *Learning and Individual Differences, 35*, 62–69. https://doi.org/10.1016/j.lindif.2014.07.005.

Scott-Clayton, J. (2012). *Do high-stakes placement exams predict college success?* New York, NY: Columbia University, Teachers College, Community College Research Center.

Scott-Clayton, J., & Stacey, G. W. (2015). *Improving the accuracy of remedial placement.* New York, NY: Columbia University, Teachers College, Community College Research Center.

Shannon, H. D., & Smith, R. C. (2006). A case for the community college's open access mission. *New Directions for Community Colleges, 2006* (136), 15–21. https://doi.org/10.1002/cc.255.

Shapiro, D., Dundar, A., Huie, F., Wakhungu, P. K., Yuan, X., Nathan, A., & Hwang, Y. (2017). Tracking transfer: Measures of effectiveness in helping community college students to complete bachelor's degrees (National Student Clearinghouse Research Center, Signature Report No. 13). Retrieved from https://nscresearchcenter.org/wp-content/uploads/SignatureReport13.pdf.

Shaw, E. J. (2018). The core case for testing: The state of our research knowledge. In J. Buckley, L. Letukas, & B. Wildavsky (Eds.). *Measuring success: Testing, grades, and the future of college admissions* (pp. 40–63). Baltimore, MD: Johns Hopkins University Press.

Student Right-to-Know Act (1990), Pub. L. No. 101-542, Title I, §101, 104 Stat. 2381.

US Census Bureau. (2017a). CPS historical time series tables: Table A-2. Percent of people 25 years and over who have completed high school or college, by race, Hispanic origin, and sex: Selected years 1940 to 2017. Retrieved from www.census.gov/data/tables/time-series/demo/educational-attainment/cps-historical-time-series.html.

(2017b). CPS historical time series tables on school enrollment: Table A-2. Percentage of the population 3 years old and over enrolled in school, by age, sex, race, and Hispanic origin: October 1947 to 2016. Retrieved from www.census.gov/data/tables/time-series/demo/school-enrollment/cps-historical-time-series.html.

US Department of Education. (2012). United States education dashboard. Retrieved from http://dashboard.ed.gov/about.aspx.

CHAPTER 5

Character-Based Admissions Criteria in the United States and in Europe: Rationale, Evidence, and Some Critical Remarks

A. Susan M. Niessen and Rob R. Meijer

Globally, the importance of effective and fair college admissions procedures, on both an individual and a societal level, should not be underestimated. College admissions decisions are often based on high school grades (as, for example, in Europe), scores on standardized tests (as, for example, in China and India), or a combination of both (as, for example, in the United States). Although both grades and cognitively oriented standardized test scores are good predictors of academic performance in higher education (Berry, 2015; Westrick et al., 2015), colleges and other stakeholders seem increasingly interested in including character-based criteria in admissions procedures (Hoover, 2013). In this chapter, we discuss the rationale, practice, evidence, and effects of character-based college admissions from US and European perspectives.

Character-based admissions criteria include indications of personality, motivation, study skills and habits, and other behavioral tendencies. Other commonly used terms are noncognitive, intra- and interpersonal, and non-academic traits or skills. Because many of the different traits and skills that are defined within these catch-all terms are not entirely unrelated to cognitive or academic skills (Borghans et al., 2011; von Stumm & Ackerman, 2013), we chose to use the term "character-based" in this chapter.

The higher education admissions literature is dominated by US studies and perspectives. The academic discipline of psychology, especially the field of individual differences, has had a large influence on educational selection and admissions procedures in the United States. The influence of cognitive testing is predominant in large-scale admissions tests such as the SAT® and the ACT® tests (Lemann, 1999). In addition, the US literature on character-based traits and skills in college admissions relies on the study of individual differences in terms of intra- and interpersonal skills and traits. Examples include the "Big Five" personality traits: motivation, study skills, self-efficacy, integrity, and leadership (Credé & Kuncel, 2008; Kyllonen et al., 2014; Le et al., 2005; Oswald et al., 2004; Schmitt,

2012; Sedlacek, 2004). Kuncel, Tran, and Zhang (in this volume) provide more detail on character-based tests and some of the challenges associated with them.

In Europe, admissions procedures are generally less oriented toward the psychology of individual differences and related psychological constructs, although there are exceptions, such as the Cito test (see Bartels et al., 2002) for admissions to secondary education in the Netherlands, and the Swe-SAT (Swedish Scholastic Aptitude Test)in Sweden (e.g., Lyren, 2008). This more practice-driven (rather than theory-driven) approach to admissions adopted in Europe may be one of the reasons why there is less scientific literature on the rationale and effectiveness of educational selection outside the United States.

There is limited European-based literature that answers questions such as: Which institutional goals provide the basis on which to select students? Which instruments and criteria are used to select students? How are admissions decisions reached? Nevertheless, literature oriented in US admissions practices also influences the public debate and admissions practices in Europe, including the trend to use alternatives to the traditional admissions criteria such as previous educational performance. Examples are holistic assessment (Allman, 2009; Witzburg & Sondheimer, 2013) and the use of character-based admissions criteria (Stemler, 2012; Sternberg, 2016), assessed through interviews, motivation letters, or questionnaires. However, the research, conclusions, and policies provided in the literature based in the United States do not always provide a good fit to education systems in Europe.

In this chapter, we provide: (a) a brief description of admissions practices in the United States and Europe; (b) different rationales for implementing character-based admissions criteria in admissions testing; (c) the empirical evidence of the validity and fairness of character-based admissions tools; and (d) the process of how academic and character-based admissions criteria are combined.

5.1 A Brief Overview of Admissions Practices

5.1.1   US Practices

When applying to undergraduate programs in the United States, students typically apply to colleges or universities without declaring their major right away, although there are exceptions. The degree of selectivity varies depending on the college or university. Admissions procedures in the

United States are typically based on a meritocracy model (see Wikström & Wikström, in this volume, for a description). Academic merit, usually assessed through scores on standardized tests such as the SAT® or ACT® and high school grades, are the most important determinants of admissions decisions. However, merit in domains such as the arts, music, sports, community service, and personal development are also often considered (National Association for College Admission Counseling, 2017; Zwick, 2017a). Those non-academic merits are often assessed through personal statements, recommendations, essays, résumés, and interviews (for excellent discussions of college admissions in the United States, see Camara, 2009; Zwick, 2017b).

5.1.2   European Practices

Providing a complete description of European admissions practices is an almost impossible task, so we do not attempt to do so here. Instead, we try to provide some typical practices and procedures, all of which include many exceptions. We also give examples, and we mostly focus on Western Europe.

European secondary education is often stratified into different levels and completed through centrally organized final exams. The first admissions requirement is usually a high school diploma at the highest level of secondary education, where students complete the most academically demanding track. This leads to a strong pre-selection on scholastic achievement before applying to college, which results in relatively homogenous applicant pools with respect to general cognitive or scholastic skills. Therefore, it is more difficult to differentiate between applicants based on standardized tests that measure such skills (Crombag, Gaff, & Chang, 1975; Resing & Drenth, 2007). That is probably why large-scale standardized tests are rarely used in European admissions (Sweden is the exception with the use of the SweSAT).

When this minimum-level requirement is fulfilled, high school grades play a major role in selective admissions in Europe. However, the degree of selectivity differs widely per country and mostly depends on the study program rather than on the university (England is an exception). In countries such as Denmark, Belgium, France, Luxembourg, and the Netherlands, most programs are not selective and admit all students that have the required high school diploma (Orr et al., 2017).[1] Sometimes,

---

[1]   The Grand écoles, the most prestigious higher education institutes in France, are an exception and are highly selective.

additional requirements are in place, such as students having taken specific courses relevant to the course of study, like physics, chemistry, and math for science programs. Medicine and other health-related disciplines are generally selective and are among the most selective programs in many countries. Others that are often (more) selective are psychology programs (in the Netherlands, Germany, Denmark, Finland, and Sweden) and the arts, music, and sport programs, with their own distinct admissions requirements.

In addition to high school grades, discipline-related admissions examinations assessing existing subject-matter knowledge are used in England, Belgium, and the Netherlands. Also, curriculum samples that provide a small simulation of the study program and require substantial preparation are used in the Netherlands, Germany, and Finland (de Visser et al., 2017; Kunina et al., 2007; Lievens & Coetsier, 2002; Niessen, Meijer, & Tendeiro, 2018; Valli & Johnson, 2007).

Admissions procedures in Europe are also mostly merit-based (see Wikström & Wikström, in this volume). Explicit character-based criteria are typically not included in admissions procedures in Europe. When they are included, they are mostly focused on motivation and fit and assessed through motivation letters, personal statements, and interviews. Examples can be found in the Netherlands, Denmark, Germany, Finland, and Sweden and in top universities in England (Cremonini et al., 2011; Steenman, 2018). The use of tests or questionnaires to assess character-based traits and skills such as motivation and personality is also rare; they are most commonly used in the Netherlands (Steenman, 2018). However, character-based admissions is gaining ground in Europe. For example, the German constitutional court has recently decided that the strong emphasis on high school grades in admissions to medical school is not fair and should not be the only criterion. They recommended the use of at least one other non-grade-based admissions criterion (Tagesschau, 2017). In addition, Dutch higher education programs are now required to adopt at least two distinct criteria in selective admissions procedures, one of which is preferably character-based (Ministry of Education, Culture, and Science, 2014).

5.2   The Rationale of Character-Based College Admissions

The aims of college admissions procedures can vary across colleges and countries, ranging from selecting candidates who will perform well academically, selecting candidates to optimize ethnic and social background diversity, or crafting a class of students with a wide variety of special talents. The three most common arguments to include character-based assessment align with those aims (see Niessen & Meijer, 2017).

5.2.1   Predictive and Incremental Validity

The first argument is that they have incremental validity above traditional admissions criteria, such as high school grade point average (GPA) and standardized test scores for predicting academic achievement (Credé & Kuncel, 2008; Oswald et al., 2004; Richardson, Abrahams, & Bond, 2012; Robbins et al., 2004). This seems to be the dominant argument for considering character-based admissions in Europe, where the main aim of admissions procedures seems to be to select those students that will perform best academically (Steenman, 2018). As a result, character-based admissions criteria in Europe are more closely linked to the demands of the specific study program or the future profession. Examples are integrity-based assessments for medical school (de Leng et al., 2018) and motivation for the study program of interest (Busato et al., 2000; Wouters et al., 2017). Such measures are thus mostly aimed at predicting domain-specific academic performance or future job performance in the profession of interest.

5.2.2   Predicting Broader Outcomes

A second argument is that character-based admissions criteria are more suitable to predict outcomes beyond academic achievement as defined by first-year GPA. Examples of such broader outcomes are educating future leaders, promoting active citizenship, critical thinking, creativity, and innovation (Oswald et al., 2004; Stemler, 2012; Sternberg, 2016). This is commonly argued in the United States, where the more prestigious universities largely select students to promote institutional and societal goals such as leadership, active citizenship, and athletic performance (Sternberg, 2016; Zwick, 2017a). Therefore, admissions officers may also consider "legacies [i.e., children of alumni]; leaders for school publications, student government, and other areas of student life; children of influential families; those with special talents such as musicians, athletes, and public speakers; and students from under-represented ethnic groups and geographical areas" (Zwick, 2013, p. 15).

5.2.3   Reducing Adverse Impact

A third argument is that character-based criteria may reduce adverse impact, increase diversity (Schmitt et al., 2009; Sedlacek, 2005; Sinha et al., 2011), and reduce selection system bias (Keiser et al., 2016; Mattern, Sanchez, & Ndum, 2017). This argument is also most commonly encountered in the US-based literature. Character-based admissions is typically not implemented to reduce adverse impact in Europe (Orr et al., 2017). One reason may be that achievement in high school is mostly used as an admissions criterion in Europe as opposed to standardized admission-test scores in the United States. Thus, adverse impact starts to play a significant role well before admission to higher education due to the stratification in secondary education in many European countries. For example, in the Netherlands, pupils are placed in one of three main educational tracks (which may have a number of sub-tracks or combination tracks), mostly depending on scholastic performance at the age of 11 or 12. And in Finland pupils are placed in an academic or a vocational track at age 15. Underrepresented minorities are less likely to complete higher-level secondary education or to apply to a university (Lamb et al., 2011; Organisation for Economic Co-operation and Development, 2010). However, there is a growing interest in this perspective, especially in admissions to medical school (Lievens & Coetsier, 2002; Stegers-Jager, 2018). Another example can be found in Denmark, where a small proportion of applicants is admitted based on work experience and motivation in addition to educational achievement. This provides applicants who did not start college directly after finishing high school better chances of admission (Cremonini et al., 2011). The SweSAT was introduced in Sweden for this reason (Cliffordson, 2008), which is interesting given the common adverse-impact-related criticism on cognition-oriented tests.

Broadly speaking, there are two common reasons to include character-based criteria in college admissions. The first reason is improved prediction, mostly of academic performance in Europe, and also of broader outcomes, such as leadership and citizenship, in the United States. The second reason is reducing adverse impact and increasing diversity in colleges.

5.3 Validity and Fairness of Character-Based Admissions Procedures

5.3.1 *Predictive Validity*

The predictive validity of the most common admissions criteria such as high school grades and scores on standardized tests in the United States is well documented (Kuncel & Hezlet, 2010; Westrick et al., 2015; Zwick, 2017b). It is, however, very difficult to obtain empirical studies on the validity of other frequently used admissions instruments to assess character-based admissions criteria. Common instruments used to assess character-based criteria in admissions are personal statements, interviews, motivation letters, letters of recommendation, and questionnaires (see Kuncel, Tran, & Zhang, in this volume). In general, there is a scarcity of studies that provide empirical evidence for the predictive validity of these kinds of instruments. The studies that are available show that most of these instruments tend to have little predictive and incremental validity for academic achievement (Dana, Dawes, & Peterson, 2013; Goho & Blackman, 2006; Kuncel, Kochevar, & Ones, 2014; Murphy et al., 2009; Patterson et al., 2016).

For assessing character-based admissions criteria, there seems to be too much faith in procedures that seem to be valid (Highhouse, 2008; Jones, 2011). For example, the idea that unstructured in-depth interviews can have high predictive power seems ineradicable among admissions officers and applicants. In a recent study, Niessen, Meijer, and Tendeiro (2017a) investigated the preferences of students for admissions to a psychology program. Interviews were rated most favorably, whereas lottery admissions and high school GPA were rated least favorably. Similarly, Kelly et al. (2018) found favorable stakeholder reactions to interviews and situational judgment tests (SJTs), but less favorable perceptions of cognitive-ability tests and academic records. Dana et al. (2013) showed that information obtained from an unstructured interview, when added to more reliable and valid instruments, could even reduce the predictive power of the assessment procedure. Structured interviews may have value in selection procedures, although most validity studies on the use of structured interviews were conducted in the context of personnel selection (Cortina et al., 2000; Schmidt & Hunter, 1998).

In addition, the use of motivation letters, personal statements, and interviews is generally not theory-driven. However, in the admissions literature, there are studies on carefully designed SJTs, biodata scales, and questionnaires to measure character-based traits and skills, both in the United States (Schmitt, 2012; Shultz & Zedeck, 2012; Wagerman & Funder, 2007) and in Europe (Busato et al., 2000; de Leng et al., 2018; Patterson et al., 2017; Schwager et al., 2014). These studies show that character-based admissions criteria can have incremental validity over traditional admissions criteria (Credé & Kuncel, 2008; Oswald et al., 2004; Richardson et al., 2012; Robbins et al., 2004) and can have predictive validity for broader outcomes like job performance and active citizenship (Oswald et al., 2004; Stemler, 2012; Sternberg, 2016).

However, most of these studies were conducted in low-stakes settings. The generalization of these predictive validity results to high-stakes settings is not straightforward.

5.3.2 Measuring Character in High-Stakes Contexts

One of the main issues in the generalization of research findings to high-stakes admissions procedures is the possibility of faking, due to the self-report nature of most character-based instruments. Griffin and Wilson (2012) showed that applicants scored much more favorably on self-report questionnaires compared to completing the same questionnaire for research purposes. In addition, Niessen, Meijer, and Tendeiro (2017b) found that the predictive and incremental validities of scales measuring personality, study skills, and study habits were substantially lower when they were administered in an admissions context. Anglim et al. (2018), also found lower predictive validity of conscientiousness scores when obtained in a high-stakes admissions context.

The forced-choice format was recently revived as a solution to the faking problem (e.g., Markle et al., 2013; Salgado & Táuriz, 2014), after a scoring method that results in non-ipsative data was designed (Brown & Maydeu-Olivares, 2013). However, the results on whether forced-choice items are indeed substantially more resistant to faking are mixed, and some studies found that faking ability on forced-choice questionnaires depends on cognitive ability. This high cognitive saturation of forced-choice character-based assessments can even increase their predictive validity, but likely hinders their incremental validity over more cognitively loaded criteria (Christiansen, Burns, & Montgomery, 2005; Vasilopoulos et al., 2006).

One of the few studies using a character-based instrument that was conducted in high-stakes admissions testing was the use of SJTs measuring interpersonal skills in admissions to medical school in Belgium (Lievens, 2013; Lievens & Sackett, 2012). The SJT scores were statistically significant but showed low predictive and incremental validity for interpersonal GPA, internship performance, and job-performance. Thus, they would add little utility in terms of increased doctor performance in practice (Niessen & Meijer, 2016).

An alternative method that is not based on self-reports is the multiple mini-interview (MMI). MMIs consist of several highly structured interviews or role plays, typically assessed by multiple examiners or raters (Eva et al., 2004). Moderate-to-high predictive validities were obtained using MMIs in high-stakes admissions to medical school (Husbands & Dowell,

2013). However, as with all observation-based assessments, close attention should be paid to minimizing rater errors, bias, and subjectivity (Till, Myford, & Dowell, 2013) – for example, by using behaviorally anchored rating scales (Lee et al., 2017).

While results obtained in low-stakes contexts are promising, the predictive and incremental validity results based on self-report instruments have thus far not generalized to actual high-stakes admissions procedures (Thomas, Kuncel, & Credé, 2007). Instruments based on actual behavior rather than self-reports show some promising results but are more time-consuming to develop and administer.

5.3.3   *Increasing Diversity through Character-Based Admissions Criteria*

Another reason to include character-based criteria in admissions procedures is their alleged lower-adverse impact as compared to traditional admissions criteria such as standardized tests and high school GPA (Schmitt et al., 2009; Sedlacek, 2005; Sinha et al., 2011). However, faking and coaching (Ramsay et al., 2006) could pose a threat to realizing this promise as well, due to inequality in resources in support, practice, and preparation (Kyllonen, Walters, & Kaufman, 2005; Zwick, 2017a). In addition, measures with higher cognitive saturation (that is, a strong correlation with cognitive ability) also tend to show more adverse impact (Dahlke & Sackett, 2017). Therefore, the higher cognitive saturation of the more fake-resistant forced-choice items probably also yield more adverse impact (Christiansen et al., 2005). Furthermore, an often-overlooked alternative explanation may be that the lower adverse impact of character-based admissions criteria is an artifact caused by the lower reliability of the instruments used to measure them (see Zwick, 2017b, p. 153).

While adding character-based admissions criteria with smaller mean subgroup differences can have some merit, it probably does not yield such drastic reductions of adverse impact as is often implied (Sackett & Ellingson, 1997). For example, the scores on the SJT developed by Oswald et al. (2004) showed virtually no subgroup differences between Black and White students, and showed no relationship with standardized test scores, which are ideal results in terms of minimizing adverse impact and maximizing incremental validity. Using these results as an example, let us assume that the standardized mean difference (as indicated by Cohen's d) on the SJT for the Black and White applicants equals $d = 0$ on the SJT, and that the correlation between the SJT scores and standardized-test scores equals

$r = 0$. Standardized admissions tests often yield substantial score differences of, say, $d = 1$ between Black and White students (Sinha et al., 2011). Sackett and Ellingson (1997) developed tables to find the resulting d-value of a unit-weighted composite of the two tests (in this case, the SJT and standardized admissions test scores) based on the sum of the d-values of both tests and the correlation between the scores on both tests. Based on Sackett and Ellingson's (1997) tables, we can find that a unit-weight composite based on this ideal example would yield a standardized mean difference of $d = 0.71$. This is only a modest reduction compared to using only the standardized test scores with $d = 1$. So, while adverse impact would be reduced by adding this SJT to the admissions procedure, the effect of adding an instrument that showed no adverse impact at all would be surprisingly small. Furthermore, the resulting d-value of composite measures is lower when the correlation between the scores on both tests is higher (Sackett & Ellingson, 1997). This shows a trade-off between reducing adverse impact and maximizing incremental validity. Adding character-based criteria to assessment procedures that also contain traditional criteria such as standardized tests or high school grades will thus likely have only modest effects on adverse impact.

5.4 Combining Academic and Character-Based Admissions Criteria

Using several different admissions criteria requires the integration of different sources of information to make predictions and decisions. This integration procedure also deserves attention. A popular method to integrate a variety of information about an applicant's abilities, skills, background, and character is often referred to as "holistic assessment" (Horn, 2005; Witzburg, & Sondheimer, 2013; Wouters, 2017). Holistic assessment is based on the idea that by considering all the interactions between relevant information through expert judgment, a good impression of the person as a whole can be obtained, as compared to the limited information provided by standardized test scores (Highhouse & Kostek, 2013). However, as is known from Meehl (1954; also see Dawes, 1979; Highhouse & Kostek, 2013; Kuncel et al., 2013), statistical prediction according to a predefined decision rule is almost always superior to clinical, or holistic, prediction. In clinical prediction, information from different sources is combined (in the mind) to form a hypothesis about a candidate, and then based on this hypothesis: "we arrive at a prediction [as to] what is going to happen" (Meehl, 1954, p. 4). Although the superiority of statistical prediction is a very solid finding in the psychological decision-making literature, admissions officers from some colleges seem to be proud not to use statistical prediction.

In our view, it is indeed ironic that many stakeholders (admissions officers, candidates, and parents) can be very critical about admissions criteria such as high school grades and standardized test scores, and at the same time unquestioningly embrace alternatives such as an unreliable, unstructured interview (e.g., Allman, 2009) and opaque holistic procedures. As Dana, Dawes, and Peterson (2013) discussed:

> The ability to sensemake combined with the tendency for biased testing allows unstructured interviewers to feel they understand an interviewee almost regardless of the information they receive. Unfortunately, a feeling of understanding, while reassuring and confidence-inspiring, is neither sufficient nor necessary for making accurate assessments. (p. 514)

In addition, we should realize that although traditional admissions criteria like high school grades and standardized tests are often defined as cognitive, they are not pure measures of cognitive or academic ability. A substantial amount of the variance in high school grades can be explained by variables that we would refer to as character-based, such as conscientiousness, grit, and self-efficacy (Borghans et al., 2016; Deary et al., 2007; Dumfart & Neubauer, 2016). Because of "their apparent value in measuring students' tenacity and commitment," Zwick (2017b, p. 193) recommended that high school grades should play a key role in admissions. Even scores on standardized tests have been shown to be related to such character-based traits (Borghans et al., 2011; von Stumm & Ackerman, 2013).

5.5   Conclusion and Discussion

Educational selection should be valid and unbiased. In our view, admissions officers, psychologists, and others who are involved in selective admissions should be very careful when including character-based criteria through methods like interviews, questionnaires, assignments, and holistic evaluations, because they can easily be misused. As Zwick (2017b) stated: "the less clear the admission criteria, the more likely they are to benefit the wealthier, more savvy candidates" (p. 193).

Recently, several medical institutions and federations adopted lists of lower-value services – that is, healthcare that is considered to be of no or limited value. These ineffective medical activities include some medical surgeries, tests, and procedures (Wammes et al., 2016). These activities had no scientific basis but were based on what was considered common sense and tradition. It was advised not to use these procedures at all or not to use them routinely. As Wammes et al. (2016) indicated, the quality of healthcare is reflected by "the degree to which health services for individuals and populations increase the likelihood of desired health outcomes and are consistent with current professional knowledge" (p. 2). There is a parallel between this medical practice and the practice of college admissions. In our view, admissions procedures are guided too much by intuition-based decisions, and there is a large gap between what we know about optimal decision-making and decisions made in practice, especially when it comes to character-based assessment. This scientist–practitioner gap has received a lot of attention in the field of personnel selection (Anderson, Herriot, & Hodgkinson, 2001; Drenth, 2008) and we think that it is also time to address this issue in higher education admissions. It is, therefore, extremely important that colleges should be transparent about how they select students and how their admissions criteria relate to later performance or other outcomes that one would like to predict. Zwick (2017a) warned against the risks of the use of character-based admissions criteria and suggested first to investigate the possible implications of these admissions criteria on the behavior of different stakeholders like students and parents and to conduct pilot studies to evaluate character-based admissions criteria.

Many studies have shown that the most common admissions criteria – high school GPA and standardized test scores – are good predictors of academic performance, although admittedly they have their drawbacks. Character-based admissions criteria may be able to deal with those drawbacks and, therefore, may be rightfully defined as the next frontier in college admissions (Hoover, 2013).

However, the main problem is that we need much more research to find effective methods to measure character in high-stakes testing. In addition, it is surprising that there is such little evidence available about admissions procedures outside the United States and that there are few studies that provide compelling evidence that other commonly used or recommended admissions criteria predict academic performance or other relevant outcomes. In our view, we should address this scientist–practitioner gap by conducting more studies in operational–admissions settings in collaboration with admissions officers and emphasizing that procedures with such high-societal impact be evidence-based. We advocate for more transparency by sharing information and results in international journals or other platforms to build a broader evidence-based educational-selection literature that can inform further research, policies, and practice, especially for character-based measures.

REFERENCES

Allman, M. (2009). Quintessential questions: Wake Forest's director gives insight into the interview process. Retrieved from http://blog.rethinkingadmissions .wfu.edu/2009/08/quintessential-questions-wake-forest%E2%80%99s-admission-director-gives-insight-into-the-interview-process/.

Anderson, N., Herriot, P., & Hodgkinson, G. P. (2001). The practitioner–researcher divide in industrial, work and organizational (IWO) psychology: Where we are now, and where do we go from here? *Journal of Occupational and Organizational Psychology*, *74*, 391–411. https://doi.org/10.1348/096317901167451.

Anglim, J., Bozic, S., Little, J., & Lievens, F. (2018). Response distortion on personality tests in applicants: Comparing high-stakes to low-stakes medical settings. *Advances in Health Sciences Education: Theory and Practice*, *23*, 311–321. https://doi.org/10.1007/s10459-017-9796-8.

Bartels, M., Rietveld, M. H., Van Baal, G. M., & Boomsma, D. I. (2002). Heritability of educational achievement in 12-year-olds and the overlap with cognitive ability. *Twin Research*, *5*, 544–553. https://doi.org/10.1375/136905202762342017.

Berry, C. M. (2015). Differential validity and differential prediction of cognitive ability tests: Understanding test bias in the employment context. *Annual Review of Organizational Psychology and Organizational Behavior*, *2*, 435–463. https://doi.org/10.1146/annurev-orgpsych-032414-111256.

Borghans, L., Golsteyn, B. H., Heckman, J., & Humphries, J. E. (2011). Identification problems in personality psychology. *Personality and Individual Differences*, *51*, 315–320. https://doi.org/10.1016/j.paid.2011.03.029.

(2016). What grades and achievement tests measure. *PNAS Proceedings of the National Academy of Sciences of the United States of America*, *113*, 13354–13359. https://doi.org/10.1073/pnas.1601135113.

Brown, A., & Maydeu-Olivares, A. (2013). How IRT can solve problems of ipsative data in forced-choice questionnaires. *Psychological Methods*, *18*, 36–52. https://doi.org/10.1037/a0030641.

Busato, V. V., Prins, F. J., Elshout, J. J., & Hamaker, C. (2000). Intellectual ability, learning style, personality, achievement motivation and academic success of psychology students in higher education. *Personality and Individual Differences*, *29*, 1057–1068. https://doi.org/10.1016/S0191-8869(99)00253-6.

Camara, W. J. (2009). College admission testing: Myths and realities in an age of admissions hype. In R. P. Phelps (Ed.). *Correcting fallacies about educational and psychological testing* (pp. 147–180). Washington, DC: American Psychological Association. https://doi.org/10.1037/11861-004.

Christiansen, N. D., Burns, G. N., & Montgomery, G. E. (2005). Reconsidering forced-choice item formats for applicant personality assessment. *Human Performance*, *18*, 267–307. https://doi.org/10.1207/s15327043hup1803_4.

Cliffordson, C. (2008). Differential prediction of study success across academic programs in the Swedish context: The validity of grades and tests as selection instruments for higher education. *Educational Assessment, 13*, 56–75. https://doi.org/10.1080/10627190801968240.

Cortina, J. M., Goldstein, N. B., Payne, S. C., Davison, H. K., & Gilliland, S. W. (2000). The incremental validity of interview scores over and above cognitive ability and conscientiousness scores. *Personnel Psychology, 53*, 325–351. https://doi.org/10.1111/j.1744-6570.2000.tb00204.x.

Credé, M. & Kuncel, N. R. (2008). Study habits, skills, and attitudes: The third pillar supporting collegiate performance. *Perspectives on Psychological Science, 3*, 425–453. https://doi.org/10.1111/j.1745-6924.2008.00089.x.

Cremonini, L., Leisyte, L., Weyer, E., & Vossensteyn, J. J. (2011). *Selection and matching in higher education: An international comparative study.* Enschede: Center for Higher Education Policy Studies (CHEPS).

Crombag, H. F., Gaff, J. G., & Chang, T. M. (1975). Study behavior and academic performance. *Tijdschrift voor Onderwijsresearch, 1*, 3–14.

Dahlke, J. A., & Sackett, P. R. (2017). The relationship between cognitive-ability saturation and subgroup mean differences across predictors of job performance. *Journal of Applied Psychology, 102*, 1403–1420. https://doi.org/10.1037/apl0000234.

Dana, J., Dawes, R., & Peterson, N. (2013). Belief in the unstructured interview: The persistence of an illusion. *Judgment and Decision Making, 8*, 512–520.

Dawes, R. M. (1979). The robust beauty of improper linear models in decision-making. *American Psychologist, 34*, 571–582. https://doi.org/10.1037/0003-066X.34.7.571.

de Leng, W. E., Stegers-Jager, K. M., Born, M. P., & Themmen, A. N. (2018). Integrity situational judgment test for medical school selection: Judging "what to do" versus "what not to do." *Medical Education, 52*, 427–437. https://doi.org/10.1111/medu.13498.

de Visser, M., Fluit, C., Fransen, J., Latijnhouwers, M., Cohen-Schotanus, J., & Laan, R. (2017). The effect of curriculum sample selection for medical school. *Advances in Health Science Education, 22*, 43–56. https://doi.org/10.1007/s10459-016-9681-x.

Deary, I. J., Strand, S., Smith, P., & Fernandes, C. (2007). Intelligence and educational achievement. *Intelligence, 35*, 13–21. https://doi.org/10.1016/j.intell.2006.02.001.

Drenth, P. J. D. (2008). Psychology: Is it applied enough? *Applied Psychology: An International Review, 57*, 524–540. https://doi.org/10.1111/j.1464-0597.2008.00337.x.

Dumfart, B., & Neubauer, A. C. (2016). Conscientiousness is the most powerful noncognitive predictor of school achievement in adolescents. *Journal of Individual Differences, 37*, 8–15. https://doi.org/10.1027/1614-0001/a000182.

Eva, K. W., Reiter, H. I., Rosenfeld, J., & Norman, G. R. (2004). The ability of the multiple mini-interview to predict pre-clerkship performance in medical school. *Academic Medicine, 79*, 40–42. https://doi.org/10.1097/00001888-200410001-00012.

Goho, J., & Blackman, A. (2006). The effectiveness of academic admission interviews: An exploratory meta-analysis. *Medical Teacher, 28*, 335–340. https://doi.org/10.1080/01421590600603418.

Griffin, B. & Wilson, I. G. (2012). Faking good: Self-enhancement in medical school applicants. *Medical Education, 46*, 485–490. https://doi.org/10.1111/j.1365-2923.2011.04208.x.

Highhouse, S. (2008). Stubborn reliance on intuition and subjectivity in employee selection. *Industrial and Organizational Psychology: Perspectives on Science and Practice, 1*, 333–342. https://doi.org/10.1111/j.1754-9434.2008.00058.x.

Highhouse, S., & Kostek, J. A. (2013). Holistic assessment for selection and placement. In K. F. Geisinger, B. A. Bracken, J. F. Carlson, J. C. Hansen, N. R. Kuncel, S. P. Reise, & M. C. Rodriguez (Eds.). *APA handbook of testing and assessment in psychology* (Vol. 1) *Test theory and testing and assessment in industrial and organizational psychology* (pp. 565–577). Washington, DC: American Psychological Association. https://doi.org/10.1037/14047-031.

Hoover, E. (2013). Noncognitive measures: The next frontier on college admissions. *Chronicle of Higher Education.* Retrieved from www.chronicle.com/article/Noncognitive-Measures-The/136621.

Horn, C. (2005). Standardized assessments and the flow of students into the college admission pool. *Educational Policy, 19*, 331–348. https://doi.org/10.1177/0895904804274057.

Husbands, A., & Dowell, J. (2013). Predictive validity of the Dundee Multiple Mini-Interview. *Medical Education, 47*, 717–725. https://doi.org/10.1111/medu.12193.

Jones, B. M. (2011). Assessing admission interviews at residential STEM schools. *NCSSSMST Journal, 16*, 20–29.

Keiser, H. N., Sackett, P. R., Kuncel, N. R., & Brothen, T. (2016). Why women perform better in college than admission scores would predict: Exploring the roles of conscientiousness and course-taking patterns. *Journal of Applied Psychology, 101*, 569–581. https://doi.org/10.1037/apl0000069.

Kelly, M. E., Patterson, F., O'Flynn, S., Mulligan, J., & Murphy, A. W. (2018). A systematic review of stakeholder views of selection methods for medical schools admission. *BMC Medical Education, 18*, 139. https://doi.org/10.1186/s12909-018-1235-x.

Kuncel, N. R., & Hezlett, S. A. (2010). Fact and fiction in cognitive ability testing for admissions and hiring decisions. *Current Directions in Psychological Science, 19*, 339–345. https://doi.org/10.1177/0963721410389459.

Kuncel, N. R., Klieger, D. M., Connelly, B. S., & Ones, D. S. (2013). Mechanical versus clinical data combination in selection and admissions decisions: A meta-analysis. *Journal of Applied Psychology, 98*, 1060–1072. https://doi.org/10.1037/a0034156.

Kuncel, N. R., Kochevar, R. J., & Ones, D. S. (2014). A meta-analysis of letters of recommendation in college and graduate admissions: Reasons for hope. *International Journal of Selection and Assessment, 22,* 101–107. https://doi.org/10.1111/ijsa.12060.

Kunina, O., Wilhelm, O., Formazin, M., Jonkmann, K., & Schroeders, U. (2007). Extended criteria and predictors in college admission: Exploring the structure of study success and investigating the validity of domain knowledge. *Psychology Science, 49,* 88–114.

Kyllonen, P. C., Lipnevich, A. A., Burrus, J., & Roberts, R. D. (2014). Personality, motivation, and college readiness: A prospectus for assessment and development (ETS Research Report No. RR-14-06). https://doi.org/10.1002/ets2.12004.

Kyllonen, P. C., Walters, A. M., & Kaufman, J. C. (2005). Noncognitive constructs and their assessment in graduate education: A review. *Educational Assessment, 10,* 153–184. https://doi.org/10.1207/s15326977ea1003_2.

Lamb, S., Markussen, E., Teese, R., Polesel, J., & Sandberg, N. (2011) *School dropout and completion.* Dordrecht: Springer. https://doi.org/10.1007/978-90-481-9763-7.

Le, H., Casillas, A., Robbins, S. B., & Langley, R. (2005). Motivational and skills, social, and self-management predictors of college outcomes: Constructing the student readiness inventory. *Educational and Psychological Measurement, 65,* 482–508. https://doi.org/10.1177/0013164404272493.

Lee, J., Connelly, B. S., Goff, M., & Hazucha, J. F. (2017). Are assessment center behaviors' meanings consistent across exercises? A measurement invariance approach. *International Journal of Selection and Assessment, 25,* 317–332. https://doi.org/10.1111/ijsa.12187.

Lemann, N. (1999). *The big test: The secret history of the American meritocracy.* New York, NY: Farrar, Straus, and Giroux.

Lievens, F. (2013). Adjusting medical school admission: Assessing interpersonal skills using situational judgment tests. *Medical Education, 47,* 182–189. https://doi.org/10.1111/medu.12089.

Lievens, F., & Coetsier, P. (2002). Situational tests in student selection: An examination of predictive validity, adverse impact, and construct validity. *International Journal of Selection and Assessment, 10,* 245–257. https://doi.org/10.1111/1468-2389.00215.

Lievens, F., & Sackett, P. R. (2012). The validity of interpersonal skills assessment via situational judgment tests for predicting academic success and job performance. *Journal of Applied Psychology, 97,* 460–468. https://doi.org/10.1037/a0025741.

Lyren, P. (2008). Prediction of academic performance by means of the Swedish scholastic assessment test. *Scandinavian Journal of Educational Research, 52,* 565–581. https://doi.org/10.1080/00313830802497158.

Markle, R., Olivera-Aguilar, M., Jackson, T., Noeth, R., & Robbins, S. (2013). Examining evidence of reliability, validity, and fairness for the SuccessNavigator™ assessment (ETS Research Report No. RR-13-12). Retrieved from www.ets.org/Media/Research/pdf/RR-13-12.pdf.

Mattern, K., Sanchez, E., & Ndum, E. (2017). Why do achievement measures underpredict female academic performance? *Educational Measurement: Issues and Practice, 36*(1), 47–57. https://doi.org/10.1111/emip.12138.

Meehl, P. E. (1954). *Clinical versus statistical prediction: A theoretical analysis and a review of the evidence*. Minneapolis: University of Minnesota

Ministry of Education, Culture, and Science (2014, August 29). *Informatie over de afschaffing van loting bij numerusfixusopleidingen* [Information concerning the abolishing of lottery admission]. Kamerbrief [Government information]. Retrieved from www.rijksoverheid.nl/documenten-en-publicaties/kamerstuk ken/2014/08/30/kamerbrief-met-informatie-over-de-afschaffing-van-loting-bij-numerusfixusopleidingen.html.

Murphy, S. C., Klieger, D. M., Borneman, M. J., & Kuncel, N. R. (2009). The predictive power of personal statements in admissions: A meta-analysis and cautionary tale. *College and University, 84*(4), 83–86.

National Association for College Admission Counseling (2017). *State of College Admission*. Retrieved from www.nacacnet.org/globalassets/documents/publi cations/research/soca17final.pdf.

Niessen, A. S. M., & Meijer, R. R. (2016). Selection of medical students on the basis of non-academic skills: Is it worth the trouble? *Clinical Medicine, 16*, 339–342. https://doi.org/10.7861/clinmedicine.16-4-339.

(2017). On the use of broadened selection criteria in higher education. *Perspectives on Psychological Science, 12*, 436–448. https://doi:10.1177/1745691616683 05.

Niessen, A. S. M., Meijer, R. R., & Tendeiro, J. N. (2017a). Applying organizational justice theory to admission into higher education: Admission from a student perspective. *International Journal of Selection and Assessment, 25*, 72–84. https://doi.org/10.1111/ijsa.12161.

(2017b). Measuring non-cognitive predictors in high-stakes contexts: The effect of self-presentation on self-report instruments used in admission to higher education. *Personality and Individual Differences, 106*, 183–189. https://doi.org/10.1016/j.paid.2016.11.014.

(2018) Admission testing for higher education: A multi-cohort study on the validity of high-fidelity curriculum-sampling tests. *PLoS ONE 13*(6), 1–21. https://doi.org/10.1371/journal.pone.0198746.

Organisation for Economic Co-operation and Development (2010). *OECD reviews of migrant education: Closing the gap for immigrant students; policies, practice and performance*. Paris: Organisation for Economic Co-operation and Development.

Orr, D., Usher, A., Haj, C, Atherton, G, & Geanta, I. (2017). *Study on the impact of admission systems on higher education outcomes* (Vol. 1): *Comparative report*. Brussels: European Commission. Retrieved from https://publications .europa.eu/en/publication-detail/-/publication/9cfdd9c1-98f9-11e7-b92d-01aa75ed71a1.

Oswald, F. L., Schmitt, N., Kim, B. H., Ramsay, L. J., & Gillespie, M. A. (2004). Developing a biodata measure and situational judgment inventory as predictors of college student performance. *Journal of Applied Psychology, 89,* 187–207. https://doi.org/10.1037/0021-9010.89.2.187.

Patterson, F., Cousans, F., Edwards, H., Rosselli, A., Nicholson, S., & Wright, B. (2017). The predictive validity of a text-based situational judgment test in undergraduate medical and dental school admissions. *Academic Medicine, 92,* 1250–1253. https://doi.org/10.1097/ACM.0000000000001630.

Patterson, F., Knight, A., Dowell, J., Nicholson, S., Cousans, F., & Cleland, J. (2016). How effective are selection methods in medical education? A systematic review. *Medical Education, 50,* 36–60. https://doi.org/10.1111/medu.12817.

Ramsay, L. J., Schmitt, N., Oswald, F. L., Kim, B. H., & Gillespie, M. A. (2006). The impact of situational context variables on responses to biodata and situational judgment inventory items. *Psychology Science, 48,* 268–287.

Resing, W. C. M., & Drenth, P. J. D. (2007). *Intelligentie: Weten en meten* [Intelligence: Measuring and knowing]. Amsterdam: Uitgeverij Nieuwezijds.

Richardson, M., Abrahams, C., & Bond, R. (2012). Psychological correlates of university students' academic performance: A systematic review and meta-analysis. *Psychological Bulletin, 138,* 353–387. https://doi.org/10.1037/a0026838.

Robbins, S. B., Lauver, K., Le, H., Davis, D., Langley, R., & Carlstrom, A. (2004). Do psychosocial and study skill factors predict college outcomes? A meta-analysis. *Psychological Bulletin, 130,* 261–288. https://doi.org/10.1037/0033-2909.130.2.261.

Sackett, P. R., & Ellingson, J. E. (1997). The effects of forming multi-predictor composites on group differences and adverse impact. *Personnel Psychology, 50,* 707–721. https://doi.org/10.1111/j.1744-6570.1997.tb00711.x.

Salgado, J. F., & Táuriz, G. (2014). The five-factor model, forced-choice personality inventories and performance: A comprehensive meta-analysis of academic and occupational validity studies. *European Journal of Work and Organizational Psychology, 23,* 3–30. https://doi.org/10.1080/1359432X.2012.716198.

Schmidt, F. L., & Hunter, J. E. (1998) The validity and utility of selection methods in personnel psychology: Practical and theoretical implications of 85 years of research findings. *Psychological Bulletin, 124,* 262–274. https://doi.org/10.1037/0033-2909.124.2.262.

Schmitt, N. (2012). Development of rationale and measures of noncognitive college student potential. *Educational Psychologist, 47,* 18–29. https://doi.org/10.1080/00461520.2011.610680.

Schmitt, N., Keeney, J., Oswald, F. L., Pleskac, T. J., Billington, A. Q., Sinha, R., & Zorzie, M. (2009). Prediction of 4-year college student performance using cognitive and noncognitive predictors and the impact on demographic status of admitted students. *Journal of Applied Psychology, 94,* 1479–1497. https://doi.org/10.1037/a0016810.

Schwager, I. T. L., Hülsheger, U. R., Lang, J. W. B., Klieger, D. M., Bridgeman, B., & Wendler, C. (2014). Supervisor ratings of students' academic potential as predictors of citizenship and counterproductive behavior. *Learning*

and Individual Differences, 35, 62–69. https://doi.org/10.1016/j.lindif
.2014.07.005.

Sedlacek, W. E. (2004) *Beyond the big test: Noncognitive assessment in higher education.* San Francisco, CA: Jossey-Bass.

(2005). The case for noncognitive measures. In W. J. Camara, E. W. Kimmel, W. J. Camara, & E. W. Kimmel (Eds.). *Choosing students: Higher education admissions tools for the 21st century* (pp. 177–193). Mahwah, NJ: Lawrence Erlbaum Associates Publishers.

Shultz, M. M., & Zedeck, S. (2012). Admission to Law school: New measures. *Educational Psychologist, 47,* 51–65. https://doi.org/10.1080/00461520.2011.610679.

Sinha, R., Oswald, F., Imus, A., & Schmitt, N. (2011). Criterion-focused approach to reducing adverse impact in college admissions. *Applied Measurement in Education, 24,* 137–161. https://doi.org/10.1080/08957347.2011.554605.

Steenman, S. C. (2018). Alignment of admission: An exploration and analysis of the links between learning objectives and selective admission to programmes in higher education (Doctoral dissertation). University of Utrecht.

Stegers-Jager, K. M. (2018). Lessons learned from 15 years of non-grades-based selection for medical school. *Medical Education, 52,* 86–95. https://doi.org/10.1111/medu.13462.

Stemler, S. E. (2012). What should university admissions tests predict? *Educational Psychologist, 47,* 5–17. https://doi.org/10.1080/00461520.2011.611444.

Sternberg, R. J. (2016). *What universities can be: A new model for preparing students for active concerned citizenship and ethical leadership.* Ithaca, NY: Cornell University Press.

Tagesschau (2017). Medizin-Zulassung muss überarbeitet werden [Admission to medical school must be revised]. Retrieved from www.tagesschau.de/inland/medizinstudium-verfassungsgericht-101.html.

Thomas, L. L., Kuncel, N. R., & Credé, M. (2007). Noncognitive variables in college admissions: The case of the non-cognitive questionnaire. *Educational and Psychological Measurement, 67,* 635–657. https://doi.org/10.1177/0013164406292074.

Till, H., Myford, C., & Dowell, J. (2013). Improving student selection using multiple mini-interviews with multifaceted Rasch modeling. *Academic Medicine, 88,* 216–223. https://doi.org/10.1097/ACM.0b013e31827c0c5d.

Valli, R., & Johnson, P. (2007). Entrance examinations as gatekeepers. *Scandinavian Journal of Educational Research, 51,* 493–510. https://doi.org/10.1080/00313830701576631.

Vasilopoulos, N. L., Cucina, J. M., Dyomina, N. V., Morewitz, C. L., & Reilly, R. R. (2006). Forced-choice personality tests: A measure of personality and cognitive ability? *Human Performance, 19,* 175–199. https://doi.org/10.1207/s15327043hup1903_1.

von Stumm, S., & Ackerman, P. L. (2013). Investment and intellect: A review and meta-analysis. *Psychological Bulletin, 139,* 841–869. https://doi.org/10.1037/a0030746.

Wagerman, S. A., & Funder, D. C. (2007). Acquaintance reports of personality and academic achievement: A case for conscientiousness. *Journal of Research in Personality, 41*, 221–229. https://doi.org/10.1016/j.jrp.2006.03.001.

Wammes, J. G., van den Akker-van Marle, M. E., Verkerk, E. W., van Dulmen, S. A., Westert, G. P., van Asselt, A. I., & Kool, R. B. (2016). Identifying and prioritizing lower value services from Dutch specialist guidelines and a comparison with the UK do-not-do list. *BMC Medicine, 14*, 1–9. https://doi.org/10.1186/s12916-016-0747-7.

Westrick, P. A., Le, H., Robbins, S. B., Radunzel, J. R., & Schmidt, F. L. (2015). College performance and retention: A meta-analysis of the predictive validities of ACT scores, high school grades, and SES. *Educational Assessment, 20*, 23–45. https://doi.org/10.1080/10627197.2015.997614.

Witzburg, R. A., & Sondheimer, H. M. (2013). Holistic review: Shaping the medical profession one applicant at a time. *New England Journal of Medicine, 368*, 1565–1567. https://doi.org/10.1056/NEJMp1300411.

Wouters, A. (2017). Effects of medical school selection on the motivation of the student population and the applicant pool (Doctoral dissertation). VU University, Amsterdam.

Wouters, A., Croiset, G., Schripsema, N. R., Cohen-Schotanus, J., Spaai, G. G., Hulsman, R. L., & Kusurkar, R. A. (2017). A multi-site study on medical school selection, performance, motivation and engagement. *Advances in Health Sciences Education: Theory and Practice, 22*, 447–462. https://doi.org/10.1007/s10459-016-9745-y.

Zwick, R. (2013). *Disentangling the role of high school grades, SAT scores, and SES in predicting college achievement.* (Research Report No. RR-13-09). Princeton, NJ: Educational Testing Service. https://doi.org/10.1002/j.2333-8504.2013.tb02316.x.

(2017a). The risk of focusing on character in admissions. *Chronicle of Higher Education, 63*(42). Retrieved from www.chronicle.com/article/The-Risks-of-Focusing-on/240787.

(2017b). *Who gets in? Strategies for fair and effective college admissions.* Cambridge, MA: Harvard University Press. https://doi.org/10.4159/9780674977648.

CHAPTER 6

Cross-Cultural and Global Competencies and Their Role in Admissions Policies and Practices

Stephanie McKeown, Adrienne Vedan, Jackson Traplin,
Leah Sanford, and Cynthia Bourne

Equity, diversity, and inclusion are areas of priority for higher education institutions in Canada. Recently, academic leaders across Canada have committed to advancing equity, diversity, and inclusion on their campuses (Universities Canada, 2017). In response, many Canadian institutions are rethinking their access to education and admissions policies and practices, and are considering what it means to have greater participation in higher education and greater success for traditionally under-represented populations (Higher Education Quality Council of Ontario, 2017). This commitment to equity, diversity, and inclusion challenges higher education institutions to confront many systemic issues and make choices that nurture diverse and inclusive campus climates.

Higher education campuses around the world are becoming more diverse than ever before. Diversity includes differences in gender, gender identity and expression, ethnicity, sexuality, religion, culture, nationality, socioeconomic status, mental and physical ability, life experiences, skills, and knowledge. It is present in the different ways in which individuals and groups "see, categorize, and understand" the world (Page, 2007). Diverse students bring a wide range of abilities and backgrounds, and admissions assessments should be appropriate and fair to these students (Sedlacek, 2004). Not all individuals have the same needs and circumstances. Through equity-related policies, the goal is to lessen and ultimately remove obstacles to accessing higher education that may result from one's personal or social circumstances and support students in achieving their academic successes (Sedlacek, 2004). Thus, it is important that higher education institutions enact admissions policies and practices that account for and value the ways in which people are different, which will improve access for all individuals (Blessinger, Hoffman, & Makhanya, 2018). Such equity-related initiatives must be fundamental to ensure that these commitments are at the heart of academic policies. However, campus attitudes and systemic practices can sometimes foster alienating and individualistic values (Caxaj et al., 2018). So, the opportunity set forth in front of Canadian higher education is to review admissions policies and practices that consider the realities and experiences of our applicants. As a result, there are three key themes currently playing out in Canadian higher education that are changing the fabric of our learning environments: indigenization, internationalization, and globalization.

Indigenous youth are the fastest growing part of the population in Canada. Although the proportion of Canadian Indigenous high school graduates and the numbers of Indigenous students entering into the postsecondary system have been increasing, the Indigenous postsecondary attainment rate remains significantly lower than that of non-Indigenous learners (Munro, 2014). The education gap is particularly great among those earning a university credential (Gordon & White, 2014; Statistics Canada, 2011). In response to the calls to action by the Truth and Reconciliation Commission of Canada (Truth and Reconciliation Committee, 2015), as well as Canada's adoption of the *United Nations Declaration on the Rights of Indigenous Peoples* (United Nations, 2008), many institutions are pledging to improve access to education, the learning environment, and educational attainment levels, to better meet the needs of Indigenous learners (Colleges and Institutes Canada, 2014; McKeown et al., 2018; Pidgeon, 2014; Universities Canada, 2015).

Increasingly, academic leaders are recognizing the sociocultural impact international students have on campus communities and their contributions on expanding student learning outcomes to include cross-cultural and global knowledge (Hegarty, 2014). International students strengthen the learning environment at higher education institutions as well as the Canadian communities in which they live. They bring a mix of cultures, backgrounds, and perspectives that contributes to the diverse Canadian landscape and the quality of the educational experiences of all students (Luo & Jamieson-Drake, 2013; Soria & Troisi, 2014). Between 2010 and 2018, there was a 154 percent increase in international students studying in Canadian higher education institutions (Canadian Bureau for International Education, 2018). Many institutions aim to have at least 20 percent of their student population comprised of international students from a variety of countries. To achieve this goal, admissions policies for international students are under review, particularly in relation to the English-language requirement for university admissions when prospective students meet all other admissions requirements for degree programs.

Internationalization and globalization have increased student mobility around the world; business, trade, and knowledge-exchange have sharply increased, leading students to travel globally in hopes of experiencing a unique educational opportunity and enhance their future employment prospects. With the focus on educating globally aware and knowledgeable students, many argue that Canada is falling behind its peers in sending students on global learning experiences (Knight-Grofe & Deacon, 2016). Therefore, the Canadian government has prioritized significantly growing the number of Canadian students who participate in global learning experiences, such as studying abroad, internships, international practicums, work–study programs, and global service-learning opportunities (Biggs et al., 2015).

Using these three themes of indigenization, internationalization, and globalization as the framework of our chapter, we focus our discussions on cross-cultural and global competencies and how they may contribute to a more equitable, diverse, and inclusive campus if they are integrated with admissions policies and practices. First, we provide a brief overview of higher education in Canada and the focus on cross-cultural and global skills and competencies. Then, we provide a discussion of Indigenous students in Canada and how culturally inclusive approaches to admissions can contribute to decolonizing practices in higher education. Next, we provide a summary on the significant growth and demand of international student mobility to Canadian universities and the admissions policies and practices that are encouraging this growth. Finally, we discuss the potential for cross-cultural and global competencies to be used in admissions processes for programs that include global experiences for Canadian students.

6.1   Higher Education in Canada

Most higher education institutions in Canada are public universities, colleges, polytechnics, institutes, and *Cégeps* (*Collèges d'enseignement général et professionnel*) in the province of Quebec. The Constitution Act in 1982 assigns responsibility for higher education institutions to the provincial or territorial governments, resulting in unique systems of education within each province or territory. At the national level, higher education public institutions are represented by two associations: Universities Canada (UC) and Colleges and Institutes Canada (CICan). UC represents 96 universities across Canada, while CICan represents 420 campuses of colleges and institutes and 80 additional learning, training, or access centers. Institutional membership in each of these organizations is voluntary. These associations promote and advocate for higher education in Canada, as well as provide data and share information on higher education trends.

Admission in Canadian higher education is almost always to a program rather than to an institution and entry is usually more competitive for some programs than for others, while other programs may have open-entry policies. Until recently, most higher education institutions in Canada considered only high school grades to determine the eligibility of students admitted to their programs (Tancock, 2017). Increasingly, however, many institutions are using a combination of noncognitive and cognitive approaches in their admissions practices to provide a more holistic under-standing of the applicant, particularly for selective or highly competitive programs. Researchers have discussed the benefits of including noncogni-tive measures combined with cognitive measures in admissions practices to increase admissions of under-represented populations in higher education (Oliveri & Ezzo, 2014; Sedlacek, 2004). Whether in engineering, business, or medicine, at the undergraduate or graduate levels applicants are being asked through personal essays, portfolios, and video statements to describe their contributions to their communities and what they value. This supplemental admissions information is used to understand the applicant's non-academic attributes and, together with their high school grades, is used to make a decision on their admission status to a program.

Typically, using a rubric, evaluators are instructed to look for certain character traits in written or video submissions – including leadership potential, knowledge in a field or creativity, ability to deal with adversity, and community service – and then assign a score from zero to three for each trait (Tancock, 2017). A score of three in community service would mean that a student has shown "strong evidence of activity/identification with community; significant contributions over time." A score of zero would mean "no meaningful answer" was provided. But these more subjective admissions criteria are raising concerns that bias could interfere with the selection process and that students who have higher levels of socioeconomic status could have an unfair advantage because they are well connected in their community and are more comfortable describing them-selves. In addition, there are differences in how these profiles and grades are weighted by admissions personnel, which can vary significantly by institution and by program. For some applicants, strong evidence of desirable noncognitive attributes could support their admission to a pro-gram when their grades are on the low end of the admissions acceptance score (Tancock, 2017). Many higher education institutions that include noncognitive aspects to admissions practices tend to ask applicants to provide a personal statement or respond to general questions and assess their responses related to attributes of leadership, problem-solving, commitment to community, and readiness to learn, rather than including questions about cross-cultural or global competencies.

6.2   Cross-Cultural and Global Competencies

Prioritizing students' awareness as global citizens and preparing them for careers in a globalized labor market has resulted in a focus on cross-cultural and global knowledge in higher education (Chakma, 2016). The role of higher education institutions is to prepare students with the skills necessary to solve complex dynamic problems needed for students to be successful in a competitive, globally connected, and technologically intensive world (Ontario Public Service, 2016). Students are expected to develop these skills through a variety of experiences intended to enable them to appreciate and respect cultural differences, to demonstrate compassion and concern for others, to understand world cultures and events, and to analyze global systems. The goal, then, is to integrate this learning into their lives as citizens so that they may thrive, contribute to, and lead in a global society (Gregersen-Hermans, 2017; What Is Global Citizenship, 2011).

Many leaders in higher education believe that cross-cultural and global communication, collaboration, knowledge, and understanding are critical skills and competencies that students should learn to be successful in the twenty-first century. Much of the higher education research on cross-cultural and global competencies has been focused on students and their learning outcomes (Kruse, Rakha, & Calderone, 2018). These studies have been concerned with what a student is expected to know, understand, and demonstrate at the end of their period of learning that will make them successful as civically responsible global citizens. Institutional programs and practices regarding cross-cultural and global competencies are often offered to students after they have been admitted to their programs through specific orientation programs, student support programs and resources offered on campus, welcoming spaces built and developed for students, and food options on campus. Until recently, however, many Canadian universities neglected to explicitly include cross-cultural and global attributes in admissions policies and practices. Rather, we believe the onus should be on institutions to articulate how they improve access to higher education for under-represented groups and create a positive learning environment. Institutions themselves need to demonstrate the cultural and global competencies required to encourage diversity and inclusion on our campuses by widening participation initiatives for all individuals. The following sections on indigenization, internationalization, and globalization highlight some examples of how institutional policies have changed to appreciate and respect cultural differences, demonstrate compassion for others, and better understand world cultures.

6.2.1 Indigenization

In consultation with its members and partners in Indigenous communities, Colleges and Institutes Canada (CICan) (2014) developed an Indigenous Education Protocol, which is founded on seven principles that aim to reaffirm the importance of Indigenous education. This document underscores the structures and approaches required to address Indigenous peoples' learning needs and support self-determination and socioeconomic development of Indigenous communities (Colleges and Institutes Canada, 2014). Similarly, in 2015, UC adopted 13 principles on Indigenous education. These principles recognize the need for institutional commitment at every level to develop opportunities for Indigenous students, greater indigenized curricula, Indigenous leadership within university communities, as well as the vital work needed to create resources, spaces, and approaches to promote discussion and intercultural engagement between Indigenous and non-Indigenous students (Universities Canada, 2015).

Challenges to Indigenous students' successful educational journeys are embedded in both a historical as well as a contemporary context. Colonial ideologies informed the Indian Act and resulting policies, which have defined the ability for Indigenous people to access and participate in higher education. Additional ambiguity between federal and provincial jurisdiction regarding Indigenous higher education initiatives have created barriers for Indigenous learners (Stonechild, 2004). With the introduction of the Indian Act in 1876, a range of aggressively assimilative policies were implemented that included the restriction of freedom of movement, suppression of cultural beliefs and practices, and the forced removal of children to residential schools (Stonechild, 2004).

The specter of the Indian residential school (IRS) system, where a majority of Indigenous children had been sent by the federal government to be assimilated into the dominant culture (ending with the last IRS closure in 1996), continues to haunt the minds and hearts of Indigenous learners navigating higher education (Charbonneau, 2017; King, 2008). Additionally, up until the Indian Act of the 1920s, if an Indigenous individual attended university, they could face automatic enfranchisement, meaning that they would lose their status as Indians: "Therefore, it was difficult, if not impossible, for them to pursue university education on their own accord" (Stonechild, 2004, p. 5).

In this historical context, Indigenous knowledge systems were dismantled, and family units were disrupted over generations; this effect reverberates into the present day. Many Indigenous students are the first in their family to attend a higher education institution (Melville, 2017). Government funding for Indigenous students is usually distributed only to Indigenous persons who qualify as status of Indian or Inuit under the Indian Act. This system of recognition inevitably ignores non-status Indigenous and Métis populations, thereby limiting these groups' access to higher education funding resources (Holmes, 2006). One recent report indicates that an overwhelming number of Indigenous students have experienced instances of racism within the institutions, resulting in negative effects on these students' higher education learning outcomes (Restoule et al., 2013).

6.2.1.1   *Cross-Cultural Competencies as a Decolonizing Practice*

Access is a key component of Indigenous educational attainment in Canada, with only a small percentage of high school graduates earning the prerequisites to enroll in further education. More than 60 percent of Indigenous students have utilized bridging programs to help transition them to higher education (Ottmann, 2017). Many institutions have implemented various programs and policies to increase access and widen participation for Indigenous learners; the University of Manitoba has one of the longest standing initiatives to provide access to engineering programs for Indigenous learners who do not have the prerequisites to apply for direct admission. Since this program started in 1985, it is one of the most successful in Canada, with more than 100 graduates. As part of the application process, Indigenous students need to provide two references, proof of Indigenous ancestry (Status, Non-Status, Métis, or Inuit), as well as fill out an application form that includes sections for community and life history and an autobiographical section. The program provides students with programs and services to meet the needs of the whole student – academic, personal, financial, and social (University of Manitoba, 2017).

Another approach adopted by Mount Royal University was to establish Indigenous admissions targets, which set out to increase the percentage of self-identified Indigenous students from 3.4 percent in 2013 to 7 percent by 2025 (Mount Royal University, 2013). Applicants who qualify to be considered under this admission category must self-identify as an Indigenous applicant, meet the definition of an Indigenous applicant (Canadian who is a Status Indian/First Nations, Non-Status Indian/First Nations,

Métis, or Inuit), and meet the minimum general university admissions requirements as well as program requirements. The designated seats are filled on a competitive basis. There are several activities that are measured toward their success against their strategic 2025 goals, including an increased understanding of Indigenous culture and issues as demonstrated by faculty, staff, and management; inclusion of Indigenous content and perspective in all degree-program curricula; and an increased number of Indigenous faculty and staff attracted to and retained at the university (Mount Royal University, 2016).

The University of Alberta has formally acknowledged that Indigenous learners are under-represented in higher education and are working toward having an Indigenous student population that is at least proportionate to the Indigenous population of the province (University of Alberta, 2018). To fulfill this goal, the university states: "additional qualified applicants may be considered over and above the Aboriginal students who are admitted in the regular competition for places in a Faculty" (University of Alberta, 2018). Students who are not eligible for admission may be eligible to enroll through the university's Transition Year program. Through the university's governance structure, Indigenous enrollment in each faculty is reported annually and monitored and evaluated (University of Alberta, 2018).

At the University of British Columbia's (UBC) Okanagan campus, there is a supported admissions process for Indigenous students. Three categories are used to admit applicants: (a) applicants who are directly admissible to a degree program and those whose average of admission may be slightly below the competitive threshold, but whose admission is endorsed by faculty; (b) applicants who are not directly admissible to a degree program, but who have demonstrated competency in key subject areas and whose average of admission is within a certain range; and (c) applicants who are not admissible to a degree program, but are invited to enroll in Aboriginal Access Studies through a personalized offer letter. Aboriginal students can apply directly to the Aboriginal Access Studies pathway program and students who cannot be admitted to a degree program are given automatic eligibility to enroll. Students who successfully complete a minimum of 18 credits (6 courses) through the Aboriginal Access Studies, in addition to meeting program requirements, are able to transfer into a degree program at the university's Okanagan campus. About 80 percent of students enrolled in the Aboriginal Access Studies program have transitioned into degree programs at UBC as well as other institutions. Through the supported admissions programs, the offer of admissions includes recommendations regarding course load and tutorial participation. In addition, contact information for a designated faculty liaison and an adviser is included. The intake of Indigenous students enrolling in supported admissions to nursing and engineering programs has more than doubled, with a more than 90 percent retention rate.

The province of Ontario has taken steps to increase Indigenous student access in partnership with Indigenous communities by passing the Indigenous Institutes Act. This legislation is the first legislation in Canada to recognize Indigenous Institutes as both independent and complimentary to the public higher education system. The Act allocates key functions and oversight of Indigenous Institutes to Indigenous people. It provides the framework to ensure that higher education credentials, such as diplomas and degrees offered from Indigenous Institutes, will meet the same standards as those offered from public higher education institutions (Ontario Ministry of Training, Colleges and Universities, 2018).

Pidgeon (2014) placed the onus on Canadian higher education institutions to transform the existing academy through Indigenization, which includes empowering Indigenous self-determination, addressing decolonization, and reconciling systemic and societal inequalities between Indigenous and non-Indigenous peoples. These practices would help to ensure that the curriculum is culturally relevant and applicable to Indigenous students' needs and develop courses and programs that are more open to Indigenous methods of learning, teaching, and researching. In addition, researchers have argued that all members of the higher education community benefit by engaging students, faculty, and staff in conversations where they learn about Indigenous histories; the inequities and barriers Indigenous individuals face; recognize rights, gain respect for, cooperate with, and form partnerships (Aboriginal Nurses Association of Canada, 2009; British Columbia Ministry of Advanced Education, 2012; Timmons, 2009).

6.2.2   Internationalization

By 2025, the global demand for international higher education is expected to grow to more than 7.2 million students worldwide (James-MacEachern & James-MacEachern, 2017; Organisation for Economic Co-operation and Development, 2017). Today, the number of international students studying abroad totals close to 5.5 million, compared to 4.5 million in 2011, 2.1 million in 2000, and 1.3 million in 1990 (Organisation for Economic Co-operation and Development, 2017). International students have become critical global consumers, and many apply to institutions in more than one country (Knight-Grofe & Klabunde, 2009). The top choice countries in which students wish to pursue their international education experience include the United States, the United Kingdom, Australia, France, and Canada (Adamoski, 2015; Organisation for Economic Co-operation and Development, 2017).

There has been a significant increase to the growth of international students enrolling in Canadian institutions over the past several years (Beck, 2012). In 2018, there were 572,415 international students studying in Canada, which was a 15 percent increase over the previous year (Canadian Bureau for International Education, 2018). A majority of this growth, 86 percent, is concentrated in the provinces of Ontario, British Columbia, and Quebec. It is expected that these numbers will continue to rise, as 95 percent of international students recommended Canada as a destination for their higher education (Canadian Bureau for International Education, 2018; Singer, 2017). Institutions that will be successful in recruiting and admitting international students will be those where admissions policies acknowledge and celebrate diversity and promote intercultural and inclusive campus environments.

International students are choosing to study in Canada because of the environmental, political, and social climates as well as visa availability (Chen, 2007; Simmons, 2018). Research findings, moreover, show that visa and immigration considerations are of great importance in choosing Canada for particular demographics of students (Chen, 2007). Fifty-one percent of international students plan to apply for permanent residency in Canada, while more than 65 percent plan to apply for postgraduate work permits to remain in Canada for three years after graduating, commonly leading to them applying for permanent residency (Canadian Bureau for International Education, 2018; Chen, 2007; Knight-Grofe & Klabunde, 2009). Canada has recently gained momentum with its newest, progressive immigration policies where students can now work part-time while studying without a separate work permit. In addition, points are now specifically awarded to candidates with Canadian education experience, which, in turn, strengthens their application for permanent residency (Singer, 2017).

Higher education institutions have seen the economic impact and value in admitting a diverse international student body. Global Affairs Canada (2016) reported international students in Canada spent approximately 11.4 billion dollars on tuition, accommodations, and other discretionary spending. Canada's economy continues to benefit from international students (Canadian Magazine of Immigration, 2017) and this will continue as both provincial and federal international-education strategic plans aim to double the number of international students in higher education by 2020. However, the contributions of international students go well beyond their economic impacts. Studying and engaging with individuals from around the world enriches the lives of Canadian students and increases their comfort with different cultures – something they will increasingly need if they are to excel in the global economy (Chakma, 2016). Such competencies in today's global workforce are seen as crucial, and higher education has an important role to play in ensuring that graduating students are prepared for the growing challenges of an increasingly diverse global community (Jayakumar, 2008). Universities are producing cross-culturally competent citizens by admitting a diverse international student population; the mere presence of having international students is no longer in addition to the general student body but rather a vital component of it (Hegarty, 2014).

Recent studies in higher education have highlighted why admitting and retaining diverse international students is beneficial for institutions and their communities. Luo and Jamieson-Drake (2013) found that students who interacted with international students gained new cultural perspectives, as well as empathy, and demonstrated increased cross-cultural competencies. Similarly, Soria and Troisi (2014) concluded that Canadian students acquired enhanced intercultural, global, and international competencies when provided with opportunities to learn about diverse global and international cultures through formal and informal interactions with international students on campus. Moreover, these researchers found that internationalization in home activities positively influenced students' development of cross-cultural competencies as much as, if not more than, study-abroad programs.

Improved communication and critical-thinking skills have also been tied to a diverse campus community. Jayakumar (2008) found that exposure to racial diversity in higher education institutions has long-term benefits in preparing students to understand multiple perspectives, negotiate conflict, and relate to different worldviews. Luo and Jamieson-Drake's (2013) research built upon both Astin (1993) and Chang's (1996) findings which concluded that conversations and/or serious discussions with international students: (a) improved critical thinking abilities of both groups of students, (b) positively affected students' abilities to think critically about a subject, (c) led to a greater openness to diverse perspectives, and (d) contributed to students' serious questioning and challenging of their own values and beliefs (Pascarella et al., 1996). Academically, Hegarty (2014), Chakma (2016), and Kounalakis (2015) measured how international students are a vital component of research universities. Their findings concluded that international students contribute to an increase in institution patent applications (Hegarty, 2014).

UBC's Vantage College offers unique admissions pathways for international students who do not yet meet the English-language admissions requirements but who do meet the competitive admissions score on the prerequisite courses required for their degree program. The objective of the Vantage One program is to support the transition of international students from high school to the second year of a UBC degree. It is an 11-month program that combines first-year coursework with additional academic mentorship and English-language resources, so each student is prepared to progress successfully into the second year of their chosen UBC degree. The Vantage One program offers four streams of study, including management, arts, engineering, and science, enhanced by academic-English classes. Similarly, the English Foundation Program offered at UBC's Okanagan campus is an accredited program that provides university admission to students who meet all academic requirements for their degree program, but do not yet meet UBC's English-language admission standard.

6.2.3   *Globalization*

The third area where higher education in Canada has worked to appreciate and respect cultural differences is in its interest in expanding opportunities for students to study or learn abroad. Exchange programs, study abroad, and other forms of experiential learning, such as service-learning, international practicums and internships, and volunteering, have grown in popularity. Thus, internationalization efforts are not confined to incoming students; outbound students are also part of the internationalization process. Indeed, there is a widespread belief that Canada's role in the global economy would benefit by greatly increasing the percentage of students who participate in global-learning experiences (Biggs et al., 2015). However, to participate, students need to have access to both higher education and the financial resources required to travel and live abroad (Admit Project Team, 2002). Interwoven with outbound student mobility is higher education's obligation to see that such programs advance cultural and global competencies.

Recent reports suggest that Canada is falling behind compared to other countries when it comes to the number of outbound students sent abroad each year. The current rate of participation is approximately 3 percent and has been at that level for more than a decade. The Centre for International

Policy Studies (CIPS) at the University of Ottawa (Biggs et al., 2015; Paris & Biggs, 2017) suggests it is a matter of strategic importance that Canada increase its total number of outbound students engaging in global experiences. As a result, CIPS proposes increases of 25 percent to 30 percent by 2025. These are lofty numbers given current low participation rates, but for any level of increase to happen interest will need to build in these programs, beginning with the recruitment and admissions process and continuing throughout a student's undergraduate career (Paris & Biggs, 2017).

To address this gap in outbound student mobility, a recent initiative in 2017 brought together representatives from Canadian universities, colleges, and government to create a strategic plan to increase the number of students who engage globally. The conclusions resulting from these discussions are represented in a report authored by Paris and Biggs (2017). The report recommends that Canada craft "and adequately fund [a] national strategy that sets clear targets and responsibilities" (p. 4). The report provides 20 recommendations that include prioritizing developing (or emerging) countries, increasing accessibility to programs with a global component, reducing barriers within institutions through curricular changes, creating an overarching brand similar to that of Europe's Erasmus program or Australia's Colombo programs, and providing a national investment fund to support these initiatives.

Funding is a key issue for many students. While economics and the development of a globally competent workforce may guide Canadian policymakers' interest in increasing the number of outbound students, personal economics are often the main barrier for students who may wish to study or volunteer abroad (Association of Universities and Colleges of Canada, 2014; Biggs et al, 2015). To participate in a global experience, students need access to the financial resources required to travel and live abroad (Admit Project Team, 2002). Some universities have undertaken steps to support their students financially in the form of small bursaries or awards to offset student costs, such as UBC's Go Global Award (https://students.ok.ubc.ca/finance/financial-support/awards/exchange.html) and Sir Wilfrid Laurier's International Fund (https://students.wlu.ca/academics/global-engagement-and-exchanges/financial-assistance.html). In the case of Sir Wilfrid Laurier University, the Arts Global Experience program offers specific support through its Global Studies Education Abroad fund, and also requires participating students to develop a fundraising strategy through one of its required courses. However, adequate funding options remain a challenge for most students.

Paris and Biggs (2017) also stress the need for quality assurance, beginning with a platform on which to share best practice and "establish common standards" (p. 3). With institutional metrics for success often centered on the number of students who participate in a global experience, there is less attention paid to the implications of creating meaningful cultural experiences and preparing students to get the most out of engaging with a host culture. As a result, the literature is rife with examples of underprepared students participating in a global experience. This can be particularly concerning in emerging or developing countries, where students engage in service or volunteer activities. Issues such as cultural imperialism, extensive use of resources, use and abuse of photography and social media (Epprecht, 2004), an inflated sense of expertise (Tiessen, 2012), and inappropriate behavior (McDonald, 2017) all point to a lack of preparation that can have unintended negative consequences on both students and hosts (Crabtree, 2013). Unfortunately, the potential for developing cross-cultural competencies are often compromised in such situations.

As noted earlier in this chapter, admissions in higher education in Canada is generally conducted on a program-by-program basis, and so too are the approaches to how global experiences are designed. Most structured preparation rests with individual programs rather than on a distinct pedagogical or learning outcomes framework (Paris & Biggs, 2017). At the institutional level, preparation is generally limited to safety protocols and institutional requirements for academic transfer and credit rather than cultural competency (Epprecht, 2004). Overall, there tends to be little attention paid to programming that can help students develop critical reflective skills. Gaudelli and Laverty (2015) point out that higher education "enthusiastically embraces activities associated with global learning without introducing a new order of conceptions to support them" (p. 14). They suggest a need for guidelines that go beyond logistics and planning to reflect real learning opportunities, contending "that without due attention to the nature of experiences and implied reflective spirit to accompany study abroad, the full potential of these efforts may not be realized" (p. 14).

Adequately preparing students for a global experience requires time and commitment on the part of both students and the institution. Commonly, students do not need to plan much in advance to participate in a global experience. A typical example, at Saint Francis Xavier University, students apply in their second year to participate abroad in their third year (www.stfx.ca/academics/international-exchange). Specific programs that center around a global experience, such as Wilfrid Laurier University's Global Studies Program are more intentional, providing time for preparation opportunities for students to "think critically about the possibilities" of their placement (www.wlu.ca/programs/arts/undergraduate/global-stud ies-ba/arts-global-experience.html, para. 3). Phillion et al. (2009) build in a comprehensive pre-departure program for their international teaching practicum situated in the Honduras. In this program, students are introduced to the contextual challenges of teaching in under-resourced classrooms and are encouraged to reflect critically on global inequality and privilege.

In another model of a global experience for undergraduates, Trent University's International Development program, *Trent in Ghana*, collaborates directly with universities in Ghana. In this model, students can spend an academic year in-country that combines a full semester of programming in a partner university with 12 weeks of field experience on a development project. Canadian participants study alongside Ghanaian students, participate in an intense language program, and are housed through a home-stay program that is flexible after the first month (www .trentu.ca/ids/year-abroad-programs/trent-ghana/academics). The combination of field work and study abroad through the Trent program offers a rich cultural experience for student participants, and competition for the program is high given that the program accepts only 15 students per year (P. Shaffer, personal communication, January 14, 2019).

Some programs introduce the option of a global experience early in their recruitment process, providing students with the opportunity to engage in long-term planning, both financially as well as through course electives. One example of such programming is UBC's Okanagan School of Nursing's Global Health Practicum which sends 12 or more students each to Ghana and Zambia (https://students.ok.ubc.ca/global/outgoing/gsp/cur rent-programs/2019nursing.html). Students are introduced to the option of a global practicum during the recruiting process:

> Information about global health starts in recruitment, and then again at CREATE and first year orientation. We have a number of students who choose UBCO because of our Global health stream, and the Global Health Practicum options. (J. Vinek, personal communication, October 29, 2018)

The UBC School of Nursing is an example of an approach to a global experience that begins at recruitment and is reflected throughout the academic course of the program. Students participate in a short pre-departure program prior to embarking and can build capacity for their global experience through course electives and leadership projects related to their Community Engagement course (https://nursing.ok.ubc.ca/under graduate-program-overview/).

In a recent global service-learning opportunity for teacher-candidates in UBC Okanagan's Faculty of Education program, one of the authors sought intentionally to prepare students through a structured pre-departure program (Bourne, Crichton & Yakong, 2016). Using a design-thinking process (IDEO, 2015; Stanford University, 2009) that considered the potential for unintended negative consequences, the project intro-duced a pre-departure program for Ghana that discussed the historical, geographical, and cultural background to the setting, included activities that provoked critical reflection of power and privilege, and provided opportunities to learn basic greetings in the local dialect. In addition, students from previous projects shared their experiences.

Higher education in Canada appears committed to increasing out-bound mobility, but to do so requires intentional design, resources, and commitment. The policy recommendations represented in *Global Edu-cation for Canadians* (Paris & Biggs, 2017) provide a framework for that intentional design and represent a promising start. The next step is for provincial and national governments to support such a framework, which in turbulent economic times can be difficult. These recommendations can and should also be embraced by participating universities as a way of meeting their institutional mandates of global engagement and should be part of the admissions process into programs offering global oppor-tunities.

6.3   Conclusion

In conclusion, the higher education landscape in Canada is rapidly changing and needs to reconsider access to education for non-traditional and previously under-represented learners. Increased diversity on campuses brings a wider range of abilities and backgrounds, and admissions assess-ments should be appropriate and fair to these students. Thus, admissions processes, practices, and policies should be reviewed critically to examine access to education for these populations and to demonstrate a commit-ment to equity, diversity, and inclusion. This will require examining systemic issues and barriers that perpetuate division and inequity in higher education and widening participation through intentional admissions strategies. Such initiatives must be fundamental to ensure diversity and inclusion are at the heart of academic policies. We argue that the onus should be on institutions to articulate how they improve access to higher education for under-represented groups and demonstrate institutional cross-cultural and global competency. Thus, it is important higher education institutions focus their attention on revising admissions policies and practices that account for and value the ways in which people are different (Charvat, 2009).

Three key themes addressed in this chapter were indigenization, internationalization, and globalization. All require a significant transformation in Canadian higher education policies and practices to be sustainable. Challenges to Indigenous students' success in higher education include the intergenerational and ongoing effects of the Indian Residential School. Indigenous youth are the largest growing population in Canada and will become a large proportion of the workforce. Programs geared toward supporting Indigenous students' transition to higher education are critical to ensuring Canada's economic and social success. A significant increase in international students to Canadian higher education also demands attention for interconnectedness. Studying and engaging with individuals from around the world will enrich the lives of Canadian students and enhance their cross-cultural and global knowledge while studying in their home institutions. Finally, Canada is falling behind its peers when it comes to the number of students studying beyond its borders. With significant growth in this area set as a priority, it must be ensured that students are well prepared to engage responsibly and to contribute positively to the global society.

In summary, we believe Canada must actively demonstrate its commitment to the principles developed by UC and CICan, as well as reflect on and identify how to promote equity, diversity, and inclusion in our admissions processes and policies. By engaging in dialogue, we can assess the feasibility of implementing supportive admissions programs at more Canadian institutions by interpreting the unique and specific barriers that different applicants and learners face. Cross-cultural and global competencies can be used as more than learning outcomes of what we want students to be able to achieve after being enrolled in our programs. They can be used to help change our admissions practices and policies so that we can truly reach our goal of providing an equitable, diverse, and inclusive learning environment. While many Canadian universities, colleges, and institutes have made progress over the past few decades, academic leaders in Canada recognize that there is more we can do to truly achieve inclusive excellence in higher education.

REFERENCES

Aboriginal Nurses Association of Canada. (2009). Cultural competence and cultural safety in nursing education. Retrieved from www.cna-aiic.ca/~/media/cna/page-content/pdf-en/first_nations_framework_e.pdf.

Adamoski, R. (Ed.). (2015). BC International student survey: Final report. Retrieved from www.Adamoski.ca/pubs/ISSReport2015.pdf.

Admit Project Team. (2002). Higher education admissions and student mobility: The admit research project. *European Educational Research Journal, 1*, 151–172. https://doi.org/10.2304/eerj.2002.1.1.6.

Association of Universities and Colleges of Canada. (2014). *Canada's universities in the world.* (AUCC Internationalization Survey). Ottawa: AUCC.

Astin, A. W., (1993). Diversity and multiculturalism on the campus. *Change: The Magazine of Higher Learning, 25*(2), 44–49. https://doi.org/10.1080/00091383.1993.9940617.

Beck, K. (2012). Globalization/s: Reproduction and resistance in the internationalization of higher education, *Canadian Journal of Education, 35, 3*, 133–148.

Biggs, M., McArthur, J., Higgins, K., Maloney, D., Sanchez, J., & Werker, E. (2015). *Towards 2030: Building Canada's engagement with global sustainable development* (Centre for International Policy Studies Report). Ottawa: University of Ottawa, Centre for International Policy Studies.

Blessinger, P., Hoffman, J., & Makhanya, M. (2018, 9 March). Towards a more equal, inclusive higher education. *University World News.* Retrieved from www.universityworldnews.com/post.php?story=20180306102731111.

Bourne, C., Crichton, S., & Yakong, V. (2016). Exploring the influence of design principles to create a global service-learning project for teacher-candidates in the Upper East Region, Ghana West Africa: A case study. In A. Tinkler, B. Tinkler, J. R. Strait, & V. M. Jagla (Eds.). *Service learning to advance social justice in a time of radical inequality* (pp. 221–264). Charlotte, NC: Information Age Publishing, Inc.

British Columbia Ministry of Advanced Education. (2012). Indigenous post-secondary education and training policy framework and action plan: 2020 vision for the future. Retrieved from www.aved.gov.bc.ca/Indigenous/docs/Indigenous_Action_Plan.pdf.

Canadian Bureau for International Education. (2018). Facts and figures: Canada's performance and potential in international education. Retrieved from https://cbie.ca/media/facts-and-figures.

Canadian Magazine of Immigration. (2017, July). The benefits of international students to Canada. Retrieved from http://canadaimmigrants.com/benefits-international-students-canada/.

Caxaj, S. C., Chau, S., Lee, R., & Parkins, I. (2018). *Campus diversity report: Experiences of Indigenous and/or racialized and/or LGBTQ+ students at UBC Okanagan.* Kelowna: University of British Columbia, Okanagan.

Retrieved from https://nursing.ok.ubc.ca/wp-content/uploads/sites/6/2015/08/campusdiversityreport-web-1.pdf.

Chakma, A. (2016). Making the world our students' classroom. Policy. Retrieved from www.policymagazine.ca/pdf/21/PolicyMagazineSeptemberOctober-2016-Chakma.pdf.

Chang, M. J. (1996). Racial diversity in higher education: Does a racially mixed student population affect educational outcomes? (Doctoral dissertation). University of California–Los Angeles.

Charbonneau, J. (2017). The educational gap between Indigenous and non-Indigenous people in Canada. *Journal of Student Affairs, 26*, 83–89. Retrieved from https://scholar.google.ca/scholar?hl=en&as_sdt=0%2C5&q=educational+gap+between+indigenous+and+non-indigenous&btnG.

Charvat, L. J. (2009). Exemplary Practices in Equity and Diversity Programming. Retrieved from https://equity.ubc.ca/files/2010/06/exemplary_practices_in_-equity_-and_diversity_programming_UBCV.pdf.

Chen, L. (2007). Choosing Canadian graduate schools from afar: East Asian students' perspectives. *Higher Education, 54*(5), 759–780. https://doi.org/10.1007/s10734–006-9022-8.

Colleges and Institutes Canada. (2014). Indigenous education protocol for colleges and institutes. Retrieved from www.collegesinstitutes.ca/policyfocus/Indigenous-learners/protocol/.

Crabtree, R. (2013). The intended and unintended consequences of international service-learning. *Journal of Higher Education Outreach and Engagement, 17* (2), 43-66.

Epprecht, M. (2004). Work-study abroad courses in international development studies: Some ethical and pedagogical issues. *Canadian Journal of Development Studies, 4*(25), 687–706.

Gaudelli, W., & Laverty, M. (2015). What is a global experience? *Education and Culture, 31*(2), 13–26. https://doi.org/10.1353/eac.2015.0018.

Global Affairs Canada. (2016, October 12). Economic impact of international education in Canada: 2016 Update. Retrieved from www.international.gc.ca/education/report-rapport/impact-2016/index.aspx?lang=eng.

Gordon, C. E., & White, J. P. (2014). Indigenous educational attainment in Canada. *The International Indigenous Policy Journal, 5*(3). https://doi.org/10.18584/iipj.2014.5.3.6.

Gregersen-Hermans, J. (2017). Intercultural competence development in higher education. In D. K. Deardorff & L. A. Arasaratnam-Smith (Eds.). *International approaches, assessment and application* (pp. 1–16). Abingdon: Routledge. https://doi.org/10.4324/9781315529257-7.

Hegarty, N. (2014). Where are we now: The presence and importance of international students to universities in the United States. *Journal of International Students, 4*, 223–235.

Higher Education Quality Council of Ontario. (2017). Access. Retrieved from www.heqco.ca/en-ca/OurPriorities/Access/Pages/home.aspx.

Holmes, D. (2006). *Redressing the balance: Canadian university programs in support of aboriginal students*. Ottawa: Association of Universities and Colleges of Canada.

IDEO (2015). *The field guide to human-centered design* (1st ed.). San Francisco, CA: IDEO.org.

James-MacEachern, M., & James-MacEachern, D. (2017). Exploring factors influencing international students' decision to choose a higher education institution. *International Journal of Education Management, 31*(3), 343–363. https://doi.org/10.1108/IJEM-11-2015-0158.

Jayakumar, U. (2008). Can higher education meet the needs of an increasingly diverse and global society? Campus diversity and cross-cultural workforce competencies. *Harvard Educational Review, 78,* 615–651. https://doi.org/10.17763/haer.78.4.b60031p350276699.

King, T. (2008). Fostering aboriginal leadership: Increasing enrollment and completion rates in Canadian post-secondary institutions. *College Quarterly, 11*(1), 1–16.

Knight-Grofe, J., & Deacon, L. (2016). Canada's global engagement challenge: A comparison of national strategies. *International Journal, 71,* 129–143. https://doi.org/10.1177/0020702015622994.

Knight-Grofe, J., & Klabunde, N. (2009). *Canada first: The 2009 Survey of International Students* (Ed. J. Humphries). Retrieved from https://Users/leahsanford/Downloads/244205_2018-04-25_102622.pdf.

Kounalakis, M. (2015). International students at American universities benefit all. Retrieved from www.thenewstribune.com/opinion/article26275591.html.

Kruse, S. D., Rakha, S., & Calderone, S. (2018). Developing cultural competency in higher education: An agenda for practice. *Teaching in Higher Education, 23,* 733–750. https://doi.org/10.1080/13562517.2017.1414790.

Luo, J., & Jamieson-Drake, D. (2013). Examining the educational benefits of interacting with international students. *Journal of International Students, 3,* 85–101.

McDonald, M. (2017). *Making volunteering abroad a more ethical experience. University Affairs/Affaires universitaires.* Retrieved from www.universityaffairs.ca/features/feature-article/making-volunteering-abroad-ethical-experience/.

McKeown, S., Vedan, A., Mack, K., Jacknife, S., & Tolmie, C. (2018). *Indigenous educational pathways: Access, mobility, and persistence in the BC post-secondary system.* Vancouver: BC Council on Admissions and Transfer.

Melville, A. (2017). Educational disadvantages and Indigenous law students: Barriers and potential solutions. *Asian Journal of Legal Education, 4,* 95–115. https://doi.org/10.1177/2322005817700202.

Munro, D. (2014). Skills and higher education in Canada: Towards excellence and equity. Retrieved from http://canada2020.ca/wp-content/uploads/2014/05/2014_Canada2020_Paper-Series_Education_FINAL.pdf.

Mount Royal University. (2013). *Learning together, leading together: Mount Royal University's strategic plan to 2025.* Retrieved from www.mtroyal.ca/cs/groups/public/documents/pdf/mru_strategic_plan.pdf.

(2016). Indigenous strategic plan 2016–2021. Retrieved from www.mtroyal.ca/
IndigenousMountRoyal/indigenous-strategic-plan/index.htm

Oliveri, M. E., & Ezzo, C. (2014). The role of noncognitive measures in higher
education admissions. *Journal of the World Universities Forum, 6,* 55–65.
https://doi.org/10.18848/1835-2030/CGP/v06i04/56838.

Ontario Ministry of Training, Colleges and Universities. (2018). Indigenous
Institutes Act, 2017. Retrieved from www.tcu.gov.on.ca/pepg/publications/
framework.html.

Ontario Public Service. (2016). 21st century competencies: Foundation document for discussion. Phase 1. Towards defining 21st century competencies
for Ontario. Retrieved from www.edugains.ca/resources21CL/About21st
Century/21CL_21stCenturyCompetencies.pdf.

Organisation for Economic Co-operation and Development. (2017). Education
at a Glance 2017. Retrieved from www.oecd-ilibrary.org/education/educa
tion-at-a-glance-2017_eag-2017-en.

Ottmann, J. (2017). Canada's Indigenous peoples' access to post-secondary education: The spirit of the "new buffalo." In J. Frawley (Ed.). *Indigenous pathways,
transitions and participation in higher education* (pp. 95–117). Calgary: University of Calgary. https://doi.org/10.1007/978-981-10-4062-7_7.

Page, S. E. (2007). *The difference: How the power of diversity creates better groups,
firms, schools, and societies.* Princeton, NJ: Princeton University Press.

Paris, R., & Biggs, M. (2017). *Global education for Canadians: Equipping young
Canadians to succeed at home and abroad.* Report of the Study Group on
Global Education. Ottawa: Centre for International Policy Studies, Univer-
sity of Ottawa.

Pascarella, E. T., Edison, M., Nora, A., Hagedorn, L. S., & Terenzini, P. T.
(1996). Influences on students' openness to diversity and challenge in the
first year of college. *Journal of Higher Education, 67,* 174–195. https://doi
.org/10.1080/00221546.1996.11780255.

Phillion, J., Malewski, E., Sharma, S., & Wang, Y. (2009). Reimagining the
curriculum: Future teachers and study abroad. *Frontiers: The Interdisciplinary
Journal of Study Abroad, 18,* 323–339.

Pidgeon, M. (2014). Moving beyond good intentions: Indigenizing higher education in British Columbia universities through institutional responsibility
and accountability. *Journal of American Indian Education, 53,* 7–28.

Restoule, J., Mashford-Pringle, A., Chacaby, M., Smillie, C., & Brunette, C.
(2013). Supporting successful transitions to post-secondary education for
Indigenous students: Lessons from an institutional ethnography in Ontario,
Canada. *The International Indigenous Policy Journal, 4*(4), 1–10. https://doi
.org/10.18584/iipj.2013.4.4.4.

Sedlacek, W. E. (2004). *Beyond the big test: Noncognitive assessment in higher
education.* San Francisco, CA: Jossey-Bass.

Singer, C. R. (2017, August 31). New immigration policies attract international
students to Study in Canada. Retrieved from www.Singer, 2017/new-immi
gration-policies-entice-international-students-study-canada/.

Simmons, L. (2018). *B.C. university pilots competency-based admissions program. University Affairs/Affaires universitaires.* Retrieved from www.universityaffairs.ca/news/news-article/bc-university-pilots-competency-based-admissions-program/

Soria, K. M., & Troisi, J. (2014). Internationalization at home alternatives to study abroad. *Journal of Studies in International Education, 18,* 261–280. https://doi.org/10.1177/1028315313496572.

Stanford University. (2009). The new city experience: An introduction to design thinking. Facilitator's guide. Retrieved from https://dschool-old.stanford.edu/sandbox/groups/dtbcresources/wiki/bdb3f/attachments/e3cfa/NewCity-Facilitators-Guide-March2014-(V6).pdf?sessionID=8a36f7a15079a8053bd6f424e621f46e9692f705.

Statistics Canada. (2011). National household survey: The education attainment of Aboriginal peoples in Canada. Retrieved from www12.statcan.gc.ca/nhs-enm/2011/as-sa/99-012-x/99-012-x2011003_3-eng.cfm.

Stonechild, B. (2004). *The new buffalo: The struggle for Aboriginal post-secondary education in Canada.* Winnipeg: University of Manitoba Press.

Tancock, K. (2017). Beyond grades: University entrance essays, tests and portfolios. Retrieved from www.macleans.ca/education/facing-extra-requirements/?utm_source=macleans&utm_medium=organic&utm_campaign=recirc&utm_content=tag_list.

Tiessen, R. (2012). Motivations for learn/volunteer abroad programs: Research with Canadian youth. *Journal of Global Citizenship and Equity Education, 2* (1), 1–21.

Timmons, V. (2009). Retention of Aboriginal students in post-secondary institutions in Atlantic Canada: An analysis of the supports available to Aboriginal students. Retrieved from http://en.copian.ca/library/research/ccl/retention/retention.pdf.

Truth and Reconciliation Committee. (2015). *Truth and reconciliation commission of Canada: Calls to action.* Winnipeg: Truth and Reconciliation Commission of Canada.

United Nations. (2008). *United Nations Declaration on the Rights of Indigenous Peoples.* Retrieved from www.un.org/esa/socdev/unpfii/documents/DRIPS_en.pdf.

Universities Canada. (2015). Universities Canada principles on Indigenous education. Retrieved from www.univcan.ca/media-room/media-releases/universities-canada-principles-on-Indigenous-education/.

(2017). Universities Canada principles on equity, diversity, and inclusion. Retrieved from www.univcan.ca/media-room/media-releases/universities-canada-principles-equity-diversity-inclusion/.

University of Alberta. (2018). University of Alberta calendar 2018–2019. Retrieved from https://calendar.ualberta.ca/content.php?catoid=28&navoid=6975&hl=%22aboriginal%22&returnto=search.

University of Manitoba. (2017). Engineering access program (ENGAP). Retrieved from http://umanitoba.ca/faculties/engineering/programs/engap/index.html.

What Is Global Citizenship? (2011). In Y. Harlap (Ed.). *Road to global citizenship: An educator's toolbook* (pp. 7–10). Toronto: UNICEF.

Country-Specific Admissions Practices

Cathy Wendler

A top priority for many countries is to ensure a well-educated population. Higher levels of education result in many benefits to both individuals and society at large. For individuals, more education can lead to increased career opportunities, less chance of unemployment, and economic stability (Carnevale, Rose, & Cheah, 2011). For society, higher levels of education impact how individuals behave within and support the priorities of the society. For example, studies have shown that college-educated individuals are more likely to engage in philanthropic activities, are more active in civic and political affairs, show increased levels of community involvement, and are less reliant on government public assistance than those having less education (Trostel, 2015). While Trostel reported on data primarily from the United States, many of these societal benefits are seen as universal and are echoed in a number of chapters elsewhere in this volume (see, for example, Wikström & Wikström; Williams & Wendler; McKeown, Vedan, Traplin, Sanford, & Bourne), and are discussed as well in the chapters in this section.

College admissions practices are not developed or used in isolation but reflect societal values of a country. The underlying philosophy regarding who should be allowed to go to college or university, the criteria believed to be important in determining which applicants get in and which do not, and how fairness and diversity are perceived often contribute to the shape of admissions procedures. The chapters in this section detail country-specific higher education admissions practices. These chapters present only a sampling of countries and should in no way be seen as representative of practices used by all countries around the globe. But the countries represented in this section do present many different and unique practices, each reflecting that country's values associated with higher education.

Despite the uniqueness of each chapter, a number of common themes emerge, including access to college, diversity, and fairness, and the validity of the decision-making criteria used in college admissions.

Access to college: Who has the right to attend higher education is an overarching concern in many of the chapters. The chapter by Lyrén and Wikström demonstrates how Sweden's strong beliefs in equal opportunities for all individuals and lifelong learning, regardless of an individual's age, influence its educational system and views on higher education access. The chapter by Pham and Sai details the movement of higher education in Vietnam from an elite system available only to some individuals to one that is accessible to a greater number of individuals.

In some countries, access to higher education is embedded within a historical context that has driven beliefs about access as well as fairness and equity. The chapters by Jappie on South Africa and by Oanda on other African nations, for example, clearly detail the role of major political changes on higher education equity and access. Allalouf, Cohen, and Gafni also discuss the impact of changing political scenes on access to higher education in Israel.

Diversity and fairness: Ensuring that fairness and diversity are part of the admissions process is another common concern. For many countries, fairness and diversity are still addressed in more traditional ways. For example, Koljatic and Silva describe the fairness issues surrounding the use of the college admissions test used in Chile, and Jappie describes equity issues seen by discrepancies in higher education participation rates of students from different population groups in South Africa.

However, fairness does not necessarily have the same meaning across all countries. As pointed out in the chapter by Papanastasiou and Michaelides, fairness in Cyprus is defined in terms of public perception. They describe fairness as a type of test security: A test is fair if no individual, as part of test preparation, test development, or test scoring, has an unfair advantage over any other student.

For many countries, immigration has made issues of diversity and fairness even more complicated. The chapters by Allalouf, Cohen, and Gafni and by Lyrén and Wikström discuss how increased immigration has stressed the philosophical beliefs about fairness in Israel and Sweden.

Validating decision-making criteria: The validity issues surrounding the use of secondary school grades, teacher evaluations, and specialized tests as part of admissions to higher education programs continue to be of concern in many countries. Oanda addresses the various selection criteria and mechanisms used in a number of African countries that still result in less than desirable consequences. The potential bias in secondary school grades and teacher evaluations and the challenges that have emerged from their use is acknowledged in chapters by Allalouf, Cohen, and Gafni and by Lyrén and Wikström.

As a result of potential bias in grades or teacher evaluations, many countries use specialized tests either separately or in conjunction with other criteria, such as grades. However, tests carry with them their own challenges and validity concerns. In particular, the chapters on Chile (Koljatic & Silva), Israel (Allalouf, Cohen, & Gafni), Sweden (Lyrén & Wikström), and Vietnam (Pham & Sai) contain discussions of these issues and suggest solutions.

The practices described in the chapters in this section provide a rich source of information. It is hoped that readers will learn from these chapters and consider both the positive and negative aspects of these approaches as a way of broadening educational opportunity for all students at a global level.

REFERENCES

Carnevale, A. P., Rose, S. J., & Cheah, B. (2011). *The college payoff: Education, occupations, lifetime earnings.* Washington, DC: Georgetown University Center on Education and the Workforce.

Trostel, P. (2015). *It's not just the money.* Indianapolis: IN: Lumina Foundation. Retrieved from www.luminafoundation.org/files/resources/its-not-just-the-money.pdf.

CHAPTER 7

Admissions Policies and Practices and the Reshaping of Access Patterns to Higher Education in Africa

Ibrahim Oanda

Higher education gross enrollment rates (GER) in Africa remain the lowest in the world, averaging 8.9 percent of the eligible cohort in 2015 (United Nations Educational Scientific and Cultural Organization [UNESCO] Institute for Statistics, 2015). The continent is also experiencing an increase in population and an increasing demand for access to higher education. Projections show that Africa will account for 1.2 billion of the 2.4 billion expected increase in the global population by 2050 and will experience a dramatic increase in its working-age population, thereby creating public and policy pressure for widened access to quality and relevant higher education (Caerus Capital, 2018). The low GER in the midst of increased demand for access has resulted in a complex mix of public policies that regulate admissions to and standards for higher education institutions. Higher education on the continent, on the other hand, remains largely public with an increasing number of private universities having limited enrollment capacities.

Over the last two decades, public universities in a majority of the countries introduced admission of private students who pay tuition fees similar to those they would pay if they attended private for-profit institutions. This strategy, meant to help the institutions generate funds to support operational costs, means that the institutions operate dual-admission policy tracks: one set of admissions policies for students who receive public funding and the other for private students. This has added to the complexity in existing admissions practices and outcomes.

Given the expanse of the continent, varied higher education traditions, and existence of multiple admissions and selection procedures, this chapter will highlight some of the common trends in admissions to higher education institutions and implications for access and equity. The discussions will also be limited to the university sector of higher education given that the technical and vocational sector of higher education in Africa has not attracted much demand for access compared to the university sector.

Throughout the continent, the scramble for admissions is in the university sector of higher education. The technical, vocational education, and training sector (TVET) has expanded slowly and with little government support. To try to reduce the pressure for university admissions, governments have resorted to changing most technical and related middle-level institutions into universities. By 2014, the TVET sector enrolled only 2.8 million students compared to 7.8 million in universities in sub-Saharan Africa (Caerus Capital, 2018).

This chapter is organized into four parts. First is a discussion of the contextual background for understanding the design of admissions policies in Africa. The chapter does not include discussions about South Africa as there is a separate chapter on that country (see Jappie, in this volume). Second is an overview of the design and nature of admissions policies. Third, is a discussion of salient institutional selection policies and practices regarding admissions. Fourth is a discussion of the institutional structures and personnel dealing with admissions. Last, is a conclusion highlighting the implications of admissions policies and practices for access and participation.

7.1   Contextual Background

The nature of admissions policies and trends in participation rates in African universities should be understood in the context of prevailing dominant public provision for university education. Throughout Africa, higher education is largely provided through publicly funded institutions. Across most of the continent, the perception that getting credible, affordable qualifications means getting admitted to a public university still prevails. On the other hand, the economies of most of the countries have not expanded fast enough to secure enough resources for the expansion of publicly funded higher education systems. This has resulted in admission pressures on a slowly expanding system. Given the pressure for access, admissions policies, especially to public universities, are designed to admit the number of students who can be funded by the public as opposed to the number of students who merit admission to the institutions. The population per capita served by one university in Africa's most populated countries is as high as 1.5 million in Egypt, 1.2 million in Nigeria, 890,000 in the Democratic Republic of Congo, 480,000 in Ethiopia, and 390,000 in South Africa (Dahir, 2017). The fully publicly financed free university education model applicable in many countries accounts for most of this stagnation in expansion.

Gross participation rates in African higher education remain the lowest in the world, averaging 8.9 percent, according to the latest data, though the continent has had the fastest growth in enrollment in the last three decades (Darvas et al., 2017; UNESCO Institute for Statistics, 2015). Demand for access to higher education, however, continues to increase in a context where capacity to broaden access is constrained by lack of resources. Available data show that, by 2017, there were 7.8 million students enrolled in tertiary education institutions in sub-Saharan Africa, compared to 7.2 million in 2000 and fewer than 400,000 students in 1970 (Caerus Capital, 2018; UNESCO Institute for Statistics , 2010). However, the GER for tertiary education grew at an average annual rate of 4.3 percent between 1970 and 2013 compared to a global annual average increase of 2.8 percent over the same period (Darvas et al., 2017). North African countries, however, with the exception of Mauritania (Algeria, Egypt, Libya, Morocco, and Tunisia) had higher GER participation rates compared to the sub-Saharan countries. Libya had the highest participation rate (estimated at over 50 percent), Algeria at 18 percent, Morocco at 12 percent, Egypt at 28 percent, and Tunisia at 34 percent in 2013 (African Union Commission, 2014). Like their sub-Saharan counterparts, the North African countries have a strong public higher education-funding model. Rising demand for tertiary education across sub-Saharan Africa has, however, taken place alongside expanding disparities across income groups, with students from the top wealth quintile enrolling more frequently compared to those from the lowest and middle quintiles (Darvas et al., 2017). As a result, Africa has the highest percentage increase in the number of students seeking access to tertiary education but remains one with the lowest participation rates.

Limited access is compounded by a lack of developed private higher education institutions across Africa. This is both in terms of the number of private higher education institutions, their capacities to enroll a high number of students, the number of courses offered, and the lack of private funding sources that can advance tuition loans to students in private universities. Many of the few private universities on the continent are established largely as nonprofit institutions that rely either on private funding or tuition fees for funding. In practice, however, public funding is increasingly used to support students in private universities as a way of increasing access to higher education. In some countries, such as Kenya and the five North African countries cited above, public funding is often given to support students in private universities as a strategy to increase access (Hammound, 2010; Kenya Universities and Colleges Central

Placement Services [KUCCPS], 2014). This makes the provision of higher education largely a public-sector activity, which also influences the nature of policies for access and participation even in private universities. On average, public provision for higher education accounts for 80 percent across the continent (Caerus Capital, 2018; Hammoud, 2010; Mohamedbhai, 2017).

In terms of practice, access to institutions remains competitive and admissions practices play a limiting rather than facilitative role. The practices do not reflect students' aptitudes, but the funding available from the public and institutional-level strategies to attract more private students to public universities, as a way of boosting their revenues. Although several African countries have approved policies to support the growth and expansion of private universities to ease the pressure for admissions from public institutions, private universities remain small both in physical size and program offerings. Countries with more private institutions still have publicly regulated admissions practices and reflect inefficient management of admissions and access patterns similar to public colleges and universities.

The literature on higher education and admissions practices on the continent is more often dominated by the word "crisis," characterized by not only having one but a series of malfunctioning processes and practices. For instance, there is a lack of institutional autonomy to manage the admissions process. Even when admissions policies exist, it is possible for political interference and other forms of influence peddling to take center stage in determining who is admitted to which institutions. Admission to what are considered elite universities and academic programs is contested and, consequently, there is much evidence from available literature that the process of designing admissions policies is manipulated to the disadvantage of certain sectors of society (Anyan, 2016; Kanyip, 2013). In some cases, competitive examinations, coupled with discipline-specific requirements, are not enough to guarantee one a place at a university, and political patronage is sought. In other cases, external bodies fix the minimum requirements while universities fix the admissions requirements for institutions and disciplines. In between formal admissions practices and informal mechanisms such as political patronage, are practices rooted in history, the influence of professional associations, and the frameworks developed by regional associations. Examples of such frameworks include regional qualifications frameworks to facilitate student mobility within regional institutions and the influence of external practices such as the Bologna Process that has reshaped admissions practices in many of the anglophone universities. Still, Africa is a large continent with numerous institutions and, despite broad admissions policies, institutional practices and selection mechanisms differ even within the same countries. This chapter will therefore highlight what are seen as common trends in admissions and access patterns.

7.2 Admissions Policies

Generally, higher education admissions policies in most of Africa reflect various influences, such as the legacy of colonialism, new emerging trends in regionalization and harmonization of higher education institutions, institutional capacities to take students, and prevailing funding models. Moreover, there has been an increase in educational attainment levels putting pressure on institutions to admit more students, as growth in public universities is constrained by financial limitations and growth of private universities has been slow and cautious. Consequently, low participation rates, increased pressure for access, and the need to distribute available spaces with a sense of equity means that public bodies appointed by governments have overall responsibility for designing higher education admissions policies and overseeing their implementation.

Ministries of education or their designated agents or departments within ministries largely undertake the responsibility of designing broad policy frameworks guiding admissions to institutions. In recent years, however, with trends toward greater governance autonomy for higher education institutions and political advocacy for higher education harmonization at regional levels, the responsibility for designing policies and oversight is shared across national and regional higher education regulatory bodies. Some of these regional bodies include the Southern Africa Regional Universities Association, Inter-University Council for East Africa, the Middle East and North Africa Association for Institutional Research, the African and Malagasy Council on Higher Education initiative for French-speaking African countries, and the Association for West African Universities for West Africa. Governments, though, continue to uphold a steering role, even when there are independent external bodies established to oversee admissions processes. Ministries of Education provide overall policy direction. This direction includes establishing affirmative action, admissions quotas, and caps regarding how many students must be admitted and publicly funded. The subsequent parts of this section discuss how specific admissions policies are designed and implemented within each region.

7.2.1   North Africa

The North African countries of Algeria, Morocco, Tunisia, Egypt, and Libya have much higher gross participation rates in higher education compared to sub-Saharan African countries. Higher education participation rates increased between 2013 and 2017 for Algeria, Morocco, and Tunisia, and by 2017 higher education participation rates were roughly 48 percent, 34 percent, and 32 percent, respectively (UNESCO Institute for Statistics, 2019). Egypt had a gross enrollment rate of 34 percent in 2016 and Libya 61 percent by 2003 (UNESCO Institute for Statistics, 2019). (More recent enrollment data for Libya is not available.) In these countries, the higher education sector is dominated by public institutions, and public funding for higher education institutions is higher compared to other countries. For example, public spending on higher education as a percentage of the total education budget was about 27 percent in Algeria in 2008, 20 percent in Morocco in 2009, 20 percent in Tunisia in 2010, and 28 percent in Egypt in 2015 (UNESCO Institute for Statistics, 2019). This higher spending has meant centralized government control over admissions processes and distribution of students across the various higher education institutions.

In terms of admissions policies, five North African countries (Algeria, Libya, Mauritania, Morocco, and Tunisia) have adopted the license/bachelor's-master's-doctorate (LMD) structure of education influenced by the Bologna Process. Admission to undergraduate programs is open and public higher education is free of restrictive tuition expenses to all students who score at least 65 percent in the secondary education certificate (European Commission, 2017a; 2017b; 2017c; 2017d; 2017e; 2017f; Hammoud, 2010). Minimal selection is, however, undertaken at the institutions for students wishing to enroll in specialized professional courses such as medicine and engineering. Some of the admissions practices that are common across the region include the use of standardized testing for ensuring equity and equal opportunity at the entry level, use of more than one criterion for admissions, granting concessions to certain disadvantaged groups and less-developed geographical areas, and providing more than one admission opportunity in a year (Hammoud, 2010, p. 69).

In Egypt, approximately all of the students who qualify for admissions are admitted and distributed among public universities through the University Coordination Office of the Ministry of Higher Education. The Coordination Office considers the students' grades, their choices of the type of discipline to study, the total number of secondary school graduates, the spaces available at public universities, and the geographical distribution to make a final determination as to which institution and course to admit each student. Egypt allows private universities to administer their own admissions examinations, but under the supervision of a public body, the Supreme Council of Private Universities (Hammoud, 2010).

In practice, however, transition from secondary schools to universities in North Africa is not as open as it appears. Rather, governments, through a system of largely funded public higher education, control the number of students graduating from secondary schools that go to universities. This control is achieved through specifying the number of spaces available at each university or in degree courses, using a centralized system of admissions to distribute the students, and having overall control in the administration of qualifying examinations (Hammoud, 2010). The countries also operate various forms of affirmative-action practices. In Tunisia, information technology student-services systems are provided by the government in the rural areas to offer convenient registration services to students to seeking admission to public universities, while at the same time serving as career guidance centers to guide students in the selection of universities and courses that match their aspirations (European Commission, 2017f). To encourage students to seek admission to universities located in their home areas, Tunisia and Algeria award up to 7 additional percentage marks for students who select institutions within their locality.

Sudan has a more encompassing admissions process and affirmative-action intervention. Students who are qualified to attend a university after passing the secondary school examinations are distributed as follows (Hammoud, 2010, p. 75). Universities from the least-developed states allocate 50 percent of their enrollment capacities to local students from the states. These students are also allowed to enroll in professional disciplines. Another 5 percent of the least-developed states' university capacities are allocated to applicants from regions with mobile populations (especially pastoralists) and those from multilingual regions in Southern Sudan. All universities in the country admit disabled students according to their scores in competitive examinations, and they are exempted from paying tuition fees. While a large number of students enrolled in the universities are supported through public funding, the government allows universities to admit an additional number of not more than 25 percent of the total capacity for each year who do not receive public funding and have to pay tuition fees.

7.2.2   West Africa

The West African region has countries that use English as the medium of instruction in educational institutions (anglophone) and those that use French (francophone). Admissions policies to higher education institutions within the region are shaped by a combination of: (a) regional policies drawn by the Economic Community of West African States (ECOWAS) through the ECOWAS Education Protocol (Economic Community of West African States, 2003); (b) the influence of francophone and anglophone models in the region; and (c) national regulatory frameworks. The ECOWAS protocol emphasizes commitments to enhance accessibility to education and training for all. In particular, it emphasizes the need to: (a) provide scholarships or bursaries for girls from disadvantaged communities to create gender equity; (b) harmonize and standardize admissions requirements for institutions of higher learning and vocational training institutions; and (c) recognize certificates and other qualifications. The protocol also requires partner states to direct the heads of universities and other tertiary institutions of their countries to: (a) reserve at least 5 percent of admissions for students from other ECOWAS countries; (b) strive to harmonize and standardize admissions requirements; (c) prevent expensive duplication of courses by directing universities to devise mechanisms to facilitate the inter-university transfer of credits; (d) acknowledge the need to work toward the harmonization of the academic year to facilitate staff and student transfers; and (e) undertake to grant students from other ECOWAS countries the same privileges as their own students in terms of fees and accommodations within a period of five years from the date of the enforcement of this protocol (ECOWAS, 2003).

Beyond the above regulations, the five anglophone countries of Gambia, Ghana, Liberia, Nigeria, and Sierra Leone have a common curriculum and a common regional examination body – the West African Examination Council (WAEC), located in Accra, Ghana. The WAEC develops, administers, and grades the regional West African Senior School Certificate Examination (WASSCE) in all five countries, in addition to national examinations in select countries at lower grade levels. It also conducts examinations for third-party international examination boards and professional licensing bodies. The examination is standardized across all WAEC member countries and is offered after completion of the three-year Senior Secondary School curriculum. The WAEC countries use the WASSCE results to select students for admission to universities, and also to screen students for admission to other non-university institutions of higher learning. University admissions in member countries are based in part or wholly on performance in the WASSCE. Some countries, Nigeria most notably, also require a separate centralized university entrance examination, with eligibility based on performance on the WASSCE. Individual universities in member countries may also administer separate entrance examinations (Clark, 2015). The discussions hereunder regarding admissions practices in Nigeria and Ghana illustrate these multiple selection practices.

The various admissions regulations and agencies in anglophone West Africa means that students from these countries seeking admission to universities must undergo a three-tiered screening process. One tier requires passing the regional examination with a specified score that students need to qualify for admissions. The second tier entails passing with a specified score the matriculation examination set and administered by individual universities to select students to the more prestigious universities. Matriculation examinations are, in this case, used for purposes of distributing qualified students to different universities. First-generation universities established during the colonial period in most of Africa have better academic reputations, are more prestigious, and have better established academic infrastructures compared to second-generation universities. Students scramble to be admitted to first-generation universities and, therefore, institutions have had to introduce a selection mechanism. The third level of selection often includes students sitting for examinations in order to qualify to be registered for certain professional courses such as medicine and engineering. Failing these examinations disqualifies students from entry into the courses and they must register for alternative general courses.

The existence of several selection hurdles has made admissions into higher education institutions in most of the West African region largely accessible only to students from elite and middle-class backgrounds. This is because most of the selection examinations require better and higher-quality preparation at previous levels of education. Such higher quality is usually available from private primary- and secondary school academies that only rich families can afford.

In Nigeria, the federal government, through the National Universities Commission (NUC), designs, regulates, and monitors admissions to tertiary institutions, considering the regional regulatory policies. In practice, the policies are developed by the NUC and the Joint Admission and Matriculation Board (JAMB). The NUC and the JAMB are the two main bodies that oversee admissions policies for federal and state universities in

Nigeria. Because of limited government funding and the number of students such funding can support, prevailing federal admissions policies are focused on equal representation of students from all regions/states in public higher education institutions. Hence, admissions guidelines specify that merit, determined through examination performance; institutional carrying capacity; preference for students coming from the locality where the university is located; and quotas for educationally disadvantaged states be used as criteria for admissions (Kanyip, 2013). Accordingly, 45 percent of admissions are based on merit, 35 percent on locality of the students, and 20 percent on educationally less-developed states (Moti, 2010). But, like elsewhere in Africa, the regulations are meant not to broaden access, but to limit the number of students who would claim a place in the universities, given limited places compared to demand. To illustrate, out of thousands of applicants who sit annually for the JAMB examinations, less than 20 percent, on average, gain admissions into the universities (Kanyip, 2013). Besides, the policies create a situation where some candidates who may be admitted based on merit are denied admissions in preference to weaker candidates who come from the locality of the university.

Admissions policies in Ghana have been developed by the National Commission for Tertiary Education and the National Accreditation Board. When students submit individual applications for admissions to universities, qualification for admissions is based on a student passing with six credits on the WAEC examinations. About 400,000 students from senior high school seek admission into public universities annually, competing for fewer than 100,000 available places. This situation is made worse with over 50,000 protocol requests from more affluent and influential parents – which are often granted – thus further disadvantaging students from poor backgrounds (Anyan, 2016). This is because parents whose children are not fortunate to be admitted through the government-supported stream have to apply as full-fee-paying students or international students and have to pay higher tuition fees paid in foreign currencies. The academic-user fee is well above the income of the average Ghanaian worker (Anyan, 2016).

Within francophone West African countries, the trend has been toward harmonizing higher education study structures and admissions practices and cycles. Through the adoption of the Bologna principles, the countries have adopted the bachelor's-master's-doctorate system used by all French universities. Admissions to universities are open to all students who pass the baccalaureate, which is the entry qualification to universities supported by public funding (Darvas et al., 2017). A few francophone countries such as Mali, due to capacity limitations, control the number of student admissions through other institutional selection processes (Gioan, 2008).

The concern regarding admissions policies in both anglophone and francophone West African countries is that the application of merit-based systems that benchmark admissions on examination performance are often blind to the socioeconomic background of students. This has resulted in higher education participation trends remaining largely elitist, as admissions policies favor students from urban and wealthy families (cf. Darvas, et al., 2017).

7.2.3 East Africa

In East Africa, education ministries provide overall guidelines regarding the nature and goals of higher education admissions policies. However, the actual design and operationalization of the policies is undertaken by autonomous bodies, usually serving under higher education regulatory councils. In Uganda, for example, the overall responsibility for designing admissions policies is coordinated by the Department of Higher Education in the Ministry of Education and Sports. The functions of the Department include to undertake, through the Joint Admissions Board (JAB): (a) the admission of students to tertiary institutions; (b) the formulation of policies on admissions to institutions; (c) the execution of policies, procedures, and regulations pertaining to scholarships and admissions to higher education institutions; and (d) the coordination of services for the relevant organizations (Republic of Uganda, 2018). But the Department of Higher Education does not undertake this responsibility alone. The Uganda National Council for Higher Education (NCHE) provides an overall governance framework for university education, including guidelines for admissions to all higher education institutions. University-level admissions processes are guided by the University and Other Tertiary Institutions Act (Republic of Uganda, 2001), which has been developed by the NCHE. The NCHE sets and reviews minimum entry requirements for admissions to universities or other tertiary institutions.

The government of Tanzania, under provisions made by the Tanzania Commission for Universities (TCU) in The Universities Act (Republic of Tanzania, 2013), has developed a centralized admissions system of admitting students to public and private higher education institutions. Part IV: Admissions Procedures of the Act spells out broad policy guidelines that institutions have to follow with regard to criteria and qualifications of students for admission to institutions and academic programs, procedures to advance the goals of equitable access, and provisions to ensure good governance and transparency in admissions processes. The Act provides for two modes of admissions, either through direct-entry or indirect-entry qualifications in a relevant field of study. For equity purposes, the Act requires universities to design specific affirmative-action measures to broaden access and ensure equity. The affirmative-action measures are targeted at promoting gender equity in the institutions, addressing educational challenges of people with special needs and other challenges associated with socioeconomic factors, and promoting girls' admission into science and technology courses. Universities are also required to put in place administrative measures to avoid corruption and other malpractice in the admissions process. All admissions services to university-level education (both public and private) are handled through a central admissions system approved by the Tanzania Commission for Universities (TCU). These policies are enforced by the TCU through its mandate as outlined in the Universities Act. An annual admissions guidebook developed by the TCU provides basic information to applicants pertaining to the admissions process to higher education institutions through the central admissions system (Tanzania Commission for Universities , 2018).

In Kenya, the responsibility for developing admissions policies for both public and private universities is with the Commission for University Education (CUE), established under the Universities Act No. 42 of 2012 (Republic of Kenya, 2012). Before 2012, admissions policies were developed by the Commission for Higher Education and placement to the institutions overseen by a committee of vice-chancellors for public universities who constituted themselves as the Joint Admissions Board. The 2012 Act left the responsibility of developing policy and requirements for admissions to universities with the Commission for University Education. Besides developing and reviewing admissions policies, the commission also licenses student recruitment agencies operating in Kenya and acts as the official agency for approving and recognizing academic credentials conferred or awarded by foreign universities and institutions for students seeking admissions to universities in Kenya.

While the Commission for University Education develops admissions policies, actual placement and distribution of students to various higher education institutions is undertaken by the KUCCPS. In executing this responsibility, the Act creating the Central Placement Service requires that the service designs strategies of promoting equity and access to university and college education, by, among other things, developing criteria for affirmative action for the marginalized, minorities, and persons with disabilities (KUCCPS, 2016). The placement board also seeks to establish a criterion to ensure that, as much as possible, students are registered in the courses for which they applied considering their qualifications and the courses they listed as priorities.

7.3   Institutional Admissions Practices

Despite the existence of admissions policies promoting equity and broadening of access, the limited capacity in the institutions and inadequate public funding mean that most universities in Africa admit less than 30 percent of qualified applicants annually. National-level admissions policies promising equity, therefore, exist side by side with institutional-level selection practices that end up closing out a high number of qualified students from accessing higher education. The huge pool of qualified applicants and inadequate public funding of public universities in Africa has resulted in the introduction of a second-stream admissions process in the institutions. Second-stream admissions are considered revenue-generation streams for the universities. There are lower academic requirements for admissions to institutions and professional courses, but students pay higher tuition fees compared to those supported by the government. This admissions practice is referred to as "dual track admissions." The first track is the government-supported stream that is competitively admitted but beneficiaries pay lower tuition fees. The second track refers to institutionally managed admissions and admits students with lower academic grades compared to the first group, but who pay higher tuition fees. Concerns continue to emerge that the flexibility associated with the admissions process of second-stream students – especially those based on one's ability to pay – has opened a second avenue for students from rich families to monopolize professional programs. A higher percentage of the students in public universities in East Africa fall under this second category and their flexible admission continues to raise concerns regarding equity and quality.

Various practices associated with the second institutional-level admissions end up compromising the transparency of admissions processes in a number of countries. This is because even though, in theory, students who are admitted under both streams are those who have met minimum academic qualifications, competition for places in reputable universities and professional courses often leads to other non-merit-based considerations. Institutions end up with two groups of students: those admitted and distributed by national agencies and those admitted by individual universities. This second group of students constitutes the majority of students in public universities as institutions have come to depend on them to generate funding that they need to bridge shortfalls from governments. And because the capacity to pay often is the first consideration for the second-track admissions, malpractice creeps in, thus compromising the integrity of the admissions processes and the quality of academic outputs. We briefly discuss examples from Nigeria, Kenya, and Uganda to illustrate how these dual-track admissions work in the institutions.

7.3.1   Nigeria

In Nigeria, each of the states has at least one federal university and one or more state or private universities, but there is limited space for students. So, even after students are eligible to enter university according to admission rules set by regional and national bodies, universities administer a matriculation examination to determine final admissions. The number of applications for admission each year is slightly more than two million, but only three out of 20 applicants get places – if admissions are evenly distributed. However, admissions are never evenly distributed, but skewed by universities, parents' ability to lobby and pay for education, institutions' size, and government interferences (Kanyip, 2013). This is because students in Nigeria who have passed the WAEC examinations do not have a direct entry to the universities. Instead, they must pass another screening examination administered by the Universities and Tertiary Institutions Matriculation Board. It is the Matriculation Board that approves the placement of the recommended candidates into the various institutions. Regardless of the best grades a student scored at the WAEC, failing the matriculation examination disqualifies a student from joining a university, or getting into a university and course of choice. It is at this level that malpractice has been documented, with parents buying examinations in advance or bribing university authorities to award their children higher marks to increase chances of admission (Oshemughen & Oghuvbu, 2013). Students are also forced to apply to sit for the matriculation examinations in several universities to increase their chances of admissions, a process which disadvantages poor students as they need money for travel and application fees to facilitate multiple applications. What this means is that final eligibility for admission to Nigerian universities may actually depend on and be influenced by factors not stipulated in national admissions policies. Available data for the period 2010 and 2015 from the Nigerian

Bureau of Statistics and the JAMB show that of the 10 million students who applied for admission into Nigerian tertiary institutions, only 26 percent were successful (Kazeem, 2017). The large number of prospective students who do not gain admission into any institution drives a majority of them and their parents to resort to forms of corruption to get access, thus undermining the integrity of the admissions process.

7.3.2   Uganda

In Uganda, there is competition to access the few public scholarships for public universities funded by government sponsorship. There are two policy guidelines upon which universities base their admissions processes (Republic of Uganda, 2017). First, 75 percent of the places in public universities are earmarked for programs that the National Council for Higher Education determines to be critical for national development and, therefore, need to be funded by government. Second, of the remaining 25 percent of slots, 40 slots are allocated for talented sports students, 64 slots are allocated to students with disabilities, and 896 slots are competed for through district quotas, based on district population.

Actual selection and placement of students is done by the Public Universities JAB, which ensures that admissions policies follow university admissions lists aligned with limits on institutional space. The existence of the Public Universities JAB is anchored in a provision by the University and Other Tertiary Institutions Act (Republic of Uganda, 2001) which requires senates of universities to advise their councils on eligibility and qualifications of candidates for admission. The JAB is therefore comprised of representatives from public universities who converge every June to select students who qualify for the government scholarship scheme. Students who do not qualify for government support are admitted by individual universities following admissions guidelines provided by the Department of Higher Education, the NCHE, and the Act regarding the qualifications one is required to attain to be admitted to a university. In determining final selection and admissions, JAB awards marks for subjects that a student has passed, based on a cluster of subjects developed by the NCHE. There are three clusters of subjects. The first consists of essential subjects which are determined to be core to the program the student has selected to pursue. Science-based programs, for example, will have mathematics and chemistry or mathematics and physics as essential subjects. Each of these subjects, if passed, is weighted 3 points. The second cluster is comprised of subjects that are considered relevant to the program the student has selected. These subjects are categorized along the lines of pure sciences or social sciences and arts subjects and each is weighted 2 points. The final cluster consists of desirable subjects, or those that provide a student with broad-based skills regardless of the student's program of specialization. These subjects include computer studies and a general paper (the equivalent of a liberal arts program) and are weighted 1 point.

Subjects are considered "essential," "relevant," or "desirable," depending on the program for which the student intends to register. For example, a student intending to pursue a bachelor of science in agricultural engineering may be required to pass either mathematics or physics as their essential subject, have one subject where the student scores their highest grades in chemistry, agriculture, economics, geometry, or mechanics, as the relevant subject, and either a general paper or computer studies as their desirable subject (Republic of Uganda, 2018). These guidelines are issued annually to guide students in the choices they make before they sit the advanced certificated examinations that they need to pass to qualify for admission to a university.

The admissions policy is structured so that every candidate is assessed across three subjects studied in high school, and only one subject can belong to each category for purposes of selection. This means only one subject can be categorized as essential for admissions. Candidates are selected on merit from those who apply for a program as their first choice followed by those who apply for the program as second, third, and fourth choice. Students who are not admitted to programs of their first choice are considered for their second and third choices until all students are placed.

While detailed, the admissions process in Uganda is such that candidates would miss admission to an institution or academic program of choice if they fail to take into consideration the subject clusters and weighting when selecting academic programs for study. Passing the advanced certificate examination in this respect does not guarantee candidates admission.

7.3.3   Kenya

Admissions policies in Kenya, including the criteria and requirements for entry to both public and private universities, are developed by the CUE. Actual admissions and distribution of students to various public universities, colleges, and academic programs on public funding are managed through KUCCPS. Individual universities manage admissions for private (second-stream) students.

The first stage in the admissions process starts with each university declaring its capacity for publicly funded students. Universities also provide the placement service with capacities for each academic program. Based on declared capacities, the KUCCPS decides on two issues. First is the number of eligible students for admissions to universities – both public and private – based on a policy criterion set by the CUE. The second determination is to set the cut score (or pass score) that students need to achieve to be admitted to given universities and programs. The more reputable, first-generation universities require higher cut scores for students to be admitted to professional courses compared to newer universities. The cut score is determined every other year depending on the public funding available and the number of students who have scored the minimum admissions grades set by CUE. The cut score may be lowered to admit more students or increased to admit fewer students on government support. In practice, this means that students in the same program within a five-year cohort would have varied qualification marks depending on if they were admitted in a year with lower or higher cut scores (Nakweya, 2018). The third stage in the admissions process takes place at the institutional level, as institutions determine the qualifications students need for particular degree programs or subjects.

But, like many other African countries, Kenya also experiences malpractice in admissions processes to higher education institutions. The malpractice occurs mainly at two levels. First is at the level of competition to get better grades at the school certificate level and secure a place in the reputable public universities and professional programs. The competition has made wealthy parents invest in private primary and secondary education and, often, schools and parents engage in examination cheating to help their students score the best grades. The second level at which malpractice occurs is in the admissions process of private students to public and private universities. By 2018, Kenya had 84 universities: 31 public universities, 16 public constituent colleges, 18 private chartered universities, 5 private constituent colleges, and 14 universities with letters of interim authority to operate while awaiting accreditation. Over the last 5 years, on average, public universities have been admitting about 47 percent of qualified students on public funding support. That leaves about 53 percent of qualified students that both public and private universities must scramble for, especially because all the institutions rely heavily on tuition fees paid by private students for their operation. It is at this level that some universities bend rules and admit unqualified students or charge lower tuition fees and sacrifice the quality of the teaching process. When fewer students qualify for admission to universities compared to the capacities declared by the institutions, the competition for students and associated malpractice also increase.

After a decade-long expansion of public universities, Kenya began, in 2013, to give more support to the establishment of diploma-level technical institutions as a strategy to curb the scramble for university places, channeling students to the technical-level institutes to acquire technical skills and addressing the challenge of youth employability (Oxford Business Group, 2016). Enforcing higher cut scores for university admissions is partly meant to support this trend. However, the practice has resulted in situations where universities do not have enough students to fill even half the capacities they declare. On the other hand, students are unwilling to take up places in the technical and other non-university higher education institutions. For example, in 2015, only 11,523 students applied for admission to middle-level colleges, which had a combined capacity of 41,550 students (Oxford Business Group, 2016).

7.4   Institutional Personnel and Infrastructure

What cadre of staff serve as admissions officers in several universities in Africa and what infrastructures exist in the institutions to manage admissions processes? Universities in many African countries do not have professional higher education admissions officers partly because higher education as a disciplinary area is rarely included in the curriculum of higher education institutions. So, across the universities, academics hold various leadership positions with no prior training in leadership. Often university academic registrars, assisted by committees of deans and heads of departments, perform the work of admissions officers, assisted by a secretariat of nontrained administrative staff. Along the same lines, offices in charge of admissions, career guidance, or student affairs may not have professional staff (Pansiri & Sinkamba, 2017).

The lack of trained, professional staff accentuates the lack of appreciation for higher education administration as a professional discipline. Academics with administrative responsibilities rarely have any professional background in student administration. Since such administrators are charged with designing institutional-level admissions policies, such policies are most likely to lack breadth, limiting student admissions to just being let into the institutions without consideration of anything else. This issue has implications on the quality of student services and the added value that university programs have on students' later careers. The lack of data in most of the institutions in Africa regarding actual enrollment figures, time to graduation for particular cohorts, and the socioeconomic profile of students points to how marginal the admissions process is in the majority of the institutions. In Kenya, for example, with recent incidents of terrorist attacks on campuses, the department of immigration, not the universities, has set out new regulations for admissions of foreign students to Kenyan universities. The requirements include candidates seeking admission first through the Director of Immigration, indicating the course they intend to pursue and its duration, copies of their academic certificates, proof of funds, and a commitment letter from their sponsor (Ligami, 2017). The department of immigration may not, however, have the capacity to determine the genuineness of academic credentials, and this would further erode any professionalism in the admissions process. A large-scale professionalization of various aspects of higher education leadership and management, more especially those dealing with student affairs, is needed.

7.5 Conclusion

African countries have designed broad higher education admissions policies advocating for inclusion, equity, and broadening of access. For the most part, this has not changed patterns of access and participation to higher education institutions from what they were two or three decades ago. Higher education is still largely offered on a supply basis with the government being the main supplier and regulator. A combination of public-funding abilities, limited institutional capacities, and increasing demand for publicly supported higher education even from the rich quartiles of society has turned admissions processes into a highly selective game where the rich and politically influential often outplay those from poor backgrounds at various levels, making good higher education a privilege of the wealthy. The lack of professional higher education admissions officers in a majority of the institutions accentuates this chaotic situation.

North African countries, with a controlled system of admitting students to universities and middle-level tertiary institutions and ensuring that a large number of the students graduating from the middle-level tertiary colleges get employed, have managed to register higher participation rates. The admissions crisis in sub-Saharan African countries is, in this respect, exacerbated by governments' negligence of middle-level tertiary institutions.

Prospective students and their families have negative perceptions of the middle-level institutions, thus creating a scramble for admissions to university-level institutions. Governments also have not helped as they have responded to pressure for more university places by conferring university status on the middle-level colleges without any extra resources to raise the standards and quality processes in the institutions. Students therefore focus first on seeking admission to the best universities before they resort to the new universities, and finally the few available private universities. The capacity of universities is also generally low compared to the number of qualifying students as a consequence of growing populations. Consequently, both the government and institutions employ numerous selection mechanisms, not to test students' aptitude but to rationalize to the students why they have failed to secure admission. On the other hand, African countries continue to spend higher budgets on the university sector – 20.1 percent of total government expenditure on education compared to a world average of 21.3 percent (World Bank, 2013). This has meant that most of the countries cover almost 80 percent of the costs of students' tertiary education, most of whom come from wealthier backgrounds, given the selection mechanisms that favor this group of students, as has been argued here. This means that admissions processes as conducted contribute to widening social inequalities instead of higher education working to stem such inequalities. The challenge that persists throughout the continent is how to create an articulated system of higher education institutions where a correct balance is struck between students admitted to middle-level tertiary institutions and universities and admissions processes that consider equitable access to institutions and academic programs.

REFERENCES

African Union Commission. (2014). *AU Outlook on Education Report. Arab Maghreb Union*. Addis Ababa: African Union Commission.

Anyan, J. (2016). Persistent elitism in access to higher education in Ghana. (Doctoral dissertation). University of Helsinki.

Caerus Capital. (2018). The business of education in Africa. Retrieved from https://edafricareport.caeruscapital.co/.

Clark, N. (2015). A common anglophone curriculum under the West African Examinations Council. *World Education News + Reviews*. Retrieved from https://wenr.wes.org/2015/03/common-anglophone-curriculum-west-afri can-examinations-council.

Dahir, A. L. (2017, January). Africa has too few universities for its fast-growing population. Retrieved from https://qz.com/africa/878513/university-educa tion-is-still-a-dream-many-in-africa-are-yet-to-attain.

Darvas, P., Gao, S., Shen, Y., & Bawany, B. (2017). *Sharing higher education's promise beyond the few in sub-Saharan Africa*. Washington, DC: World Bank. Retrieved from https://doi.org/10.1596/978-1-4648-1050-3.

Economic Community of West African States. (2003). ECOWAS Protocol A/P3/ 1/03 on education and training. ECOWAS, Department of Education, Culture, Science and Technology. Retrieved from www.esc.comm.ecowas .int/wp-content/uploads/2016/04/protocol-on-education-and-training1 .pdf.

European Commission. (2017a). *Overview of the higher education system: Algeria.* Brussels: Education, Audiovisual, and Culture Executive Agency.

(2017b). *Overview of the higher education system: Egypt.* Brussels: Education, Audiovisual, and Culture Executive Agency.

(2017c). *Overview of the higher education system: Libya.* Brussels: European Union, Education, Audiovisual, and Culture Executive Agency.

(2017d). *Overview of the higher education system: Mauritania.* Brussels: European Union, Education, Audiovisual, and Culture Executive Agency.

(2017e). *Overview of the higher education system: Morocco.* Brussels: European Union, Education, Audiovisual, and Culture Executive Agency.

(2017f). *Overview of the higher education system: Tunisia.* Brussels: European Union, Education, Audiovisual, and Culture Executive Agency.

Gioan, A. P. (2008). *Higher education in francophone Africa: What tools can be used to support financially sustainable policies?* Washington, DC: World Bank. Retrieved from https://doi.org/10.1596/978-0-8213-7470-2.

Hammoud, R. (2010). Admission policies and procedures in Arab Universities. In B. Lamine (Ed.). *Towards an Arab higher education space: International challenges and societal responsibilities.* Proceedings of the Arab regional conference on higher education (pp. 69–92). Beirut: UNESCO Office Beirut and Regional Bureau for Education in the Arab States.

Kanyip, B. P. (2013). Admission crises in Nigerian universities: The challenges youth and parents face in seeking admission (Doctoral dissertation). Retrieved from https://scholarship.shu.edu/dissertations/1908/.

Kazeem, Y. (2017). Only one in four Nigerians applying to university will get a spot. *Quartz Africa.* Retrieved from https://qz.com/africa/915618/only-one-in-four-nigerians-applying-to-university-will-get-a-spot/.

Kenya Universities and Colleges Central Placement Services. (2014). Placement policy. Retrieved from www.kuccps.net/sites/default/files/Placement%20Policy %20Aug.pdf.

(2016). Admission of 10,000 government sponsored students to degree courses in private universities. Retrieved from www.kuccps.net/?q=content/admission-10000-government-sponsored-students-degree-courses-private-universities.

Ligami, C. (2017, October 19). Authorities tighten rules for foreign student admissions. *University World News.* Retrieved from www.universityworld news.com/article.php?story=20171018093135418.

Mohamedbhai, G. (2017, May 17). Institutional massification in African universities [Blog post]. *Inside Higher Ed.* Retrieved from www.insidehighered .com/blogs/world-view/institutional-massification-african-universities.

Moti, U. G. (2010). The challenges of access to university education in Nigeria. *DSM Business Review 2* (2), 27–56.

Nakweya, G. (2018, February 23). Kenya: University admissions reform: What effect will it have? *University World News, 4*, 494. Retrieved from www.universityworldnews.com/post.php?story=2018022009222839.

Oshemughen, H. O., & Oghuvbu, E. P. (2013). Implications of scrapping JAMB and UTME from tertiary education admission process: The educational administrators' perspective. *Academic Research International, 4*(4), 469–476. Retrieved from www.savap.org.pk/journals/ARInt./Vol.4(4)/2013(4.4-50).pdf.

Oxford Business Group. (2016). Future developments and systemic reforms for Kenya's education sector. Retrieved from https://oxfordbusinessgroup.com/overview/improving-access-and-quality-education-has-been-promoted-key-sector-future-development-and.

Pansiri, B. M., & Sinkamba, R. (2017). Advocating for standards in student affairs departments in African Institutions: University of Botswana experience. *Journal of Student Affairs in Africa, 5*(1), 51–62. Retrieved from www.journals.ac.za/index.php/jsaa/article/view/2482.

Republic of Kenya. (2012). Universities Act No. 42 of 2012. Retrieved from www.education.go.ke/index.php/downloads/file/91-the-universities-act-no-42-of-2012.

Republic of Tanzania. (2013). The Universities Act. Retrieved from www.tcu.go.tz/images/documents/GN%20226-%20UNIVERSITIES%20GENERAL%20REGULATIONS(1).pdf.

Republic of Uganda. (2001). Universities and Other Tertiary Institutions Act. Retrieved from https://ulii.org/system/files/legislation/act/2001/2001/universities%20and%20tertiary%20institutions%20Act%202001.pdf.

(2017). *Ministry of Education and Sports admission guidelines to universities.* Retrieved from www.education.go.ug/.

(2018). Information on public universities admissions, 2016/2017 academic year. Retrieved from https://news.mak.ac.ug/sites/default/files/downloads/MoES-Mak-AR-PUJAB-Notes-To-Schools-2017-18-FULL.pdf.

Tanzania Commission for Universities. (2018). *Revised admissions guidebook for 2018/2019 form six applicants.* Retrieved from www.tcu.go.tz/images/documents/Revised_AdmissionGuidebook_2018_F6_8_10_2018.pdf.

United Nations Educational Scientific and Cultural Organization Institute for Statistics. (2010). *Trends in tertiary education in sub-Saharan Africa.* Retrieved from http://uis.unesco.org/sites/default/files/documents/fs10-trends-in-tertiary-education-sub-saharan-africa-2010-en.pdf.

(2015). Sub-Saharan Africa: School enrollment, tertiary (% gross). Retrieved from https://data.worldbank.org/indicator/SE.TER.ENRR?locations=ZG.

(2019). Tertiary enrolment: World development indicators. Retrieved from https://data.worldbank.org/indicator/se.ter.enrr.

World Bank. (2013). Expenditure per student, tertiary (% of GDP per capita). Retrieved from http://data.worldbank.org/indicator/SE.XPD.TERT.PC.ZS.

CHAPTER 8

Chile's Admissions Tests: Pending Changes and Revisions

Mladen Koljatic and Mónica Silva

8.1 Chile's National and Centralized University Admissions System

Chile has a national, centralized admissions system that selects students for 41 public and private universities that partake of the Unified Admission System (SUA) of the Council of Rectors of Chilean Universities (CRUCh).[1] The CRUCh is composed of the rectors of publicly funded universities, most of which were created prior to 1981. The CRUCh controls the centralized admissions process and designates the head of the SUA to control, supervise, and evaluate the tests, among other functions. The agency that runs the full testing operation – testing, scoring, application, and selection processes – is DEMRE (Departamento de Evaluación, Medición y Registro Educacional [Department of Evaluation, Measurement, and Educational Registration]), a division within the Universidad de Chile, the largest and oldest public university in the nation.

DEMRE experts develop the tests, administer them once a year, calculate scores, and run the application and selection process. In 2018, the agency assigned approximately 115,000 slots for 1,741 programs through a simultaneous selection process based on a Gale–Shapley-type algorithm (Gale & Shapley, 1962).

The process is financed by testing fees from applicants and the Ministry of Education (MoE). The fee for students that graduate from publicly funded high schools and who take the tests for the first time, are paid by the MoE. The fee for students attending private high schools and repeat test-takers are not covered by the MoE. Traditionally, Universidad de Chile receives all testing fees, which are only partly invested in DEMRE (Grondona & Luz, 2016).

---

[1] This section was adapted, with the author´s permission, from a working paper by Varas (2018).

The Prueba de Selección Universitaria (PSU), currently Chile's national test for university admissions, tests the vast content of the high school curriculum (9th to 12th grades) and is required for all universities that take part in the SUA. The yearly admissions process at the CRUCh's SUA universities involves major logistical challenges required to coordinate the participation of 25,000 collaborators, including proctors and police officers to guard the testing facilities. In 2018, the PSU was simultaneously administered to approximately 300,000 test-takers across the nation, including applicants with sensory and motor disabilities. DEMRE has handled the logistics of the wide-scale yearly application since the advent of standardized admissions testing in the nation in 1966.

Approximately a month after applicants take the admission tests, they check their scores on DEMRE's website and, if their scores in the mandatory language and mathematics tests are above the cut score defined by the CRUCh's SUA, they can proceed to apply to a maximum of ten programs of their choice. Applicants rank their preferences from most-preferred to least-preferred, and if they are assigned to a program all the lower-ranked choices are dropped.

In addition to test scores, selection factors include high school grade point average (GPA) and a class rank measure (included in 2013) that represents the relative standing of a student within his or her school. These selection factors are weighted and pooled into a final application score.

The weight assigned to selection factors varies depending on the program, and, consequently, the same student may have different application scores for similar programs offered by different universities. Such would be the case if University A's medical school weighs test scores at 0.50 while University B's medical school assigns test scores a weight of 0.60.

No other criteria, such as essays or letters of recommendation, are included in the regular admissions process, although some artistic programs require applicants to take additional tests developed at their own institutions. In those cases, DEMRE includes those scores along with the rest of the selection factors.

Direct admission is restricted, and universities can assign up to 15 percent of their slots outside the regular admissions process run by DEMRE. In practice, the 15 percent of special admissions is a mechanism whereby universities can waive some or all admissions requirements for individuals or selected groups of applicants – for example, athletes and students from disadvantaged groups who may not achieve the cut scores specified for the regular process.

Because of its high-stakes implications, the national centralized admissions process draws considerable attention from the press even though it only involves 24 percent of the total enrollment of the higher education system in Chile.

8.2   The PSU

The most questioned feature of the admissions system is the PSU, a battery of multiple-choice achievement tests that examine extensive high school curricular topics. In 2003, the PSU replaced the Prueba de Aptitud Académica (PAA) and the Pruebas de Conocimientos Específicos (PCE) (similar to the American SAT® and SAT Subject Tests™) that had been used since 1966. The PAA assessed verbal and mathematical reasoning through selected basic topics, while the PCE examined advanced topics in specific subjects required by a few of the more prestigious university programs.

To date, the PSU battery consists of two mandatory tests – language (Spanish) and mathematics – and two additional optional tests that examine content in science and social science, the choice of which depends on specific program requirements. In the science PSU, students have a choice between tests that examine biology, physics, or chemistry.

The transition from the PAA and PCE battery to the PSU was led by two faculty members from prestigious CRUCh universities, but who had little if any experience in the development of high-stakes tests (Phelps, 2014; Guzmán, 2013).

To justify the change of tests they employed the same arguments that Atkinson (2002) invoked in the United States to push for revisions to the SAT. Among the benefits, the project leaders claimed their new tests would improve school learning by strengthening the link between the high school curriculum and the university selection process. They also claimed the new tests would increase equitable access for socioeconomically deprived students since these would examine content covered in high school, making expensive coaching programs less necessary (El Diario Austral de Valdivia , 2002). However, no solid evidence was provided to support that such benefits would be accrued, and many voices pointed out the risks entailed in an unstudied and premature change (Beyer, 2002a; 2002b; Eyzaguirre & Lefoulon, 2002; Labarca, 2002). Their arguments went unheeded.

Unknown to the general public, the new tests were being designed to fulfill a double purpose: to select students for university admissions and assess the outcomes of an iconic educational reform (the first after the return to democracy) and guarantee its sustainability (Comisión Nuevo Currículum, 2000; World Bank, 2001).

The supporters of the reform movement aimed to improve quality and equity in education. Funded by a loan from the World Bank, officials at the Ministry of Education were faced with the task of evaluating the educational outcomes of the secondary school reform, but instead of implementing a NAEP-type test in the senior year of high school they opted to change the admission tests to accommodate both purposes (World Bank, 2001). Some influential CRUCh rectors, reluctant at first to embrace the change, finally acquiesced (Urzúa, 2002).

The double purpose pursued by the test was a mistake, according to one of the leading experts in educational measurement:

> If a test measured the curriculum that was taught and the students learned the skills, the score distribution would be negatively skewed. This would be expected and desirable. For admission tests, however, the goal is to spread out the scores to maximize the reliability and validity of the scores for predicting success, hence a symmetrical and bell-shaped distribution of scores would be expected and desired. It is unlikely, to say the least, that the two purposes – admission selection and outcomes evaluation – could be well accomplished via a single instrument. (Hambleton, personal communication, 2004)

However, to the non-specialists that led the project to change the tests, the notion of the dual purpose appeared like a good way to easily fulfill two different needs.

In addition, the decision to turn the admissions tests into instruments for assessing learning outcomes in secondary education proved to be detrimental for the neediest segment of high schoolers.

8.3   Equity Issues in the PSU

The double purpose of the PSU – particularly the fact that it was designed to focus primarily on one of the two official national high school curricula in the nation – eventually became its Achilles heel. The two national curricular tracks, Scientific–Humanistic (SH) and Technical–Professional (TP) differed widely in the two last years of high school (i.e., in 11th and 12th grades). Students attending the TP track – the one that educated the poorest in the nation – were disadvantaged by the PSU since it was targeted to measure SH contents covered in the last two years of high school (Pearson Education, 2013). Sadly, the disadvantage for TP students was anticipated by the MoE, some CRUCh rectors, and the project leaders in 2001. Two years before the new tests were implemented they were cognizant that the new tests would leave students from the TP track (and older students too) at a disadvantage, as revealed by the minutes of a meeting that took place before the implementation of the PSU (Minuta Reunión de Trabajo Gabinete Sra. Ministra de Educación, 2001).

Approximately 40 percent of high school students in 2015 attended the TP track in their last two years of high school (Agencia de la Calidad de la Educación, 2016) and less than 10 percent wished to enter the labor force immediately after graduation. The rest aspired to continue studies, whether at technical institutes or universities, many of which required the PSU. In 2018, almost 80,000 TP students registered to take the PSU, a test for which they were largely unprepared (Varas, 2018).

The use of the PSU violated the principle of opportunity to learn for TP students, as spelled out in the *Standards for educational and psychological testing* (American Educational Research Association [AERA], American Psychological Association [APA], & National Council of Measurement in Education [NCME], 2014). The fairness of the PSU and its legitimate use for TP students was questioned by an international audit of the admissions tests conducted by Pearson Education (2013). In addition, ministry documents revealed that the curricular coverage differed significantly for SH and TP students, with TP students receiving less curricular coverage and less time on tasks in the mandatory subjects examined in the PSU (Centro de Estudios Mineduc, 2013).

The equity deficits of the PSU had been pointed out prior to the Pearson Report (Koljatic & Silva, 2006; 2010; 2011; Beyer, 2007; 2009; Vargas, 2009). However, the CRUCh rectors – owners and main users of the PSU – failed to correct the tests. As a consequence, in 2012, a local non-governmental organization lodged a constitutional remedy action through the local courts against the use of the PSU, but the Santiago court of Appeals dismissed it, so the case ended up in the Inter-American Commission of Human Rights (IACHR) (see Muñoz, 2012). Following its initial review, the IACHR opened the petition for processing in April of 2018 (*Venegas Ovalle* v. *Chile*, 2018).

8.4 Predictive Validity and Other Deficits

In addition to the questionings of fairness issues, the 800-page Pearson Report on the PSU (Pearson Education, 2013) included 122 recommendations to improve the tests, among them predictive validity. The findings of the Pearson Report made headlines, particularly since its conclusions were at odds with previous official reports and claims by CRUCh rectors and their advisers regarding the merits of the PSU (La Segunda, 2013; *La Segunda*, 2013; Guzmán, 2013).[2]

The early appointment by the CRUCh rectors of the leaders of the PSU project to chair a committee to supervise DEMRE and act as main evaluators of the tests was an unwise decision because of the obvious conflict of interest and the threat to objectivity entailed in their designation. For years, the leaders of the PSU project presented official reports published by the CRUCh that can be best described as "pseudoevaluations," according to the definition by Stufflebeam (2001). In their reports, the authors failed to provide a valid assessment of the merit and worth of the PSU tests, focusing instead on broadcasting a favorable, albeit misleading, impression of the quality of the tests while silencing its deficits. In their six official reports, they overstated the quality of the tests and omitted analyses for the TP students (Bravo et al., 2005; 2008; 2010a; 2010b; Manzi et al., 2006; 2008). In addition, they did not address questions regarding the fairness of its use for the TP group (Abud, 2013; Echecopar, 2013; Koljatic & Silva, 2010; 2011; Koljatic, Silva, & Cofré, 2012; Vargas, 2009) and the protests from independent researchers who complained of restricted access to test data (Beyer, 2007; Castro, 2006; Prado, 2008).

The Pearson Report left no doubt as to the predictive deficits of the tests and concluded that "in no instance did PSU tests achieve prediction validity indexes close to the lower bound observed internationally" (Pearson Education, 2013, p. 452). The conclusions applied to analyses conducted for university performance in the first- and second-year GPA, as well as university completion. The authors of the Pearson Report asked: "If the PSU tests do not predict university outcomes, then why are we using them?" (p. 64). The issues of fairness, particularly for the TP group, were also extensively addressed in the report, which even cited a source from the MoE that acknowledged that the PSU "emphasize(d) the Scientific–Humanistic curricular branch" (Pearson Education, 2013, p. 54).

A few months before the Pearson Report was released to the public and knowing that the findings would not reflect well on the quality and fairness of the PSU, the CRUCh dictated that a class rank measure be applied that same year in the admissions process in addition to the students high school

---

[2] Prior to the Pearson Report of the PSU, two previous reports by OECD and The World Bank (2009) and the Educational Testing Service (2005) recommended changes to the PSU that were not implemented.

GPA. The impromptu measure, aimed at allowing for a reduction of the relative weight of the PSU in the selection process, was harshly criticized by the Minister of Education and by some school principals for its hasty implementation and for changing the rules of the admissions process for students at the last minute (Beyer, 2013).

Notwithstanding the arguments and protests from applicants and faculty who saw the rules of the game changed in the middle of the game, the CRUCh rectors agreed to assign at least a weight of 0.10 to the newly established class rank measure, but university officials were free to decide whether the weight of the class rank measure would be subtracted from test scores or high school GPA. In the years that followed the introduction of the class rank measure, some universities significantly increased its weight as a selection factor.

In addition to poor prediction and equity shortcomings of the test, Pearson experts highlighted the inadequate difficulty level of the PSU mathematics test for the population of test-takers (present since its first application and aggravated in recent years), the faulty scoring of the science PSU (declared to be untenable), and the inadequate use of PSU scores to determine cut scores to assign financial aid and to rank the quality of schools, to name a few.

8.5   Aftermath of the Pearson Report

After the release of the Pearson Education Report on the PSU (2013) and the public outcry that followed, the rectors opted to create a new entity to steer the admissions system, evaluate the tests, and oversee DEMRE's operation, but the changes were mostly cosmetic. The CRUCh refused to reform the governance of the admissions system to protect the rights of test-takers as spelled out in a proposal from the MoE (Melo, 2013). A few weeks later the Minister of Education, a respected expert who did not belong to any political party and had served as adviser to several presidents, was impeached by congress and ousted from office, not for any good reason but to score political points (*The Economist*, 2013).

With the uncomfortable presence of the Minister removed, the CRUCh agreed to introduce only minor changes in the PSU but did not allow DEMRE to implement the most relevant changes recommended by Pearson experts in order to advance fairness for the TP groups and improve predictive validity. These were: (a) to depart from the policy of using the curricular framework as the basis for the development of the PSU tests, focusing instead on the aptitudes required for successful performance at the university and (b) to reduce the content assessed in the tests to that relevant for prediction and common to the SH and TP curricula.

In addition, DEMRE experts were not allowed to correct the faulty scoring of the PSU science and the inadequate difficulty level of the PSU mathematics tests (Muñoz & Yévenes, 2018). Other pending changes, promoted by DEMRE officials but prevented by the CRUCh, included the enactment of regulations to protect the confidentiality of students' test data (Yevenes, 2018) and the eradication of the use of PSU scores to assign student benefits, such as scholarships.[3]

8.6   Reflections on How to Improve the Admissions System

An examination of the process of how the PSU came to be, how it evolved, and the obstacles to correct its deficits as a selection battery can provide useful lessons to nations that aim to build an effective and fair admissions system and insulate it from conflicts of interest. Learning can accrue from the study of successful experiences and also from failures.

The suggestions that follow stem from reflecting on the barriers that prevented the correction of the deficits in the PSU and the institutional mechanisms that should have been in place to promote test changes in line with good testing practices.[4]

8.6.1   An Autonomous and Professional Agency Should Be in Charge of Testing

In the past, researchers in policymaking in developing nations have stressed the need for the professionalization of testing in university admissions and have warned that "test development can be done in a haphazard manner, but the negative technical and political consequences are serious" (Heyneman, 1987, p. 257).

Since testing as a profession is highly susceptible to political interference, the quality of tests rests, to a large extent, on the ability of a testing agency to pursue professional ends autonomously. The endeavor requires substantial investment, thus income from the testing fees should remain within the testing agency (Heyneman, 1987; Heyneman &

---

[3] The National Association for College Admission Counseling (2008) explicitly cautions against this potential misuse of test scores.

[4] Some of the suggestions in this section build on the ideas of others, particularly Steven Heyneman (Heyneman, 1987; Heyneman & Fagerlind, 1988).

Fagerlind, 1988). This is not the case in Chile, since DEMRE does not receive all fees.

An independent and professional agency staffed with psychometric specialists is in a better position to put a limit on political meddling in testing. Although it may be "unrealistic to imagine that the real world of testing would ever be devoid of politics" (Swanson, 1997, p. 116), there is a limit to what should be tolerated. Psychometric specialists should be prepared to follow sound psychometric practices and defend them, even if it means defying the political establishment.

Psychometric specialists agree on the centrality of validity and fairness considerations in testing. Good practice entails substantial attention to these two dimensions in test construction so that admissions tests serve their purpose well: To predict university performance without providing an unjustified edge to any group in the population. In these two dimensions – prediction and fairness – there is ample room for improvement in the PSU tests.

In recent years, the head of DEMRE has defied the political establishment represented by the CRUCh. Yet, lacking in autonomy, DEMRE experts have been unable to bring about changes in the tests to make them more predictive and fair for all test-takers (Muñoz & Yevenes, 2018).

8.6.2   *Independent Board of Local Experts*

Chile is a case where the national admissions tests bear very high stakes for applicants. Among the benefits of the centralized system are the lower financial and emotional costs for students, since they do not have to go through the grueling process of being tested at every university to which they apply. The drawback is that all applicants to universities that are part of the CRUCh´s SUA system are required to take a questionable PSU. The test, in fact, functions as a monopoly, and with no competition there is little in the way of incentives to foster improvement.

This is not the case in the United States, where students have a choice between admissions tests for those universities that require test scores; and the competition can operate as an incentive to make improvements in the tests. The role of a board is probably more important to guarantee test quality in nations like Chile, where admissions tests operate as a monopoly.

The initial designation by the CRUCh rectors of the PSU project leaders as test evaluators was an unwise decision. There is an evident conflict of interest if those who create a program are put in charge of evaluating it, worse so if access to data is restricted for independent researchers. Conflict of interest in the composition of the board should be avoided, since it compromises objectivity and increases the likelihood of pseudoevaluations. An independent board should consider the best interests of all major stakeholders, not only those of university rectors or the ministry of education. Admissions tests affect test-takers, their families, and the high school system. The members of the board should evaluate the quality of the work performed by the testing agency, monitor test performance, and promote an active search to identify negative impacts associated to test use in order to minimize them.

The search for negative impacts should be among the top priorities. As Brighouse et al. (2018) state: "Rarely are there only winners and no losers from any proposed reform, however desirable that reform may be . . . [and] those keen to 'sell' a reform may well find it strategic to talk only about the good bits or to come up with feel-good rhetoric that highlights the upside while concealing the downside" (p. 5).

In the case of Chile's PSU, negative outcomes for the TP group and older students were anticipated before the new tests were implemented. Consequently, MoE officials, the CRUCh rectors, and test creators had a moral duty to pay close attention to the groups placed at risk by the change of tests. Yet they failed to do so.

8.6.3   Periodic Audits by an International Panel of Experts

A panel composed of international experts should conduct periodic in-depth reviews of the tests and the other measures employed in the selection process. Its role should be to provide an overview of the testing program and the admissions system, its outcomes, strengths, and weaknesses. The panel's reports should be made public, and the data used in their analyses should be made available to independent researchers to foster transparency, albeit taking measures to protect the confidentiality of individuals' data.

Tests are not written in stone, nor should they be. Changes occur in the university system, at the school level, and also in the population of students that apply for admissions. Consequently, tests should be revised periodically. Major test revisions and the addition of new selection instruments or measures should be a matter of serious deliberation and con-ducted according to the best psychometric practices. This was not the case in Chile, where the PAA and PCEs were eliminated without garnering validity evidence for the use of the PSU, and the class rank measure was imposed without an evaluative framework to assess its contribution to prediction and equity. Neither of these can be considered minor changes, and both merited rigorous study and deliberation.

The international testing community relies on standards and guidelines, for example those spelled out by organizations such as AERA, APA, NCME, and the International Test Commission (ITC). These are considered the yardstick for what is appropriate in test development, psychometric analyses, test administration, score reporting, and test usage (Buckendahl & Hunt, 2005). Had there been periodic audits in place, conducted by international experts, the improvisation and trial-and-error approach that characterized the changes in the admissions system might have been averted.

The development and assessments of the PSU showed the disregard for international testing standards that should orient decision-making, particularly for high-stakes tests. Schools of education in Chilean universities, particularly those offering doctoral programs, should strengthen the instruction of psychometric methods and ethical development and use of tests. The International Test Commission Guidelines (2013) and the AERA, APA, and NCME *Standards for educational and psychological testing* (2014) should be required material in order to foster good practice in the field.

An institutional scheme such as the one proposed here – an autonomous testing agency, a local board that oversees it, and an international board to conduct periodic audits – is probably more important in nations such as Chile, a nation that has very little, if any, statutory control over test use and its consequences for those tested.

Even if there are no laws that defend the rights of aggrieved test-takers, there is still a moral obligation of test users – and those who mandate its use – actively to regulate and stimulate good practices. Errors are bound to happen; the problem arises when these are concealed instead of acknowledged and corrected.

In summary, a centralized admissions system can have many benefits for relevant stakeholders: Students can benefit from not having to take a number of different admissions tests, universities can delegate selection on a specialized agency, reducing the costs entailed in running the process, and, if transparent and free of corruption, a centralized admissions system can contribute to social cohesion and social trust. The system should work better if the testing agency is selected via a transparent process, provided with adequate funding, reports on its use of funds, and is held accountable for the quality of its work.

REFERENCES

Abud, V. (2013, January 6). Los diez años de la PSU: Crónica de un daño anunciado [The ten years of PSU: Chronicle of an announced damage]. *El Mercurio*, p. A2.

Agencia de la Calidad de la Educación (2016). Panorama de la educación media técnico profesional en Chile [Overview of the secondary technical–professional education in Chile]. Retrieved from http://archivos.agenciaedu cacion.cl.

American Educational Research Association, American Psychological Association, & National Council on Measurement in Education. (2014). *Standards for educational and psychological testing*. Washington, DC: American Educational Research Association.

Atkinson, R. (2002). Achievement versus aptitude in college admission. *Issues in Science and Technology, 18*(2), 31–36.

Beyer, H. (2002a, April 25). Sobre las pruebas de ingreso a las universidades [About college entrance tests]. *El Mercurio*, p. A2.

(2002b, May 3). Nuevas pruebas de ingreso a la universidad [New college entrance tests). *El Mercurio*, p. A2.

(2007, January 17). Equidad en la PSU [Fairness in the PSU]. *El Mercurio*, p. A2.

(2009). Igualdad de oportunidades y selección a las universidades. Puntos de referencia, 303 [Equality of opportunities and selection to the universities. *Reference points, 303*]. Santiago: Centro de Estudios Públicos. Retrieved from www.cepchile.cl.

(2013, January 15). Beyer califica al sistema de admisión a universidades de "una locura" y dice que ranking de notas se aplicó "sin protocolo" [Beyer describes the system of admission to universities as "crazy" and says that ranking of grades was applied "with no protocol"]. *La Tercera*, p. 26.

Bravo, D., Bosch, A., del Pino, G., Donoso, G., & Manzi, J. (2010a). *Validez diferencial y sesgo de predictividad de las pruebas de admisión a las universidades chilenas* [Differential validity and prediction bias in the Chilean university admissions tests]. Santiago: Comité Técnico Asesor, Consejo de Rectores de las Universidades Chilenas.

Bravo, D., del Pino, G., Donoso, G., Hawes, G., Manzi, J., & Martínez, M. (2005). *Resultados de la aplicación de pruebas de selección universitaria admisión 2004* [Results of the application of university selection admissions tests 2004]. Santiago: Comité Técnico Asesor, Consejo de Rectores de las Universidades Chilenas.

Bravo, D., del Pino, G., Donoso, G., Manzi, J., Martínez, M., & Pizarro, R. (2008). *Resultados de la aplicación de pruebas de selección universitaria admisión 2006–2008* [Results of the application of university selection admissions tests 2006–2008]. Santiago: Comité Técnico Asesor, Consejo de Rectores de las Universidades Chilenas.

(2010b). *Resultados de la aplicación de pruebas de selección universitaria admisiones 2006–2010* [Results of the application of university selection admissions tests 2006–2010]. Santiago: Comité Técnico Asesor, Consejo de Rectores de las Universidades Chilenas.

Brighouse, H., Ladd, H., Loeb, S., & Swift, A. (2018). *Educational goods: Values, evidence and decision-making*. Chicago, IL: University of Chicago Press. https://doi.org/10.7208/chicago/9780226514208.001.0001.

Buckendahl, C., & Hunt, R. (2005). Whose rules? The relation between the "rules" and the "laws" of testing. In R. Phelps (Ed.). *Defending standardized testing* (pp. 147–158). Hillsdale, NJ: Lawrence Erlbaum Associates.

Castro, R. (2006, December 12). Evaluación de la PSU [Evaluation of the PSU]. *El Mercurio*, p. A2.

Centro de Estudios Mineduc. (2013). Implementación del currículum de enseñanza media en Chile [Implementation of the Chilean high school curriculum]. *Serie Evidencias*, 2(21). Retrieved from https://centroestudios.mineduc.cl/wp-con tent/uploads/sites/100/2017/06/A2N21_Curriculum_EMedia.pdf.

Comisión Nuevo Currículum de la Enseñanza Media y Pruebas del Sistema de Admisión a la Educación Superior. (2000). Informe sometido en consulta previa a la Ministra de Educación [Commission for the new curriculum for secondary education and tests for higher education]. Report submitted in consultation with the Minister of Education. Unpublished document.

Demoledor informe sobre la PSU desata presión por cambios. (2013, February 1). [Demolishing report on PSU unleashes pressure for changes]. *La Tercera*, pp. 1, 8, 9.

El Diario Austral de Valdivia (2002, July 21). El SIES comenzará a ser aplicado a contar del 2003 [The new system of admission to higher education will be administered starting from 2003]. Retrieved from www.australvaldivia.cl/ site/edic/20020721080919/pags/20020721083134.html.

Echecopar, R. (2013). Egresados de la educación media técnico-profesional en Chile: Articulación con la educación superior y efectos de la implementación de la PSU [Graduates of Chile's TP high school education: Articulation with higher education and the effects of the implementation of the PSU]. Thesis, Pontificia Universidad Católica de Chile.

The Economist (2013, April 18). Beyer gets the boot: A good minister is sacked apparently for political reasons. Retrieved from www.economist.com/amer icas-view/2013/04/18/beyer-gets-the-boot.

Eyzaguirre, B., & Lefoulon, C. (2002). El SIES: Un proyecto prematuro [The SIES: A premature project]. *Revista Estudios Públicos*, 87, 39–53.

Gale, D., & Shapley, L. S. (1962). College admission and the stability of marriage. *American Mathematical Monthly*, 69, 9–14. https://doi.org/ 10.1080/00029890.1962.11989827.

Grondona, M., & Luz, C. (2016, January 24). El Organismo que elabora la PSU en la mira de los expertos [The Organization that prepares the PSU in the spotlight of the experts]. *El Mercurio*, p. D7.

Guzmán, J. A. (2013). El cambio de la PAA a PSU fue liderado por gente con militancia política, pero nadie experto en evaluación ni en educación [The change from the PAA to the PSU was led by individuals with political militance, but none of them experts in evaluation nor in education]. *Ciper Chile*. Retrieved from https://ciperchile.cl/2013/02/13/%E2%80%9Cel-cambio-de-la-paa-a-psu-fue-liderado-por-gente-con-militancia-politica-pero-nadie-experto-en-evaluacion-ni-en-educacion%E2%80%9D/.

Heyneman, S. (1987). Uses of examinations in developing countries: Selection, research, and education sector management. *International Journal of Educational Development*, *7*, 251–263. https://doi.org/10.1016/0738-0593(87) 90023-X.

Heyneman, S., & Fagerlind, I. (Eds.). (1988). *University examinations and standardized testing principles, experience, and policy options* (World Bank Technical Paper No. 78). Washington, DC: World Bank.

International Test Commission (2013). ITC guidelines on test use. Retrieved from www.intestcom.org/files/guideline_test_use.pdf

Koljatic, M., & Silva, M. (2006). Equity issues associated with the change of college admission tests in Chile. *Equal Opportunities International*, *25*, 544–561. https://doi.org/10.1108/02610150610714385.

(2010). Algunas reflexiones a siete años de la implementación de la PSU [Some reflections seven years after the implementation of the PSU]. *Estudios Públicos*, *210*, 125–146.

(2011). Acceso y equidad en las demandas estudiantiles [Access and equity in student demands]. *Administración y Economía UC*, *71*, 24–29 Retrieved from https://issuu.com/economiayadministracionuc/docs/revista_a_e_n__71.

Koljatic, M., Silva, M., & Cofré, R. (2012). Achievement versus aptitude in college admission: A cautionary note based on evidence from Chile. *International Journal of Educational Development*, *33*, 106–115. https://doi.org/10.1016/j.ijedudev.2012.03.001.

Labarca, R. (2002, December 4) Al Simce lo que es del Simce y a la PAA lo que es de la PAA. [Simce and PAA: To each its own]. *El Mostrador*. Retrieved from www.elmostrador.cl/noticias/opinion/2002/04/12/al-simce-lo-que-es-del-simce-y-a-la-paa-lo-que-es-de-la-paa/?php%20bloginfo(%27url%27);%20? %3E/cultura.

Manzi, J., Bravo, D., del Pino, G., Donoso, G., Martínez, M., & Pizarro, R. (2006). *Estudio acerca de la validez predictiva de los factores de selección a las universidades del Consejo de Rectores* [Study about the predictive validity of the selection factors to the universities of the Council of Rectors]. Santiago: Comité Técnico Asesor, Consejo de Rectores de las Universidades Chilenas.

(2008). *Estudio acerca de la validez predictiva de los factores de selección a las universidades del Consejo de Rectores, Admisiones 2003 a 2006* [Study about the predictive validity of the selection factors to the universities of the Council of Rectors, Admissions 2003 to 2006]. Santiago: Comité Técnico Asesor, Consejo de Rectores de las Universidades Chilenas.

Melo, F. (2013, March 11). Beyer responde a rectores sobre rechazo a propuesta PSU: "Se están defendiendo intereses corporativos" [Beyer replies to rectors about PSU proposal refusal: "This is a corporate defense of their interests"]. *La Tercera*. Retrieved from www.latercera.com/noticia/beyer-responde-a-rec tores-sobre-rechazo-a-propuesta-psu-se-estan-defendiendo-intereses-corporativos/

Minuta Reunión de Trabajo Gabinete Sra. Ministra de Educación. (2001, June 25). *Minuta anexada a Acta 431 del CRUCH* [Minutes from a work meeting at the office of the Minister of Education, Document attached to CRUCh Session 431].

Muñoz, A. (2012, September 17). Denuncia por PSU en Comisión Interamericana de Derechos Humanos [Complaint by PSU in the Inter-American Commission on Human Rights]. *El Mercurio*, p. C4.

Muñoz, D., & Yevenes, P. (2018, June 1). Rectores critican al DEMRE por presiones para cambiar la PSU [Rectors criticize DEMRE for pressure to change the PSU]. *La Tercera*, p. 22.

National Association for College Counseling. (2008). Report of the Commission on the Use of Standardized Tests in Undergraduate Admission. https://files .eric.ed.gov/fulltext/ED502721.pdf.

Organisation for Economic Co-operation and Development & World Bank. (2009). *Tertiary education in Chile: Reviews of national policies for education*. Paris: OECD.

Pearson Education. (2013, January 22). Evaluation of the Chile PSU-final report. Retrieved from www.educacion2020.cl/sites/default/files/201301311057540 .chile_psu-finalreport.pdf.

Phelps, R. (2014). Evaluaciones de gran escala en Chile: ¿Son necesarias? [Large-scale evaluations in Chile: Are they necessary?]. Retrieved from https:// ciperchile.cl/2014/02/06/evaluaciones-educacionales-de-gran-escala-en-chile-%C2%BFson-necesarias/.

Prado, S. (2008, August 18). PSU, predicción y transparencia [PSU, prediction and transparency]. *El Mercurio*, p. A2.

La Segunda. (2013, January 31). Informe revela que PSU tiene severas fallas y no cumple estándares internacionales. [Report reveals that PSU has severe failures and does not meet international standards], p. 2.

Stufflebeam, D. (2001). Evaluation models. *New Directions for Program Evaluation*, 2001(89), 7–98. https://doi.org/10.1002/ev.3.

Swanson, R. (1997). The politics of standardized testing. Retrieved from https:// images.pearsonassessments.com/images/NES_Publications/1997_13Swan son_380_1.pdf.

Urzúa, R. (2002). La U y la USACH tomarán PAA en admisión 2003 [The U and the USACH will take PAA in admission 2003]. *Las Últimas Noticias*, 6.

Varas, L. (2018, July). Bringing about changes in national admission tests. Paper presented at the 11th Conference of the International Test Commission, Montreal, Canada.

Vargas, G. (2009, February 2). PSU y la educación técnica [PSU and technical education]. *El Mercurio*, p. A2.

Venegas Ovalle v. *Chile*. (2018). Case 13,575, Inter American Commission on Human Rights.

World Bank. (2001). Implementation completion report (CPl-38830; SCL 38836) on a loan in the amount of U.S. $35 million to the republic of Chile for a CLl-secondary education (Report No. 22979). Retrieved from http://documents.worldbank.org/curated/en/469921468239115337/pdf/multiopage.pdf.

Yevenes, P. (2018, August 31). CRUCh revierte medida que restringía entrega de datos de postulantes a Ues [CRUCh reverses measure that restricted delivery of data from applicants to Universities]. Retrieved from www.latercera.com/nacional/noticia/psu-cruch-revierte-medida-restringia-entrega-datos-postulantes-ues/302016/.

CHAPTER 9

Issues of Perceived Fairness in Admissions Assessments in Small Countries: The Case of the Republic of Cyprus

Elena C. Papanastasiou and Michalis P. Michaelides

The Republic of Cyprus gained its independence in 1960 and joined the European Union (EU) in 2004 and the Eurozone in 2008. According to its constitution, Greek and Turkish are the official languages, although English is also widely used. With an area of 9,251 square kilometers, it is the third largest island in the Mediterranean Sea, but one of the smallest countries in the EU. With a population of approximately 800,000, it represents only 0.2 percent of the population of the EU (Statistical Service of Cyprus, 2016). This makes Cyprus the country with the third lowest population in the EU, ranking only above Malta and Luxembourg.

The educational system in the Republic of Cyprus is highly centralized. The Ministry of Education and Culture (MoEC) is responsible for: (a) the enforcement of education laws and the preparation of new legislation relative to public and private education at all levels; (b) the formulation of the intended curriculum for all subjects in grades K–12; and (c) the prescription of syllabi, curricula, and textbooks for all subjects in public schools. Public as well as private primary, secondary, and tertiary education institutions operate on the island and are all accountable to the MoEC. The MoEC is also in charge of organizing the University Entrance Examinations (UEE) that are used as the sole criterion for entry into the public universities in Cyprus, as well as into the public tertiary institutions in Greece.

Primary education begins at the age of five years and eight months, changing to six years in 2021, and lasts for six years. The main aim of primary education is to offer educational opportunities to all children, regardless of age, sex, family, and social background, as well as to achieve balanced cognitive, emotional, and psychomotor development for these students (Ministry of Education and Culture, 2014).

Secondary general education is available to all primary school graduates through public and private secondary schools. Public secondary education is free for all six grades, but it is compulsory for Grades 7–9 only. Private secondary schools are comprised of either six or seven years of schooling (Grades 7–12 or 7–13).

During the 2014–2015 school year there were 167 secondary education institutions and 57,161 secondary school students (Statistical Service of Cyprus, 2017). Public secondary general schools are organized into two, three-year cycles: The Gymnasium (Grades 7–9) and the Lyceum (high school; Grades 10–12). The Gymnasium cycle places emphasis on a common-core curriculum for all students, whereas the Lyceum cycle allows students to select groups of specialization courses, depending on the preferences, skills, and interests of students. As an alternative to Lyceums, students can choose to attend secondary technical and vocational schools starting from Grade 10.

The first university in Cyprus was established in 1992; before that, most Cypriots studied in colleges or postsecondary institutions in Cyprus (e.g., the pedagogical academy), in Greek universities, as well as in other countries (e.g., the United States, the United Kingdom, Germany). Currently, tertiary education – college-level education – is provided by three public and five private universities and 41 postsecondary institutions and colleges. Public universities are tuition free for undergraduate students; private universities charge fees for all degrees. Yet, many Cypriot students, especially those who attend private high schools, tend to study in universities abroad.

The relatively large number of tertiary institutions in Cyprus compared to the size of the country signifies the important role that tertiary education plays in Cyprus. Cyprus ranks second in the EU in regard to the proportion of the population aged 30–34 with tertiary education degrees. Specifically, 54.7 percent of the population has a degree from a tertiary institution, which is above the 46 percent target of the Europe 2020 strategy (Statistical Service of Cyprus, 2016). Moreover, Cyprus ranks third among the EU countries in regard to public expenditure on all levels of education as a percentage of the Gross Domestic Product. Both of these statistics point to the emphasis that is placed on higher education in the country.

9.1 Assessment and the University Entrance Examinations in Cyprus

Assessment is viewed as an indispensable part of the teaching and learning process in Cypriot curricula (Ministry of Education and Culture, 2010) and serves as a means for improving teaching practice. Survey evidence indicates that teachers and students agree with the view that the primary purpose of assessments is to improve teaching practice and student learning (Michaelides & Solomonidou, 2019; Michaelides & Theodorou, 2014). However, besides the importance placed on assessment, the Cypriot educational system can be considered as low stakes in terms of testing (Lamprianou, 2012; Michaelides, 2014).

There are no national, high-stakes exams administered in public primary and secondary schools. In primary education, assessments are classroom-based, with the aim of monitoring the progress of students. In secondary education, end-of-year exams are school-based and used for promotion to the next grade (Solomonidou & Michaelides, 2017). The examination at the end of 12th grade is the first instance of a nationwide, high-stakes examination given to students (Brown & Michaelides, 2011).

The UEE, also known as the Pancyprian Examinations, are the main criterion for entrance into the free public universities in Cyprus. Scores from these examinations form the basis of a selective system used to gain admission to specific programs and universities. The UEE are taken by students who attended high schools that followed the national curriculum but students from other backgrounds, such as from private schools, are also eligible to take these tests. The UEE have a dual role, acting as both end-of-year exams and college entrance exams, and all graduating students from high schools that followed the national curriculum are required to take the examinations. The dual role of these examinations will cease in the next few years, so only students who wish to be considered for entry into public tertiary institutions in Cyprus (or Greece) will take the UEE.

Each high school graduate has the option to participate in at least four examinations of their choice for admission into specific university majors. Students can take separate combinations of subjects, depending on the requirements of the major to which they would like to apply. For example, a student who would like to study mathematics would have to take exams in modern Greek, mathematics, physics, and in a fourth subject chosen from chemistry, biology, computer science, and technology (Ministry of Education and Culture, 2018). A student who would like to study political science would have to take exams in modern Greek, history, English, as well as in a fourth subject selected from ancient Greek, Latin, mathematics, French, biology, or political economy. Students who would like to apply for admission to two different majors would have to take exams in more than four subjects in order to meet the requirements for each major.

The scores that each student receives are linearly scaled, transformed to fit a prespecified score distribution, and then averaged in order to receive an access score. However, students who have applied for admissions in more than one major that will require different combinations of subjects will receive different access scores based on the requirements for each major (Lamprianou, 2012). Only the students who have received the highest access scores among the candidates who applied for the same major can be accepted, until the prespecified number of applicants are admitted into the program. In very competitive majors, such as medicine and law, a student's admission could even be decided based on the second decimal place of their access scores. Consequently, the very competitive nature of these examinations means afternoon private tutoring is considered necessary by both students and parents – often to the detriment of the family budget and students' free time (Michaelides, 2014).

9.2 Test Development Process

The psychometric properties of admissions assessments used for entry into public universities are not the main parameters considered during the test development process. For practical, historical, and political reasons, issues of perceived fairness related to test security procedures are considered critical factors in the testing process. Consequently, the test development process in Cyprus is very different compared to that of other countries.

All of the processes that are followed concerning the UEE are described in the annual *Guide to the Pancyprian Examinations* (*Guide*) (Ministry of Education and Culture, 2018). As described in the *Guide*, toward the end of each academic year, the Examinations Service Office of the Department of Higher and Tertiary Education has the responsibility of forming committees in charge of the development of the examination. Typically, about 50 separate committees are formed, each of which typically consists of 5 individuals who are selected among school inspectors, principals, vice principals, experienced public high school teachers, and/or academics with expertise that corresponds to the subject of each test. An additional person is invited to each committee as a reviewer. The role of the reviewer is to answer the test questions to identify any mistakes, omissions, or any other types of problems that may not have been detected by the original committee. Knowledge of measurement or item writing is not a requirement for participation in these committees.

Before being officially assigned to a test-preparation committee, all individuals have to sign a form acknowledging that they do not have any relatives (up to the fourth degree) who will be participating in the UEE and that they had not offered any private lessons to examinees during the same academic year. This step is one of the most important procedures of the test preparation process, since it ensures that no individuals will be unfairly advantaged by being informed of the test content before the administration of the examinations.

Once the committees are formed, their members are required to meet up to 24 hours before the administration of the exam for the test development process. This usually takes place in a hotel where the committee members are isolated from the outside world with no access to the Internet or phone lines. During this period, they are expected to develop the test questions and the examination script, as well as prepare the grading (scoring) rubrics and exemplary answers/solutions for each test question. The committee is also expected to ensure that:

- the examination papers do not contain errors, shortcomings, or ambiguities;
- the examination papers include questions that are based on the curriculum that was listed in the *Guide*;
- the examination can be completed by the examinees within the predetermined timeframe;
- the examination papers include questions of various difficulty levels; and
- the examinations have the highest possible degree of reliability and validity. (Ministry of Education and Culture, 2018)

However, no additional information is provided in the *Guide* regarding how to ensure the highest possible degree of reliability and validity.

Finally, according to the *Guide*, the committee is also in charge of overseeing the process of typesetting the examinations, copying them, and sealing the envelopes with the examinations that will be sent to the examination centers. The committees are only allowed to leave the hotel one hour after the examinations have started. All of these activities are organized in a manner that ensures the security of the test preparation process and ensures that the public views the examinations as fair.

9.3 The Grading Process

As described in the *Guide*, after the examinations take place, the tests are gathered in a specific location where the grading will take place. The examiners or raters are typically selected among experienced secondary schoolteachers who have many years of teaching experience, especially in teaching a specific subject in the final year of high school. Teachers apply to become raters so that they can grade tests and are selected on their years of teaching experience and their previous grading experience. Based on the submitted applications, a subject-matter school inspector selects a group of raters. These then have to be approved by the MoEC.

After the raters are selected, and before the grading process begins, each is required to sign a form indicating that they have no relatives up to the fourth degree who have participated in the UEE that year. Each rater is also required to undergo a training session before they are assigned a specific number of tests that need to be graded. The names of the examinees are hidden on each script, so the raters do not have access to identifying information that could potentially influence their grading.

The tests are mostly composed of open-ended questions. Raters are provided with the grading rubric for each question and are requested to grade each question without making any marks on the answer sheet. After the grades for each question are submitted, they are summed up and hidden from view so that a second reviewer can proceed with the grading. Subsequently, the ratings of both graders are compared. If the grades submitted by the two raters vary by less than 10 percent of the maximum score, the grades of the two reviewers are averaged. Otherwise, if they differ by more than 10 percent, a third rater is assigned to also grade the test. In cases where a third rater has been invited, the final score assigned to the student is the average score of all raters. This grading process has been developed in a way that ensures that no examinee will be unfairly advantaged by subjective and lenient scoring by raters who know certain examinees or who can identify an examinee's script.

9.4 Psychometric Quality of the Examinations

The *Guide* includes no specifications about the degree of reliability or validity of the test results. Moreover, no psychometric data are considered or evaluated when developing the test questions. The only requirements that exist are that the examinations should cover content covered in the national curriculum for Grade 12 and that the students should be able to complete the test in three hours. The only reference regarding reliability and validity is that the examinations should have the highest possible degree of reliability and validity. However, no further information is included as to how these claims can be evaluated.

Despite the lack of psychometric evidence in regard to the UEE, the tests are considered fair. Consequently, due to their perceived fairness, their quality is accepted by the Ministry of Education, as well as by the general public.

9.5 Perceptions of Fairness in Examinations

In the 1999 *Standards for educational and psychological testing* (American Educational Research Association [AERA], American Psychological Association [APA], & National Council of Measurement in Education [NCME], 1999), fairness in examinations was defined as a lack of bias, the equitable treatment of examinees, and the provision of equal opportunities to learn the content measured by the assessments. Based on this definition, an important component in fairness is the evaluation of test-question content to determine if the questions and tests are fair to different groups (e.g., people of color, people with disabilities, people from both genders) (Zwick, 2006). This can typically be examined in two ways. The first way is by experts who perform a sensitivity review during the test development process (Zwick, 2006). The purpose is to ensure that the content of each question is not offensive or controversial, does not reinforce stereotypes of certain groups, and is not derogatory toward any group (Educational Testing Service, 2017). The second way to evaluate fairness is by examining whether differential item functioning (DIF), or bias, exists in any items. The goal of such analyses is to examine whether equally proficient members of different groups have different success rates on certain items (Camilli, 2006).

The definition of fairness changed, however, in the 2014 version of the *Standards for Educational and Psychological Testing* (AERA, APA, & NCME, 2014). According to the 2014 standards, "the term fairness has no single technical meaning, and is used in many different ways in the public discourse" (p. 49). In the case of Cyprus, the issue of fairness is not associated with bias (which is typically a central threat to fairness in testing), neither is it associated with whether or not certain questions are offensive or controversial for subgroups of examinees, nor is it examined through DIF analyses. The issue of bias is also not associated with opportunities to learn the appropriate content, since all public schools in Cyprus are required to cover the same material from the same curriculum. Rather, the issue of fairness in the UEE in Cyprus seems to depend exclusively on test security. The definition of fairness could be expanded to include the process of ensuring that no individuals who participate in the examinations (either those teachers who develop the tests or the examinees who take them) have prior knowledge of any test questions and that no examinees get differential treatment during the grading process. This issue is of grave importance in a country such as Cyprus, where people tend to be suspicious of those whom they suspect might be connected in some degree with individuals involved in the testing process and might, therefore, have an unfair advantage compared to others with no such connections.

To remedy such concerns, and to ease the public's worries, the MoEC has purposely provided a detailed description of: (a) the responsibilities of the question-writing committees; (b) the responsibilities of the raters; (c) the responsibilities of other examination center personnel; and (d) additional procedural details related to the process of copying, transporting, and distributing the examinations. It is noteworthy that this information is covered in the very beginning of the *Guide*, signifying the importance that is placed on these issues. Our interpretation of the reason for including this information at the beginning of the *Guide* is to gain the public's trust in the examination procedures and to demonstrate that it is unlikely that any examinee will be unfairly advantaged due to any security breach or weakness of the examination procedures.

This trust in the test security procedures serves as a type of social contract through which society accepts the examinations as a fair filter that controls the distribution of educational resources (Lamprianou, 2009). Evidence from student examinees in Cyprus shows that their perceptions of examination fairness, non-discrimination, and objectivity contributes to an overall positive evaluation of the system. Interviews conducted with high school graduates who had recently participated in the UEE highlighted the importance of a reliable, credible, and fair selection process to determine access to higher education (Michaelides, 2014). These attributes were assured by procedural characteristics such as the nondisclosure of questions due to the confinement of the test developers during the preparation of the examinations, the strict proctoring procedures used during administration, and the anonymity of the students' responses during grading. Although not entirely understood by the interviewees, the score transformation methodology was considered necessary to account for the differential difficulty of the subject tests. In an unpublished study with Lyceum teachers, the examination system was also lauded as fair and meritocratic (Michaelides, 2010). Even the teachers who were critical of the UEE as incompatible with broader educational and pedagogical goals, or as a suboptimal system for assessing high school achievement, acknowledged the fairness and necessity of this selection mechanism for higher education admissions.

9.6 Conclusion

The Republic of Cyprus provides an interesting case in terms of the evolution of high-stakes assessment within a small country. By placing a strong emphasis on test security issues, the Ministry has established society's trust in the fairness of these examinations. This is confirmed by the fact that, to date, no instances have been reported regarding individuals who have been unfairly disadvantaged by the examinations. When society, as well as examinees, trust the examination process, all stakeholders tend to invest their best effort in the process without being distracted by groups that lobby against it. In this way, students can focus on studying for the examinations with the belief that their preparation is the only factor that influences their performance. Moreover, students avoid being sidetracked by debates regarding any extraneous factors that can interfere with their success in these examinations. Teachers also accept this process and put their efforts into appropriately preparing students for the UEE rather than scrutinizing technical or procedural characteristics.

The success of the security of the examination process has made the Ministry reluctant to change any significant aspect of the test development and testing process. This notion is in accord with Lamprianou (2009), who stated that "once societies strike a 'consensus' on a working model of examinations (and usually the simpler the examination system the better), they usually stick with it, even though some criticisms may arise from time to time" (p. 221). In the case of Cyprus, the emphasis seems to be on the perceptions about procedural aspects of test development and administration, with little or no interest in empirical evidence on test interpretation and use. Therefore, regardless as to whether or not the test is the most appropriate for the purpose for which it is intended, what seems to matter is the public's acceptance of the testing process and perceptions of quality, instead of providing empirical evidence of the effectiveness and psychometric quality of the UEE. Similar results were also found in the United Kingdom, where trust in examinations tended to be based on the perceptions of the public rather than on actual facts (Simpson & Baird, 2013). Based on this issue, Newton (2005) has argued in favor of educating the public regarding the properties of tests, in particular, error and measurement inaccuracy, as such education is necessary to avoid the gradual loss of public confidence in examinations.

This is in contrast to other countries, where, once a system has been in place, scientific and empirical investigations to improve the testing process tend to focus on the technical and procedural characteristics of the assessment and to ignore other important aspects of testing (Klinger & Rogers, 2011). For example, in the case of countries with strong testing cultures, the focus tends to be on the technical characteristics of an assessment program, starting even before the pilot testing of the items. This includes psychometric practices, such as standard setting, equating, DIF analyses, selection of scoring models, and reliability analyses. Often, less emphasis is placed on how the public, educators, and examinees perceive the tests, the consequences these tests have on a country's educational system, and how this climate affects student results.

The UEE are high-stakes for the participating students. The educational system in Cyprus is otherwise low accountability and this may be an additional factor that has led to the perpetuation of the test development process described above. Since schools and teachers are not held accountable for their students' performance in the UEE, they have less of an incentive to criticize and demand changes in the test development and grading process. It is possible that if teachers were held accountable for their students' results, they might be more likely to scrutinize this process to ensure its fairness as well as the accuracy of their students' results.

Another factor that might perpetuate the existing test development process in Cyprus is that the Examinations Service Office is located under the MoEC. Because of this centralization, there are no other organizations (e.g., private testing companies) with whom they could compete to undertake this process. Consequently, there is no need for the MoEC to become more transparent in order to prove its quality or to provide detailed evidence supporting the degree of validity and reliability of its results to the public and to its competitors.

An additional consequence of the centralization of the Examinations Service Office is that only public servants are involved in the testing process, irrespective of their training in the field of assessment. Most public servants who work in the Ministry have a background either in primary education, or pre-primary education, or in a specific subject that is taught at the secondary education level (e.g., mathematics, Greek, physics). The extent to which these public servants have completed courses in measurement or assessment is not clear, since the majority of universities that these public servants graduated from do not require such courses. As a result, there is no push from within the Examinations Service Office to make any drastic changes to the examination process.

A possible drawback of this situation is that no analyses are being performed to evaluate the psychometric quality of the examinations or to look deeper into the validity of the examination data. For example, what are the psychometric properties of the UEE and how do they differ from subject to subject and from year to year? What is the extent of the predictive validity of data? Are the most appropriate people selected into each major? Is there a better way of selecting individuals into each major? The need to answer these questions is in accord with Kane (2013), who states that in addition to validating the interpretation of test scores it is also important to validate their use. Similarly, Haertel (2013) states that testing professionals should extend validity arguments to include decisions and implications of test-score inferences. Therefore, fairness arguments should be integrated in argument-based validation (Xi, 2010).

Another drawback of this process is that the focus on fairness from the perspective of test security ignores the examination of bias for subgroups of examinees. For example, are there groups that are unfairly disadvantaged by the UEE? What types of group differences typically exist in the various subject matters?

Overall, in order to be able to examine the validity of scores from any testing program, evidence needs to be collected from various sources, including stakeholders' inputs. This goes beyond the mere evaluation of perceived fairness of an examination by the general society, as well as beyond just attending to the psychometric properties of a test. The evaluation of a testing program needs to be performed through multiple perspectives, while considering the context within which the examinations take place. Adopting a unified validity framework (Messick, 1989), and by collecting evidence that supports score meaning and score use (e.g., as in the form of construct or predictive validity) should be required along with evidence related to the social consequences of score use and its value implications.

REFERENCES

American Educational Research Association, American Psychological Association, & National Council of Measurement in Education. (1999). *Standards for educational and psychological testing*. Washington, DC: American Educational Research Association.

(2014). *Standards for educational and psychological testing*. Washington, DC: American Educational Research Association.

Brown, G.T.L., & Michaelides, M.P. (2011). Ecological rationality in teachers' conceptions of assessment across samples from Cyprus and New Zealand.

European Journal of Psychology of Education, 26, 319–337. https://doi.org/ 10.1007/s10212–010-0052-3.

Camilli, G. (2006). Test fairness. In R. L. Brennan (Ed.). *Educational measurement* (4th ed.) (pp. 221–256). Westport, CT: American Council on Education.

Educational Testing Service. (2017). Fairness guidelines. Retrieved from www.ets .org/about/fairness/guidelines.

Haertel, E. H. (2013). How is testing supposed to improve schooling? *Measurement: Interdisciplinary Research and Perspectives, 11,* 1–18. https://doi.org/ 10.1080/15366367.2013.783752.

Kane, M. T. (2013). Validating the interpretations and uses of test scores. *Journal of Educational Measurement, 50,* 1–73. https://doi.org/10.1111/jedm.12000.

Klinger, D. A., & Rogers, W. T. (2011). Teachers' perceptions of large-scale assessment programs within low-stakes accountability frameworks. *International Journal of Testing, 11,* 122–143. https://doi.org/10.1080/15305058.2011.552748.

Lamprianou, I. (2009). Comparability of examination standards between subjects: An international perspective. *Oxford Review of Education, 35,* 205–226. https://doi.org/10.1080/03054980802649360.

    (2012). Unintended consequences of forced policy-making in high stakes examinations: The case of the Republic of Cyprus. *Assessment in Education: Principles, Policy & Practice, 19,* 27–44. https://doi.org/10.1080/ 0969594X.2011.608348.

Messick, S. (1989). Validity. In R. L. Linn (Ed.). *Educational measurement* (3rd ed.) (pp. 13–103). New York, NY: Macmillan.

Michaelides, M. P. (2010, July). High stakes assessments and their impact as perceived by high school teachers. Poster session presented at the Seventh Conference of the International Test Commission, Hong Kong.

    (2014). Validity considerations ensuing from examinees' perceptions about high-stakes national examinations in Cyprus. *Assessment in Education: Principles, Policy & Practice, 21,* 427–441. https://doi.org/10.1080/0969594X.2014.916655.

Michaelides, M. P. & Solomonidou, G. (2019). Factorial structure, gender invariance and predictive validity of the students' conceptions of assessment-VI inventory. *European Journal of Psychological Assessment, 35,* 248–254. https://doi.org/10.1027/1015-5759/a000383.

Michaelides, M. P., & Theodorou, C. (2014, October). Teachers' conceptions about assessment: Adaptation of a scale on a Cypriot sample. *Proceedings of the 13th Pedagogical Association of Cyprus meeting* (pp. 265–275). Nicosia: PEK.

Ministry of Education and Culture. (2010). Αναλυτικά προγράμματα προδημοτικής, δημοτικής, και μέσης εκπαίδευσης. [Curriculums of kindergarten, elementary, and secondary education]. Nicosia: Ministry of Education and Culture.

    (2014). *Annual report 2014.* Retrieved from www.moec.gov.cy/en/annual_ reports.html.

    (2018). *Guide to the Pancyprian examinations.* Retrieved from www.moec.gov .cy/ypexams/panexams/odigoi-exetaseon.html.

Newton, P. E. (2005). The public understanding of measurement inaccuracy. *British Educational Research Journal, 31*, 419–442. https://doi.org/10.1080/01411920500148648.

Simpson, L., & Baird, J. (2013). Perceptions of trust in public examinations. *Oxford Review of Education, 39*, 17–35. https://doi.org/10.1080/03054985.2012.760264.

Solomonidou, G., & Michaelides, M. P. (2017). Students' conceptions of assessment purposes in a low stakes secondary-school context: A mixed methodology approach. *Studies in Educational Evaluation, 52*, 35–41. https://doi.org/10.1016/j.stueduc.2016.12.001.

Statistical Service of Cyprus. (2016). *Cyprus in the EU scale.* The Press and Information Office for the Statistical Service. Retrieved from www.cystat.gov.cy.

(2017). *Statistics of education 2014/2015.* Nicosia: Republic of Cyprus.

Xi, X. (2010). How do we go about investigating test fairness? *Language Testing, 27*, 147–170. https://doi.org/10.1177/0265532209349465.

Zwick, R. (2006). Higher education admissions testing. In R. L. Brennan (Ed.). *Educational measurement* (4th ed.) (pp. 647–679). Westport, CT: American Council on Education.

CHAPTER 10

Higher Education Admissions Practices in Israel

Avi Allalouf, Yoav Cohen, and Naomi Gafni

10.1 Background: Higher Education in Israel

The higher education system in Israel is governed by The Council for Higher Education (CHE), which is responsible for allocating public funds to universities and colleges. CHE also grants accreditation to higher education institutions (HEIs) and to various departments within them. In 1990, the higher education sector in Israel consisted of seven research universities, an open university, five budgeted (public) academic colleges (offering mostly undergraduate studies), seven teacher-training colleges, and only one private college. Since 1990, as a result of the population growth in Israel (from 4.7 to 8.8 million) and increasing demands for higher education, the higher education system has undergone dramatic changes that are reflected in the number of students and in the number and types of HEIs.

As of 2018, the higher education sector in Israel consists of eight research universities, an open university, 20 budgeted (public) academic colleges, 21 teacher-training colleges, and 13 private colleges. The colleges also offer a growing number of graduate study programs. In 2018, 55 percent of undergraduate students were enrolled in academic colleges and the remainder were pursuing studies at the universities (Council for Higher Education, 2019).

10.2 Higher Education Admissions Practices in Israel

Admission to HEIs is based mostly on merit (see Wikström & Wikström, in this volume, for more detail on the merit-based admissions model). Over the past decades, admissions have been based on two criteria, usually equally weighted: matriculation exams (Bagrut Certificate [BC]) administered by the Ministry of Education (MoE) and the Psychometric Entrance Test (PET), administered by the National Institute for Testing and

Evaluation (NITE). The BC is a prerequisite for all HEIs except the Open University. The PET is developed in Hebrew and translated into Arabic and six other languages. Often, the universities (but not necessarily the other HEIs) publish the previous year's admissions cutoff scores, thus giving candidates a good indication of their chances of being accepted. Admissions criteria differ across HEIs and departments within the HEIs.

Higher education admissions officers at universities for undergraduate studies seldom use criteria such as personal interviews (except for medicine), application essays, letters of recommendation, or evidence of extracurricular activities, and never consider an applicant's parent being an alumnus of the HEI in their admissions decisions. As of 2017, the acceptance rate was about 73 percent for universities (Central Bureau of Statistics, 2018a) and about 82 percent for colleges (Central Bureau of Statistics, 2018b).

10.2.1 The Need for a Standardized, Non-Curriculum-Based, Translated/Adapted Test

Until the late 1960s, there was a single criterion for admissions: the BC score, comprised of the average of scores on external tests administered by the MoE and internal tests administered by each high school. Around 1970, the growing demand for additional selection criteria such as the use of the PET (a standardized, non-curriculum-based, translated/adapted test) emerged for four reasons, some of which are unique to Israel (see Beller, 2001). First, the BC, as a non-standardized test, did not have sufficient validity to support high-stakes inferences. Combining the BC with the PET would improve confidence in score-based inferences, especially in fields with low acceptance rates (e.g., medicine, law, and psychology). Second, the PET was needed because the BC was not comparable across populations such as students who completed the BC in Hebrew and those who completed it in other languages (e.g., Arabic). Third, admissions for immigrant populations was problematic and criteria for non-Hebrew speakers (e.g., Russian, French, English, and Spanish speakers) was needed (Beller, 1995). Fourth, the PET provided a second chance for students who did not pay much attention to studies during high school; therefore, the PET was introduced. The PET is a scholastic aptitude test constructed and administered by the National Institute for Testing and Evaluation (NITE) since 1983. It was based on similar tests that had been designed by the universities during the 1970s and early 1980s. Since 1990, PET contains three domains: verbal reasoning (V), quantitative reasoning (Q), and English as a Foreign Language (E). Considering the country's large Arab minority (21 percent of the population), the PET is translated into and adapted for Arabic.

The language of higher education instruction in Israel is Hebrew. Therefore, university candidates who do not take the PET in Hebrew are usually required to take a Hebrew proficiency test, which is used for determining admissions and placement decisions. All candidates are required to take an English placement test. The PET's E section can be used for this purpose, but there is also an English placement test that is administered separately.

10.2.2   Predictive Validity of the Admissions Tools

In contrast to the BC, the PET was created with one purpose in mind: to predict academic success. As such, the test has proved quite successful. It has been found to be a good predictor of academic success in most areas of higher education studies. Many research studies have examined the predictive validity of the PET and the BC with respect to academic performance – first-year grade point average (FPGA) and grade point average at the end of undergraduate studies (UGPA). Table 10.1 summarizes predictive validity studies (Kleper & Turvall, 2016; Kleper, Turvall, & Oren, 2014; Oren et al., 2014), based on about 100,000 students in the years 2002–2009, corrected for range restriction (Gulliksen, 1987). The predictive validity-added value of the PET over that of the BC is noteworthy: 0.09–0.10 (from 0.36 to 0.46, from 0.38 to 0.47 – an increase of 8 percent to 9 percent in explained variance).

Retention is another important criterion against which to evaluate validity. Both the PET and the BC were found to predict student retention at the universities (Haimovich & Ben-Shakhar, 2004).

One study tested the assumption that predictive validity applies to the full range of ability (and not only to the restricted range of the students

Table 10.1 *Predictive validity correlation coefficients of the admissions tools (Bagrut Certificate [BC] and Psychometric Entrance Test [PET]) against First-Year GPA (FGPA) and Undergraduate GPA (UGPA)*

Criterion	BC+PET	BC	PET and its components			
			PET	V	Q	E
FGPA	0.46	0.36	0.43	0.36	0.37	0.32
UGPA	0.47	0.38	0.41	0.34	0.33	0.31

who were above the admissions cutoff score). In that study, a random sample of applicants below the admissions cutoff score was admitted (the teachers did not have any information regarding their scores). It was found that, indeed, students who were admitted, despite poor performance on the PET, did less well than students who were above the admissions cutoff score (Ben-Shakhar, Kiderman, & Beller, 1996).

10.3 The Bagrut Certificate

In 1949, the BC was modeled after the British Advanced Level (A Level) General Certificate of Education (GCE). It is the result of a compromise between several goals and concerns. First, the BC is used as a summative assessment of a student's high school achievements. Second, the MoE uses it to control the content and the quality of secondary schooling. Third, it is required for entry to HEIs – a student's ticket to higher education and an academic degree. The three main purposes of the BC dictate its structure. The certificate has two major parts. One part reports internal evaluations of subject areas that are not externally tested. The other part reports the grades in those subject areas that are tested externally; some of these are compulsory and others elective. Each grade in the second part is a composite score, half of which is determined by an external grade and the other half by a school-based (internal) evaluation.

10.3.1 Summative Assessment of a Student's School Achievements

In order to serve its purpose as a summative assessment of students' high school achievements, the BC should reflect all of the students' coursework and academic interests. Educators insist on including every instructional activity and all forms of school assessment – examinations, teacher evaluations, portfolios, and written papers, among others. Moreover, scores of both compulsory and elective subjects are included. Thus, the BC is not standardized, and its meaning differs greatly across students.

10.3.2 Controlling Content and Quality of Secondary Schooling

The media, which have easy access to the data, frequently use the results of the BC – the number of students awarded a BC and the grades they obtained – to rank teachers, schools, and districts. These rankings seldom consider prior circumstances, such as students' academic level when entering high school.

The high stakes associated with the BC for students, teachers, and principals make it convenient for the MoE to use it as a vehicle to encourage reforms. If an external BC is based on a new syllabus, then, understandably, teachers and schools quickly follow suit. Since the purpose is to gauge the state of the education system, it is of national concern if fewer students earn the BC. On the other hand, an increasing number of students earning the BC is considered a sign of improvement in the education system.

There is, on average, a continuing increase in the proportion of students who earn the BC. The proportion of students earning the BC at the end of high school increased from 51 percent in 2000 to 64 percent in 2016 (Central Bureau of Statistics, 2018c). Although this trend is encouraging, there are doubts as to whether it represents genuine improvement in the education system. The trend could also reflect a steady decrease in the BC's difficulty level. Various changes and reforms have been made in the BC system, which might account for the increase in the proportion of BC holders. Some of the reforms were not related to instructional quality but rather to technical aspects of granting the certificate.

10.3.3   Prerequisite for Higher Education Admissions

When used as part of HEI's admissions criteria, the BC should be as objective, fair, and standardized as possible, which includes ensuring that all students taking it are evaluated on a single scale. This use conflicts directly with the demand for plurality in subject areas and assessment approaches. HEIs considering the BC for admissions purposes usually give more weight (bonus points) to grades in the compulsory subject areas. In addition, there is no way to guarantee that BCs of different cohorts will be comparable, and there is no built-in method for equating different forms of BC external tests. The use of the BC as an instrument in higher education admissions confers high-stakes status on it, which puts pressure on teachers to raise their students' grades.

10.3.4   Flexibility and Complexity

The current BC system is, on the one hand, designed to be flexible, permitting high school students to choose their preferred course of study. It is also a lenient system in the sense that students' failures are not remembered forever. Once students have retaken a test, their prior failures or low grades will not affect their chances when they apply to HEIs. The BC is meant to be a non-punitive system of positive reinforcement.

On the other hand, the system is complicated. Most students, teachers, and principals do not fully understand its intricacies. Planning a course of study in high school becomes a major problem of optimization. It is not always clear what course of study is optimal in terms of time and effort, or how it corresponds to the students' interests and strengths. This complexity also has social implications – as the system becomes more complex, the more privileged schools and students will benefit, as has been seen in other contexts. Moreover, because there are multiple ways to earn a BC and multiple combinations of fields and levels of study from which the students can choose, the BC suffers from the lack of standardization – and is therefore limited as a higher education admissions tool.

10.3.5 Bagrut Reforms

Part of the complexity of the BC is the result of the number of reforms it has undergone. Over the years, members of the Israeli parliament and Ministers of Education have initiated changes to the BC. Members of parliament accumulate political capital by exhibiting social awareness, reducing gaps between sectors of the population, and smoothing the way for students to obtain it. Ministers of Education want to make a mark early on, knowing their tenure is limited. Some of the more interesting reforms, motivated by political, social, and pedagogical concerns include the following.

10.3.5.1 Increasing Accessibility (1975)
The reform vastly increased the choices that were open to students and teachers. Instead of a small number of subject areas, students could, in theory, devise a personalized syllabus. In addition to the compulsory subjects, students could add areas of study at different levels.

10.3.5.2 Taking BC Tests Prior to the Senior Year (1993)
Originally, students were required to take all the BC tests in their senior year (Grade 12). The idea of allowing students to take certain tests in Grade 11 or even Grade 10, was aimed at enabling them to concentrate on fewer subject areas at a time. As a result of the reform, the number of students who earned the BC increased.

10.3.5.3 Lottery (1995)
The lottery reform was based on the approach that learning is more important than test performance. The Minister of Education decided that three of the seven tests in compulsory subjects would be cancelled each

year. The decision regarding which tests to cancel would be made by lottery one month before the scheduled test date. Teacher evaluations of the students' knowledge would replace the cancelled tests for the subjects in question. The result, according to this approach, would be that learning would take place up to a month before the beginning of the test season, at which time the students could concentrate their efforts on the four subjects for which Bagrut tests would be held. The result was a significant increase in average grades and in the number of students who earned a certificate. This reform, despite the clever rationale behind it, met with harsh criticism, and the lottery system was discontinued within a couple of years.

10.3.5.4 Focusing (1997)

The next reform was initiated for both pedagogical and political reasons. Cancelling the lottery meant that the students would be tested on a heavier syllabus. The majority of high school students saw this as a burden and objected to the cancellation of the lottery. The compromise was that students would have to sit all seven examinations, but each would focus on only four-sevenths of the syllabus. Exactly which parts of the syllabus were to be the focus of the exam would be decided and publicized one month before the beginning of the testing season.

10.3.5.5 Changing the Weight of Internal Assessment (2014)

A recent reform was motivated by pedagogical concerns as one of the main goals behind it was to increase the autonomy of schools in determining the curriculum. As was mentioned above, the grades on the BC were composed of internal and external test averages, equally weighted. One change was that 70 percent of the grade in each subject matter would be determined as before, and 30 percent would be determined by internal assessment on a syllabus, which the school was free to devise. The result was that the weight of external assessment was reduced to 35 percent.

The frequent changes in the structure and content of the BC tests (including some not listed above), as well as the lack of standardization, explain, in part, the inclusion of PET scores as a key tool in the higher education admissions process.

10.4 The Psychometric Entrance Test

The second admissions criterion for HEIs is the PET (Beller, 1994; Oren et al., 2014). It is administered four times a year, and the test forms (within and across years) are equated. A unique feature of the PET is that parallel forms are available in Hebrew, Arabic, English, French, Russian, Spanish, Italian, and Portuguese. A special version also is available for examinees whose native language differs from those above; the questions appear in Hebrew and English with difficult terms translated into additional languages. To create equivalent forms, the versions are linked. One may take the PET an unlimited number of times. The results are valid for at least seven academic years following the test date. Results are reported to the examinees, to all the universities, and to other HEIs the examinee requested as score recipients.

In 2018, the test consisted of three timed sections in V, Q, and E. The V domain has 46 multiple-choice (MC) questions and an essay. The Q and E sections have 40 and 44 MC questions, respectively. The V domain assesses verbal skills and the ability to analyze and understand complex written material, to think clearly and systematically, and to perceive fine distinctions of meaning among words and concepts. The Q domain tests the ability to use numbers and mathematical concepts to solve problems and analyze information presented in different forms, such as graphs, tables, and charts. Mathematical reasoning rather than mathematical knowledge is assessed; hence, only a relatively basic knowledge of mathematics is necessary. The E domain tests the skills involved in understanding academic-level texts in English.

Three PET General scores on a common scale are computed and reported: PET General is weighted 2V+2Q+E; PET Verbal is weighted 3V+Q+E; and PET Quantitative is weighted 3Q+V+E. Each HEI decides which PET score to use for admissions decisions. In addition to the paper-and-pencil forms, there are computerized adaptive (CAT) forms intended for examinees with learning disabilities (Cohen et al., 2008; Gafni et al., 2009). The indices for internal consistency of the total score reach .95 (Kennet-Cohen, 2016). Test–retest reliability is about .90 when the retest takes place no more than one year after the initial test. The three domains of the PET are relatively unidimensional, and the factorial structure of the test is relatively stable (Kleper & Saka, 2017).

10.4.1 PET Fairness

10.4.1.1 Language, Cultural, and Social Subgroups.
There is ongoing debate, both within and outside HEIs, as to what constitutes proper admissions procedures. Advocates for certain social groups, such as Israeli Arabs, new immigrants (mainly from Ethiopia),

and students from lower socioeconomic backgrounds, argue that the admissions process is biased against these groups. While it is true that these groups are under-represented in higher education, careful examination reveals (see below and Section 10.4.1.2) that their scores for admissions purposes are usually on a par with their academic achievement, both at the end of freshman year and at graduation. However, universities are not oblivious to social issues and reserve a small proportion of places for admissions by affirmative action. Test fairness is an important issue. The fairness of the PET and the BC for various social groups has been examined in previous research: Studies have found the PET to be unbiased toward, or, sometimes, even biased in favor of, Arab-speaking examinees (Kennet-Cohen, Turvall, & Oren, 2014) and Russian-speaking examinees (Gafni & Bronner, 1998; Kennet-Cohen, 1993). As of 2017, women comprised about 54 percent of the candidates for the universities, compared to 57 percent for the colleges (Central Bureau of Statistics, 2018d). The PET has been found to favor men, while the BC has been found to favor women; however, the combined score, which is generally used for admissions – (BC+PET)/2 – was found to be fair to both genders (Azen, Bronner, & Gafni, 2002; Kennet-Cohen, Turvall, & Oren, 2014).

While the Cleary model of differential prediction (Cleary, 1968) was used in all studies, additional definitions of fair selection also were examined. For example, boundary conditions for differential prediction (Linn, 1984), and the difference between Cohen's d (Cohen, 2013), which is derived from the Constant Ratio Model (Darlington, 1971; Thorndike, 1971), were added in the more recent research (Kennet-Cohen, Turvall, & Oren, 2014).

10.4.1.2   Test Accommodations
Another area which is related to fairness is test accommodations. NITE evaluates clinical diagnostic reports and provides test accommodations to examinees recognized as having learning disabilities. Many of the examinees use the MATAL – a computer-based test battery for the diagnosis of learning disabilities (Ben-Simon et al., 2008). Most accommodations take the form of modifications in the administration of the test (e.g., extended testing time, breaks between chapters, enlarged test forms, and use of a computerized adaptive version of the PET). The validity and fairness of the PET accommodations were studied and found to be satisfactory (Kleper et al., 2013).

10.4.1.3   Coaching
There is a thriving industry of PET coaching, and because the courses are quite expensive, coaching has become a major source of the criticism

directed at PET and of the frequent calls to eliminate the test. The popular argument is that the rich (who can afford coaching) score higher and thus have an unfair advantage over the rest of the students. Examinees believe that taking a course is a must. As a result, currently, about 90 percent of PET examinees complete a coaching course before taking the test. Several studies have shed light on the perceived necessity of taking a course and on how a course affects the test outcome. It was found that the gains from short-term coaching are no greater than those achieved by repeat testing, and that coaching courses have a rather small impact on score gains, as compared to self-preparation: about 10 points, which is equal to one-tenth standard deviation (Goldzweig, Oren, & Saar, 2014). In addition, and perhaps more importantly, it was found that coaching does not reduce the predictive validity of the test (Allalouf & Ben-Shakhar, 1998).

10.4.2   PET Reform

The PET, which has undergone fewer changes than the BC, has been the target of both public and political criticism. Members of Israel's parliament continually criticize the test's content and question its necessity as a selection tool in addition to the BC. Over the years, parliament members have introduced numerous proposals to abolish the PET, but none has been accepted. In 2003, by way of compromise in response to yet another proposal in parliament to abolish the test (and to improve the admissions chances of disadvantaged candidates), the universities agreed to a change regarding scores used for admissions purposes. Instead of accepting applicants based on a single combined score (average of BC and PET), universities accepted them on the basis of the higher of the two: BC or PET. Thus, the PET was no longer mandatory, but optional. The new system was less valid and less fair; candidates with high, and likely inflated, BC were accepted in larger proportions. Furthermore, the change did not necessarily improve the chances of admitting disadvantaged applicants. Not surprisingly, the previous system – the average of BC and PET – was reinstated only one year later.

However, given the pace of change in the Israeli political system, there is always the possibility that the admissions method will flip back again. When first introduced in 1983, the test comprised five MC-based subtests – verbal, quantitative, English, figures, and general knowledge. Several key changes have been made to the PET since that time.

10.4.2.1   Eliminating Figures and General Knowledge (1990)
In the light of cumulative predictive validity results, it was decided in 1990 to revise the PET and restructure it. The components that were

found to have greater validity – verbal, quantitative, and English – were expanded, while the components found to be relatively less valid (general knowledge and figures) were eliminated (Beller, 1994).

10.4.2.2 Three Changes (2011/2012)

During the years 1990–2010, numerous proposals to abolish the PET were presented in the Israeli parliament. All were withdrawn. In 2010, a member of parliament garnered considerable support for a new law to abolish the PET. However, she withdrew her proposal after NITE modified the PET to strengthen the connection between test scores and the proficiencies needed for academic studies. These changes had, in fact, already been discussed by NITE; the political pressure secured them. Three changes were introduced (see Oren et al., 2014):

- Calculating three general scores (instead of one) makes it possible to give greater weight to either the quantitative score (for admissions to engineering and the sciences) or the verbal score (for admissions to law and the humanities).
- Several item types with lower face validity were removed from the verbal and quantitative subtests. One of the item types removed was vocabulary, in response to widespread criticism related to the many hours spent by examinees on rote memorization of lists of words and their meanings.
- Adding a writing task to the verbal domain was the major change. The examinees are given a single prompt of up to ten lines and are required to write an essay (30–50 lines) in 30 minutes. The essay can be written in any of the PET languages. The essay is assessed by two examiners or raters, and its weight is 25 percent of the verbal score (see Cohen, 2017, for a study regarding intra-rater reliability for the PET writing task).

It seems that these three changes achieved their goals. The examinees, although faced with a new, unfamiliar situation – the writing task – accepted this change with no negative response. Some of the HEIs now use the new general scores. The media response was also positive. Reliability and predictive validity were not affected (Kennet-Cohen & Saar, 2017).

10.5   Alternative and Additional Admissions Routes

In an attempt to resolve some of the conflicting pressures of academic requirements and social need, HEIs in Israel use various alternative routes for admissions, some of which are quite recent.

- Bagrut Only. Candidates whose BC score is above a certain threshold are admitted without being required to take the PET. This method is not employed in the more competitive and selective areas of study, such as medicine and computer science. It is used more in the colleges than in the universities.
- Best 5 Percent. There is a possibility for the best 5 percent of students from high schools to be admitted. Some faculties (e.g., law) admit candidates whose score on the BC is among the top 5 percent at their school, regardless of which school it is.
- Different Admissions Tools. A different admissions test may be used for certain populations, such as new immigrants from Ethiopia. Those who are admitted are entitled to academic mentoring as well as financial aid, which is essential. This method is used in a few HEIs.
- Noncognitive Tools. For certain fields (e.g., medicine), additional non-cognitive admissions tools may be used, such as a standardized personal questionnaire, as well as multiple mini-interviews and behavioral simu-lations (Gafni et al., 2012; Hadad et al., 2016; Kennet-Cohen et al., 2016; Moshinsky, Ziegler, & Gafni, 2017; Ziv et al., 2008).
- Pre-Academic Preparatory Programs. In some cases, the BC or PET scores may be replaced by those received in pre-academic preparatory programs.
- Open University Courses. Admissions to some areas of study can be on the basis of certain courses offered by the Open University.
- Using MOOCs (Massive Open Online Courses). This is the most recent route. In some of the faculties in one university, successful completion of three MOOCs (above a certain score) can replace the PET score.

10.6 Conclusion

Admission to HEIs in Israel is mainly merit-based. This chapter has described the basic requirements for acceptance to bachelor's degree pro-grams in Israel: The BC, PET, and the Hebrew Proficiency test for non-Hebrew-speaking candidates (in accordance with the criteria set by the particular university and department). Certain institutions and depart-ments have additional requirements (e.g., personal interviews or additional tests). Certain faculties and departments, such as medicine, dental medi-cine, law, psychology, engineering, and pharmacy have rather demanding admissions requirements.

The BC is a national certificate issued by the MoE. The PET is an examination, which was established at the behest of the universities in Israel and developed by NITE. In general, university admissions offices use the combined score of the BC and PET, which was found to be a good predictor of both academic achievement and student retention. The predictive validity of this combined score has proved to be better than that of either of the two scores taken alone. The added value of the PET over that of the BC to the predictive validity correlation has been substantial. The issues we face in Israel are similar to those in other countries. Testing, particularly high-stakes testing for admissions purposes and in the certification and ranking of schools, is strongly associated with social issues and thus with the political domain. The two admissions tools mentioned have been the target of both public and political criticism and have undergone reforms that stemmed from the need to find a compromise between conflicting interests. On one hand, the aim is to provide education for as many people as possible and in particular for those from lower socioeconomic backgrounds; on the other hand, there is the desire to attain as high a level of academic achievement as possible.

Although the BC was created with noble intentions and high expectations, over time, it has become complicated, expensive, and expansive. In trying to serve multiple goals, it has grown into an unmanageable system, which can serve none of those goals satisfactorily. The main problem with using the BC alone is that it is a non-standardized tool. It was for this reason that the PET, a standardized and valid tool, was introduced for use in addition to the BC. The fairness of the PET and the BC for various social groups has been studied in previous research; in general, combining BC and PET has been shown to be fair.

During the last ten years, Israeli higher education has undergone changes. Rather than choosing from among seven research universities, students now have access to some 60 public and private institutions. In trying to resolve the conflicting pressures of academic requirement and social need, HEIs in Israel use additional alternative routes for admissions. The expansion of the system has led to more competition among the institutions seeking to attract candidates, which, in turn, has resulted in an easing of acceptance criteria and, unfortunately, a lowering of the level of studies.

REFERENCES

Allalouf, A., & Ben-Shakhar, G. (1998). The effect of coaching on the predictive validity of scholastic aptitude tests. *Journal of Educational Measurement, 35,* 31–47. https://doi.org/10.1111/j.1745-3984.1998.tb00526.x.

Azen, R., Bronner, S., & Gafni, N. (2002). Examination of gender bias in university admissions. *Applied Measurement in Education, 15*, 75–94. https://doi.org/10.1207/S15324818AME1501_05.

Beller, M. (1994). Psychometric and social issues in admissions to Israeli universities. *Educational Measurement: Issues and Practice, 13*(2), 12–20. https://doi.org/10.1111/j.1745-3992.1994.tb00791.x.

(1995). Translated versions of Israel's inter-university Psychometric Entrance Test (PET). In T. Oakland & R. K. Hambleton (Eds.). *International perspectives on academic assessment* (pp. 207–218). Boston, MA: Kluwer. https://doi.org/10.1007/978-94-011-0639-9_12.

(2001). Admission to higher education in Israel and the role of the psychometric entrance test: Educational, social, and political dilemmas [Special issue]. *Assessment in Education: Principles, Policy & Practice, 8*, 317–337. https://doi.org/10.1080/09695940120089125.

Ben-Shakhar, G., Kiderman, I., & Beller, M. (1996). Comparing the utility of two procedures for admitting students to liberal arts: An application of decision-theoretic models. *Educational and Psychological Measurement, 56*, 90–107. https://doi.org/10.1177/0013164496056001006.

Ben-Simon, A., Beyth-Marom, R., Inbar-Weiss, N., & Cohen, Y. (2008). *Regulation of learning disability diagnosis and test accommodation provision in institutions of higher education* (Report No. 383). Jerusalem: National Institute for Testing and Evaluation.

Central Bureau of Statistics. (2018a). *Statistical abstracts of Israel 2018: table 8.56. Applicants for first year studies toward a first degree in universities, by first preferred field of study, sex, age, population group, and by results of application.* Retrieved from https://old.cbs.gov.il/reader/shnaton/templ_shnaton.html?num_tab=sto8_56&CYear=2018.

(2018b). *Statistical abstracts of Israel 2018: table 8.57. Applicants for first year studies toward a first degree in academic colleges, by first preferred field of study, sex, age, population group, and by results of application.* Retrieved from https://old.cbs.gov.il/reader/shnaton/templ_shnaton_e.html?num_tab=sto8_57&CYear=2018.

(2018c). *Statistical Abstracts of Israel 2018: table 8.19. Students in 12th Grade: Matriculation examinees and those entitled to a certificate.* Retrieved from https://old.cbs.gov.il/reader/shnaton/templ_shnaton_e.html?num_tab=sto8_19&CYear=2018.

(2018d). *Statistical Abstracts of Israel 2018: table 8.61. Students in universities, academic colleges and academic colleges of education by degree, sex, age, population group and district of residence.* Retrieved from https://old.cbs.gov.il/reader/shnaton/templ_shnaton_e.html?num_tab=sto8_61&CYear=2018.

Cleary, T. A. (1968). Test bias: Prediction of grades of Negro and white students in integrated colleges. *Journal of Educational Measurement, 5*, 115–124. https://doi.org/10.1111/j.1745-3984.1968.tb00613.x.

Cohen, J. (2013). *Statistical power analysis for the behavioral sciences.* Philadelphia, PA: Routledge, Taylor, and Francis.

Cohen, Y. (2017). Estimating the intra-rater reliability of essay raters. *Frontiers in Education*. https://doi.org/10.3389/feduc.2017.00049.

Cohen, Y., Ben-Simon, A., Moshinsky, A., & Eitan, M. (2008). *Computer-based testing (CBT) in the service of test accommodations*. Jerusalem: National Institute for Testing and Evaluation.

Council for Higher Education. (2019). *Collection of data for start of year: table 1. Students in institutions of higher education by level of degree and type of institution*. Retrieved from https://che.org.il/en/statistical-data/.

Darlington, R. B. (1971). Another look at "cultural fairness." *Journal of Educational Measurement, 8,* 71–82. https://doi.org/10.1111/j.1745-3984.1971.tb00908.x.

Gafni, N., & Bronner, S. (1998). *An examination of criterion-related bias in the testing of Hebrew- and Russian-speaking examinees in Israel*. Jerusalem: National Institute for Testing and Evaluation.

Gafni, N., Cohen, Y., Roded, K., Baumer, M., & Moshinsky, A. (2009). *Applications of CAT in admissions to higher education in Israel: Twenty-two years of experience*. Jerusalem: National Institute for Testing and Evaluation.

Gafni, N., Moshinsky, A., Eisenberg, O., Ziegler, D., & Ziv, A. (2012). Reliability estimates: Behavioral stations and questionnaires in medical school admissions. *Medical Education, 46,* 277–288. https://doi.org/10.1111/j.1365-2923.2011.04155.x.

Goldzweig, Oren, & Saar, Y. 2014).
התועלת של קורסי הכנה מסחריים לבחינה הפסיכומטרית בהשוואה להכנה בקרב עצמית נבחני עברית וערבית, [The effect of commercial coaching courses for PET in comparison to self-coaching in Hebrew and Arabic] (Report 405). Jerusalem: National Institute for Testing & Evaluation.

Gulliksen, H. (1987). *Theory of mental tests*. Hillsdale, NJ: Erlbaum.

Hadad, A., Gafni, N., Moshinsky, A., Turvall, E., Ziv, A., & Israeli, A. (2016). The multiple mini-interviews as a predictor of peer evaluations during clinical training in medical school. *Medical Teacher, 38,* 1172–1179. https://doi.org/10.1080/0142159X.2016.1181730.

Haimovich, T., & Ben-Shakhar, G. (2004).
סיום תואר ונשירה בחינת הבגרות ומבחן הכניסה הפסיכומטרי לאוניברסיטאות כמנבאי [The matriculation certificate grades (Bagrut) and the score on the Psychometric Entrance Test (PET) as predictors of graduation and attrition]. *Megamot, 43,* 446–470.

Kennet-Cohen, T. (1993). *An examination of predictive bias: The Russian version of the psychometric entrance test for Israeli universities*. Jerusalem: National Institute for Testing and Evaluation.

(2016). The reliability and validity of PET. Retrieved from https://nite.org.il/files/rel_val.pdf.

Kennet-Cohen, T., & Saar, Y. (2017). *Adding a writing task to a university admissions test: An evaluation of short-term consequences*. Paper presented at the annual AEA-Europe Conference, Prague, Czech Republic.

Kennet-Cohen, T., Turvall, E., & Oren, C. (2014). Detecting bias in selection for higher education: Three different methods. *Assessment in Education: Principles, Policy & Practice, 21*, 193–204. https://doi.org/10.1080/0969594X.2013.877871.

Kennet-Cohen, T., Turvall, E., Saar, Y., & Oren, C. (2016). The predictive validity of a two-step selection process to medical schools. *Journal of Biomedical Education, 2016*, 1-6. http://dx.doi.org/10.1155/2016/8910471.

Kleper, D. & Turvall, E. (2016). ניתוח-על של תוקף הניבוי של הבחינה הפסיכומטרית [A meta-analysis of the predictive validity of the Psychometric Entrance Test] (RR16–02). Jerusalem: National Institute for Testing and Evaluation.

Kleper, D., Turvall, E., & Oren, C. (2014).
בוגר תוקף הניבוי של כלי המיון לאוניברסיטאות בישראל מול ממוצע תואר [Predictive validity of the PET in predicting higher first year GPA]. (RR 403) Jerusalem: National Institute for Testing and Evaluation.

Kleper, D., & Saka, N. (2017). General ability or distinct scholastic aptitudes? A multidimensional validity analysis of the psychometric higher education entrance test. *Journal of Applied Measurement, 18*, 194–214.

Kleper, D., Turvall, E., Kennet-Cohen, T., & Oren, C. (2013)
מבקשי תנאים מותאמים בבחינה הפסיכומטרית הוגנות מערכת המיון להשכלה הגבוהה כלפי [Examining the fairness of higher education admissions for applicants who request test accommodations] (RR-386). Jerusalem: National Institute for Testing and Evaluation.

Linn, R. L. (1984). Selection bias: Multiple meanings. *Journal of Educational Measurement, 21*, 33–47.

Moshinsky, A., Ziegler, D., & Gafni, N. (2017). Multiple mini-interviews in the age of the Internet: Does preparation help applicants to medical school? *International Journal of Testing, 17*, 253–268. https://doi.org/10.1080/15305058.2016.1263638.

Oren, C., Kennet-Cohen, T., Turvall, E., & Allalouf, A. (2014). Demonstrating the validity of three general scores of PET in predicting higher education achievement in Israel. *Psicothema, 2*, 117–126. https://doi.org/10.7334/psicothema.2013.257.

Thorndike, R. L. (1971). Concepts of culture fairness. *Journal of Educational Measurement, 8*, 63–70.

Ziv, A., Rubin, O., Moshinsky, A., Gafni, N., Kotler, M., Dagan, Y., & Mittelman, M. (2008). MOR: a simulation-based assessment centre for evaluating the personal and interpersonal qualities of medical school candidates. *Medical Education, 42*, 991–998. https://doi.org/10.1111/j.1365-2923.2008.03161.x

CHAPTER 11

Access, Equity, and Admissions in South African Higher Education

Naziema Jappie

Promoting student access in higher education institutions (HEIs) in South Africa remains a challenge given the limitations and resources those institutions face. The 1997 Education White Paper 3: "A programme for transformation of higher education," stated that there is an "inequitable distribution of access and opportunity for students and staff along lines of race, gender, class, and geography. There are gross discrepancies in the participation rates of students from different population groups" (Republic of South Africa Department of Education [DOE], 1997, p. 8). In addition, the 2001 National Development Plan (NDP) clearly intended to develop a system of higher education that will "promote equity of access and fair chances of success to all who are seeking to realise their potential through higher education, while eradicating all forms of unfair discrimination and advancing redress for past inequalities" (Republic of South Africa DOE, 2001, p. 6).

More than two decades after apartheid, the higher education sector is still struggling to strike a balance between access and success, which is evident in high drop-out rates and low graduation rates. The regulation and management of access and admissions in higher education is a complex and challenging issue. Given the complexities of the transition from apartheid and the transformation agenda in higher education, this chapter first provides a brief historical context of South African education that gave rise to the challenges of access and admissions to higher education. The new democratic transition of educational policies and practices is explained next, showing the intention of transformation in higher education admissions practices. The chapter concludes with remarks about the future of postsecondary education in South Africa.

11.1 Historical Context

Prior to the 1800s, higher education was commonly reserved for those who could travel to Europe. In 1829, the government established the first institution of higher education, the South African College, which later became the University of Cape Town (UCT). Subsequently, the independent state of the Transvaal (1852) and the Orange Free State (1854) established their own institutions. The Grey College became the University of Free State in 1855 and today is known as the University of the Free State. In 1869, the Christian College in Potchefstroom was established. It was later incorporated into the University of South Africa and renamed Potchefstroom University for Christian Higher Education (Byrnes, 1997).

In 1959, the Extension of University Education Act prohibited universities from accepting most Black students, although the government did establish universities for Black, Colored, and Indian students (Ocampo, 2004). During apartheid, between 1948 and 1994, HEIs were reserved for different racial, ethnic, and linguistic groups. Both historically White and historically Black institutions were products of apartheid planning and functionally differentiated to maintain the ideology of separate development. This racially structured differentiation was accompanied by a set of conditions that included finances and infrastructure that disadvantaged the historically Black institutions. The fiscal allocation in terms of race, where the education of Whites enjoyed more funding, resulted in wide-scale disparities with regard to all aspects of education.

By 1994, there were 36 racially divided HEIs in South Africa. With the constitutional democracy created in 1994, all South African HEIs had to be liberated from the apartheid policies. The Republic of South Africa Department of Education (1997) noted that many of the institutions required consolidation or retooling for new missions and goals. The policy also noted that there was a need to diversify the educational system in terms of the mix of institutional missions and programs that were required to meet national and regional needs in terms of social, cultural, and economic development.

In 1994, a process of restructuring post-apartheid higher education began by merging and creating 23 institutions by 2005. Three other institutions were subsequently established, bringing the total to 26. Although South Africa has 11 official languages, English is the medium of instruction at almost all institutions, with a few institutions still teaching some programs in Afrikaans.

The present higher education institutional landscape is a major advance compared to that of 1994. However, in the absence of development strategies and institutional redress to enable them to build their capabilities and capacities to address social and educational needs, historically Black institutions have had concerns that a policy of differentiation and diversity could continue the old historical patterns of disadvantage and advantage. There was scope for inter-university collaboration with differentiated research, teaching, technological, and comprehensive universities. Universities had to examine their course and degree offerings so that there could be mobility of students between the different universities.

Interestingly, enrollment figures have doubled since 1993, at which time there were 473,000 students. Black students constituted 52 percent and women 43 percent of the total. In 2009, of the 837,000 students, 78 percent were Black and 57 percent were women (Republic of South Africa Department of Higher Education and Training [DHET], 2015). In 2016, there were 26 public HEIs and 123 registered private HEIs. Enrollment at public and private HEIs reached 1.1 million in 2015, with public institutions enrolling 975,837 students. The target set out by the National Development Plan (NDP), which was launched in August 2012, is 1.6 million students to be enrolled in HEIs by 2030.

11.2 Transition toward Fair and Equal Admissions to Higher Education

11.2.1 The Higher Education Act of 1997

The Higher Education Act 101 of 1997 (Republic of South Africa, 1997) applies to higher education in the Republic of South Africa. Under the Act, the Minister of Education is tasked with establishing a Council on Higher Education (CHE) to determine higher education policy. The Minister must also publish such policy by notice in the *Government Gazette*.

The Preamble to the Act (1997) states as follows:

> *Establish* a single coordinated higher education system which promotes co-operative governance and provides for programme-based higher education;
> *Restructure and Transform* programmes and institutions to respond better to the human resource, economic and development needs of the Republic;
> *Redress* past discrimination and ensure representivity and equal access;
> *Provide* optimal opportunities for learning and the creation of knowledge;
> *Promote* the values which underlie an open and democratic society based on human dignity, equality and freedom;
> *Respect* freedom of religion, belief and opinion;
> *Respect* and encourage democracy, academic freedom, freedom of speech and expression, creativity, scholarship and research;
> *Pursue* excellence, promote the full realisation of the potential of every student and employee, tolerance of ideas and appreciation of diversity;

Respond to the needs of the Republic and of the communities served by the institutions;

Contribute to the advancement of all forms of knowledge and scholarship, in keeping with international standards of academic quality;

And whereas it is desirable for higher education institutions to enjoy freedom and autonomy in their relationship with the State within the context of public accountability and the national need for advanced skills and scientific knowledge. (pp. 1–2)

11.2.2 Functions of the Council on Higher Education

The CHE may advise the Minister on any aspect of higher education on its own initiative and must advise the Minister on any aspect of higher education at the request of the Minister. The key functions of the CHE are to promote quality assurance, accredit programs, and publish information regarding developments in higher education for the promotion of access of students to higher education. The CHE also provides structure and planning, allocates funding, and examines governance issues for higher education. Moreover, it monitors and evaluates the progress of transformation within the higher education sector and provides regular reports on the admission, program enrollment, and graduation rates of the sector. It is mandatory that every publicly funded science, research, and professional council, and every HEI provides the CHE with such information as the CHE may reasonably require for the performance of its functions in terms of this Act.

11.3 Admissions Policies, Practices, and Criteria

In South Africa, each university has the authority to decide how and who to admit based on the policies and published criteria, which must be available to everyone. In order to be admitted, the student must meet particular requirements to be eligible for admissions. In addition, students have to undergo rigorous interviews, produce portfolios, and, in some cases, pass a standardized assessment at a proficient level. Eligibility for admissions does not give an automatic right of entrance in certain areas of study such as medicine, engineering, performing arts, and science.

11.3.1 National Senior Certificate

In South Africa, matriculation (or matric) is used to refer to the final year of high school and the qualification received on graduating from high school. The school-leaving exams, which are government administered, are known as the matric exams. Obtaining a matric is the minimum qualification required for university entrance. Officially, the qualification obtained at the end of secondary schooling is the National Senior Certificate (NSC), and the school-leaving examinations are the Senior Certificate Examinations. The NSC was first issued in 2008 and implemented beginning in January 2009.

Learner performance is reported by level according to system national codes and descriptors which explain what each percentage mark received means:

- Level 7: 80–100% (Outstanding achievement)
- Level 6: 70–79% (Meritorious achievement)
- Level 5: 60–69% (Substantial achievement)
- Level 4: 50–59% (Adequate achievement)
- Level 3: 40–49% (Moderate achievement)
- Level 2: 30–39% (Elementary achievement)
- Level 1: 0–29% (Not achieved: Fail)

Students who fulfill certain requirements (who receive an achievement rating of 4: Adequate achievement, or better, in four designated subjects) on their senior certificate results also receive a matriculation endorsement/bachelor's pass on their certificates (Department of Education, 2005a). This endorsement is the legal minimum requirement for admission to a bachelor's degree at any South African university. Students applying to a South African university with foreign school qualifications can obtain a matriculation exemption to show that they meet the same standards.

This multiple meaning can lead to confusion. For example, the statement that a person *passed matric* or *has their matric* may mean either that they received a senior certificate (i.e., they finished high school) or that they received a senior certificate with matriculation endorsement (i.e., they are eligible to enter university).

11.3.2   *Minimum Requirements for Admissions*

The Department of Education (1997) proposed a single qualifications framework for higher education. The purpose of the National Qualifications Framework is to provide guidelines on the statutory minimum admission requirements in terms of the NSC, whose specifications were approved by the Minister of Education. There are three types of programs at the undergraduate higher education level: higher certificate, diploma, and bachelor's degree. Each of these has specific admissions criteria (Republic of South Africa Department of Education, 2005b).

11.3.2.1 Higher Certificate

For the higher certificate, the minimum admission requirement is an NSC, with a minimum of 30 percent (2: Elementary achievement) in the language of learning and teaching of the higher education institution, as certified by the Council for General and Further Education and Training (known as Umalusi). Institutional and program needs may require additional combinations or recognized NSC subjects and levels of achievement. For example, an institution may determine that a higher certificate in architectural design requires, in addition to the NSC, a specified level of attainment in design and an associated recognized subject.

11.3.2.2 Diploma

For the diploma, the minimum admission requirement is an NSC with a minimum of 30 percent (2: Elementary achievement) in the language of learning and teaching of the higher education institution, as certified by Umalusi, coupled with an achievement rating of 3: Moderate achievement, or better, in four recognized 20-credit subjects. Institution and program needs may require additional combinations of recognized NSC subjects and levels of achievement. For example, a diploma in data metrics might require a pass score at a specified level in mathematics or information technology.

11.3.2.3 Bachelor's Degree

In November 2018, the Minister of Higher Education and Training amended the minimum admissions requirement for a bachelor's degree (Department of Higher Education and Training, 2018). The new requirement was applied retroactively to August 1, 2018.

The biggest change impacts the 20-credit NSC subject requirement. Previously, matrics needed to pass four subjects from a designated list of 18 subjects: accounting, agricultural sciences, business studies, dramatic arts, economics, engineering graphics and design, geography, history, consumer studies, information technology, languages, life sciences, mathematics, mathematical literacy, music, physical sciences, religion studies, and visual arts. In March 2018, the Department of Higher Education revoked the country's designated list of subjects, effectively making all 20 credit-bearing subjects offered as part of the NSC of equal status, with the exception of the subject life orientation. Requirements for bachelor's entry now include a National Senior Certificate (NSC) with a minimum of 30 percent (2: Elementary achievement) in the language of learning and teaching of the higher education institution, as certified by Umalusi, and an achievement rating higher than 50 percent (4: adequate achievement) for any other four subjects, excluding life orientation.

These requirements work with the pass requirements to achieve the NSC, making the following the minimum requirements to gain entry to a bachelor's degree program:

- Receive a minimum of 30 percent (2: Elementary achievement) in the language of learning and teaching of the higher education institution, as certified by Umalusi,
- Pass one official language at home language level at 40 percent (3: Moderate achievement), or more,
- Pass four subjects at 50 percent (4: Adequate achievement), or more, excluding life orientation, and
- Pass two other subjects at a minimum of 30 percent (2: Elementary achievement) (Department of Higher Education and Training, 2018).

However, HEIs are entitled to specify an appropriate level of subject achievement for a particular program. The change in policy by the minister has been criticized by some universities saying that it would make it easier for matrics to now attain entry into a bachelor's program (BusinessTech, 2018). Each year, universities are faced with challenges related to admissions of students to various programs for the bachelor's degree.

It must be noted that each HEI has its own set of admissions policies. One of the key aspects of the admissions policy is to ensure transformation to address issues of equity and fairness. Each HEI also has a set of criteria to indicate a student's eligibility to be considered for admissions, which are based on requirements for the degree program. Professor Saleem Badat (2011) stated that "an admissions policy needs to reflect the engagement of the University with the apartheid legacy, the current social structure, constitutional, legislative, and other social imperatives, and the institution's engagement with the concepts of social equity and redress." Therefore, it can be argued that institutions with admissions policies that confine themselves to addressing academic success only must also take into consideration issues of race, class, and gender, thus helping to erode social inequalities.

11.3.3   The National Benchmark Tests

Many South African universities use standardized entrance tests of linguistic, numerical, and mathematical ability, called the National Benchmark Tests (NBTs). The NBTs contains two tests, the Academic Literacy and

Quantitative Literacy Test (AQL) and the Mathematics Test. The NBT is forward-looking in that it assesses the learner's potential and ability to succeed in their first year at the university. Scores are presented in three levels: proficient, intermediate, and basic. These provide guidelines to universities on how to interpret the NBT scores.

The objectives of the test are to

- assess the entry-level academic literacy and quantitative literacy and mathematics proficiency of students,
- assess the relationship between higher education entry-level requirements and secondary-school-level exit outcomes,
- provide a service to HEIs that require additional information to assist in selection and placement of students in appropriate curricular routes (e.g., regular, extended, augmented, or other), and
- assist with curriculum development, particularly in relation to foundational and augmented courses.

11.3.4 Policy Considerations

Each university has a vision, a mission, and a values statement that describe their transformation agenda for access and admissions. For example, the University of Cape Town adopted the following:

> We are committed to utilising our resources to widen educational and social opportunities, enhance the quality of life of individuals and communities, build an equitable social order based on respect for human rights, and advance the public good through knowledge generation, teaching and active engagement with key challenges facing our society – South African, continental and global. (University of Cape Town, 2016, p. 5)

Other institutions have also published their statements on their institutional websites.

The Higher Education Act 101 of 1997 (Republic of South Africa, 1997) ensures that HEI policies, including admissions policies, are created with due regard for their relationship to and influence on education and training in other sectors. Institutions' admissions requirements, policies, and practice are expected to advance the objectives of the Higher Education Act and the National Qualifications Framework and must be consistent with the Minister's policies in terms of the Act. In particular, such requirements, policies, and practices are expected to advance the objectives of redress, equity, and quality in higher education. Badat (2011) asserts that commitment to social equity and diversity of the student body, and

affirmative action as a strategy to achieve their realization, have implications for student recruitment, admissions, and support. Consequentially,
the Act outlines the statutory minimum or threshold norms for admission
to the undergraduate higher certificate, diploma, and bachelor's degree
programs. Such norms apply to all public and private higher education
institutions.

Although the NSC is the primary gateway between school and higher
education, it does not guarantee a learner's admission to any program of
study in higher education. Moore (2005) argues that there is widespread
misunderstanding of the issues of eligibility and admission. As she notes,
"the first step in the admissions process is determining the eligibility of
applicants. All students must be eligible to be considered for admission,
meaning they must meet all of the quantitative university requirements
before they can apply." Within the context of this policy, the right of HEIs
to set specific admissions requirements to particular programs is confirmed
in Section 37 of the Higher Education Act (Republic of South Africa, 1997).

Many adult learners who have not achieved an NSC or equivalent
qualification can benefit from higher education. In keeping with the
objectives of the National Qualifications Framework, the Ministry of
Education supports wider and more diverse access to higher education
and fairer progression pathways within the system. As a result, institutional
admissions policies must allow for alternative routes of entry that are
equivalent to the NSC standard, including the assessment of an adult
learner's capacity to benefit from a particular program by the Recognition
of Prior Learning (South African Qualifications Authority, 2009) for
professional development.

11.4   Access, Success, and Sustainability

Access to higher education is an aspiration of every youth in the country
who views this as a pathway to a brighter future. In South Africa, students
from lower socioeconomic backgrounds find it challenging to gain access
to higher education, for various reasons, such as poor schooling, and many
students are unable to meet the minimum requirements for admissions
and funding. This is a serious problem, especially since university fees are
high and financial aid not readily available. Poor academic preparation at
school has been known to disadvantage students who pursue higher
education. Manik (2015) has commented that the price that HEIs in
South Africa pay in increasing access to students who have poor matric

results is the domino effect of their dropout rates. That is, while these students have been provided with an opportunity to be in a university, they lack the preparedness for sustained study in a higher education environment, which demands that students be independent learners.

Even with all the policies and criteria in place, the level of learner performance continues to be a serious problem in higher education. A report from a task team of the Council on Higher Education (2016) has shown that about 50 percent of registered students drop out of their studies and only about 25 percent obtain their degrees in the required time. The failure effectively to develop intellectual talent in South Africa has serious consequences for the country's progress and stability. There-fore, improving the number, quality, and mix of graduates is increasingly accepted as being essential for economic and social development, as well as for revitalizing the education system as a whole. The importance of an expanded number of high-quality graduates to the well-being of the country was also highlighted by the National Planning Commission and by the establishment of new national initiatives such as the National Education Collaboration Trust to facilitate and strengthen efforts to improve South Africa's education system at all levels.

These circumstances create two interlinked imperatives for higher edu-cation. First, given the pervasive effects of poverty and inequality on attainment at school, it is critical to be able to identify students from disadvantaged backgrounds who have the potential to succeed in higher education. Second, it is necessary to provide supportive learning oppor-tunities in higher education that enable these students to gain the academic foundations for succeeding in advanced studies.

The #FeesMustFall protests of 2015–2016 raised questions about how and for whom the government should invest in higher education. The argument for investing more in higher education is strengthened to the extent that this investment is seen as not only improving the quality of higher education – and, thus, of the opportunities for the few – but also ultimately contributing to greater equity in access to higher education and thus in success and opportunities for later social and economic mobility. Granting access through free education is very promising, but if students do not graduate, there is likely to be no return on investment for the government. The success rates remain worryingly low, and although there are various interventions in place there is a need for a rigorous examination of the causes of this. A report submitted by Dr. Wangenge-Ouma (2013, p. 5) stated that "even though access has generally increased, high drop-out rates at both undergraduate and postgraduate levels remain a huge concern with approximately 50 percent of students (undergraduates and postgraduates) not completing their qualifications." In 1977, the Department of Education (1997, sect. 2.29) stated that increased access must not lead to a revolving-door syndrome for students with high failure and dropout rates. The issue of student success is currently a top priority in higher education.

11.5 Conclusion

It is generally accepted that a fair and transparent higher education admissions system is essential for all applicants. A report from the Admissions to Higher Education Steering Group (2004) stated that higher education is a valuable commodity: It can affect salary, job security, and power to influence society.

Notwithstanding some major achievements in terms of facilitating legislation, national and institutional policies and practices, certain significant initiatives by the state, and the increase in enrollment of Black and women South Africans in higher education, institutions are still facing serious challenges. In the current context of transformation in university admissions, administrators are challenged to articulate explicitly the educational purpose and benefits of diversity. Badat (2011) maintains that the pace of social equity and redress in higher education continues to be severely constrained by adverse conditions in South African schooling. This needs serious attention. Furthermore, it must be noted that not all students leaving secondary school are eligible for university study, but due to a popular view that a university degree bestows class and status, universities have become the destination of choice for those who pursue tertiary education. The Department of Education and Training diverted attention to the Technical Vocational Education and Training (TVET) colleges. The Minister pledged funding to ensure another pathway for students to post-secondary education.

Recently, the government decided to inject a large amount of funding into free education to students from households below a certain income threshold. While this might be good for access, institutions are facing the challenge of high dropout rates and students not graduating for other reasons. Many HEIs lack the resources to ensure adequate academic support programs for students at risk and simultaneously for institutional redress. It is important that institutions seek to correct the injustices of the past by striving to minimize barriers for applicants that are irrelevant to satisfying admissions requirements. An institution's structures and processes should be designed to facilitate a high-quality, efficient admissions system, and a professional service to all applicants. As an education sector, institutions regularly review their admissions policies with the intention of ensuring equality of opportunity and success within the legal framework.

REFERENCES

Admissions to Higher Education Steering Group (2004). Fair admissions to higher education: Recommendations for good practice. In *Admissions to higher education review*. Nottingham: Department for Education and Skills Publications. Retrieved from http://dera.ioe.ac.uk/5284/1/finalreport.pdf.

Badat, S. (2011). Redressing the colonial/apartheid legacy: Social equity, redress, and higher education admissions in democratic South Africa. Retrieved from www.ru.ac.za/media/rhodesuniversity/content/vc/documents/Redressing%20the%20Colonial%20or%20Apartheid%20Legacy.pdf.

BusinessTech. (2018, November 30). Government changes minimum entry requirements for a bachelor's degree in South Africa. *BusinessTech*. Retrieved from https://businesstech.co.za/news/government/288442/government-changes-minimum-entry-requirements-for-a-bachelors-degree-in-south-africa/.

Byrnes, R. M. (1997). *South Africa: A country study*. Washington, DC: Federal Research Division.

Council on Higher Education. (2016). South African higher education reviewed: Two decades of democracy. Retrieved from http://che.ac.za/sites/default/files/publications/CHE_South%20African%20higher%20education%20reviewed%20-%20electronic_1.pdf.

Manik, S. (2015). Calibrating the barometer: Student access and success in South African public higher education institutions [Special edition]. *Alternation*, *17*, 226–244. Retrieved from http://alternation.ukzn.ac.za/Files/docs/22%20SpEd17/12%20Manik%20F.pdf.

Moore, J. (2005). Why isn't eligibility part of the affirmative action debate? Retrieved from https://diverseeducation.com/article/4887/.

Ocampo, L. (2004). Global perspectives on human language: The South African context. Timeline of education and apartheid. Retrieved from https://web.stanford.edu/~jbaugh/saw/Lizet_Timeline.html.

Republic of South Africa. (1997). Higher Education Act 101 of 1997. Retrieved from www.che.ac.za/sites/default/files/publications/act101.PDF.

Republic of South Africa Department of Education. (1997). Education white paper 3: A programme for the transformation of higher education. Retrieved from www.che.ac.za/sites/default/files/publications/White_Paper3.pdf.

(2001). National development plan for higher education in South Africa. Retrieved from www.dhet.gov.za/HED Policies/National Plan on Higher Education.pdf.

(2005a). National senior certificate: A qualification at level 4 on the national qualifications framework. Retrieved from www.saide.org.za/resources/Library/DoE%20-%20NSCNQF4.pdf.

(2005b). Minimum admission requirements for higher certificate, diploma and bachelor's degree programmes requiring a national senior certificate. Retrieved from www.dhet.gov.za/HED%20Policies/Minimum%20Admission%20Requirements%20for%20Higher%20Certificate,%20Diploma%20and%20Bachelor's%20Degree.pdf.

Republic of South Africa Department of Higher Education and Training. (2015). Statistics on post-school education and training in South Africa. Retrieved from www.dhet.gov.za/DHET%20Statistics%20Publication/Statistics%20on%20Post-School%20Education%20and%20Training%20in%20South%20Africa%202015.pdf.

(2018). Minimum admission requirements for higher certificate, diploma and bachelor's degree programmes requiring a national senior certificate: Amendment to the minimum admission requirements for entry into bachelor's degree programmes for holders of the national senior certificate. Retrieved from www.gov.za/sites/default/files/gcis_document/201812/42100gon1369.pdf.

Republic of South Africa Minister of Higher Education and Training. (2013). The higher education qualifications sub-framework. Retrieved from www.uj.ac.za/corporateservices/quality-promotion/Documents/quality%20docs/national/Revised%20HEQSF%20Jan2013%20FINAL.pdf.

South African Qualifications Authority (2009). National Qualifications Framework Act 67. Retrieved from www.saqa.org.za/list.php?e=Legislation.

University of Cape Town. (2016). Strategic planning framework. Retrieved from www.uct.ac.za

Wangenge-Ouma, G. (2013). *Widening participation in South African higher education: Report submitted to HEFCE and OFFA*. Bristol: Higher Education Funding Council for England. Retrieved from www.voced.edu.au/content/ngv%3A59466.

CHAPTER 12

Admissions Practices in Sweden

Per-Erik Lyrén and Christina Wikström

This chapter gives an account of the admissions system to higher education in Sweden with special focus on the criteria used in the selection process: upper secondary school grades and scores from the Swedish Scholastic Aptitude Test (SweSAT). The Swedish educational system in general and the admissions system specifically have some unique features that may interest the reader. Primarily, the educational system, from preschool to higher education, has a comparatively high degree of centralization. Most higher education institutions are governed and funded by the state. This reflects on both the admissions process and the education that is provided by the universities. Other typical characteristics are strong beliefs in equal opportunities, lifelong learning, and second chances, all of which influence the educational system in numerous ways. Higher education selection regulations are pervaded by meritocratic principles (see Wikström and Wikström, in this volume, for a discussion), but there are also expectations and demands for diversity in the student body.

The chapter first describes higher education institutions in Sweden, followed by sections on admissions regulations and the selection criteria. Then, we give an account of reform efforts. We end the chapter with some concluding remarks.

Higher education in Sweden is, to a large extent, a state-mandated activity. Currently, there are 47 higher education institutions, of which 30 are state-owned public authorities, and 17 are owned by foundations, associations, or other private bodies (Universitetskanslerämbetet, n.d.). Institutions are classified as either universities (universitet: 14 public, 2 private), university colleges (högskola: 16 public, 2 private), or independent education providers (enskilda utbildningsanordnare: 13 in total, all private). University colleges have less authority than universities when it comes to awarding advanced degrees, such as master's and doctorates, and independent education providers generally award degrees in only one or a few subjects, such as in nursing/health care, religious studies, or psychotherapy.

12.1   Admissions Regulations

Although higher education in Sweden is centrally regulated, there are some differences between public and private institutions. Public institutions are regulated mainly through the Higher Education Act (HEA) (Högskolelag, 1992) and the Higher Education Ordinance (HEO) (Högskoleförordning, 1993), while private institutions are regulated through a specific law concerning degree-awarding powers for such institutions and a few sections in the HEA and the HEO.

When it comes to admissions, the most important regulations are found in one chapter of the HEO. This means that admissions regulations determined by the Government or Parliament only apply to public institutions. Private institutions are free to set their own admissions policies and procedures as long as they do not violate other fundamental regulations, such as the Discrimination Act (Diskrimineringslag, 2008). However, since private institutions constitute a relatively small part of higher education in Sweden, we will not provide details regarding their admissions procedures in this chapter. The HEO chapter specifies a number of requirements that institutions must meet. Apart from some differences in regulations depending on candidates' previous experience (i.e., if they are already students in higher education or if they are new entrants) and on the level of studies, the regulations are the same for all applicants; there are no special routes based on, for example, scholarships or affirmative action.

One example of the centralization of the educational system is that Sweden has a nationally coordinated admissions procedure. There are degrees of local autonomy, as described below, but all applications are administered centrally, meaning that applicants do not have to submit separate applications if they apply to several universities or programs.

12.1.1   Eligibility

Another difference from many other systems is that Swedish admissions regulations distinctly separate eligibility and selection. While selection instruments are only used when there are more eligible applicants than available study places, all applicants must meet certain eligibility requirements. Basic eligibility is usually achieved by graduating from upper secondary school (or equivalent). This means passing the main part of courses where certain courses in Swedish, English, and mathematics are mandatory. Required courses are included in programs with an academic orientation, while those enrolled in vocationally oriented programs may have to take additional courses to meet the requirements. Although graduation is the standard way of meeting the basic eligibility requirements, other ways that show the person has acquired the required knowledge and skills necessary to benefit from the course or study program can be accepted.

In addition to the basic requirements, some courses and programs have specific requirements that constitute special eligibility. For instance, applicants to certain programs in the medical field (e.g., medicine, dentistry, and veterinary medicine) must have pursued certain courses in biology, chemistry, physics, and mathematics (Universitets- och högskolerådet, 2016). These requirements are, according to the HEO, "absolutely essential for the student's ability to benefit from the education." This implies that institutions cannot use special eligibility for the sole purpose of gaining a more able pool of applicants.

12.1.2   Selection

When there are more applicants who meet the eligibility requirements than there are study positions available, selection takes place. Selection among new entrants is based on one of the following criteria:

- grades (upper secondary school grade point average [USGPA])
- SweSAT scores, or
- local selection criteria

For students who are not new entrants, selection is based not only on the rank ordering of the three criteria above, but also on prior course performance in higher education.

Selection is carried out through a quota system, in which a certain proportion of the admitted candidates are selected using the different criteria. The regulations state that at least one-third of the candidates are to be admitted based on grades, at least one-third based on SweSAT scores, and, at most, one-third based on criteria determined by the institution, referred to as *local criteria*. There are exceptions to this quota rule for courses or programs in the fine, applied, or performing arts, which may allocate all study places based on local criteria. Also, under special circumstances, institutions can be granted other quota proportions by the Swedish Council for Higher Education (the government body responsible for admissions issues; hereafter referred to as "the Council").

In general, most institutions admit one third of their applicants based on SweSAT scores, and most of the remaining applicants are selected on the USGPA (Statens offentliga utredningar, 2017). Local selection criteria are rarely used. In 2015, more than one-third of the institutions did not use local criteria at all and the rest used it for very few courses and programs (Statens offentliga utredningar, 2017).

12.2   Selection Criteria

To give a better understanding of the selection criteria in Swedish admissions and how they are used, this section will start with a short historical background.

Access to upper secondary school and higher education was for a long time limited only to privileged groups in Swedish society. This gradually changed during the post-war era of the twentieth century, due to two strong mechanisms: One driven by societal and egalitarian ambitions and the other by needs of the labor market and industry needing educated workers (Lundahl et al., 2010). The number of places in upper secondary schools increased considerably during the second half of the century, a trend later seen in higher education as well (Öckert, 2001). The expansion of the educational sector also called for reliable and valid admissions procedures and instruments for selection. Since grading practices varied considerably between schools and over time, the school grades were recognized as highly problematic for this purpose. This made the grades difficult to use both for giving information on previous achievement and particularly for rank ordering applicants (Andersson, 1999). To achieve more comparable grades that could be used for fair selection to higher education, a norm-referenced grading system was introduced in the 1960s, with nationally administered tests used for grade calibration. These grades proved to work rather well for selection. However, many students did not have such grades from their previous education. This did not go well with the aim of providing educational opportunities for all. The main argument for also giving access to students who did not have a traditional study background was to decrease social gaps in society; but, it was also assumed that there was a hidden ability reserve in this group, that is, students with a high potential for further education (Husén & Härnqvist, 2000).

After the norm-referenced grade system had been introduced, the arguments for a general admissions test became weaker, and the focus shifted toward introducing an instrument that could be used for giving nontraditional students access to higher education. In 1977, the SweSAT was introduced for this purpose. Its design was strongly inspired by the American SAT®, but with a different purpose and use: The SweSAT was open only to students who were at least 25 years old and who had at least four years of work experience. Age and work experience constituted basic eligibility for this group.

Providing this separate route was soon criticized as being unfair to other students who also needed, or wanted, other options than to compete with previous grades. In 1991, the system was changed again so that the same regulations applied to all applicants. Consequently, the SweSAT became the second chance for anyone with an uncompetitive USGPA. However, to continue with the goal of broadening recruitment, extra credit points for work experience were added to the test score. This was removed in 2008 as it became evident that new students at Swedish universities were among the oldest in the world (Statens offentliga utredningar, 2017). The test has since been used in the same way, but with some changes to the test content, as described below. School grades have, on the other hand, been reformed a couple of times after the introduction of the separate routes. Perhaps the most significant reform was during the 1990s, when the entire school system was decentralized, and the grading system was changed from norm-referenced to criterion-referenced, in spite of concerns about how a criterion-referenced system would work for calculating USGPAs and rank ordering applicants.

12.2.1   Grades

The Swedish school system, from preschool to upper secondary school, is regulated by the Swedish Education Act (Skollag, 2010) and the national curriculum. Assessment and grading are criterion-referenced and based on the syllabi and grading criteria attached to the national curriculum. The syllabi define content and performance levels for courses and subjects, and the grading criteria define grade levels and what should be assessed. However, even if the system is centrally regulated, much authority is given to the schools and to the teachers, who have the sole responsibility for assessing and grading their students. This means that teachers' ability to interpret the criteria, identify the standards for each grade level, assess the students with appropriate methods, and integrate the information to create a summative decision is of great importance for valid assessments and for maintaining standards.

Grades are assigned on a scale from F to A, where E is the first pass grade. While grades above a pass grade (E) are irrelevant for eligibility, high grades are important for selection. In order to calculate the USGPA, the letter grades are transformed to a numerical scale, where E = 10 credits, D = 12.5, C = 15, B = 17.5, and A = 20. The USGPA is a weighted average and the grades in different courses are weighted proportionally to the length of the course that has been taken. There is also a system with merit courses, where some courses – in most cases advanced courses in modern languages, English, and mathematics – give extra credits. The merit courses can give an additional 2.5 credits, resulting in a USGPA with a maximum of 22.5. Without extra credits, the maximum USGPA is 20.

12.2.2   The SweSAT

As noted earlier, the SweSAT serves as an alternative route into higher education, an optional second chance. The test is a shared responsibility between the Council and the higher education institutions. The Council is responsible for tasks that are contracted to external parties, such as test development, printing, scoring, and score reporting. The institutions are responsible for test-day administration, including test-taker registration and providing appropriate facilities and test proctors. The Council is also empowered to make more detailed regulations regarding the test (e.g., determining allowed equipment, the nonuse/use of mobile phones, and the right to testing accommodations).

The overall purpose of the SweSAT is to predict academic success, although the definition of the construct upon which the test is based has changed over time. It was originally described as *scholastic aptitude* (*studielämplighet*) and based on four broad domains: aptitude, abilities, knowledge, and personality. The test is now mainly designed to measure general verbal and quantitative skills and abilities that are regarded important in higher education (see Wedman, 2017 for a more thorough description of the history and the theoretical model of the test). Today, the test is composed of two sections, with 80 items each: verbal (subtests: vocabulary, Swedish reading comprehension, sentence completion, and English reading comprehension) and quantitative (subtests: mathematical problem-solving; quantitative comparisons; data sufficiency; and diagrams, tables, and maps). The two sections are scaled separately (range 0.0–2.0) to allow for differential quantitative and verbal weighting depending on the discipline of the specific course or program, which is to be implemented as a trial during 2019–2021 (Förordning om försöksverksamhet med viktat högskoleprovsresultat vid urval, 2018). Only the average of the two section scores is currently used in the admissions, but both normed scores and raw subscores are reported to test-takers. A test score is valid for five years. There is no restriction regarding repeated test-taking, and, for repeaters, the best score counts.

12.2.3   Local Criteria

The third route into higher education selection is the institutions' option to select students based on criteria other than the USGPA and SweSAT scores. The institutions can choose between: (a) tests other than the SweSAT; (b) knowledge or experience of particular merit for the course or program applied for; and (c) other objective circumstances that are relevant for the program. As noted earlier, most institutions tend to use this option to a very limited extent. However, in 2018, the Government commissioned the Council to promote the use of local criteria in admissions.

12.2.4   Validity Issues and Criticism

Most validity discussions regarding selection to higher education in Sweden have focused on predictive validity and group differences, the latter with particular focus on gender differences in test performance (see Wolming & Wikström, 2010, for an overview; see Section 12.2.5 for a lengthier discussion on diversity issues). Overall, research has shown that there are both similarities and differences in how well the criteria work: There are significant correlations between the selection criteria and, also, between the criteria and academic achievement. However, the USGPA seems to work better than the SweSAT in terms of predictive validity (see, e.g., Cliffordson, 2006; 2008; Cliffordson & Askling, 2006; Lyrén et al., 2014). A common explanation for the difference in prediction is generally that grades capture aspects that are relevant for academic performance, such as industriousness, or motivation, among other constructs. While the test is criticized for having lower predictive validity, grades have proved to be problematic in terms of comparability and fairness, as they tend to vary across teachers, schools, and time. Proposed explanations for this are complex, including the use of vague criteria and variations in teachers' ability to assess their pupils in a valid and reliable way (Klapp Lekholm, 2008; Vlachos, 2018), often in combination with external pressure for high grading due to school competition and school accountability (Björklund et al., 2010; Wikström, 2005; Wikström & Wikström, 2005).

A validity issue that has emerged over the past decade is score reporting. This is due to the relatively recent quantitative/verbal-partitioning of the SweSAT, and an increased interest in subscores in general. A study on the version of the SweSAT before 2011 showed that most subscores (in this case, subtest scores) had so-called added value (Lyrén, 2009), which was not the case with many other high-stakes tests (Sinharay, Haberman, & Wainer, 2011; Sinharay, Puhan, & Haberman, 2010). A study on the current version of the test (Wedman & Lyrén, 2015) showed that the two section scores have added value over the total score, which is some evidence in support of differential weighting of these scores. However, most subtest scores do not have added value over the section scores, and this raises concerns about the current score-reporting practices.

12.2.5   Group Differences and Diversity

It is well known that tests and grades work differently for different students, which is also the case for the Swedish selection criteria. Wikström and Wikström (2017) found, in line with previous research, that males had higher SweSAT scores than females, while females and students with an immigrant background had higher USGPAs. The score difference between men and women on the SweSAT is usually about 0.4 standard deviations in total, with 0.5 on the quantitative section and 0.2 on the verbal section (Lyrén, 2017). The general pattern of the gender differences seems stable over time and revisions, and they are assumed to relate more to formatting rather than content. For example, studies have shown that test-takers differ in strategies or test anxiety (Stenlund, Eklöf, & Lyrén, 2017; Stenlund, Lyrén, & Eklöf, 2018). Also, while there are systematic group differences in SweSAT scores at the test level, differential item functioning between women and men does not seem to be a problematic issue (Wedman, 2018).

   Group differences in the selection instruments is one factor that affects diversity in the student body, and selection mechanisms is another. Table 12.1 displays characteristics of applicants and admitted students. First, we note that individuals' backgrounds differ between programs. For example, compared to all professional degree programs, those admitted to preschool teaching are more often women, older, and less often have parents with tertiary education, while those admitted to civil engineering more often are men, less often have immigrant status, more often have parents with tertiary education, and are younger. In other words, there are self-selection mechanisms involved in admissions. Second, if we look at admissions to the professional degree programs in general, there are higher proportions of women, Swedish natives, and people with parents having tertiary education. The student body is also younger compared to all applicants. However, there are differences between programs in this case as well, where, for example, admissions to some programs leads to a higher proportion of men (civil engineering, medicine). Also, while admissions to

Table 12.1 *Distribution on background variables (sex, foreign background, parents' education, and age) for admitted students and applicants to a selection of professional degree programs for the academic year 2012–2013*

Program	Sex (percentage) Women	Immigration status[a] (percentage)	Parents' education (percentage) LS	US	TE	Age (years) M	SD
All professional degree programs (41)							
Applicants	60	21	7	45	49	25.5	7.7
Admitted	61	18	5	41	54	24.2	6.8
Biomedical science							
Applicants	74	50	9	44	47	24.8	7.3
Admitted	77	46	10	50	41	24.2	6.5
Civil engineering							
Applicants	32	19	2	32	65	21.0	3.4
Admitted	30	15	2	29	69	20.7	2.4
Medicine							
Applicants	57	29	4	27	69	22.9	5.5
Admitted	55	17	1	20	79	22.7	4.7
Preschool teaching							
Applicants	90	22	11	59	31	26.7	7.8
Admitted	94	15	8	58	33	25.8	7.1
Social work							
Applicants	82	29	9	51	40	24.8	6.8
Admitted	85	19	6	47	47	24.0	6.8

Source: Data are taken from Lyrén et al. (2014).
[a] 1st- and 2nd-generation immigrants.
LS = lower secondary education; US = upper secondary education; TE = tertiary education.
M = mean; SD = standard deviation.

most programs results overall in a lower proportion of immigrant students, the effect is stronger for some programs (e.g., medicine, social work) than others (e.g., biomedical science, civil engineering). Therefore, the general pattern is that the Swedish admissions system seems to over-select traditional student groups. Still, it selects nontraditional students to a larger extent than some other countries (Bron & Agelli, 2000; Schuetze & Slowley, 2002).

12.3   Reform and Other Developments

Currently, future reforms are discussed intensely, but little has been decided. A report from a recent government commission on entrance to higher education, which presented its final report in March 2017 (Statens offentliga utredningar, 2017, p. 20), could have had a potentially large impact on admissions; however, most of the proposals were not mentioned in the Government's proposition on entrance to higher education the following year (Proposition 2017/18:204).

12.3.1   Eligibility

The current regulations in the HEO state how the basic requirements can be met, for example, through an upper-secondary school diploma, but they do not state what kind of competencies that form these requirements. One proposal is that basic eligibility requirements would reflect competencies in six areas: (a) Swedish and English; (b) scientific approach; (c) the ability to illustrate issues from several perspectives; (d) problem-solving ability; (e) the ability to draw conclusions and make a case for them; and (f) other competencies that are necessary to benefit from higher education. A related proposal is to introduce the opportunity for applicants to meet the basic eligibility requirements through a standardized test that would test these competencies. To avoid conflict with the normal schooling procedure, the test would be available only to applicants who are at least 24 years old. This suggestion, and the rationale behind it, resembles the reasoning behind the introduction of the SweSAT in the early 1970s. Both proposals were acknowledged in the Government's proposition. There were also proposals regarding special eligibility; however, these regulations are too intricate to discuss in this chapter.

12.3.2   Selection

The commission suggested that of the available study places, the majority should be allocated based on grades and no more than 15 percent should be allocated based on SweSAT scores (compared to the current one-third). In addition, the minimum proportion rule for grades and the maximum proportion rule for local criteria should be abolished. The Government did not acknowledge this proposal; instead, it declared that the current distribution of places should be the principal rule.

The commission finds it problematic that pupils even at the beginning of upper secondary school can take the test and argues that a very good score would reduce the motivation for aiming higher than an E grade in the remaining courses in upper secondary school. There is, however, little or no evidence that this is a problem in practice. Still, the commission proposed a lower age limit of 19 years for taking the test, which in practice would mean that the first test-taking opportunity would be during the final semester of upper secondary school. This was included in the Government's most recent changes to the HEO to come in effect in 2022; however, the age limit was set at 18 instead of 19 years.

Other proposals were: (a) to abolish the system of additional credits for merit courses; (b) to introduce differential weighting of SweSAT quantitative and verbal scores (as described in Section 12.2.2); (c) to make scores valid for three years instead of five; (d) to limit repeated test-taking by allowing candidates to take the test only three times during any three-year period; and (e) to make grades and SweSAT scores open for use as the basis for local selection criteria, as long as they are used in ways other than in the grade and SweSAT quota groups. These proposals were not mentioned in the proposition mentioned earlier, but they may very well be included in future legislation.

12.4   Concluding Remarks

The Swedish educational system, including admissions to higher education, is highly characterized by a belief in lifelong learning and in the importance of equal opportunity in education, through free education and several routes into higher education. Consequently, Swedish students are generally older and more diverse when it comes to socioeconomic background compared to students in many other countries (see Hauschildt, Vögtle, & Gwosć, 2018). Still, increasing achievement gaps in elementary and secondary schools (Organisation for Economic Co-operation and Development, 2015), and the fact that diversity is only considered important as long as meritocracy is upheld, makes broad recruitment difficult. For example, affirmative action is not illegal, but has been very difficult to implement in practice.

Another complex and complicated issue is the changing population. In recent years, immigration has increased, which leads to new challenges for the educational system. The system is expected to find ways to assess these potential students' previous knowledge, to give them a fair chance to compete in the admissions, and to give admitted students an education that will make them competitive on the job market. It is likely that tests for assessing previous knowledge for eligibility as well as general achievement tests for selection will become increasingly important in giving these students the chance to be admitted to higher education. This will introduce new routes for entering Swedish higher education in the future.

REFERENCES

Andersson, H. (1999). *Varför betyg? Historiskt och aktuellt om betyg* [Why grades? Grades in past and present]. Lund: Studentlitteratur.

Björklund, A., Fredriksson, P., Gustafsson, J.-E., & Öckert, B. (2010). *Den svenska utbildningspolitikens arbetsmarknadseffekter: vad säger forskningen?* [Labor market effects of the Swedish educational policy: What does the research say?] (IFAU Rapport 2010:13). Uppsala: Institutet för arbetsmarknadspolitisk utvärdering.

Bron, A., & Agelli, K. (2000). Nontraditional students in higher education in Sweden: From recurrent education to lifelong learning. In H. G. Schuetze & M. Slowley (Eds.). *Higher education and lifelong learners: International perspectives on change* (pp. 83–100). London: Routledge.

Cliffordson, C. (2006). Selection effects on applications and admissions to medical education with regular and step-wise admission procedures. *Scandinavian Journal of Educational Research, 50,* 463–482. https://doi.org/10.1080/00313830600823811.

(2008). Differential prediction of study success across academic programs in the Swedish context: The validity of grades and tests as selection instruments for higher education. *Educational Assessment 13*(1), 56–75. https://doi.org/10.1080/10627190801968240.

Cliffordson, C., & Askling, B. (2006). Different grounds for admission: Its effects on recruitment and achievement in medical education. *Scandinavian Journal of Educational Research, 50,* 45–62. https://doi.org/10.1080/00313830500372026.

Diskrimineringslag [Discrimination Act]. (2008). SFS 2008:567. Stockholm: Kulturdepartementet

Förordning om försöksverksamhet med viktat högskoleprovsresultat vid urval [Ordinance Regarding Trials on Weighting SweSAT Scores for Selection]. (2018). SFS 2018:1511. Stockholm: Utbildningsdepartementet.

Hauschildt, K., Vögtle, E. M., & Gwosć, C. (2018). *Social and economic conditions of student life in Europe: Eurostudent VI (2016–2018) synopsis of indicators.* Bielefeld: Bertelsmann. Retrieved from https://ec.europa.eu/epale/en/resource-centre/content/eurostudent-vi-2016-2018-synopsis-indicators.

Högskoleförordning [Higher Education Ordinance]. (1993). SFS 1993:100. Stockholm: Utbildningsdepartementet.

Högskolelag [Higher Education Act]. (1992). SFS 1992:1434. Stockholm: Utbildningsdepartementet.

Husén, T., & Härnqvist, K. (2000). *Begåvningsreserven En återblick på ett halvsekels forskning och debatt* [The ability reserve: A look back at half a century of research and debate]. Uppsala: Föreningen för svensk undervisningshistoria.

Klapp Lekholm, A. (2008). Grades and grade assignment: Effects of student and school characteristics (Doctoral dissertation). Gothenburg University.

Lundahl, L., Erixon Arreman, I., Lundström, U., & Rönnberg, L. (2010). Setting things right? Swedish upper secondary school reform in a 40-year perspective. *European Journal of Education*, *45*, 49–62. https://doi.org/10.1111/j.1465-3435.2009.01414.x.

Lyrén, P.-E. (2009). Reporting subscores from college admission tests. *Practical Assessment, Research & Evaluation*, *14*(4). Retrieved from http://pareonline.net/getvn.asp?v=14&n=4.

(2017). *Högskoleprovet våren och hösten 2016: Provtagargruppens sammansättning och resultat* [The SweSAT in the spring and fall of 2016: Composition and results of the test-taking group] (BVM No. 65). Umeå: Department of Applied Educational Science, Umeå University.

Lyrén, P.-E., Rolfsman, E., Wedman, J., Wikström, C., & Wikström, M. (2014). *Det nya högskoleprovet: samband mellan provresultat och prestation i högskolan* [The new SweSAT: Association between test results and performance in higher education]. Umeå: Department of Applied Educational Science, Umeå University.

Öckert, B. (2001). Effects of higher education and the role of admission selection (Doctoral dissertation). Stockholm: The Swedish Institute for Social Research at Stockholm University.

Organisation for Economic Co-operation and Development. (2015). Improving schools in Sweden: An OECD perspective. Retrieved from www.oecd.org/edu/school/Improving-Schools-in-Sweden.pdf.

Proposition 2017/18:204. (2017). Fler vägar till kunskap: en högskola för livslångt lärande [More routes to knowledge: A higher education for lifelong learning].

Schuetze, H. G., & Slowley, M. (2002). Participation and exclusion: A comparative analysis of non-traditional students and lifelong learners in higher education. *Higher Education*, *44*, 309–327. https://doi.org/10.1023%2FA%3A1019898114335.

Sinharay, S., Haberman, S. J., & Wainer, H. (2011). Do adjusted subscores lack validity? Don't blame the messenger. *Educational and Psychological Measurement*, *71*, 789–797. https://doi.org/10.1177/0013164410391782.

Sinharay, S., Puhan, G., & Haberman, S. J. (2010). Reporting diagnostic scores in educational testing: Temptations, pitfalls, and some solutions. *Multivariate Behavioral Research*, *45*, 553–573. https://doi.org/10.1080/00273171.2010.483382789–797.

Skollag [Education Act]. (2010). SFS 2010:800. Stockholm: Utbildningsdepartementet.

Statens offentliga utredningar. (2017). *Tillträde för nybörjare: ett öppnare och enklare system för tillträde till högskoleutbildning* [Admission for new entrants:

A more open and simple system for admission to higher education] (Statens offentliga utredningar, 2017:20). Stockholm: Wolters Kluver.

Stenlund, T., Eklöf, H., & Lyrén, P.-E. (2017). Group differences in test-taking behaviour: An example from a high-stakes testing program. *Assessment in Education: Principles, Policy & Practice, 24*, 4–20. https://doi.org/10.1080/0969594X.2016.1142935.

Stenlund, T., Lyrén, P.-E., & Eklöf, H. (2018). The successful test-taker: Exploring test-taking behaviour profiles through cluster analysis. *European Journal of Psychology of Education, 33*, 403–417. https://doi.org/10.1007/s10212–017-0332-2.

Universitetskanslerämbetet. (n.d.). Facts about higher education. Retrieved from http://english.uka.se/facts-about-higher-education.html.

Universitets- och högskolerådet. (2016). Tabell för områdesbehörigheter [Table for field-specific requirements]. Retrieved from www.uhr.se/globalassets/_uhr.se/studier-och-antagning/tilltrade-till-hogskolan/tabell-for-omradesbe horigheter-2016.pdf.

Vlachos, J. (2018). Trust-based evaluation in a market-oriented school system (Working Paper 1217). Stockholm: Research Institute of Industrial Economics. http://hdl.handle.net/10419/183446.

Wedman, J. (2017). Theory and validity evidence for a large-scale test (Doctoral dissertation). Retrieved from http://urn.kb.se/resolve?urn=urn:nbn:se:umu:diva-138492.

(2018). Reasons for gender-related differential item functioning in a college admissions test. *Scandinavian Journal of Educational Research, 62*, 959–970. https://doi.org/10.1080/00313831.2017.1402365.

Wedman, J., & Lyrén, P.-E. (2015). Methods for examining the psychometric quality of subscores: A review and application. *Practical Assessment, Research & Evaluation, 20*(21). Retrieved from http://pareonline.net/getvn.asp?v=20&n=21.

Wikström, C. (2005). Grade stability in a criterion-referenced grading system: The Swedish example. *Assessment in Education: Principles, Policy & Practice, 12*, 125–144. https://doi.org/10.1080/0969594050014381 1.

Wikström, C., & Wikström, M. (2005). Grade inflation and school competition: An empirical analysis based on the Swedish upper secondary schools. *Economics of Education Review, 24*, 309–322. https://doi.org/10.1016/j.econedurev.2004.04.010.

(2017). Group differences in student performance in the selection to higher education: Tests vs. grades. *Frontiers in Education, 2*(45). https://doi.org/10.3389/feduc.2017.00045.

Wolming, S., & Wikström, C. (2010). The concept of validity in theory and practice. *Assessment in Education: Principles, Policy & Practice, 17*, 117–132. https://doi.org/10.1080/09695941003693856.

CHAPTER 13

Revisions of Admissions Testing in Vietnam: From Elite to Mass Higher Education

Duy Ngoc Pham and Hong Cong Sai

Vietnam has a history dating back for more than 4,000 years. In 2016, this 331,230 square kilometer country in South East Asia had a population of 92.69 million (General Statistics Office of Vietnam, 2018a). In the same year, its per capita gross domestic product (GDP) was US $2,170, almost ten times more than in 1985 (World Bank, 2018). Vietnam joined the World Trade Organization in 2005 and its economy has been growing steadily since then, with annual GDP growth rates of around 6 percent (World Bank, 2018). Concomitant with growth, Vietnam has increasingly become more globalized, creating increasing demand for a more educated workforce in all sectors of the economy (Altbach, 2016). Consequently, higher education in Vietnam has experienced its fastest period of growth in two decades in terms of higher education institutions and students attending these institutions. This has transformed the higher education system from an elite to a mass system (Trow, 1973). Characteristics of the transformed higher education system include the gradual decentralization of the system as institutions gain increasing autonomy and changes made as to how students are selected. The decentralized system has seen a move away from open-ended admissions tests to a more basic and effective testing system and more flexible admissions policies. Over the past few years, colleges and universities have gained the autonomy to set up their own selection criteria and procedures to attract and recruit students.

In this chapter, we will briefly review the 1,000-year history of Vietnam's higher education system. Then, we will describe some key major revisions of admissions testing in Vietnam in recent decades. The legal framework and national practices to unify two sets of tests into a single testing system are discussed at length. In order to draw conclusions about the effectiveness of the revisions, the policy analyses will be contextualized in the long history of Vietnam's higher-learning institutions and with reference to the most recent standards for educational and psychological testing. To conclude, we will point out the main challenges to revising admissions tests during the move from elite to mass tertiary education. Some policy recommendations will be proposed to improve admissions testing in Vietnam and in countries that are in similar stages of development.

13.1   Looking Back to Move Forward

The first institution of higher learning in Vietnam was the Temple of Literature (Van Mieu Quoc Tu Giam) in Hanoi, established in the 1070s by the Ly Dynasty. The original purpose of the establishment was to worship Confucius through knowledge of his school of thought and key followers and to educate children of the King and leading mandarins (Nguyen, 2012). From that time, standardized testing was used by different dynasties to select public servants and higher-ranking government officials (World Bank, n.d.[a]). The examinations were administered in a few rounds at municipal, provincial, and national levels. Those who passed the lower levels were allowed to sign up for the next set of examinations to compete for higher credentials. Examinees who obtained the highest recognition were called Doctor (Tien-sy) and were appointed to hold important positions in the government (Nguyen, 2012). Their names and information concerning their home villages were carved in stone stelae that have been preserved in Temples of Literature in Hanoi and Hue (Nguyen, Le, & Nguyen, 2005).

From the eleventh to the eighteenth centuries, the Confucian school of thought was the main educational ideology, thus exams based on this curriculum were the main instruments used to select students for higher learning and scholars to be public servants (Nguyen, 2012; Tran, 2009). Since the start of French colonization in 1858, higher education has gone through many changes that, in part, reflect the sociopolitical context of the country in each era. The first modern university was the University of Indochina, established in 1906 by the French colonial government to educate Vietnamese intellectuals to absorb French values and serve the colony in Vietnam and the islands of Indochina (University of Indochina, 2016). Three gateways are described in the establishment charter to select students for the new university. Graduates from a few French high schools in the country at that time were the first source of students. The second source of prospective students came from those who held a baccalaurete degree with appropriate proficiency in French. And the last channel for possible admission was for those without any of the credentials mentioned above to be proposed and approved by an admissions committee (University of Indochina, 2016). During this transitional period, the content of the educational tests was gradually moving away from the influence of Confucian learning and Chinese or Chinese-based Vietnamese writing (i.e., Chu Nom, which is a way to use Chinese characters to take notes in Vietnamese dialects) to a French curriculum and language (Tran, 2009).

After French colonization, Vietnam fought in several wars with different foreign countries until 1979. Consequently, higher education and admissions policies and practices went through many temporary arrangements and changes. From 1956 to 1975, the country was divided into two parts: North Vietnam and South Vietnam. Higher education in North Vietnam followed the system used by the Soviet Union and was supported by communist countries such as the Soviet Union and China. Meanwhile, higher education in South Vietnam was Americanized and quickly moved away from its French antecedents (Le, 2006). For example, in 1974, the Republic of Vietnam adopted admissions tests that were like the SAT® to select students for admission into their colleges and universities (Nguyen, 2016). After the 1975 reunification, the higher education system in the South was converted into a unique centralized system that more closely resembled the preunification higher education system in the North. A historical analysis of the higher education system in Vietnam in the last millennium suggests that higher education and selection testing was influenced by the country's sociopolitical context and its degree of independence and resourcefulness to make decisions and implement policies in each period. In the next section, we discuss more recent movements and policies related to admissions testing in Vietnam.

13.2 A Recount of Vietnam's More Recent Higher Education Changes

The last two decades have marked the most rapid growth in higher education institutions in Vietnam after unification in 1975, with the number of institutions more than doubling, from 178 institutions in 2000 to 445 institutions in 2015 (General Statistics Office of Vietnam, 2018b). During the same period, the number of tertiary students also increased, from 889,500 in 2000 to more than two million in 2015. Along the same lines, private higher education has flourished. The first private institution was founded in 1988, and by 2000 there were 30 private colleges and universities. By 2015, 88 private colleges and universities hosted a total of about 271,400 students (Thang Long University, 2014). According to the Ministry of Education and Training (MoET), the number of universities in 2017 was 235 compared to 223 one year earlier. The number of students in these 4-year institutions has remained stable at about 1.7 million in 2016 and 2017 (Ministry of Education and Training, 2017a).

Vietnam has also made significant progress in increasing access to higher education in the last two decades and enrollment rates increased from 9.4 percent in 2000 to 28.8 percent in 2015 (World Bank, n.d.[b]; General Statistics Office of Vietnam, 2018b). A recent report by the MoET (2017a) showed that about 41 percent of high school graduates matriculated into tertiary institutions in 2017 (Le, 2017). Going along with the massification process, higher education institutions in Vietnam have also tried to improve educational quality and better serve students' needs by internationalizing their programs through collaboration with international partners and by offering joint programs. Le (2017) indicated that there were more than 500 such programs jointly offered by Vietnam's and foreign universities all over the world. Most of these programs use instructional materials provided by the foreign universities. Students entering the programs are usually expected to be at least moderately proficient in a foreign language to be able to access the materials, take courses in the institution's language of instruction, and to interact with international lecturers.

The move from elite to mass higher education seems promising on the surface as more bachelor's degree holders will graduate to supply the fast-growing economy. However, it also introduces many challenges in relation to upgrading the system's infrastructure and governance and improving its quality and effectiveness. One important change is to revise its admissions testing and student-selection processes.

13.2.1   Current Legal Framework for Admissions

In recent decades, the construction and administration of admissions tests has swung back and forth between centralized and decentralized processes. Before 1965, admissions tests were developed and administered by individual or groups of universities. From 1965 to 1990, admissions tests were centrally developed by the MoET and only constructed-response questions were used. From the 1990s to 2002, the test construction then swayed back to universities using a large set of sample tests issued by the MoET. Since 2002, the country saw its most dramatic changes in admissions testing. A national policy of three commonalities (ba chung) became the guiding principle of university admissions in which all universities administered the same tests to nationally shared schedules and used the same test scores to select incoming students. Under this framework, the MoET was responsible for preparing the tests, the universities administered them, and students used test scores to apply to a few universities of their interest. Up until 2012, all these policies were regularized by administrative decrees issued by the MoET based on a general education law passed by the National Assembly in 2005 (Education Law, 2005).

To provide a clearer legal framework for higher education, the country passed its first higher education law in 2012. This law specifies, among other things, that institutions are: (a) free to identify and publicly announce their admissions quota to attract prospective students; and (b) self-responsible for setting up admissions policies and implementing their admissions process. This law reflects the guiding principle that a more decentralized higher education system is needed so as to be more responsive to the fast-growing economy and socioeconomic changes (Law on Higher Education, 2012). Prior to this law, admissions quotas for each institution could be imposed by the MoET and admissions policies were set at a national level.

13.3 The Most Recent Revision in 2017: Triple-Purpose Testing

13.3.1 Policy Overview

In this section, we will review the details of the most recent admissions policies that were put in place for implementation from 2017. The purpose of the new decree and admissions practices is to reduce testing pressure for high school students and support higher education institutions' admissions practices. Prior to 2017, 12th graders used to take high school graduation and university admissions exams in June and July, respectively, to graduate from high schools and apply for colleges. Regulated by the new decree issued in 2017, the two exams were unified into a single one to be used: (a) to provide scores to set criteria for high school graduation; (b) to provide a common score for colleges and universities to select incoming students; and (c) to evaluate the educational quality of K–12 education for the country (Ministry of Education and Training, 2017b).

13.3.2 Test Development and Administration

13.3.2.1 Test Design

The new set of exams consists of three independent tests (mathematics, literature, and a foreign language) and two combined ones (natural and social sciences). Each of the latter two involves three independent sections, and each section covers one subject that students learn in high school. For example, the three-section natural sciences test has one section for physics, one for chemistry, and one for biology. Similarly, the social sciences exam contains sections for history, geology, and civic education. To obtain the credentials to graduate from high school, students need to take all three independent tests and at least one of the combined tests. Students already possessing a high school diploma could choose to take the tests required by the institutions for which they are going to apply. Time for each test varies from 60 minutes for foreign languages to 150 minutes for natural and social sciences. Multiple-choice questions (MCs) are used in all tests with the only exception of literature, which includes constructed-response questions scored by humans. Note that this is the first time since 1975 that all questions in the mathematics test are MCs. In terms of the testing content, the tests in 2017 covered the 12th-grade curriculum (i.e., the last year of high school). In 2018, the coverage was expanded to include the 11th-grade curriculum.

13.3.2.2   Test Construction
Due to the importance of the exam and the lack of expertise in nongovernment sectors, the MoET has usually been responsible for the construction of the test. High school teachers and university faculty are mobilized to write and review items in secured locations. Then, MCs are empirically pretested and analyzed to build operational test forms. After many rounds of internal review by content experts, MCs are then assembled in pilot form to be pretested using high school students. Pretesting data are analyzed using the Rasch model, and questions or response options of questionable statistics or parameter estimates are examined, revised, or discarded. Finalized items after pretesting are then put into item banks to build test forms. To avoid instances of cheating, multiple forms for each test using MCs are assembled to be spiraled in each test room. The questions are selected so that the forms have the same level of difficulty since the scores of different forms are used interchangeably as credentials for high school graduation and university admissions. Once the group at MoET has finalized the test forms, they are printed out and sent to groups of test administrators (known as *cum thi* in Vietnamese) as "top secret" materials to prepare for the test dates.

13.3.2.3   Test Administration
The provincial Departments of Education in each of the 64 provinces of the country are responsible for delivering the tests. High schools in each

district are usually selected to be the testing locations and test-takers usually go to the sites nearest their homes. To engage universities and colleges in the test-administration process, faculty members and staff from those institutions are mobilized to serve on the administration board of directors or as examination proctors. During two testing days, approximately one million students sit the exam and a large amount of resources are mobilized to administer the tests and guarantee security for their administration.

13.3.2.4 *Scoring and Test-Based Admissions Decisions*

All the tests using MCs are scored by machine. Number-correct scores are then converted into a 0–10 score scale by rounding to two decimal places. The literature test is scored on the same scale. Most colleges and universities use sum scores from three tests or test sections to select students. For example, acceptance to computer science programs is based upon the sum scores of the mathematics test and the physics and chemistry sections of the natural sciences test. Each institution can set their own cut scores, but they must add up to at least 15.5 for three tests and/or sections. Institutions or programs related to military, national security, or the arts usually adopt additional selection methods on top of the test scores to recruit their students.

Equal access to higher education has been a national policy since the 1975 unification. Thus, students from some special communities are given priority to increase their chances to enter colleges and universities. For example, cut scores for students whose parents were killed or wounded while serving the country are set one to a few points lower than those for other students. Students from minority groups or who live in remote or mountainous areas are also supported by this policy. Since a single-sum score is used to inform admissions decisions, lowering the cut scores for students from special communities seems to improve their access to higher education. However, additional research is needed to investigate the impact of this policy and how much lower the cut scores for those students need to be in comparison to the cuts for typical students to improve access.

Before ending this section, it is worthwhile to reiterate that, by law, recruiting students is the right and responsibility of higher education institutions (Law on Higher Education, 2012). This point is further detailed in the admissions decree of 2017 to allow institutions to set their own admissions policies. For example, institutions are not forced to use test scores of the high school graduation and admissions exams to select students. If institutions need different admissions measures, they can develop and administer their own tests to collect information to recruit students at institutional or program levels. Given the complexity and high cost of building and administering institutional tests, very few universities in Vietnam organize their own assessments for all their applicants. Most, but not all, of the institutions rely on the high school graduation and admissions test scores to select their students. This is likely to be the safest and easiest choice for them. However, given that the tests in 2017 appeared to be quite easy and not very discriminating, some highly selective universities such as the medical schools or honor programs have considered building another layer of tests. Those additional assessments, which might mimic the SAT Subject Tests™ approach as an example among similar examinations from other countries, are expected to provide additional information about applicants' levels of proficiency and readiness for institutions or programs to which they are applying.

Another trend to diversify the sources of information to select students is to use imported tests such as the SAT or ACT® test from the United States, the General Certificate of Education Advanced Level (A Level) from the United Kingdom, or the Singapore–Cambridge General Certificate of Education Ordinary Level (O Level) from Singapore to set the criteria to admit students. This trend was first announced and adopted by the Vietnam National University, Hanoi (Yen, 2018). With the increasing popularity of undergraduate programs offered in English in Vietnam, this trend seems to be more prevalent and will be employed by more universities in the years to come. Nonetheless, the validity of imported test scores can be threatened by many factors (Oliveri, Lawless, & Young, 2015). Thus, the adoption of scores from tests developed to serve admissions purposes in foreign systems to the higher education context of Vietnam warrants thorough investigation and evaluation. Uninformed use of such scores without considering the purpose of the test could result in unintended consequences. First, since high school and college curricula differ across countries, if we use scores from admissions tests from one country to select students in another one, the selection error is likely to be higher. Second, uneven educational opportunities for students with differing socioeconomic status could lead to unequal access to higher education when imported test scores are in use. Students from rural areas or lower-income families are less likely to be able to afford tutoring services and after-school classes in foreign languages to prepare and pay for tests such as the SAT and ACT tests. Consequently, their possibility of being accepted will be lowered if scores from these tests are adopted to admit Vietnamese students.

In short, the new policies and practices implemented to unify high school graduation exams and admissions tests into a single testing system in recent years seems to point Vietnam in the right direction of reducing testing pressure and cutting administrative costs. However, many questions about fairness and equal access remain unanswered and require research and systematic evaluation. In what follows, we will discuss some initial results, report one security issue, and summarize feedback from the public about the new testing and admissions system.

13.4 Some Results and Concerns

13.4.1 Some Initial Results from 2017

The most recent revision of admissions testing policy in Vietnam (starting in 2017) seems to show some positive influences on the system. From the public's perspective, the new unified testing system reduced testing pressure and coaching (Le, Thanh, & Le, 2017). This observation can be explained by the timeline, content, and format of the new tests. Indeed, in the new system, students just need to sit one testing session by the end of high school instead of taking two sets of tests within a month, as in the previous system. In addition to reducing two testing instances to one session, almost all of the MCs assess foundational content and basic skills specified and emphasized in the national 12th-grade curriculum. Especially important to note is that the MCs in the mathematics test are much less complicated and demanding than the open-ended questions used in the test before 2017.

The new system also outperformed the former one in terms of expense for families and students (Le et al., 2017). As estimated by Dr. Tung Le, CEO of FPT Education, the new way of administering the tests at communal levels instead of in provincial cities may have saved the whole country about US $40 million. Since 2017, students and their families have not had to travel to and stay for a few days in big cities to take the admissions tests in July. They can stay at home and go to the high school in their neighborhood to take the unified tests.

Another positive change associated with the new testing system is that it encourages more students from ethnic groups to take the tests. For example, in Hoa Binh, a province in which more than 70 percent of the population is made up of minorities, there were 5,683 students from ethnic groups out of 7,942 students that took the tests in 2017. This was the highest number of minority students taking the high school

Table 13.1 *Pass rates of minority students, 2014–2017*

Year	Number of students passing	Number of minority students passing	Percentage of minority students passing
2016–2017	360,024	29,079	8.08
2015–2016	340,423	20,159	5.92
2014–2015	432,305	25,602	5.92

Source: Adapted from the Department of Quality Management (Ministry of Education and Training, 2017a).

graduation tests since 1991 (Nghiem, 2017). The new testing system put in place in 2017 also allows more applicants from minority backgrounds to be eligible to access tertiary education. Indeed, Table 13.1 displays the numbers of students whose admissions scores were not less than the cut scores specified by the MoET.

As Table 13.1 indicates, the percentage of minority students whose scores met the minimum requirement to enter colleges and universities increased by about 2 percent in 2017 compared to the two previous years. This evidence shows that higher education has become more accessible to minority students since the new testing system was introduced. At this time, we do not have information from all the universities and colleges as to the number of minority students who matriculated in 2017 and previous years. Nonetheless, the fact that the new testing system encouraged more students from minority groups to take and obtain scores exceeding the pass threshold to be eligible for tertiary education illustrates another advantage of the new system. By and large, the unification of the two sets of tests and test administration at the communal level seems to have resulted in some notable improvements in terms of reducing pressure and costs and supporting minority students. However, the revisions did not come without issues, criticism, and skepticism. In the following sections, we will summarize some critiques from the public in 2017 and a security scandal in 2018.

13.4.2   Public and Security Concerns

While the initial results in 2017 appear to be promising, concerns remain about question formats, test security, and fairness. First, some prominent mathematicians in Vietnam expressed their anxiety that the move from using open-ended questions to MCs for the mathematics tests might overlook higher-order intellectual and calculation skills (Hien, 2016). Representatives of the Vietnam Mathematical Society also questioned the preparedness of the MoET to build test banks of MCs in just a few months, just before the test dates. Second, after reviewing several test forms, some teachers and content experts were skeptical about the equality of the level of difficulty of the forms (Le & Nguyen, 2017). Representatives from the MoET stated publicly that all the forms were assembled so that they would be equally difficult. Given that no equating method had been adopted, the concern of those teachers and content experts seemed to be reasonable and warrants further investigation and discussion. Third, students and parents in urban areas questioned the suitability of lowering cut scores for applicants from rural and remote districts. Depending upon where the applicants live, the cut scores can be lowered from one to a few points on the sum-score scales for acceptance to colleges and universities. This priority policy for rural students has existed for many years. Since the purpose of the tests from 2017 included their use for high school graduation and for college admissions, they seemed to be easier than the admissions tests used in previous years. The lowering of one to a few points for rural applicants was likely to put urban students in more disadvantageous situations when they applied to some of the highly selective universities or programs with many rural applicants.

Finally, there was the shocking fraud of altered test scores that happened in three provinces in 2018 (Quynh, Duong, & Phan, 2018). In Ha Giang, Son La, and Hoa Binh, government officers had changed the scoring process to increase test scores of hundreds of students. For example, in Ha Giang, the former deputy director of the province's Department of Testing and Quality Assurance had broken the security system to change answer sheets of at least 114 students to increase their scores. In Son La, violations were detected in human scoring of the literature test. Scores of 12 students had been increased by at least one score point. Remarkably, there was one student who obtained a literature score that was 4.5 points higher than his/her adjusted score after the investigation. In short, the serious concerns of the public, and the occurrence of the scandal, reconfirmed the weight that the admissions tests carry and how important they are. For the future, it is recommended that the MoET and related entities such as colleges and universities take these concerns seriously and find ways to improve the current system.

13.5   Conclusions and Policy Recommendations

As we have shown, higher education in Vietnam is changing from an elite to a mass system. A mass higher education system needs a more accessible admissions process and less-challenging examinations (Trow, 2006). The recent movement of unifying high school graduation and admissions tests in Vietnam seemed to implement that view and the Law on Higher Education (2012) was put in place to regulate admissions practices. Since the new system was introduced, some positive feedback from the public has been recorded and an outrageous scandal has occurred. In what follows, we will adopt the most recent standards for educational and psychological testing from the United States (American Educational Research Association, American Psychological Association, & National Council on Measurement in Education, 2014) to suggest some policy recommendations for Vietnam and countries (or educational systems) that are in the process of revising and improving their admissions testing and policies. We are cognizant that imposing standards developed in an American context to that of Vietnam with a long history and unique educational culture can be unfavorable. Instead of thinking of this as an imposition, we would like the reader to treat our recommendations as suggestions for policymakers and practitioners to refer to when they are working on improving their policies and practices in the area of admissions testing and selection.

The first recommendation we propose is that the MoET collects more validity evidence with respect to each intended use of the test scores of the new testing system. This recommendation is strongly suggested by the testing standards mentioned earlier. The MoET states that the new tests serve three purposes: (a) setting high school graduation criteria, (b) assisting tertiary admissions, and (c) evaluating education quality. Until now, we can find only very limited scientific evidence to support or refute any aspect of those purposes. The scarcity of validity evidence for the new tests and the long history of educational and selection testing in Vietnam are an indication that the country should pay more attention to test validation, conduct validity studies to support intended test usage and reduce any unintended consequences of testing.

Second, considering the concern of the public regarding the equivalence of the test forms, we would suggest that some type of equating should be implemented so that scores from different forms can be used interchangeably. To set the foundation for implementing some equating methods, the test developers need to move away from reporting raw score scales. A new score scale that carries some meaningful interpretation to educational stakeholders should be introduced. Raw scores from different forms should then be mapped into this score scale via equating or scaling methods to create score reports for each student. Along with equating, some score-anchoring and/or standard-setting methods should be implemented to provide meaningful cut scores to set high school graduation criteria or to admit students into higher education. With more interpretable and meaningful score scales, institutions and programs can use the score reports to select more suitable applicants.

Third, consequences of the new testing system should be investigated to inform the public and set the stage for follow-up testing and policy revisions. For instance, given that different forms within a test were unlikely to be perfectly equivalent, it is highly recommended that the difficulty of those forms and the consequence for students taking different forms should be examined. Another line of research would be to evaluate the validity of scores of imported assessments. Institutions should be informed about the impact of applying externally developed tests such as the SAT, ACT, A Level, or O Level to student selection and equality of access. Studies are needed to shed light on the validity of scores of those tests when they are used for admissions purposes in Vietnam. The framework introduced by Oliveri, Lawless, and Young (2015) can be adopted to guide such studies.

Finally, the test-fraud scandal that happened in 2018 is alarming in the sense that simply having a good reform direction is not enough if security procedures and human factors running the whole system are not functioning appropriately. For the future, we strongly recommend that the scoring process needs to be re-evaluated and overhauled. To keep human intervention regarding answer sheets to a minimum, the sheets should be processed by machines so they are anonymous when they are transferred to the scanning devices and scoring computers operated by humans. Other administrative solutions such as having answer sheets and essays (e.g., for literature) from one province scored by teachers and officials from a different province could also help mitigate scoring fraud.

In conclusion, Vietnam took bold action in 2017 to combine the high school graduation exams and admissions tests into a single system. Going along with the combination is the upgrade of admissions policies to more fully implement the new legislation enacted in 2012 to give the autonomy of admissions decisions back to institutions. This new testing system and follow-up admissions policies are likely to be stable in at least the next few years (Ministry of Education and Training, 2017a). On the one hand, we support the general direction set forth by the government due to suggestions by leading scholars in higher education (e.g., Trow, 2006), and positive feedback from educational stakeholders. On the other hand, we also agree with some major concerns raised by the public about particular technical aspects of the new system, such as test-form equivalency, using imported assessments to admit Vietnamese students, and priority policies for minority and/or rural students. Those concerns warrant more systematic and scientific investigations to inform sounder and more effective policies and practices to contribute to the successful transition from an elite to a mass higher education system in Vietnam.

REFERENCES

Altbach, P. G. (2016). *Global perspectives on higher education*. Baltimore, MD: Johns Hopkins University Press.

American Educational Research Association, American Psychological Association, & National Council on Measurement in Education. (2014). *Standards for educational and psychological testing*. Washington, DC: American Educational Research Association.

Education Law, No. 38/2005/QH11 (2005). Retrieved from www.wto.org/english/thewto_e/acc_e/vnm_e/WTACCVNM43_LEG_14.pdf.

General Statistics Office of Vietnam. (2018a). Population and employment: Area and population of Vietnam in 2016. Retrieved from www.gso.gov.vn/default_en.aspx?tabid=774.

(2018b). Education: Some statistics of Vietnam's higher education up to 2016. Retrieved from http://gso.gov.vn/default_en.aspx?tabid=782

Hien, Q. (2016, September 13). Hội Toán học phản đối thi trắc nghiệm môn toán [Vietnam Mathematical Society against standardized test using MCQs]. Retrieved from https://thanhnien.vn/giao-duc/hoi-toan-hoc-phan-doi-thi-trac-nghiem-mon-toan-743756.html.

Law on Higher Education, No. 08/2012/QH13. (2012). Retrieved from www.ilo.org/dyn/natlex/natlex4.detail?p_lang=en&p_isn=91570&p_country=VNM&p_count=532.

Le, D. P. (2006). The role of non-public institutions in higher education development of Vietnam. (Doctoral dissertation). Hiroshima University.

Le, H., & Nguyen, T. (2017, June 23). Giáo viên nhận xét đề thi trắc nghiệm môn toán THPT quốc gia [Teachers comment on the mathematics test]. Retrieved from http://vietnamnet.vn/vn/giao-duc/tuyen-sinh/giao-vien-nhan-xet-de-thi-trac-nghiem-mon-toan-ky-thi-thpt-quoc-gia-2017-379870.html.

Le, H., Thanh, H., & Le, V. (2017, June 26). "Chấm điểm" kỳ thi THPT quốc gia 2017 ["Scoring" the national high school graduation exams 2017]. Retrieved from http://vietnamnet.vn/vn/giao-duc/tuyen-sinh/ky-thi-thpt-quoc-gia-2017-duoi-goc-nhin-nha-giao-380279.html.

Le, V. (2017, August 11). Những con số "biết nói" về giáo dục đại học Việt Nam ["Speaking statistics" of Vietnam's higher education]. Retrieved from http://vietnamnet.vn/vn/giao-duc/tuyen-sinh/nhung-con-so-biet-noi-ve-giao-duc-dai-hoc-viet-nam-389870.html.

Ministry of Education and Training. (2017a). Số liệu giáo dục đại học 2017. [Statistics of universities in 2017]. Retrieved from https://moet.gov.vn/content/tintuc/Lists/News/Attachments/5137/so%20lieu%20thong%20ke%20GDDH%202016_2017.pdf.

(2017b). Thông tư ban hành ban hành Quy chế thi trung học phổ thông quốc gia và xét công nhận tốt nghiệp trung học phổ thông. [Decree to issue the regulations for national high school graduation exams and certification]. Retrieved from https://moet.gov.vn/van-ban/vanban/Pages/chi-tiet-van-ban.aspx?ItemID=1236.

Nghiem, H. (2017, July 6). Hòa Bình có 1 thí sinh dân tộc đạt 2 điểm 10 [Hoa Binh had one ethnic student who obtained two scores of 10]. Retrieved from www.tienphong.vn/giao-duc/hoa-binh-co-1-thi-sinh-dan-toc-dat-2-diem-10-1164977.tpo.

Nguyen, Q. C. T. (2012). *Khoa cu Viet Nam (Tap Thuong): Thi huong* [Educational testing in Vietnam (higher volume): provincial exams]. Hanoi: Literature Publisher.

Nguyen, P. V., Le, L. V., & Nguyen, T. M. (2005). *Lich su Thang Long Hanoi* [History of Thang Long Hanoi]. Ho Chi Minh City: Youth Publisher.

Nguyen, H. (2016, September 13). Thi trắc nghiệm môn Toán ở Sài Gòn năm 1974 [Standardized tests in Saigon in 1974]. Retrieved from http://vietnamnet.vn/vn/giao-duc/tuyen-sinh/thi-trac-nghiem-mon-toan-o-sai-gon-nam-1974-326318.html.

Oliveri, M. E., Lawless, R., & Young, J. W. (2015). *A validity framework for the use and development of exported assessments*. Princeton, NJ: Educational Testing Service.

Quynh, T., Duong, T., & Phan, A. (2018, July 19). Vietnam probes outrageous fraud in national high school exam. Retrieved from https://e.vnexpress.net/news/news/vietnam-probes-outrageous-fraud-in-national-high-school-exam-3779835.html

Thang Long University. (2014). History of Thang Long University. Retrieved from http://en.thanglong.edu.vn/about-tlu/2014-03-17-06-58-58/history-of-the-thang-long-university/148-about-tlu/profile/history

Tran, T. P. H. (2009). *Franco-Vietnamese schools and the transition from Confucian to a new kind of intellectual in the colonial context of Tonkin* (Working Paper Series). Cambridge, MA: Harvard-Yenching Institute.

Trow, M. A. (1973). *Problems in the transition from elite to mass higher education*. Berkeley, CA: Carnegie Commission on Higher Education.

(2006). Reflections on the transition from elite to mass to universal access: Forms and phases of higher education in modern societies since WWII. In J. J. Forest & P. G. Altbach (Eds.). *International handbook of higher education* (pp. 243–280). Dordrecht: Springer. https://doi.org/10.1007/978-1-4020-4012-2_13.

University of Indochina. (2016, September 11). Quá trình hình thành và phát triển của Đại học Đông Dương qua tài liệu lưu trữ [Establishment and development of University of Indochina through archives]. Retrieved from http://luutruquocgia1.org.vn/gioi-thieu-tai-lieu-nghiep-vu/qua-trinh-hinh-thanh-va-phat-trien-cua-dai-hoc-dong-duong-qua-tai-lieu-luu-tru.

World Bank. (n.d.[a]). Education in Vietnam: Development history, challenges and solutions. Retrieved from https://siteresources.worldbank.org/EDUCA TION/Resources/278200-1121703274255/1439264-1153425508901/Edu cation_Vietnam_Development.pdf.

(n.d.[b]). School enrollment, tertiary (% gross). Retrieved from https://data .worldbank.org/indicator/SE.TER.ENRR?locations=VN

(2018). GDP per capita of Vietnam in recent years. Retrieved from https:// data.worldbank.org/country/vietnam

Yen, A. (2018, February 8). Đại học tốp trên xét tuyển nhiều yếu tố. [Top universities use multiple criteria to select students]. Retrieved from http:// tuyensinh.dantri.com.vn/tuyen-sinh/dai-hoc-top-tren-xet-tuyen-nhieu-yeu-to-20180207163328589.htm.

PART III

Assessments Used in Higher Education Admissions

María Elena Oliveri

The chapters in this section provide an overview and critical discussion of the types of assessments used to help inform admissions decisions. Examples include assessments that measure academic preparation (either general or subject-specific skills), tests of language proficiency, and assessments of noncognitive and personality traits. These assessments may or may not be required of all applicants depending on the type of institution students apply to, educational model the higher education institution uses, and rigor of the admitting institution's selection criteria, among other factors. At times, these assessments are developed by outside testing agencies. At other times, government agencies or universities develop them.

Central to the use of these assessments is their ability to capture students' skills, knowledge, or personality traits accurately to predict their readiness to pursue and complete their program of study. The various authors also discuss criteria that can add value to the admissions-decision process, such as the inclusion of items on the test that assess content that students had an opportunity to learn, are not susceptible to coaching or faking, and that focus on skills students will need in their future studies.

These authors also discuss the use of multiple measures to assess higher education success given its multidimensional nature. They suggest combining or integrating data from various sources of information to optimize the decision-making process so as to inform meaningful, valid, and fair decision-making. To this end, there has been increased interest in combining traditional measures, such as scores from academic tests and prior grades (which have received the most attention in the research literature), with additional assessments. An example of emerging or more innovative measures includes the assessment of noncognitive attributes to augment the use of academic predictors as criteria for decision-making, because these attributes may be considered relevant to college success.

The chapters in this section describe the benefits, challenges, and limitations of various measures used in admissions decisions. They also provide suggestions for future research to help strengthen score-based inferences from their use. The authors of chapters in this section discuss these and other issues in detail.

The chapter by Reshetar and Pitts describes academic assessments that measure general or subject-specific skills and are used around the world. They discuss two types of assessments: exit exams used when leaving an institution and entrance exams required for admittance to an institution. The authors describe general characteristics of the tests, concerns, and psychometric challenges for their use. They also discuss future-looking trends in developing and implementing various types of academically focused assessments so that they provide valid and reliable results.

Eckes and Althaus discuss assessments of language proficiency in admissions decisions. Assessments of language proficiency are increasingly important given the rising numbers of international students traveling abroad to study, not only to English-speaking countries but also to non-English-speaking countries. Along the same lines, increasing numbers of refugees and students studying in a language that is not their best language often are asked to take language proficiency assessments to demonstrate their linguistic preparedness for academic study and inform decisions to implement language-support programs for students not meeting the requirements. The authors highlight that demonstrating a level of language proficiency that represents minimum entrance requirements, under optimal conditions, is merely a necessary – but not a sufficient – condition for academic success. Thus, the authors discuss the importance of using benchmarks and standards to inform college-admissions decisions meaningfully as well as additional challenges institutions face in predicting students' academic success.

The final chapter, by Kuncel, Tran, and Zhang, describes noncognitive assessments that measure skills and traits, such as leadership, moral character, empathy, social consciousness, and civic responsibility, that may be used in admissions decisions. The authors describe traditional measures of noncognitive factors, such as letters of recommendation, as well as more modern tools, such as situational judgment tests and biodata. They review existing research, possible sources of bias, and concerns related to their use, such as faking. They also offer recommendations for practice for the various tools discussed. One example is the triangulation of various measures and sources of information to evaluate student readiness to pursue and complete higher education studies.

Collectively, these chapters provide a comprehensive view of the various assessments used in admissions decisions. The future is bright concerning research to address the various complexities and challenges that can be raised in relation to the use of these measures and the identification of ways to combine the various sources of information provided by these, and other, criteria used in informing admissions decisions.

CHAPTER 14

General Academic and Subject-Based Examinations Used in Undergraduate Higher Education Admissions

Rosemary Reshetar and Martha F. Pitts

Test scores are an integral part of admissions systems in many countries. The focus of this chapter is on examinations in undergraduate higher education admissions that measure general academic or subject-specific skills. We provide an overview of the admissions testing landscape followed by descriptions of some of the examinations used in different countries. The descriptions include, when available, information regarding test administration and oversight, test structure, content, technical procedures, technical quality, validity, test use, and fairness. Following the descriptions of individual examinations is a more general discussion that covers considerations in developing and implementing academically focused examination programs that provide valid and reliable results.

Across the globe, there is great variety in the examinations used in higher education. A few papers provide comparisons of higher education admissions models and inclusive examinations. Helms (2008) provides a comprehensive overview of models used in admissions worldwide, grouping examinations into three primary categories: secondary leaving examinations, entrance examinations, and standardized aptitude tests. For purposes of this chapter, we classify these examinations into two primary categories. The first category is the leaving (exit) examinations, which students are required to pass in order to receive a high school diploma or certificate and make students eligible to enter higher education. The second category is the entrance examinations, which are used for selection into higher education or particular programs.

McGrath et al. (2014) provide a comparative overview of higher education entrance qualifications and examinations in ten European countries, Turkey, Australia, Japan, and the United States. They note the reliance of the European admissions systems on secondary education requirements as the main qualification for higher education admissions. A report by the Office of Qualifications and Examinations Regulation (2012) compared the demands of assessments commonly taken by students looking to enter higher education in more than a dozen countries internationally with systems they categorized as high performing with those of the General Certificate of Education Advanced Level (A Level) qualifications in the United Kingdom in the four disciplines of mathematics, chemistry, English, and history.

Examinations used in higher education vary across several noteworthy dimensions. One distinguishing factor is that of examination sponsorship and management. Some examinations are owned by independent companies, some are managed at the country level, and others are institution specific. Another factor is the content measured by the tests. Examinations may test language proficiency, personal or personality characteristics, general aptitude or academic skills, cognitive ability, general subject areas such as science and humanities, more narrowly focused subject areas, and skills such as portfolio examinations used in the arts. Other chapters in this volume focus on tests used to measure personal characteristics (see Niessen & Meijer and Kuncel, Tran, & Zhang) or language proficiency (see Eckes & Althaus). The current chapter focuses only on those examinations that are academically based and measure either general ability or knowledge in particular subject areas.

14.1   The Use of General Academic and Subject-Based Tests in Higher Education

General ability and academic examinations are those that target general verbal, quantitative, and reasoning skills. Subject-based examinations, offered individually or as parts of a battery, are typically tailored to specific subjects offered in secondary and high school curricula. The use of these examinations adds value to the extent that they enhance the quality and fairness of selection for higher education. To contribute to an equitable admissions system, the test must represent students' performance and potential accurately. They should test material that students have had an opportunity to learn, and for this reason they are often built to reflect the foundational knowledge students learn in (secondary) school.

Best-practice test development and psychometric procedures, along with equitable access to preparation materials, provide an essential foundation to support test reliability, validity, and fairness. Attention to administrative procedures, including preparation materials, test security, and access also supports the quality of the program. Guidelines and quality standards for test use and best practice in educational and psychological assessment specify areas to which attention should be given, if possible (e.g., American

Educational Research Association, American Psychological Association, & National Council on Measurement in Education, 2014; International Test Commission, 2001; 2006; 2012; 2014; 2018; Council of Chief State School Officers & Association of Test Publishers, 2013; Council of Chief State School Officers, 2014). Beyond these best practices, broader policy considerations of fairness and access to higher education are needed and are beyond the scope of this chapter.

Examinations aid admissions decisions by demonstrating predictive validity for college success. Thus, examinations can support the higher education enterprise when they are used as indicators that students are ready for higher education coursework. This allows for targeting of educational resources to enhance enrollees' probability of success and completion, and proactively to provide additional preparatory resources for students, if needed. In addition, as feasible, evaluation of the validity of claims should be part of an ongoing research agenda (Kane, 2013). As Messick (1989, p. 13) notes, "validity is an evolving property and validation is a continuing process." Examples of research that address the evidential validity argument follow.

Studies have been conducted to examine the quality and validity of the Turkish Yuksekoğretime Gecis Sınavı (YGS) and Lisans Yerleştirme Sınavı (LYS) examinations. For example, Atalmis (2016) analyzed the impact of violating item-writing guidelines on test difficulty and did not find a negative impact when items with negatively worded stems were included. Ağazade et al. (2014) conducted a concurrent validity study using data from students enrolled in education, law, and health science majors at a medium-score admission university and found low predictive validity for first-semester grade point averages. Hatipoğlu (2016) examined pre-service English language teachers' views of the effect of the English section and concluded that it had a detrimental effect on the teaching and learning of English in Turkey.

Studies of the reliability and validity of the A Level examinations tend to be subject-specific rather than focused on the entire system. For example, Stringer (2014) studied the achieved weighting of assessment objectives as a facet of validity for some A Level subjects and found examples where the achieved weights deviated from the intended weights. Insight into possible causes was offered. Shaw and Crisp (2010) evaluated the validity of the A Level examinations in geography and found considerable support for interpretation of results, along with some potential threats to validity, to inform improvements. Other research (Benton & Bramley, 2015; Sutch, Zanini & Benton, 2015; and Zanini & Williamson, 2017) focused on monitoring and improving the quality of the technical work and the impact of the recent assessment reforms on the educational system.

Studies on the Konkoor used in Iran include the predictive validity of final English examinations as a measure of success in Iranian national university entrance examination (Alavi, 2012; Sazegar & Motallebzadeh, 2017), medical students' academic performance (Farrokhi-Khajeh-Pasha et al., 2012), and a content analysis of the English section in the fields of mathematics, humanities, and natural sciences (Razmjoo & Madani, 2013). Other studies have examined predictive validity questions for the Matura in Croatia (Mundar, Kečik, & Matotek, 2015) and the SweSAT used in Sweden (Wedman, 2017). Research on the ACT® and SAT® examinations used in the United States is referenced in Section 14.2.1.4.

In a paper focused on the language-testing component of The National Center Test for University Admission used in Japan, Watanabe (2013) indicates that some information to support reliability and validity, including results of annual reviews and student performance statistics, is provided annually by the test producer. He also mentions that research that addressed the predictability of test scores is the most difficult to collect, institution specific, and urgently needed.

Keeping in mind the importance of the use and interpretation of scores from such examinations, we next provide various examples of examinations used in higher education admissions with a focus on the design and procedures of each program.

14.2   Country- or Region-Specific Examinations

In this section we discuss some general academic and subject-based examinations and examination systems used for admissions. We divide these examinations into two categories: those tests that are used to select higher education applicants into particular institutions and those tests that make students eligible for higher education. We look at the administration model and structural characteristics, including the content framework, timing, and item types. Finally, other relevant information, such as the weight given to test score(s) in the admissions process or issues of fairness and validity, are provided if available.

Some country-specific admissions practices are discussed elsewhere in this volume and include information on the examinations used in those contexts (see Oanda for a discussion on admissions practices in African nations; Koljatic and Silva for Chile; Papanastasiou and Michaelides for Cyprus; Allalouf, Cohen, and Gafni for Israel; Jappie for South Africa;

Lyrén and Wikström for Sweden; and Pham and Sai for Vietnam). In this section, we describe some additional countries not included elsewhere in the book. Ideally, a review of this type would be based on primary-source technical documentation provided by the examination sponsors or developers. In searching references, we found limitations to the information publicly available. Given these limitations, preference was given to information released by examination sponsors, published articles, and academic sources. Information obtained from *Wikipedia* or other websites is also included if it was the only available source.

14.2.1   Entrance Examinations

Many countries use separate examinations to select applicants into higher education institutions or particular programs, fields of study, or majors. This section provides information on the general academic or subject-based examinations and their contexts for the following countries that offer separate admissions examinations, including China, South Korea, Japan, the United States, Puerto Rico and Latin America, Iran, Turkey, India, and Brazil.

14.2.1.1   China

The admissions system in China is highly competitive and uses a quota system that specifies a fixed number of first-year students assigned for each university in each province. Test scores obtained on the entrance exam, The National College Entrance Examination (NCEE), commonly referred to as the Gaokao, play a decisive role in admissions selection. The admissions plan and the full examination process are under the purview of the Chinese government.

Wang (2006) presents an overview of the process used to develop and administer the NCEE. The report describes the process by which new forms are developed and administered each year under stringent security protocols and notes that because entirely new forms need to be developed each year, there are limitations for pretesting and test-equating procedures to be incorporated. For the purposes of admissions decisions, candidates are rank ordered by their test scores relative to those in their cohort.

The examination is nine hours in length and is administered once annually over a two-day period in early June. The format is referred to as 3+X. Three compulsory subjects are included: mathematics (2 hours), Chinese (2.5 hours), and a foreign language (English, Japanese, Russian, or French; 2 hours). In addition, students choose an elective subject

(2.5 hours) and take a comprehensive examination in natural science (physics, chemistry, and biology) or social science (history, politics, and geography). Some provinces add an additional local examination requirement. Test content is defined by the national curriculum and must stay within the curriculum framework. Question formats include multiple-choice, open response, polytomous (two choices) response, a writing prompt in Chinese, and writing and listening prompts in English (these require written responses). Grading (scoring) is conducted at the provincial level, usually by university staff. Constructed-response items are scored by two examiners or raters independently.

The Gaokao appears to be continually undergoing reform (for the status of the reform or to contact the Ministry of Education for the People's Republic of China regarding the reform, the reader should visit http://en .moe.gov.cn/).

14.2.1.2   South Korea

The admissions system in South Korea is similar to China's in that it is highly competitive and test scores obtained on the annual entrance examination – the College Scholastic Ability Test (CSAT) – play a decisive role in selection. Also known as the Suneung, the CSAT is fully managed by the Korea Institute of Curriculum and Evaluation (KICE) and tight security controls are in place throughout the entire process. Kwon, Lee, and Shin (2017) present a profile of the education system in Korea focusing on the CSAT and describe the test development process, which, like the process in China, is conducted under high security.

The CSAT is administered nationally once a year in November. The test focuses on thinking skills and subjects across the high school curriculum. There are five separately timed sections ranging from 40 to 102 minutes in: (a) language arts, (b) mathematics, (c) English, (d) Korean history and investigation (social studies, science, vocational education), and (e) second foreign languages and Chinese characters and classics.

Students take Korean history as a compulsory subject. The three subject areas of language arts, mathematics, and English language have mandatory and selective components. There are many selection options for subject tests within each of the investigation study areas (social studies, science, and vocational education) and foreign-language offerings. Most questions are multiple-choice, including some with listening prompts in the English section, and 30 percent of the mathematics section consists of short-answer questions (for the latest information on the logistics and format of the examination, the reader should visit www.KICE.re.kr).

Raw scores for each subject are standardized and converted to reported stanine grades, based on predetermined cut points. Student score reports include a standard score, percentile, and stanine/grade for each subject. More technical information for the CSAT is not publicly available.

As with the Gaokao in China, the CSAT is extremely high-stakes as it serves as a gatekeeper to future opportunities, and thus results in intense pressure for students, families, and teachers. Kwon, Lee, and Shin (2017) elaborate on the societal context of the CSAT use and related dilemmas for policymakers, arguing that there is a need for less reliance on a high-stakes standardized test to make positive educational reforms. Choi and Park (2013) also provide a historical analysis of the college entrance system in South Korea, critique the quality, cite limitations, and suggest improvements.

14.2.1.3 Japan

Japan has a single national admissions test. Known as the National Center Test, it is administered by each university in conjunction with the National Center for University Entrance Examinations (National Center for University Entrance Examinations, 2015). It measures basic academic achievement for applicants to national and public universities. Private universities may require candidates to take (a) only a university-developed test, (b) only the National Center Test, or (c) both the National Center Test and a university-developed test (Kuramoto & Koizumi, 2018).

The NCUEE oversees test development, testing procedures, scoring, and score reporting for the National Center Test. The two-day examination is administered annually on the same day throughout the country. Tests are offered in six subject areas, including geography and history, civics, Japanese language, several foreign languages, science, and mathematics. There are separately timed sections of approximately one to two hours for each subject test. In 2016, 30 subject tests were offered in the six areas. The National Center Test consists mainly of multiple-choice format questions. There is a written and a listening test for examinees who select English as their foreign language. Participating universities specify the tests from the National Center Test to be administered to applicants.

The NCUEE works with universities on relevant research projects aimed at improving university admissions-selection methods, including research on the National Center Test, and disseminates research bulletins (in Japanese) to the public via their website (National Center for University Entrance Examinations, 2015).

Changes are set to be introduced in 2020. English tests will be administered multiple times each year and allow applicants to submit their best score for admissions. Constructed-response questions will be included in the Japanese language and mathematics tests along with multiple-choice questions. Finally, the testing time will be extended. Kuramoto and Koizumi (2018) describe the impetus and development of the changes in the context of large-scale educational assessment in Japan.

14.2.1.4   United States

Admissions examinations play some role in the admissions process at the vast majority of 4-year higher education institutions in the United States. A 2018 survey on the state of college admissions conducted by the National Association for College Admission Counseling (Clinedinst & Patel, 2018) indicates that standardized tests are of considerable importance for 52 percent of institutions responding to the survey and that standardized tests of are moderate importance for 31 percent of the institutions that responded. The ACT test and SAT are the most common examinations used in admissions. In addition, 20 SAT Subject Tests™ are offered on specific subjects. These tests are administered multiple times throughout the year and test-takers may repeat them as often as desired. Multiple scores and subscores are reported, with scores on all forms equated to an existing score scale for each test.

Both the ACT and SAT have elaborate assessment design, development, and psychometric procedures in place. Information can be found in the technical manuals, which describe the examination; procedures for test development, psychometrics, and administration; and validity evidence (ACT, 2017a; The College Board, 2017a). A considerable body of research on the quality, fairness, and validity of the ACT and SAT tests has been conducted by the sponsoring organizations, independent researchers, and institutions using the tests in their admissions process.

ACT, Inc. develops and administers the ACT test. The ACT contains 215 multiple-choice questions in four sections: English, mathematics, reading, and science. The timing of each section ranges from 35 to 60 minutes, for a total testing time of 2 hours 55 minutes. An optional 40-minute writing examination that requires students to produce an essay in response to a particular prompt is also available.

Fairness reports describe the fairness review process, statistical analyses for bias (DIF) process, and results for each test year (e.g., ACT, 2017b). Related research made publicly available by ACT, includes, for example, research examining test validity (e.g., Huh & Huang, 2016) and broader admissions topics such as college and career readiness (ACT, 2018).

The SAT is developed and administered by The College Board. The SAT is organized into four sections: reading; writing and language; mathematics; and an optional written essay, which is a direct-writing task. The total testing time is 3 hours, without the 50-minute optional essay. There are 154 questions on the required sections of the test, the majority of which are multiple-choice, with some mathematics questions requiring students to produce and fill in their responses in a grid. Supporting research made publicly available includes, for example, validity research (e.g., Beard & Marini, 2018; Shaw, 2015) and research to inform users about the use of test scores for the redesigned examination introduced in 2016 (e.g., Marini, Beard, & Shaw, 2018; Marini, Shaw & Young, 2016).

There are 20 SAT Subject Tests in five general subject areas: English, history, languages, mathematics, and science. Each test is comprised of multiple-choice questions. Testing time for each subject test is one hour.

14.2.1.5 *Puerto Rico and Latin America.*

The PAA™ is a Spanish-language college-entrance examination developed by The College Board's Puerto Rico and Latin America Office (The College Board, 2008; Cascallar & Dorans, 2003). The PAA is designed for students in the region whose primary language is Spanish and used for admission and support of academic counseling for institutions of higher education across Puerto Rico and Latin America. The PAA is 3 hours and 15 minutes long. The Puerto Rico Department of Education administers the PAA annually to all 11th-grade students in Puerto Rico during the school day. Students may also take the PAA during one of three Saturday administrations. Scores on all forms are equated to an existing score scale for each test.

The assessment comprises four tests in three sections: reading and writing (in Spanish; 70 questions [45 and 25 respectively]); mathematics (55 questions); and English (50 questions). Four test scores (reading, writing, mathematics, and English), three section-level scores (reading and writing, mathematics, and English), and 11 subscores are reported. The reading and writing and mathematics sections are generally used as part of the admissions process. The English section was developed to evaluate the English proficiency of students whose primary language is Spanish and is recommended for placement in first-year English courses. Most test questions are multiple-choice, with some mathematics questions requiring students to produce and fill in their responses on a grid.

While the design of the PAA is similar to The College Board's SAT, it is neither a translation nor an adaptation of the SAT. Since its beginning, the

PAA has been designed by an international committee that includes experienced Latin American and Puerto Rican educators; test questions are written by Spanish-speaking subject-matter specialists with knowledge of Latin American and Puerto Rican educational systems.

A revised (fourth-generation) PAA was launched in December 2017 (The College Board, 2017b) and has been administered in Puerto Rico since then. The PAA is not required for admission to all higher education institutions in Puerto Rico. In many institutions, however, the primary admission material requirements include the PAA scores and high school grades. Even test-optional institutions may use PAA scores for placement purposes, if applicable, as well as for institutional effectiveness and accreditation purposes. In Latin America, the PAA is typically used as a standalone assessment and most institutions are still using the third generation of the PAA.

14.2.1.6 Iran

Admission to public universities is based solely on performance in the nationwide Iranian National University Entrance Examination (the Konkoor), which is administered annually in June. The Iranian Measurement Organization (IMO) creates and administers the test. The Konkoor is a norm-referenced test and students are selected for admissions based on their relative performance (Gronlund & Linn, 1990; Hudson, 2005). It is a four-and-a-half-hour multiple-choice examination that covers high school topics in five different academic areas: experimental sciences; mathematics and physics; human sciences; fine arts; and foreign languages (Kamyab, 2008). Azad University has a separate entrance examination and is considered less prestigious than the public universities (Farrokhi-Khajeh-Pasha et al., 2012).

14.2.1.7 Turkey

Admission to higher education institutions in Turkey is highly competitive. The universities in Turkey set their admissions requirements individually. For associate and bachelor's degree programs, Turkish students are required to sit for a university entrance examination organized by the government's Student Selection and Placement Center (ÖSYM) (Akkök & Watts, 2003). The examination consists of multiple-choice questions and is divided into two stages: the higher education transition exam Yuksekoğretime Gecis Sınavı (YGS) and the undergraduate placement exam Lisans Yerleştirme Sınavı (LYS). The ÖSYM publishes examination information in the Turkish language on their website (www.osym.gov.tr/).

The YGS examination is offered once each year in April. There are two relevant YGS cut scores; one is used to apply for associate degree programs and the other to qualify to sit for the LYS. If a student receives a score above the established cut score on the LYS, they are eligible to apply for bachelor's degree programs. Final scores for acceptance into bachelor's degree programs are calculated by adding 40 percent of the YGS score and 60 percent of the LYS score and then adding the sum to the student's secondary grade point average.

The YGS tests four core curricula subjects: basic mathematics, Turkish language and expression, sciences, and social sciences. Test takers are allowed 160 minutes to complete the examination, which includes 160 questions on geography, physics, history, philosophy, biology, mathematics, chemistry, Turkish language, and religion and morality.

The LYS assessment is a five-test battery, including (LYS1) mathematics, geometry; (LYS2) natural sciences (physics, chemistry, biology); (LYS3) Turkish language and literature, and geography; (LYS4) social sciences history, geography, and philosophy group (physiology, sociology, and logic); and (LYS5) foreign language (English, German, French). The five tests range from 80 to 90 questions, with testing times of 120 to 135 minutes, and are taken in multiple sessions over two weekends in June. University applicants take selected LYS tests according to the major in which they wish to specialize at college (Akbas, 2015; Hatipoğlu, 2016).

14.2.1.8 India

Most Indian universities participate in an admissions system centralized at the national and state levels. Students who pursue degrees in technology, including engineering, computer science, and healthcare, are required to complete an entrance examination for admission to higher education. Each examination has eligibility requirements, including completing courses of study and minimum/maximum ages. A brief description of some examinations follows.

There are Main and Advanced versions of the Joint Entrance Examination (JEE) which is required for students applying to the Indian higher education institutions that offer degrees in engineering, technological, and scientific disciplines. The version required depends upon the institution or institutional group for which the student seeks admission. JEE Advanced is used for admission to programs at Indian Institutes of Technology. The JEE Main is administered twice annually in January and April, and a normalization process is used to assure that candidates are neither benefited nor disadvantaged due to the difficulty level of the form.

Qualification scores on the JEE Main allow students to sit for the JEE Advanced, which is offered annually in May, in English and Hindi.

Both versions test mathematics, physics, and chemistry, via objective questions administered solely through computer-based testing (CBT).

For students applying for architecture, a paper-and-pencil section to measure drawing aptitude is added to the JEE Main. The National Aptitude Test in Architecture (NATA) is conducted twice annually by the Council of Architecture and is used for admission to bachelor's of architecture undergraduate programs at some private colleges. The examination includes a one-hour online section with 20 mathematics and 40 general-aptitude multiple-choice questions, and a two-hour paper section with two performance-based drawing questions evaluating drawing ability, imagination, and observation skill.

The National Eligibility Cum Entrance Test (UG) is required for admission to the Indian higher education institutions offering degrees in medicine and dentistry. The examination is three hours long and administered once annually in paper-and-pencil mode. It is offered in multiple languages and includes 180 multiple-choice questions in physics, chemistry, and biology (botany and zoology).

The Common Law Admission Test (CLAT) is required for admission to the National Law Universities in India and is sponsored by the Consortium of National Law Universities. The examination is two hours long and administered once annually. As of 2019, the test includes 200 multiple-choice questions in five areas: English, including comprehension and general knowledge; current affairs; elementary mathematics; legal aptitude; and logical reasoning (with 40, 50, 20, 50, and 40 questions, respectively).

14.2.1.9 *Brazil*

Both the Exame Nacional do Ensino Médio (ENEM) and the Vestibular examinations are used in Brazil for admissions. The ENEM is a non-mandatory national high school examination under the purview of the Ministry of Education that serves as a standard university entrance qualification test and is the main gateway to public universities in Brazil (Salmi & Fèvre, 2008). The ENEM is composed of 180 multiple-choice questions in five areas (natural sciences, human sciences, mathematics, Portuguese, and either English or Spanish as a foreign language), and an essay. It is administered over two days in November, for four-and-a-half hours one day and five-and-a-half hours the other.

In addition to the ENEM, some universities use a Concurso Vestibular, a competitive examination, for selection to higher education institutions

(World Bank, 2000). Individual universities and colleges often design and administer a customized entrance examination for various fields of study under general guidance from the National Education Council. The Vestibular is usually given from November to January and spans several days. It typically includes multiple-choice and essay questions and covers core secondary school subjects (Helms, 2008).

Individual institutions may choose if they want to use the ENEM, their institution's own test, or a combination of both, in their admissions selection process. The latest information regarding the ENEM is available from the Ministry of Education for Brazil; the reader should visit portal .mec.gov.br.

14.2.2 Exit (Leaving) Examinations

Examinations referred to as graduation, exit, or leaving examinations are those which students are required to pass to receive a high school diploma or certificate. They may be administered institutionally, regionally, or nationally. In some cases, receiving a particular pass mark in these examinations also makes students eligible to enter higher education. In other cases, scores on these examinations are used to rank order applicants or are combined with other application materials to create a selection index that is used for acceptance decisions. We describe a few examples below.

14.2.2.1 Matura Examinations

"Matura" is a term used by several countries to describe those examinations that allow students to exit secondary school. They are generally taken at the end of secondary school education and make students eligible to apply to higher education admissions. Countries that use a Matura examination as part of their admissions process include Albania, Austria, Bosnia, Bulgaria, Croatia, the Czech Republic, Herzegovina, Hungary, Italy, Kosovo, Liechtenstein, Macedonia, Montenegro, Poland, Serbia, Slovakia, Slovenia, Switzerland, and Ukraine. Matura examinations often include a battery of tests – general and/or subject-specific tests. They may include mandatory and optional components whereby students select which subjects to complete. The use of the scores for selection may be determined at the individual institutional level or at a higher level.

14.2.2.2 Abitur Examinations

After 12 or 13 years of studies in a German school, high school graduates receive a certificate known as the Abitur that authorizes them to study any subject at a higher education institution in Germany. The Abitur examinations are a series of written or oral tests taken in the spring over the course of two or three years coinciding with grades 11, 12, and 13 of the German public-school system. Neather (1993) provides historical, contextual information about the Abitur examinations. Three general areas must be covered: language, literature, and the arts; social sciences; and mathematics, natural sciences, and technology. Students may select specific subjects to test within each area. Each written basic-level examination takes about three hours; advanced-level examinations take four-and-a-half hours. Written examinations are in essay format and oral examinations last about 20 minutes. Papers are graded by at least two teachers at the students' schools. In some parts of Germany, students may prepare a presentation, research paper, or participate in a competition; they may take additional oral examinations to pass the Abitur if their performance on the written examination is poor. In addition to the Abitur requirement, some universities set up their own entrance examinations.

The administration is carried out by the schools, with oversight by the Ministry of Culture, and must be conducted according to the legal requirements set by the government. The scoring system for the Abitur final grades, consisting of the marks obtained in the examinations and in class performance, depends on the federal state (Bundesland) in which the Abitur is taken.

14.3   Discussion

The types of examinations, the content tested, the examination structure and scoring, the administration model, and the use of examination results differ immensely across countries. In addition, the amount of information available publicly varies by country and is often limited. A major distinction is between leaving examinations taken at the end of high school and examinations that are developed and used primarily for admissions selection. Variations in test structure are noted. They range from general standardized tests (that are a few hours in length and target more general skills and abilities) to batteries of subject-specific examinations which occur over multiple days of testing. Some examinations solely or primarily contain multiple-choice questions, some contain constructed-response questions, and some have a mixed format. Differences in sponsorship, administration, testing opportunities, and scoring procedures were described. The varied use of scores from entrance examinations includes: rank ordering students for selection and placement, the use of pass scores in a leaving examination for qualification, minimum cut score requirements for admissions, and weightings of examination scores determined by each institution.

All the factors above impact the admissions decisions and future careers of test-takers. In highly competitive programs, test sponsors must take significant measures to address test security. As noted earlier, the incorporation of best practice, as practicably feasible, provides a foundation for the use of examinations to add value to the admissions process. Assessing fairness of both the examinations and the procedures used by higher education institutions should be considered in the context of societal needs, as well as the examination program.

As higher education admissions take a future-looking perspective, the following questions might be kept in mind: How is fairness addressed in the end-to-end educational system? What is the validity argument for use of test scores, and what gaps exist? How can testing play a role in improving opportunities for access to higher education for all students? What should be emphasized in educational policy discussions in various environments? What information regarding the technical quality of the examination should be publicly shared?

Test sponsors are encouraged to consider their test design decisions and the impact for individual test-takers and to the educational system, and to release as much technical information as possible, publicly. Many programs make changes to support educational reform. Increased use of technology-based assessments is likely. By providing a look at varied and representative examination programs, it is hoped that readers will gain an appreciation of possibilities and consider them within their context and in conjunction with relevant guidelines and quality standards noted earlier.

REFERENCES

ACT. (2017a). *ACT technical manual.* Iowa City, IA: ACT.

  (2017b). *Fairness report for the ACT tests: 2015/2016.* Iowa City, IA: ACT.

  (2018). *The condition of college and career readiness, national 2018.* Iowa City, IA: ACT.

Ağazade, A. S., Caner, H., Hasipoğlu, H. N., & Civelek, A. H. (2014). Turkish university entrance test and academic achievement in undergraduate programs: A criterion-related validity study. *Procedia: Social and Behavioral Sciences 116,* 4582–4590. https://doi.org/10.1016/j.sbspro.2014.01.990.

Akbas, I. (2015). Comparison between undergraduate placement examination (LYS) in Turkey and EdEXCEL international advanced levels examination (IAL) in the world. *Green University Review of Social Sciences, 2*(2), 71–93.

Retrieved from http://green.edu.bd/wp-content/uploads/PDFs/Journals/ GURSS/v-2-i-2/Comparison_Between_Undergraduate_Placement_Examin ation_LYS_in_Turkey_and_Edexcel_International_Advanced_Levels_ Examination_IAL_in_the_World.pdf.

Akkök, F., & Watts, A. G. (2003). *Public policies and career development: Country report on Turkey*. Washington, DC: World Bank. Retrieved from http:// siteresources.worldbank.org/INTLL/Resources/Public-Policies-and-Career-Development-Policy/Turkey_report.pdf.

Alavi, T. (2012). The predictive validity of final English exams as a measure of success in Iranian National University Entrance English Exam. *Journal of Language Teaching and Research*, *3*, 224–228. https://doi.org/10.4304/ jltr.3.1.224-228.

American Educational Research Association, American Psychological Association, and National Council on Measurement in Education. (2014). *Standards for educational and psychological testing*. Washington, DC: American Educational Research Association.

Atalmis, E. H. (2016). Do the guideline violations influence test difficulty of high-stake test? An investigation on University Entrance Examination in Turkey. *Journal of Education and Training Studies*, *4*(10), 1–7. https://doi .org/10.11114/jets.v4i10.1738.

Beard, J., & Marini, J. (2018). *Validity of the SAT for predicting first-year grades: 2013 SAT validity sample*. New York, NY: The College Board.

Benton, T., & Bramley, T. (2015). *The use of evidence in setting and maintaining standards in GCSEs and A levels: Discussion paper*. Cambridge: Cambridge Assessment.

Cascallar, A. S., & Dorans, N. J. (2003). *Linking scores from tests of similar content given in different languages: Spanish language PAA and English language SAT I*. New York, NY: College Entrance Examination Board.

Choi, H. J., & Park, J.-H. (2013) Historical analysis of the policy on the college entrance system in South Korea. *International Education Studies*, *6*(11). https://doi.org/10.5539/ies.v6n11p106.

Clinedinst, M., & Patel, P. (2018). *2018 state of college admission*. Arlington, VA: National Association for College Admission Counseling.

The College Board. (2008). *The Puerto Rico and Latin America Office*. New York, NY: Author.

(2017a). *SAT suite of assessments technical manual: Characteristics of the SAT*. New York, NY: Author.

(2017b). PAA revisada: Preguntas y respuestas [Revised PAA: Questions and answers]. Retrieved from https://latam.collegeboard.org/wp-content/ uploads/2017/10/PAA-Preguntas-y-Respuestas-Puerto-Rico-2017.pdf

Council of Chief State School Officers. (2014). Criteria for procuring and evaluating high quality assessments. Retrieved from https://ccsso.org/sites/ default/files/2017-10/CCSSO%20Criteria%20for%20High%20Quality% 20Assessments%2003242014.pdf.

Council of Chief State School Officers & Association of Test Publishers. (2013). *Operational best practices for statewide large-scale assessment programs* (2013 ed.). Washington, DC: Council of Chief State School Officers & Association of Test Publishers.

Farrokhi-Khajeh-Pasha, Y., Nedjat, S., Mohammadi, A., Rad, E. M., Majdzadeh, R., Monajemi, F., & Yasdani, S. (2012). The validity of Iran's national university entrance examination (Konkoor) for predicting medical students' academic performance. *BMC Medical Education, 12*(60), 1–8. https://doi .org/10.1186/1472-6920-12-60.

Gronlund, N. E., & Linn, R. L. (1990). *Measurement and evaluation in teaching.* New York, NY: Macmillan.

Hatipoğlu, C. (2016). The impact of the University Entrance Exam on EFL education in Turkey: Pre-service English language teacher's perspective. *Procedia: Social and Behavioral Sciences, 232,* 136–144. https://doi.org/ 10.1016/j.sbspro.2016.10.038.

Helms, R. M. (2008). *University admission worldwide.* Washington, DC: International Bank for Reconstruction and Development/World Bank.

Hudson, T. (2005). Trends in assessment scales and criterion-referenced language assessment. *Annual Review of Applied Linguistics, 25,* 205–227. https://doi .org/10.1017/S0267190505000115.

Huh, N. R., & Huang, C.-Y. (2016). *Examining the validity of ACT composite score and high school grade point average for predicting first-year college GPA of special-tested students.* Iowa City, IA: ACT, Inc.

International Test Commission (2001). International guidelines for test use. *International Journal of Testing, 1,* 93–114. https://doi.org/10.1207/ S15327574IJT0102_1.

(2006). International guidelines on computer-based and internet delivered testing. *International Journal of Testing, 6,* 143–171. https://doi.org/ 10.1207/s15327574ijt0602_4.

(2012). ITC guidelines on quality control in scoring, test analysis, and reporting of test scores. Retrieved from www.intestcom.org.

(2014). International guidelines on the security of tests, examinations, and other assessments. Retrieved from www.intestcom.org/files/guideline_test_ security.pdf.

(2018). ITC guidelines for the large-scale assessment of linguistically and culturally diverse populations. Retrieved from www.researchgate.net/publica tion/315761630_ITC_Guidelines_for_the_Large-Scale_Assessment_of_Lin guistically_Diverse_Populations.

Kamyab, S. (2008). The University Entrance Exam crisis in Iran. *International Higher Education, 51,*22–23. https://doi.org/10.6017/ihe.2008.51.8010.

Kane, M. T. (2013). Validating the interpretations and uses of test scores. *Journal of Educational Measurement, 50,* 1–73. https://doi.org/10.1111/ jedm.12000.

Kuramoto, N., & Koizumi, R. (2018). Current issues in large-scale educational assessment in Japan: Focus on national assessment of academic ability and university entrance examinations. *Assessment in Education: Principles, Policy, & Practice, 25*, 415–433. https://doi.org/10.1080/0969594X.2016.1225667.

Kwon, S. K., Lee, M., & Shin, D. (2017). Educational assessment in the Republic of Korea: Lights and shadows of high-stake exam-based education system. *Assessment in Education: Principles, Policy, & Practice, 24*, 60–77. https://doi.org/10.1080/0969594X.2015.1074540.

McGrath, C. H., Henham, M. L., Corbett, A., Durazzi, N., Frearson, M., Janta, B., & Schweppenstedde, D. (2014.) Higher education entrance qualifications and exams in Europe: A comparison. Directorate-General for Internal Polices, Policy Department Structural and Cohesion Policies, European Parliament. Retrieved from www.europarl.europa.eu/thinktank/en/docu ment.html?reference=IPOL-CULT_ET(2014)529057.

Marini, J. P., Beard, J., & Shaw, E. (2018). *Student ranking differences within institutions using old and new SAT scores.* New York, NY: The College Board.

Marini, J. P., Shaw, E. J., & Young, L. (2016). *Using old and new SAT Scores for admission: A closer look at concordant scores in predictive models* (College Board Research Report No. 2016-17). New York, NY: The College Board.

Messick, S. (1989). Validity. In R. L. Linn (Ed.). *Educational measurement* (3rd ed.) (pp. 13–103). New York, NY: Collier Macmillan.

Mundar, D., Kečik, D., & Matotek, D. (2015). Relationship between enrolment criteria and first-year student' study-success. Proceedings of the 3rd Human and Social Sciences at the Common Conference, *Slovakia, 3*(1), 111–115. https://doi.org/10.18638/hassacc.2015.3.1.179.

National Center for University Entrance Examinations. (2015). *National Center for University Entrance Examinations Annual Report.* Tokyo: National Center for University Entrance Examinations. Retrieved from www.dnc.ac.jp/albums/abm.php?f=abm00006725.pdf&n=2015%E5%A4.

Neather, E. J. (1993). The Abitur examination. *Language Learning Journal, 7*, 19–21. https://doi.org/10.1080/09571739385200071.

Office of Qualifications and Examinations Regulation. (2012). *International comparisons in senior secondary assessment: Full report.* Coventry: Ofqual.

Razmjoo, S. A., & Madani, H. (2013). A content analysis of the English section of university entrance exams based on Bloom's revised taxonomy. *International Journal of Language Learning and Applied Linguistics World, 4*(3), 105–129.

Salmi, J., & Fèvre, C. (2008). Tertiary education and lifelong learning in Brazil. Retrieved from www.anped.org.br/sites/default/files/resources/SALMI_Jamil_e_F_VRE_Chlo_._Tertiary_Education_and_Lifelong_Learning_in_Brazil..pdf.

Sazegar, Z., & Motallebzadeh, K. (2017). Iranian National University Entrance Examination (Konkoor) of B.A.: An analysis of its reliability and validity. *Modern Journal of Language Teaching Methods, 3*(7), 358–365.

Shaw, E. (2015). *An SAT validity primer.* New York, NY: The College Board.

Shaw, S., & Crisp, V. (2010). How valid are A levels? Findings from a multi-method validation study of an international A level in geography. Paper presented at the Association for Educational Assessment in Europe, Oslo, Norway.

Stringer, N. (2014). *The achieved weightings of assessment objective as a source of validity evidence* (Ofqual Report No. 14/5375). Coventry: Office of Qualifications and Examinations Regulation. Retrieved from https://assets.publishing.service.gov.uk/government/uploads/system/uploads/attachment_data/file/605434/2014-02-11-the-achieved-weightings-of-assessment-objectives-as-a-source-of-validity-evidence.pdf.

Sutch, T., Zanini, N., & Benton, T. (2015). *A level reform: Implications for subject uptake.* (Cambridge Assessment Research Report). Cambridge: Cambridge Assessment.

Wang, X. B. (2006). *An Introduction to the system and culture of the college entrance examination of China* (Office of Research and Analysis Report No. RN-28). New York, NY: The College Board.

Watanabe, Y. (2013). The National Center Test for university admissions. *Language Testing, 30,* 565–573. https://doi.org/10.1177/0265532213483095.

Wedman, J. (2017). *Theory and validity evidence for a large-scale test for selection to higher education.* Umea: Umea University.

World Bank. (2000). *Brazil: Higher education sector study* (Report No. 19392-BR). Washington, DC: Human Development Department, Latin America and the Caribbean Region.

Zanini, N., & Williamson, J. (2017). *Learning aims: A preliminary exploration to monitor A/AS level reform* (Cambridge Assessment Research Report). Cambridge: Cambridge Assessment.

CHAPTER 15

Language Proficiency Assessments in Higher Education Admissions

Thomas Eckes and Hans-Joachim Althaus

Assessments of language proficiency form an important basis for decisions about admissions to higher education. For example, when it comes to deciding on admissions to undergraduate programs in a college or university in the United States, demonstration of a good working knowledge of English, in particular a high level of reading and writing skills, is often considered essential. When the admissions decisions deal with international study applicants, it is common practice also to consider the proficiency level reached in the listening and speaking test sections.

Language proficiency assessments discussed in this chapter have a clearly specified target language use (TLU) domain, that is, the higher education setting (Bachman & Palmer, 2010; Elder, 2017). The basic expectation is that applicants with sufficiently high test scores are well prepared to meet the language requirements for their course of study and, therefore, likely to show satisfactory academic performance.

Throughout the chapter, we focus on language proficiency assessments designed for international students. In other words, students' linguistic preparedness for academic study is evaluated in a language other than their best or native language. These students typically intend to leave their country of origin and migrate to another country for study purposes.

15.1 Language and International Student Mobility

According to recent international education statistics, more than 4.6 million young adults pursue higher education outside of their home countries (Organisation for Economic Co-operation and Development, 2017). In addition, since 2015, rapidly increasing numbers of refugees have been seeking access to higher education. This pattern has taken place mostly in Europe, with Syria as the largest source country of refugees worldwide due to continued conflict (Institute of International Education, 2017). The excessively high level of academic displacement has been posing unprecedented challenges to tertiary programs in European education systems, highlighting the need to assess refugees' language proficiency and implement language-support programs.

15.1.1 English-Language Proficiency Tests

Drawing on figures reported in Project Atlas (2017), the top five destination countries, hosting almost 60 percent of all foreign students, are the United States (24 percent), the United Kingdom (11 percent), the People's Republic of China (10 percent), Australia (7 percent), and France (7 percent). In this ranking, Canada (7 percent), the Russian Federation (6 percent), and Germany (6 percent) follow in the next three places. International students often study in countries where English is an official language. Furthermore, institutions in non-English-speaking countries – in particular, institutions in the Nordic countries and in the People's Republic of China – increasingly offer more English-medium programs (Organisation for Economic Co-operation and Development, 2017). As a result, English has become the most common language of instruction worldwide.

Therefore, it is not surprising that millions of international students from non-English speaking backgrounds take an English proficiency test each year. The two most frequently taken tests are the International English Language Testing System™ (IELTS) provided by the IELTS partnership between the British Council, IDP Education, and Cambridge Assessment English, and the Test of English as a Foreign Language internet-based test (TOEFL iBT®) developed by Educational Testing Service (ETS). Both tests are widely accepted by institutions all around the world (Xi, Bridgeman, & Wendler, 2014). Other tests of English for academic purposes (EAP) include the Pearson Test of English (PTE Academic), provided by Pearson Language Assessment; the College English Test (CET) in China, provided by the National College English Testing Committee (Zheng & Cheng, 2008); the Cambridge English: Advanced (CAE) and the Cambridge English: Proficiency (CPE), both provided by Cambridge Assessment English.

15.1.2 Non-English-Language Proficiency Tests

Countries that implement academic programs dominantly or exclusively in languages other than English keep attracting international students for various reasons, such as resemblance in terms of shared cultural traditions and values, geographical proximity, or high prestige of the educational system more generally. Consequently, these countries offer a great variety of non-English-language proficiency tests to examine applicants' readiness for the linguistic study requirements and to inform admissions decisions. In many countries, multiple tests of proficiency in a given language are available for this purpose (Deygers, Zeidler et al., 2018).

Considering the countries that host the largest shares of international students in comparison to their total higher education populations, six European countries, where English is not the official language, are among the top ten (Project Atlas, 2017): France (12 percent), the Netherlands (11 percent), Finland (11 percent), Germany (9 percent), Sweden (9 percent), and Spain (6 percent).

For academic programs that are not taught in English, each of these countries offers standardized language tests to prove the required level of proficiency in the national language. Examples of representative language tests for nonnative speakers include the following: For French, the Diplôme d'études en langue française and Diplôme approfondi de langue française diplomas (also called the DELF/DALF diplomas);[1] for Dutch, the Educatief Startbekwaam [Ready-to-Start Higher Education] (STRT); for German, the Test Deutsch als Fremdsprache (TestDaF);[2] for Swedish, the Test i svenska för universitets-och högskolestudier [Test in Swedish for University Study] (TISUS); and, for Spanish, the Diploma de Español como Lengua Extranjera (DELE). For Finnish, there is no special test offered for international students, because most programs are taught in English and specific language requirements are defined by the higher education institutions themselves.

In the People's Republic of China, which is attracting increasingly more international students, admission to Chinese-medium courses (i.e., courses taught in Mandarin Chinese) requires nonnative speakers to prove their Chinese-language proficiency by taking the Chinese Proficiency Test (HSK). By contrast, English-medium courses require scores from English-language proficiency tests such as IELTS or TOEFL, rather than HSK results. Native speakers of English and applicants holding an academic degree taught in English are exempt from this regulation.

---

[1] For a review of the DELF, see Elder (2018).
[2] For a review of the TestDaF, see Norris & Drackert (2018).

Table 15.1 *Fourfold decision table for language-test results and academic performance*

	Academic performance	
Language test	Fail[b]	Succeed
Fail[a]	True negative (TN)	False negative (FN)
Pass	False positive (FP)	True positive (TP)

[a] Fail indicates "has not reached the minimum entrance requirement" set for the language test. Pass indicates "has reached or exceeded the minimum entrance requirement."
[b] Fail indicates "has not reached the minimum requirement" set for academic success (e.g., a minimum GPA level). Succeed indicates "has reached or exceeded the minimum requirement" for success.
The table illustrates the basic relation between candidates' results on a language test used for admissions purposes and their later success or failure at academic study.

15.2 Language Proficiency and Academic Success

15.2.1 The Basic Structure of Admissions Decisions

One of the key questions confronting higher education admissions committees is whether candidates possess the level of language skills and proficiencies required for success in the academic study for which they apply. It is important to note, however, that demonstrating a level of language proficiency that represents minimum entrance requirements, under optimal conditions, is merely a necessary – but not a sufficient – condition for academic success (Bridgeman, Cho, & DiPietro, 2016; Graham, 1987). In fact, the relation between language proficiency and academic success is far from simple and straightforward (as discussed later).

Table 15.1 shows a two-by-two decision or contingency table (Swets, 1988) that presents the basic structure of the relationship between language proficiency and academic performance underlying admissions decisions in higher education settings. The table entries result from the dichotomization of two variables. The first variable refers to the scores candidates received on the language test, the second variable refers to the measure of academic performance, most often first-year grade point average (GPA).

15.2.2 The Accuracy of Admissions Decisions

An important issue concerns the accuracy of admissions decisions based on language-test scores. In principle, candidates who meet or exceed the minimum proficiency level (pass the test) are predicted to be successful in their future study; when this is borne out, the students constitute the group of true positive (TP) cases. Conversely, candidates who do not meet that level (fail the test), but who are nonetheless admitted on some other basis, and turn out to be unsuccessful, represent the true negative (TN) cases.[3] However, as Table 15.1 shows, TP and TN cases are only two of the four possible outcomes. There may be candidates who fail the test, but (when admitted) succeed at study, forming the group of false negative (FN) cases. Finally, candidates may pass the test, but fail at study, forming the group of false positive (FP) cases.

From these four outcome categories, two basic indicators of decision accuracy can be derived. Building on concepts from signal-detection theory, these are called "sensitivity" and "specificity" (Fawcett, 2006). Sensitivity is the true positive rate, computed as the fraction of candidates who passed the test and proved to be academically successful: sensitivity = TP / (FP + TP). On the other hand, specificity is the true negative rate computed as the fraction of candidates who failed the test and (when nonetheless admitted) did not succeed academically: specificity = TN / (FN + TN).

A test's overall decision accuracy (or predictive accuracy) is defined as the proportion of TP and TN cases in the entire sample of candidates under study. That is, predictive accuracy = (TP + TN) / n, where n is the total number of candidates in the sample. Put differently, high accuracy implies both the success of applicants scoring high on the test and the failure of applicants scoring low. From the perspective of decision-making, admissions decisions that yield high predictive accuracy achieve two goals: (a) they minimize the costs of enrolling candidates who are not sufficiently proficient in the course-relevant language, and (b) they maximize the benefits of enrolling candidates who possess the required level of language proficiency.

15.2.3   Conceptual and Methodological Challenges

Predicting students' academic success based on their test performance is complicated by several problems that are not readily resolved. Together, these problems render the notion of equating high language proficiency with high academic performance overly simplistic and grossly misleading.

---

[3] When candidates are free to take two or more recognized language proficiency tests, they may fail one test and pass another, thus being admitted on that basis.

First, language proficiency constitutes just one out of a multitude of factors that are likely to have an impact on academic success. This is especially true when considering international students. Besides general cognitive skills and content knowledge, a host of noncognitive attributes has to be considered when accounting for academic success or failure. Study habits, learning motivation, personality traits (e.g., conscientiousness, resilience), attitudes, and academic skills (e.g., digital literacy, learning styles, time management), as well as the intricacies of the processes of academic and nonacademic acculturation, may have a role to play (see e.g., Floyd, 2015; Kappe & van der Flier, 2012).

Second, the very concept of academic success is multifaceted, defying simple definitions. The most popular operational approach is to examine first-year GPA (e.g., Stemler, 2012). Yet, alternative definitions of success are also conceivable, including the acquisition of desired competencies (e.g., sociocultural knowledge and skills), persistence, graduation, time to degree, overall student satisfaction, and career success (Camara, 2013; Kuncel, Tran, & Zhang, in this volume; Niessen & Meijer, in this volume; York, Gibson, & Rankin, 2015).

Third, empirical studies of the language proficiency–academic success relation often struggle with limitations inherent in the research design and the measures used (Bridgeman, Cho, & DiPietro, 2016). Foremost among these is the restriction of range caused by the selection of candidates based on test scores. That is, academic success usually is examined only for those candidates who passed the test; those failing the test are no longer available as study participants (unless admitted for other reasons). Consequently, correlations computed for the subsample of admitted students tend to be lower than the correlations that would result for the entire applicant population, rendering questionable any conclusions drawn from the analysis (for a detailed discussion of this and other study artifacts, see Schmidt & Hunter, 2015). Also, under conditions of range restriction, it is not possible to examine the overall diagnostic accuracy of admissions decisions if passing the language test under consideration is the sole criterion for admitting candidates (because TN cases do not exist).

Building on language-test scores for admissions decisions presupposes the existence of a cut score – a point on the test score scale that separates candidates who meet or exceed the minimum proficiency level (pass) from those who do not meet that level (fail). Using first-year GPA to define academic success similarly requires a certain GPA value to distinguish between successful and unsuccessful students. The process of determining cut scores critically hinges on human judgment (Pitoniak & Morgan,

2012). Thus, it adds to the already high degree of uncertainty characterizing this field of research and its practice.

Finally, identifying candidates who are linguistically prepared to enter academic programs requires a sufficiently high reliability or precision of the language-test scores. For example, when the main assessment purpose is to separate low- from high-performing candidates, the reliability value should be at least .80 (Wright, 1996). Lower values would raise the likelihood of misclassifying candidates and, as a result, reduce the predictive accuracy of admissions decisions. A related limitation refers to the commonly low comparability of grading standards and practices across different academic programs within a given university. Frequently enough, grading standards also vary within programs of a particular institution, depending on the individual instructors' performance expectations.

15.2.4   Validity and Fairness Considerations

Kane (2013) pointed out that "test scores are of interest because they are used to support claims that go beyond (often far beyond) the observed performances" (p. 1). Within the present context, this means that language-test scores are relevant because they are used to support claims that study applicants have or lack the level of proficiency needed to succeed in their academic studies. To the extent that the claims based on language-test scores are supported by empirical evidence, the intended score interpretations and uses may be considered valid. The prerequisite for this is, of course, that the claims are stated with high precision. For example, it is one claim to propose that applicants passing a language test have sufficient linguistic skills to begin an academic program and quite a different claim to propose that such applicants will not struggle with any language-related difficulties over the course of their studies.

Regarding the fairness of assessment use, the *Standards for Educational and Psychological Testing* (American Educational Research Association, American Psychological Association, & National Council on Measurement in Education, 2014) notes that "a fair test does not advantage or disadvantage some individuals because of characteristics irrelevant to the intended construct" (p. 50). The term "intended construct" here refers to the candidates' proficiency in the language of instruction.

Test fairness is strongly related to the validity of test score interpretation and use (Kane, 2010; Xi, 2010). A case in point is examiner- or rater-mediated assessment of language performance. The writing and speaking sections of tests designed for international students typically include constructed-response items, where candidates create a response or perform a task (e.g., writing an essay). Such responses are often evaluated by human raters. However, raters' judgments are prone to errors and biases such as central tendency, halo, and differential severity or leniency toward particular groups of candidates. For example, biases may disadvantage groups defined by gender, age, first language, and cultural or ethnic membership (Eckes, 2015; Myford & Wolfe, 2003). Hence, candidates rated by severe raters may be disadvantaged compared to candidates rated by lenient raters. The result could be that some candidates appear less proficient than they actually are, leading to unfair conclusions concerning their linguistic preparedness for academic studies.

15.2.5   Language Assessment Literacy

Using language-test scores for admissions purposes presupposes a certain degree of expertise, background, or training in testing. This expertise is part of what is called language assessment literacy (Taylor, 2013). For example, when admissions officers lack the necessary testing expertise, the fairness of their test-score interpretation and use may be seriously reduced, going as far as making wrong decisions about study applicants.

Most tests of English proficiency come with detailed information about the construct being measured, the overall test design, the test sections and tasks, scoring procedures, and the use of scores for making placement and admissions decisions. Some test providers also present evidence on the relationship between different tests, drawing up concordance tables showing which scores on one test would be equivalent to scores on another test. However, these tables should be treated with caution. In a comparison between four prominent EAP tests (IELTS, TOEFL iBT, PTE, and CAE), Green (2018) demonstrated that "the tests are structured differently, target a different range of levels of proficiency, include different task types, use different approaches to scoring and have different measurement characteristics" (p. 12). This suggests that "scores from the different tests are far from interchangeable" (p. 11).

Since international students are usually free in deciding which EAP test to take, the obvious incongruence between these tests adds to the challenges facing admissions committees. This situation is exacerbated by the fact that clear-cut and unambiguous guidelines on how to compare scores from different EAP tests are lacking.

In a small-scale study, O'Loughlin (2011) examined how administrative and academic staff used the IELTS in the selection of international students for undergraduate or postgraduate entry at an Australian university. He also investigated the knowledge and beliefs these groups of test users had about the IELTS. Findings revealed a substantial degree of uncertainty and inaccuracy regarding the use of IELTS scores in the selection process.

Over the last few decades, language testing has evolved into a highly specialized profession that is replete with statistical and measurement issues as well as detailed quality-control procedures that keep moving the field ever further away from a wider public understanding of assessment principles and practices. Establishing testing standards and publishing assessment guidelines that present basic knowledge, skills, and principles in an easy-to-understand language may remedy this situation and facilitate informed decision-making in higher education (for an example of such guidelines, see International Test Commission, 2018).

15.3   The Quest for Minimum Language Proficiency Levels

15.3.1   Framing Minimum Language Requirements

Cut scores underlying admissions decisions are often determined through a standard-setting process that focuses on a particular test within a defined context of test-score interpretation and use (Cizek & Bunch, 2007). The results of this process depend on judgments provided by subject-matter experts, who have a profound knowledge of the test's design, content, and purpose, as well as the level or levels of proficiency for which cut scores are sought. Hence, this approach to standard setting adopts an internal (or context-specific) frame of reference: The complete process of determining cut scores is situated within the particular context of the test under study.

In a different approach, cut scores are established with reference to a framework that is external to the test – a framework not intrinsically related to the test's specific context or purpose. This kind of approach makes use of an external (or context-unspecific) frame of reference. The Common European Framework of Reference for Languages (CEFR) (Council of Europe, 2001) is arguably the most prominent example of such an external reference system (Chalhoub-Deville, 2009). Designed primarily for the purposes of language learning, teaching, and assessment across Europe, the CEFR has become highly influential throughout the world (Byram & Parmenter, 2012). For example, the CEFR has been adapted to the Japanese context (CEFR-J) (Negishi, Takada, & Tono, 2013) and used to recommend English-language proficiency levels for admission to English-medium programs in Vietnam (Tannenbaum & Baron, 2015).[4]

A well-known part of the CEFR is the six Common Reference Levels, which are subdivisions of three broader bands: Basic User, Independent User, and Proficient User. The levels range from A1 (the lowest) through A2, B1, B2, C1, and C2 (the highest). Each of these levels is characterized by sets of descriptors or "can-do statements." For example, the B2 level descriptors contain statements like "Can produce clear, detailed text on a wide range of subjects and explain a viewpoint on a topical issue giving the advantages and disadvantages of various options" (Council of Europe, 2001, p. 24; for a detailed discussion of the levels, see North, 2014).

The CEFR's strong impact on the field of language assessment is evidenced by the fact that well-established test providers have made every effort to relate their language tests to this framework, reporting test results (additionally, at least) in terms of CEFR levels (for a critical discussion, see Green, 2018). Since CEFR descriptors and levels refer to language proficiency in a context- and language-independent way, however, aligning (context-bound) language tests with the CEFR entails a number of challenges that are difficult to meet in practice (Kecker & Eckes, 2010; Lim et al., 2013).

No matter how closely the alignment process may follow the suggested procedures, the basic approach is likely to lead to a dilemma (Harsch, 2018). Supplementing the CEFR scales with descriptors for specific contexts and purposes and thus aiming to increase the correspondence between the language proficiency as measured by a particular test and the CEFR levels, is incompatible with the original goal of providing a sound basis for the mutual recognition of language qualifications across countries, learning traditions, and assessment settings. When, in effect, one test's B2 actually does not align with another test's B2, because they mean quite different things, nothing has been gained in terms of comparable test results (for an example, see Deygers, Van Gorp, & Demeester, 2018).

---

[4] In the People's Republic of China, a completely different approach has been taken. The focus in China is not on adoption or adaptation of the CEFR, but on the development of a new national framework for English-language education called the China Standards of English (CSE) (Jin et al., 2017).

15.3.2   Uses and Misuses of the CEFR: The European Higher Education Context

Deygers, Zeidler et al. (2018) surveyed current practices of setting CEFR-based language requirements for entrance to European institutions of higher education. The researchers conducted structured interviews with 30 respondents involved with entrance tests and policies in their respective context. Together, the respondents represented 28 European states or regions with autonomy over educational matters.

In 22 regions, there was an entrance language requirement expressed in terms of CEFR levels. The most commonly required level was B2. Specifically, in no fewer than 19 regions, B2 was the only level or one of the required levels. Depending on the academic program, C1 was required in another ten regions. Notably, there was only one region where the required CEFR level was supported by empirical evidence. The vast majority (19 respondents) answered that the required levels were not empirically founded; another three respondents reported partial empirical foundation (based on needs analysis or expert counsel). Deygers, Zeidler et al. (2018) also noted that CEFR levels were often used for marketing purposes or as a gatekeeping instrument to control university admissions. Somewhat disenchanted by these findings, they concluded that in many European states and regions the CEFR "serves as a self-administered seal of quality" (p. 12). In a similar vein, Althaus (2018) pointed out that the use of CEFR levels B2 or C1 has evolved into a widely shared cipher or code taking on a life of its own, serving to simplify what otherwise would be complex, time-consuming admissions decisions and, thus, impeding any differentiated analysis of the specific linguistic requirements of academic programs.

Besides pointing to B2 as the most favored CEFR level for setting entrance requirements across Europe, Deygers, Zeidler et al. (2018) showed that the validity of CEFR-based criteria for deciding on admissions to university is a grossly under-researched topic. Carlsen (2018) addressed this situation by examining the relationship between students' language proficiency as measured by a CEFR-based entrance test called the Advanced Test of Norwegian (ATN) and various indicators of academic success (language-specific and general success variables like academic performance). Importantly, this research included students who passed the ATN as well as students who failed the test. Based on students' ATN scores and their results on each of the success variables (self-report data), Carlsen found a multiple correlation of .34, indicating that ATN scores were indeed predictive of overall academic success. Moreover, the study showed that the B2 level represented a level of proficiency in Norwegian that international students needed to manage when entering higher education in Norway. Students not reaching B2 on the ATN reported significantly lower academic mastery than students with B2 or better. More research along these lines is needed, possibly making use of more objective measures of predictor (language proficiency) and criterion variables (academic success).

Recent research also has focused on the following question (Marks, 2015): To what extent do the linguistic knowledge and skills assessed by language tests represent the real-life communicative demands that international students encounter in their academic programs? Deygers, Van den Branden, and Van Gorp (2018) interviewed university staff members and international students in Flanders, the Dutch-speaking northern part of Belgium, about their perceptions and experiences of the relevant linguistic demands. The students had passed one of two tests measuring proficiency in Dutch as a foreign language, the STRT (Educatief Startbekwaam) or the ITNA (Interuniversitaire Taaltest Nederlands voor Anderstaligen), both of which are linked to CEFR's B2 level. Findings showed that a significant part of assessing language proficiency by the STRT and ITNA differed from real-life demands. For example, production (writing and speaking) skills seemed to be generally less important than receptive (reading and listening) skills, especially in the Flemish university students' first year. In addition, the real-life demands encountered in the university regarding listening, which are, for example, characterized by regional variations, idiosyncratic accents, and disruptions, seemed to be so great that only a few students (with proficiency level at B2 or higher) felt sufficiently prepared to follow university lectures.

Focusing on the assessment of academic writing skills, Deygers, Van den Branden, and Peters (2017) examined whether domestic (Flemish) students who were exempt from taking a university entrance language test would pass the B2 threshold (the proficiency level required from their international peers). They found that 11 percent of the domestic students failed the threshold. Moreover, the best-performing students on the writing tasks were international students. Thus, when prospective international students are formally required to pass a language test that at least some domestic students fail, serious concerns about fairness and justice are raised (Deygers et al., 2017; McNamara & Ryan, 2011).

As exemplified by these studies, setting language entrance requirements based on the CEFR levels has implications that go far beyond considerations of ensuring admitted candidates' linguistic preparedness. Indeed, what the studies highlight is the gatekeeping function that language proficiency tests serve in controlling access to higher education, thus emphasizing the sociopolitical dimension of admissions decisions.

15.4   Implications for Language Assessment Use in Higher Education

15.4.1   Qualifying the Role of the CEFR

Considering the often arbitrary ways of setting CEFR-based entrance requirements, Harsch (2018) called for a "more realistic, empirically driven use of the CEFR" (p. 105). In fact, the question of what TLU aspects the CEFR adequately represents and what aspects it under- or misrepresents has to be answered empirically.

Preconditions for aligning language tests with the CEFR, or with any other external framework, are superior psychometric test quality and a sound theoretical basis, including a precise definition of the construct measured. When a particular test does not conform to internationally accepted standards of reliability, validity, and fairness, it is meaningless at best and misleading at worst to attach a CEFR label to the test. North, Martyniuk, and Panthier (2010) put it clearly: "Relating an examination or test to the CEFR is a complex endeavor. The existence of such a relation is not a simple observable fact, but is an assertion for which the examination provider needs to provide both theoretical and empirical evidence" (p. 7).

In particular, test providers are responsible for presenting relevant empirical evidence demonstrating the quality of the proposed language test and supporting the substantive interpretations of the CEFR level or levels at which the test is aiming. Of course, those who decide on admitting candidates to academic programs need to be sufficiently literate in language assessment to be able to draw the appropriate conclusions from the CEFR levels documented on applicants' certificates or score reports.

15.4.2   Examining the Predictive Validity of Language-Test Scores

The preceding discussion has shown that the relationship between scores achieved on a language test and measures of academic success is highly intricate, with multiple factors having an impact on the extent to which candidates' performances on language tests may be generalized regarding their performances on tasks in the TLU domain (i.e., the academic setting). Moreover, where academic success is broadly defined by first-year GPA, the contribution of language proficiency to success at studying is likely to be only indirect, weak, and variable. Hence, it is not surprising that most investigations into the relationship between language proficiency and academic success have yielded mixed or inconclusive results.

Biber, Reppen, and Staples (2017) adopted a more focused approach to the definition of academic success. The authors studied candidate performance on the TOEFL writing section as a predictor of success on more specific, real-world language-related tasks, that is, disciplinary writing tasks. They found higher and more consistent correlations than often reported in studies concerned with predicting success on academic tasks more generally.

Bridgeman et al.'s (2016) study highlighted the fact that the observed strength of the relationship between language-test scores and academic performance can change substantially when taking a more detailed look at the data. The researchers found that TOEFL scores correlated more strongly with GPA when students were grouped by nationality and department as compared to the overall sample. For instance, in the overall sample, the correlation between test scores and GPA was .18; in a subsample of engineering students from China, the correlation was .58, or, after correction for range restriction, .77 (for a similar approach, see Harsch, Ushioda, & Ladroue, 2017). In another segmentation of their sample, Bridgeman et al. (2016) looked at Chinese business students who achieved much higher scores in the receptive (reading, listening) than in the productive (speaking, writing) TOEFL sections. Removing these students from the Chinese sample, the (adjusted) correlation between TOEFL scores and GPA rose from .35 to .53.

In a related study, Ginther and Yan (2018) examined the relationship between TOEFL (total and section) scores and first-year GPA of Chinese students enrolled at Purdue University across three academic years (2011, 2012, and 2013). They found that TOEFL total scores alone did not predict first-year GPA. A closer look at section scores and score profiles, however, revealed differential relationships between receptive and productive skills with first-year GPA. For example, the analysis of the 2011 and 2012 cohorts identified subsamples with a discrepant score profile of the kind reported by Bridgeman et al. (2016), that is, low scores on speaking and writing, much higher scores on reading and listening. Importantly, this particular score profile produced correlations between the receptive sections and first-year GPA that were (contrary to expectation) negative, and correlations between the productive sections and first-year GPA that were positive. Ginther and Yan (2018) concluded that "the focus of admissions practice should be shifted from total score to both subscale scores and score profiles" (p. 281).

15.4.3   Implementing Post-Admission Language Assessment

Beyond any doubt, success at higher education is also greatly determined by the implementation of language assessment and support policies after candidates have been admitted to academic programs. Deciding on admission to higher education based on language-test performance at best implies that those who achieved or exceeded the minimum-language requirement are well-prepared to start with the desired program. It does by no means imply that all language and literacy demands encountered over the course of the first years of study will be met satisfactorily. Thus, many institutions of higher education around the world face challenges in coping with the diverse language backgrounds and the less than optimal linguistic preparedness of their international students (Read, 2015).

The implementation of post-admission language-assessment instruments allows academic and administrative staff to identify students with significant needs and to advise them on how to enhance their proficiency in the language of instruction (Harsch et al., 2017). Such instruments range from language placement tests that match students to the most suitable language course (Eckes, 2017; Green, 2012) to procedures of diagnostic language assessment that identify each student's weaknesses and strengths and help to attain learning goals (Alderson, 2005; Lee, 2015).

15.5   Conclusion

Sawyer (2013) identified two goals of admissions decisions related to academic success: (a) to maximize success among enrolled students and (b) to identify accurately those applicants who are likely to be successful and to enroll as many of them as possible. Within the context of admitting international study applicants, language assessments have a key role in achieving each of these goals. Highly selective institutions can achieve the first goal by admitting only applicants with the highest scores on the language test. Such an admissions strategy maximizes the true positive rate, or the test's sensitivity, at the expense of a heightened false negative rate; that is, a relatively high proportion of applicants will be denied admission although they might have succeeded academically.

Less-selective institutions (often more or less implicitly) pursue the second goal, trying to maximize simultaneously the test's sensitivity and specificity; that is, they strive to maximize the diagnostic accuracy of the admissions decisions. Critically important in this case is the appropriate setting of a cut score, or a minimum-language requirement, building on the test's score scale or proficiency levels specified with reference to a framework like the CEFR. No less important is the implementation of language-support programs to reduce the proportion of false positive cases – that is, the proportion of students who passed the language test but turn out later to be in danger of failing their studies.

Future research needs to consider the great heterogeneity of international student samples, focusing on: (a) the psychometric quality of language tests as measures of foreign language proficiency, (b) the suitability of the criterion, or criteria, of academic success, and (c) the complexities of the relationship between these two variables. Only when research pays due attention to each of these components can admissions decisions be made on a sound basis with the highest possible degree of accuracy and fairness.

REFERENCES

Alderson, J. C. (2005). *Diagnosing foreign language proficiency: The interface between learning and assessment.* London: Continuum.

Althaus, H.-J. (2018). Warum C1 keine Lösung ist: Der Nachweis von Deutschkenntnissen für den Hochschulzugang, der GER und warum sie nicht zusammenpassen [Why C1 is not the solution: Proving knowledge of German for entrance to higher education, the CEFR, and why they do not fit together]. In A. Brandt, A. Buschmann-Göbels, & C. Harsch (Eds.). *Der Gemeinsame Europäische Referenzrahmen für Sprachen und seine Adaption im Hochschulkontext: Erträge des 6. Bremer Symposions, 2017* [The common European framework of reference for languages and its adaptation to the university context: Results from the 6th Bremen symposium, 2017] (pp. 78–98). Bochum: AKS-Verlag.

American Educational Research Association, American Psychological Association, & National Council on Measurement in Education. (2014). *Standards for educational and psychological testing.* Washington, DC: American Educational Research Association.

Bachman, L. F., & Palmer, A. S. (2010). *Language assessment in practice: Developing language assessments and justifying their use in the real world.* Oxford: Oxford University Press.

Biber, D., Reppen, R., & Staples, S. (2017). Exploring the relationship between TOEFL iBT scores and disciplinary writing performance. *TESOL Quarterly, 51,* 948–960. https://doi.org/10.1002/tesq.359.

Bridgeman, B., Cho, Y., & DiPietro, S. (2016). Predicting grades from an English language assessment: The importance of peeling the onion. *Language Testing, 33*, 307–318. https://doi.org/10.1177/0265532215583066.

Byram, M., & Parmenter, L. (Eds.). (2012). *The common European framework of reference: The globalisation of language education policy.* Bristol: Multilingual Matters. https://doi.org/10.21832/9781847697318.

Camara, W. (2013). Defining and measuring college and career readiness: A validation framework. *Educational Measurement: Issues and Practice, 32* (4), 16–27. https://doi.org/10.1111/emip.12016.

Carlsen, C. H. (2018). The adequacy of the B2 level as university entrance requirement. *Language Assessment Quarterly, 15*, 75–89. https://doi.org/10.1080/15434303.2017.1405962.

Chalhoub-Deville, M. (2009). Content validity considerations in language testing contexts. In R. W. Lissitz (Ed.). *The concept of validity: Revisions, new directions, and applications* (pp. 241–263). Charlotte, NC: Information Age.

Cizek, G. J., & Bunch, M. B. (2007). *Standard setting: A guide to establishing and evaluating performance standards on tests.* Thousand Oaks, CA: Sage. https://doi.org/10.4135/9781412985918.

Council of Europe. (2001). *Common European framework of reference for languages: Learning, teaching, assessment.* Cambridge: Cambridge University Press.

Deygers, B., Van den Branden, K., & Peters, E. (2017). Checking assumed proficiency: Comparing L1 and L2 performance on a university entrance test. *Assessing Writing, 32*, 43–56. https://doi.org/10.1016/j.asw.2016.12.005.

Deygers, B., Van den Branden, K., & Van Gorp, K. (2018). University entrance language tests: A matter of justice. *Language Testing, 35*, 449–476. https://doi.org/10.1177/0265532217706196.

Deygers, B., Van Gorp, K., & Demeester, T. (2018). The B2 level and the dream of a common standard. *Language Assessment Quarterly, 15*, 44–58. https://doi.org/10.1080/15434303.2017.1421955.

Deygers, B., Zeidler, B., Vilcu, D., & Carlsen, C. H. (2018). One framework to unite them all? Use of the CEFR in European university entrance policies. *Language Assessment Quarterly, 15*, 3–15. https://doi.org/10.1080/15434303.2016.1261350.

Eckes, T. (2015). *Introduction to many-facet Rasch measurement: Analyzing and evaluating rater-mediated assessments* (2nd ed.). Frankfurt am Main: Peter Lang.

(2017). Setting cut scores on an EFL placement test using the prototype group method: A receiver operating characteristic (ROC) analysis. *Language Testing, 34*, 383–411. https://doi.org/10.1177/0265532216672703.

Elder, C. (2017). Language assessment in higher education. In E. Shohamy, I. G. Or, & S. May (Eds.). *Language testing and assessment* (3rd ed., pp. 271–286). Cham: Springer. https://doi.org/10.1007/978-3-319-02261-1_35.

(2018). Test review. Certifying French competency: The DELF tout public (B2). *Language Testing, 35*, 615–623. https://doi.org/10.1177/0265532218781627.

Fawcett, T. (2006). An introduction to ROC analysis. *Pattern Recognition Letters*, *27*, 861–874. https://doi.org/10.1016/j.patrec.2005.10.010.

Floyd, C. B. (2015). Closing the gap: International student pathways, academic performance and academic acculturation. *Journal of Academic Language and Learning*, *9*(2), A1–A18.

Ginther, A., & Yan, X. (2018). Interpreting the relationships between TOEFL iBT scores and GPA: Language proficiency, policy, and profiles. *Language Testing*, *35*, 271–295. https://doi.org/10.1177/0265532217704010.

Graham, J. G. (1987). English language proficiency and the prediction of academic success. *TESOL Quarterly*, *21*, 505–521. https://doi.org/10.2307/3586500.

Green, A. (2012). Placement testing. In C. Coombe, P. Davidson, B. O'Sullivan, & S. Stoynoff (Eds.). *The Cambridge guide to second language assessment* (pp. 164–170). Cambridge: Cambridge University Press.

(2018). Linking tests of English for academic purposes to the CEFR: The score user's perspective. *Language Assessment Quarterly*, *15*, 59–74. https://doi.org/10.1080/15434303.2017.1350685.

Harsch, C. (2018). How suitable is the CEFR for setting university entrance standards? *Language Assessment Quarterly*, *15*, 102–108. https://doi.org/10.1080/15434303.2017.1420793.

Harsch, C., Ushioda, E., & Ladroue, C. (2017). *Investigating the predictive validity of TOEFL iBT® test scores and their use in informing policy in a United Kingdom university setting* (Research Report No. RR-17-41). Princeton, NJ: Educational Testing Service.

Institute of International Education (2017). *A world on the move: Trends in global student mobility*. New York, NY: Author.

International Test Commission. (2018). *ITC Guidelines for the large-scale assessment of linguistically and culturally diverse populations*. Retrieved from www.intestcom.org/files/guideline_diverse_populations.pdf.

Jin, Y., Wu, Z., Alderson, C., & Song, W. (2017). Developing the China Standards of English: Challenges at macropolitical and micropolitical levels. *Language Testing in Asia*, *7*(1). https://languagetestingasia.springeropen.com/articles/10.1186/s40468-017-0032-5.

Kane, M. T. (2010). Validity and fairness. *Language Testing*, *27*, 177–182. https://doi.org/10.1177/0265532209349467.

(2013). Validating the interpretations and uses of test scores. *Journal of Educational Measurement*, *50*, 1–73. https://doi.org/10.1111/jedm.12000.

Kappe, R., & van der Flier, H. (2012). Predicting academic success in higher education: What's more important than being smart? *European Journal of Psychology of Education*, *27*, 605–619. https://doi.org/10.1007/s10212-011-0099-9.

Kecker, G., & Eckes, T. (2010). Putting the manual to the test: The TestDaF–CEFR linking project. In W. Martyniuk (Ed.). *Aligning tests with the CEFR: Reflections on using the Council of Europe's draft manual* (pp. 50–79). Cambridge: Cambridge University Press.

Lee, Y.-W. (2015). Diagnosing diagnostic language assessment. *Language Testing*, *32*, 299–316. https://doi.org/10.1177/0265532214565387.

Lim, G. S., Geranpayeh, A., Khalifa, H., & Buckendahl, C. W. (2013). Standard setting to an international reference framework: Implications for theory and practice. *International Journal of Testing*, *13*, 32–49. https://doi.org/10.1080/15305058.2012.678526.

Marks, D. (2015). Prüfen sprachlicher Kompetenzen internationaler Studienan-fänger an deutschen Hochschulen: Was leistet der TestDaF? [Assessing international students' language proficiency at German institutions of higher education: How well does the TestDaF perform?] *Zeitschrift für Interkul-turellen Fremdsprachenunterricht*, *20*, 21–39. Retrieved from http://tujour nals.ulb.tu-darmstadt.de/index.php/zif/article/view/189.

McNamara, T., & Ryan, K. (2011). Fairness versus justice in language testing: The place of English literacy in the Australian citizenship test. *Language Assessment Quarterly*, *8*, 161–178. https://doi.org/10.1080/15434303.2011.565438.

Myford, C. M., & Wolfe, E. W. (2003). Detecting and measuring rater effects using many-facet Rasch measurement: Part I. *Journal of Applied Measure-ment*, *4*, 386–422.

Negishi, M., Takada, T., & Tono, Y. (2013). A progress report on the develop-ment of the CEFR-J. In E. D. Galaczi & C. J. Weir (Eds.). *Exploring language frameworks: Proceedings of the ALTE Kraków Conference, July 2011* (pp. 135–163). Cambridge: Cambridge University Press.

Norris, J., & Drackert, A. (2018). Test review: TestDaF. *Language Testing*, *35*, 149–157. https://doi.org/10.1177/0265532217715848.

North, B. (2014). *The CEFR in practice*. Cambridge: Cambridge University Press.

North, B., Martyniuk, W., & Panthier, J. (2010). The manual for relating language examinations to the common European framework of reference for languages in the context of the Council of Europe's work on language education. In W. Martyniuk (Ed.). *Aligning tests with the CEFR: Reflections on using the Council of Europe's draft manual* (pp. 1–17). Cambridge: Cambridge University Press.

O'Loughlin, K. (2011). The interpretation and use of proficiency test scores in university selection: How valid and ethical are they? *Language Assessment Quarterly*, *8*, 146–160. https://doi.org/10.1080/15434303.2011.564698.

Organisation for Economic Co-operation and Development. (2017). *Education at a glance 2017: OECD indicators*. Paris: OECD Publishing.

Pitoniak, M. J., & Morgan, D. L. (2012). Setting and validating cut scores for tests. In C. Secolsky & D. B. Denison (Eds.). *Handbook on measurement, assessment, and evaluation in higher education* (pp. 343–366). New York, NY: Routledge.

Project Atlas. (2017). *A quick look at global mobility trends*. New York, NY: Institute of International Education.

Read, J. (2015). *Assessing English proficiency for university study*. New York, NY: Palgrave Macmillan. https://doi.org/10.1057/9781137315694.

Sawyer, R. (2013). Beyond correlations: Usefulness of high school GPA and test scores in making college admissions decisions. *Applied Measurement in Education, 26,* 89–112. https://doi.org/10.1080/08957347.2013.765433.

Schmidt, F. L., & Hunter, J. E. (2015). *Methods of meta-analysis: Correcting error and bias in research findings* (3rd ed.). Thousand Oaks, CA: Sage. https://doi .org/10.4135/9781483398105.

Stemler, S. E. (2012). What should university admissions tests predict? *Educational Psychologist, 47,* 5–17. https://doi.org/10.1080/00461520.2011.611444.

Swets, J. A. (1988). Measuring the accuracy of diagnostic systems. *Science, 240,* 1285–1293. https://doi.org/10.1126/science.3287615.

Tannenbaum, R. J., & Baron, P. A. (2015). *Mapping TOEIC® scores to the Vietnamese national standard: A study to recommend English language requirements for admissions into and graduation from Vietnamese universities* (ETS RM-15-08). Princeton, NJ: Educational Testing Service.

Taylor, L. (2013). Communicating the theory, practice and principles of language testing to test stakeholders: Some reflections. *Language Testing, 30,* 403–412. https://doi.org/10.1177/0265532213480338.

Wright, B. D. (1996). Reliability and separation. *Rasch Measurement Transactions, 9,* 472.

Xi, X. (2010). How do we go about investigating test fairness? *Language Testing, 27,* 147–170. https://doi.org/10.1177/0265532209349465.

Xi, X., Bridgeman, B., & Wendler, C. (2014). Tests of English for academic purposes in university admissions. In A. J. Kunnan (Ed.). *The companion to language assessment: Evaluation, methodology, and interdisciplinary themes* (Vol. 1, pp. 318–337). Chichester: Wiley.

York, T. T., Gibson, C., & Rankin, S. (2015). Defining and measuring academic success. *Practical Assessment, Research and Evaluation, 20*(5), 1–20.

Zheng, Y., & Cheng, L. (2008). Test review: College English Test (CET) in China. *Language Testing, 25,* 408–417. https://doi.org/10.1177/0265532208092433.

CHAPTER 16

Measuring Student Character: Modernizing Predictors of Academic Success

Nathan Kuncel, Khue Tran, and Shu Han (Charlene) Zhang

Success in school is multidimensional and success is influenced by multiple student characteristics. Test scores and prior grades have received the most attention in the research literature, with varying emphasis given to tests, depending upon the country. In the United States, despite public controversy about tests (Kuncel & Sackett, 2018), grades actually get the most weight in admissions decisions, with test scores often in second place (Hawkins & Lautz, 2005). In contrast, some countries give relatively more emphasis to tests (e.g., China), while others focus more on grades and content exams (e.g., Europe). One benefit of this attention is that the field has generated a massive database that demonstrates that both grades and tests have utility in decision-making and can predict both academic and other life outcomes (Kuncel & Hezlett, 2010). Unfortunately, attention and research on other admissions tools have lagged behind. With an increasing interest in measuring and developing other characteristics like drive, resilience, teamwork, and empathy, this needs to change (see also Niessen & Meijer, in this volume).

Our goal is to start reversing this trend. In this chapter we review three traditional measures: letters of recommendation (LORs), personal statements, and interviews. We also discuss three promising modern tools: forced-choice personality assessments, situational judgment tests, and biodata. For each, we first review evidence of predictive power, bias, and applied concerns (including faking), and then offer recommendations for practice. In each case, there is also a complementary literature in organizational settings that are beyond the scope of the chapter. Finally, we comment on an often-neglected topic: data integration. Even the best admissions system can be ruined by decision biases and badly combined data.

16.1 Letters of Recommendation

16.1.1 Predictive Validity

LORs date back to at least the eighteenth century, with the letter of introduction, where a person moving to a new location would obtain letters from a person of higher status to vouch for their character and skills. Benjamin Franklin, as ambassador to France, was often asked to write letters for people he knew little about and raised many concerns about such letters that parallel the issues we face today (*Papers of Benjamin Franklin*, n.d.). However, the historical and modern intent of the letter is a portable reputation and there is good evidence that, under research conditions, authentic ratings of a person's personality by other people can be quite valuable (Connelly & Ones, 2010).

Unfortunately, letters deviate from this ideal scenario in several important ways. First, letter writers are selected by the ratee and most people pick writers who will say something favorable. As a result, most letters are very positive, with little variability. Second, letter writers are not consistent in what they discuss, leading to poor reliability and inconsistent information across letters. Finally, letter writers do not always know the person well and tend to rely on other sources of information, resulting in considerable information redundancy with other predictors like grades and personal statements (for a quantitative review, see Kuncel, Kochevar, & Ones, 2014).

As a result, letters have modest predictive power. In a review and meta-analysis of LOR predictive validity studies, correlations with grades were substantially less than what is seen for prior grades and test scores (Kuncel, Kochevar, & Ones, 2014). The relationship for college grades (.28) was better than for graduate school (.13), perhaps because high school letter writers are often academic counselors and their letters may more directly reflect the student's record. Importantly, letter ratings and graduate school degree attainment were correlated (.19). Although modest in absolute size, dichotomous outcomes that occur years in the future are inherently very difficult to predict and this relationship suggests that letters may have an especially effective role in measuring student motivation. Finally, the study results suggested that having letter writers rate student attributes directly resulted in better prediction than having a reader infer characteristics based on a written narrative.

16.1.2   Differences by Gender

Subgroup differences in LORs have mostly focused on gender differences, examining both the behavior of the letter writer as well as the letter reader. Alarmingly, as far as we know, there are no studies examining prediction bias for LORs using the gold standard Cleary model (American Educational Research Association, American Psychological Association, & National Council on Measurement in Education, 1985). The Cleary model examines whether scores on a measure are associated with the same level of subsequent performance regardless of group membership (e.g., is a recommended score of 8/10 associated with the same grade point average [GPA] in college regardless of race/ethnicity or gender?). This framework implicitly acknowledges that observing score differences between groups is insufficient evidence of bias. Unfortunately, the paucity of research examining prediction bias holds true for all of the other predictors we review here. There are some studies, however, that examine differences in scores obtained across different groups, which is a start but not a conclusion.

For LORs, a number of studies either examine how the properties of letters as written differ or conduct experiments to explore how readers react to differences in letters. One common approach has examined whether the language and content differ for men or women. In a linguistic analysis study by Watson (1987), differences in LORs for candidates for graduate studies appeared to be linked with the gender of both the writers and the applicants. Letters written for female candidates were longer and favored the recipient. In addition, female writers created longer letters than male writers (Watson, 1987). Letters written for female candidates contained more adjectives overall and more "feminine" adjectives, and only letters for females made any mention of physical appearance or attractiveness (Watson, 1987), while letters for male students tended to include greater descriptions of negative emotions and tentativeness (Houser & Lemmons, 2017). Overall, the results suggest some letter features are likely to favor each gender.

While linguistic analysis studies have the advantage of ensuring the authenticity of LORs, it may be difficult to determine whether the observed differences reflect real behavioral differences or if they reflect biases. To address this, experiments have been conducted in an attempt more directly to test effects by controlling for the content of the letters and systematically varying the genders of the writer and/or the applicant.

A few such experimental studies suggest that letters may favor women. Respondent reactions demonstrated a bias against males, such that, based on the same letters, they reported interview and admissions decisions that favor female applicants (Kryger & Shikiar, 1978). Biernat and Eidelman (2007) also examined the effect of explicit sexism in the letter on reviewer evaluations by manipulating an examiner's or rater's knowledge about whether the letter writer was sexist. The explicit sexism condition provided raters with a description of the letter writer's beliefs that women are less intelligent and less suitable for academia. Raters appeared to adjust their own perceptions such that they evaluated applicants in favor of females when the writer was explicitly sexist but evaluated applicants consistently when the writer was not sexist. In another experiment, gender and attractiveness had no effect on readers' perception of the inflated letters, while authentic letters in support of attractive women were perceived to be more successful than those of attractive men (Nicklin & Roch, 2008).

16.1.3   *Differences by Race/Ethnicity*

In a study conducted by Houser and Lemmons (2017) that compared LORs across White and non-White students with a no significant GPA difference, researchers reported differences across groups. Letters for White students applying for undergraduate research internships showed lengthier descriptions of their cognitive ability, insight, perception, productivity, and occupation, but also more cause descriptions of their behaviors and achievement and greater contradiction and discrepancy. In contrast, letters for non-White applicants contained more communal descriptions of positive emotions and affect and showed less certainty about the student's strengths.

Cross-cultural differences in the content and structure of letters remains an under-investigated topic, particularly in relation to their impact on admissions decisions (Al Ansari et al., 2015; Bouton, 1995; Precht, 1998). One study by Morgan, Elder, and King (2013) showed that LOR ratings for applicants with African American names were rated less favorably than those for applicants with Caucasian names, but this effect was eliminated when raters were required to elaborate on their judgment.

16.1.4   *Recommendations on the Use of LORs*

Despite the literature being a fraction of the size of what is seen for grades and tests, some best practices emerge. The first, obtain multiple letters and aggregate across them. Interpreting them separately likely invites confirmation biases where we unconsciously pick and choose evidence to support the reader's perspective. Beyond this general principle there are two general methods for improving letters. One approach is to make the letters more behavioral and focus the letter writer on rating/evaluating those characteristics. Standardized letters of recommendation appear to produce more reliable information (Girzadas et al., 1998). The second structured approach involves extracting adjectives from traditional narrative letters, classifying them to five attribute categories that appear to capture most of the information in letters, and then totaling their frequency to obtain scores for each of the attributes (see Aamodt, Byran, and Whitcomb, 1993 for a description and test of the method).

For the first approach, have letter writers rate students on key attributes preferably with behavioral anchors to help calibrate raters. Ratings appear to be somewhat more valid than interpreting narratives (Kuncel, Kochevar, & Ones, 2014) and appear to reduce bias (Friedman et al., 2017). A caveat is that, as both applicant and rater differences account for variability in ratings, accurate interpretation of rating scores would require a disentangling of these two sources of variance (Oliveri et al., 2017) – hence the value in having multiple raters. Third, all else equal, in practice focus letters so they provide information about attributes that are difficult to obtain from other sources. Fourth, asking letter reviewers to justify their evaluations appears to reduce bias. This is consistent with a broader literature that accountability can produce better judgments (Lerner & Tetlock, 2003). Finally, if narratives are used instead of ratings, use prompts to ask letter writers to provide specific behavioral examples and use multiple independent evaluators for each letter as both will tend to increase reliability and reduce bias.

16.2 Personal Statements and Student Essays

16.2.1 Predictive Validity

Student essays or personal statements also have a long history in admissions. Students are asked either to discuss their background and goals or they are given specific questions to answer. These essays are interpreted by readers to extract information about student personality, goals, values, skills, and, quite often, writing skill. Personal statements and essays are appealing and have strong narrative qualities and are generally rated as the third most important information source in admissions (Hawkins & Lautz, 2005) in the United States. This prominent role is not justified by the jarringly tiny scientific literature examining their predictive validity and lack of bias. And, yet, even this thin literature is alarming.

One of the authors helped conduct a meta-analysis on how personal statements were related to subsequent student outcomes (Murphy et al., 2009). Across ten studies, judges' evaluations of personal statements were related weakly with subsequent grades (.13). The relationship was even less (.09) with faculty evaluations of performance, mostly in graduate schools, across eight studies. They do not even fare well as writing samples as they demonstrated only a weak correlation with a professionally graded writing sample (Educational Testing Service, 1974) and had a somewhat larger correlation (.27) with verbal ability tests. If personal statements were the only available predictor of these outcomes, it would be worth considering them as some signal is better than none. However, not only are they the weakest predictor that is commonly used in admissions, they also demonstrate considerable overlap with other predictors, further reducing their utility (Murphy et al., 2009). The evidence of weak predictive validity is especially problematic because narratives can be very compelling (Beach, 2010). The evidence indicates that personal statements exert far more influence on who gets admitted than warranted.

16.2.2 Bias Research on Personal Statements and Student Essays

Given the scarcity of research on personal statements in general, it is not surprising that the number of studies that examined biases in personal statements is virtually nonexistent. A study evaluating the essays in a medical program found that the statements that received higher ratings from the program directors were more likely to belong to those who graduated from a medical school in the United States or Canada, female applicants, and younger applicants (Max et al., 2010). Wright and Bradley (2010) found that, for a sample consisting of 307 students, those that attended fee-paying grammar schools received higher scores on their personal statements than those from state-maintained schools. In the United Kingdom, the former group was perceived to belong to a higher social class while the latter to the working class. The working-class subgroup also was perceived to have added difficulty getting into medical schools.

Lastly, a study in 2015 examined the gender-specific differences in the content of personal statements by reviewing over 2,000 essays from applicants in medical programs in the United States (Osman et al., 2015). Male applicants tended to depict their personal qualities and skills to self-promote while female applicants expressed more emotional, communicative, and team-based skills.

However, some research suggests that bias may favor racial minorities. One experiment on the evaluation of student essays for admissions was designed around four essays which has been evaluated by experts as weak, moderate (two of the essays), or strong (Fajardo, 1985). They then assigned the essays to participants and manipulated the supposed race of the essay writer. Participant evaluations were consistent with essay quality, but all four essays were systematically rated as stronger when raters were told that they were written by Black authors than the same essays when labeled as written by White authors.

16.2.3   Recommendations on the Use of Personal Statements and Student Essays

At this time, it is difficult to recommend the use of personal statements in their current form – at all. However, it is likely that they could be better tasked to target specific application characteristics if questions are directed at those attributes and these were paired with behavioral scoring rubrics. In other words, they could be transformed into something like a take-home written version of a structured interview (described later). It is likely that this would yield more useful and valid information.

Personal statements are also used to evaluate overall fit and likelihood to matriculate. For example, graduate schools attempt to gauge whether an applicant is genuinely interested in their program or will choose to go elsewhere. It is currently unknown if personal statements can reliably help accomplish this goal. Given the low correlations with other outcomes, this seems like an unrealistic hope. This is a case where specific examples of personal statements being effective are likely to be remembered but the rate of false negatives is unknown.

16.3   Interviews

Interviews are used less commonly in admissions because of practical challenges with scalability. Larger schools need to devote considerable resources to interviewing or have a highly engaged alumni network to manage the volume. Unfortunately, the use of dispersed, poorly calibrated, and largely untrained interviewers invites low levels of predictive power and bias. Research on traditional interviews in both work and admissions settings has produced disappointing results.

Decades of research on interviewing in employment settings make clear that interviews with greater structure in process and scoring are more reliable, more valid, and less prone to bias. In contrast to low structure, estimates for the most highly structured interviews are more than twice as predictive ($r = .56$, with job performance, Huffcutt & Arthur, 1994). Recent research on structured interviewing in educational admissions demonstrates improved prediction of grades. Arguably the most important aspect of structured interviews is the use of behavioral or situational questions. These questions ask how a person has responded to a school-relevant situation in the past or how a person would respond to a hypothetical situation in the future. For example, we might not ask the reasonable school-relevant question, "How do you handle goal conflicts?" We might instead say, "Tell me about the most recent time you had too many commitments." Although both are clearly task relevant (and better than nonsense questions like "If you were a tree, what kind of tree would you be?"), the specific behavioral question yields better information.

A structured interview has two parts: content and process. Content refers to what people are asked during an interview. Process refers to how the interview is conducted. Over a dozen aspects of content and process structure have been studied; however, a review of the structured interview literature identified six components as key (see Campion, Palmer, & Campion, 1997 for a succinct review). They are: (a) conducting formal analyses of the behavioral domain (job analysis), (b) asking the same questions of all applicants, (c) using situational or behavioral questions, (d) using a scale to rate responses or the interview, (e) using a behaviorally anchored scale, and (f) training the interviewers. In addition, conducting multiple independent interviews also improves reliability and reduces idiosyncratic rater bias.

16.3.1 Bias in Interviews

As with all measures, observing differences by subgroup may alarm us; however, they may reflect real differences in the characteristics to be measured. Most research has examined interviews in medical school settings. In general, interviews do not demonstrate large group differences, and these are further reduced by using structured methods (Huffcutt & Roth, 1998).

Numerous studies affirmed limited bias in selection interviews when they are structured. In a meta-analysis, unstructured interviews tended to favor males over females ($d = .23$), but the difference became nonexistent when the interview was structured (Huffcutt et al., 2001). Little evidence of differences was found by Pau et al. (2013), who reviewed 30 studies on the Multiple Mini Interview (MMI) – a multi-rater-structured-interview method.

In the MMI, the applicants were questioned by a group of interviewers, each separately and one at a time. Interviewees are asked to rotate around numerous stations. Each station was structured and designed differently to evaluate their skills, such as critical thinking, problem-solving, and communication skills. The study found that MMI did not favor any particular subgroup.

Consistently, the use of structured interviews is associated with little to no difference in scores between racial/ethnic groups. A recent study examining medical school data for over 1,300 applicants found no appreciable differences on an MMI (Terregino, McConnell, & Reiter, 2015). Similarly, Gale et al. (2016) and Lumb, Homer, and Miller (2010), whose studies scrutinized the interview process in a medical program in the United Kingdom, found that ethnic background did not influence applicants' scores on the admissions interviews, a finding replicated in a recent study (Henderson et al., 2018).

However, one area that demonstrates a consistent bias in interviews is for physical appearance. Applicants who are physically attractive tend to receive higher ratings. For example, Shahani and Dipboye (1993) conducted an experimental design in which approximately 500 applicants were interviewed for college admissions. Then, the photographs of the applicants were judged separately and independently by three graduate students and one faculty member on a scale of facial attractiveness. The interviewers were asked to rate the candidates on a scale of 12 items, measuring their motivation and oral communication. For female applicants, attractiveness correlated .23 with interview scores, meaning that more attractive female applicants received higher interview ratings. The direction of the relationship was the same for male applicants but was smaller in magnitude ($r = .13$). Given that the description of the interview is very general, it is difficult to assess the degree of their interview structure. Overall, physical appearance appears to have a consistent influence on interview scores.

16.3.2 Recommendations for the Use of Interviews

Given the evidence, interviews should be structured. To the extent possible, they should also use multiple interviewers. Fortunately, structure is not all or nothing. Including structural elements that are feasible will tend to improve the predictive power and reduce the bias in an interview.

Schools should begin with the six key factors described by Campion et al. (1997) and consider which elements can be included. At a minimum, better questions could be developed, and interviewers could be trained, even if training is delivered remotely via video or webinar instruction. Some structural elements, like asking the same questions, are not practical in high-stakes admissions decisions. However, related sets of questions can be developed. Finally, an interview cannot reliably collect information about every aspect of the applicant. Schools should recognize this constraint, and both identify and target the most critical attributes. With respect to bias, structure seems to make a difference for multiple types of bias. Research on physical appearance suggests, for the purposes of bias, masking the appearance of applicants may be desirable. Whether this comes at the cost of obtaining better information through nonverbal behavior is not well understood at this time.

16.4   Assessments

16.4.1   *Personality, Interest, and Forced-Choice Personality Assessments*

Use of letters, personal statements, and interviews are all efforts to learn something about an applicant and we are often interested in aspects of personality. Instead of asking interviewers or letter writers to rate or comment on a person's behavior, self-report personality measures go directly to the applicant and ask them to evaluate themselves. In research studies, self-report personality assessments predict success for important school (Poropat, 2009), work (Hurtz & Donovan, 2000; Salgado, 1997), and life outcomes (Roberts et al., 2007). Similar patterns of results are also observed for vocational interests (Nye et al., 2012). In an educational setting, students who are intellectually open-minded, hardworking and organized, emotionally stable, interested in their area of study, and interpersonally skilled tend to be more successful in academic settings.

Overall, this literature indicates that traditional academic success is related to conscientiousness ($r = .22$) and openness to experience ($r = .10$) (Poropat, 2009), and these measures are largely independent of test and grade information. Both growth mindset and grit have also received considerable attention in academic contexts. In terms of academic achievement, growth mindset has actually demonstrated a comparatively weak relationship with academic achievement ($r = .10$) and has a very small effect on interventions (Sisk et al., 2018). The introduction of the grit trait has arguably stimulated an important resurgence of interest in personality assessment. A recent meta-analysis of the literature indicates that grit is a new name for the well-studied trait of conscientiousness. As one would expect of a measure of conscientiousness, measures of grit are consistently related to important academic outcomes at a level similar to conscientiousness (e.g., $r = .18$ with GPA; Credé, Tynan, & Harms, 2017). Measures of school-specific study habits, attitudes, and skills are related to personality, but are more immediately related to academic outcomes and demonstrate even stronger predictive power (correlations from .25 to .37; Credé & Kuncel, 2008). However, all of these self-report measures are potentially vulnerable to faking.

Assessing these characteristics reliably would be valuable for informing admissions because personality tests do not require lengthy administration time and are comparatively inexpensive. One major barrier has been the concern about faking and self-referent bias. Applicants could provide misleading information with the goal of obtaining admissions (although this is also true of interviews, letters, and personal statements when focused on measuring personality). We think the nature of faking on personality assessments is complex, and validity-damaging faking is not a given (Kuncel, Borneman, & Kiger, 2011; Kuncel & Tellegen, 2009); however, we also believe that the utility of personality assessments is likely to be undermined in high-stakes settings paired with a prominent coaching industry.

Fortunately, two faking-resistant methods of personality assessment have been developed that use a forced-choice approach (Brown & Maydeu-Olivares, 2013; Stark, Chernyshenko, & Drasgow, 2005). These methods reduce or avoid some of the measurement problems associated with ipsative measures and reduce the effects of faking (Huber, 2017; Pavlov, Maydeu-Olivares, & Fairchild, 2018). A measure developed for use in private middle and high school admissions demonstrated useful relationships with multiple aspects of academic success in private middle and high schools (Kuncel et al., 2018).[1] It is our opinion that for admissions a nationally administered personality assessment would need to use one of the new forced-choice methods to address coached faking and schools would need to value multiple scales on the measures when making admissions decisions.

This approach to personality assessment has the potential to obtain a faking-resistant personality profile both quickly and at low cost. However,

---

[1] The lead author was compensated for this validation study as an external researcher. Nathan Kuncel does not own or market this measure or any other forced-choice personality assessment.

two important cautions are warranted. First, as is evident from the citations, forced-choice approaches are a comparatively novel method. Although initial validation work is positive, the evidence base is not as extensive as we see for other methods. Second, although the research to date suggests faking resistance, the reality is that there are patterns of responding that result in higher scores. This fact indicates that it is not technically impossible to fake these measures. But before getting too concerned about faking, readers should remember that we already rely on methods that are subject to manipulation by the applicant, whether they are LORs, personal statements, or interviews. Obtaining a complementary source of information that is fast, inexpensive, and faking-resistant would be very desirable to improve admissions decisions.

16.4.1.1 *Bias Issues*

Meta-analyses tend to find relatively small differences in Big Five traits by race/ethnicity (Foldes, Duehr, & Ones, 2008) in adult samples, although larger effects are observed for some narrower and more specific trait measures (i.e., facets). Similarly, more frequent and larger effects are seen in gender differences for personality (Costa, Terracciano, & McCrae, 2001; Finegold, 1994), and these effects replicate cross-culturally.

Again, differences are not necessarily bias. There is research that supports that observed personality differences are real in academic settings in that they are associated with important observed school behaviors. For example, female college students obtained higher scores on conscientiousness and also outperformed male students on more discretionary aspects of course-taking behavior. They were more likely to do extra credit work and participate in discussions consistent with higher levels of conscientiousness (Keiser et al., 2016). This evidence suggests that differences are not simply the function of test content or format but can reflect real differences in how people tend to behave.

16.4.1.2 *Practice Recommendations*

Schools could consider collecting assessments that inform judgments of a student's motivation, resilience, interest, leadership, and academic curiosity. These scores should then be triangulated with other information on key student characteristics. For example, a thoughtfully developed interview, LORs, and personality assessments could all be aligned to evaluate student drive. By triangulating across multiple sources of information, prediction can be improved and the emphasis placed on any one measure can be reduced.

16.4.2   *Situational Judgment Tests*

Ideally, we would like to see, in advance, how applicants would act during school. Imagine creating a full-scale simulation of a school including classes, distractions, and social interactions that would give excellent information about how a student would perform. Such a real-life simulation would also come with a ticket price and measurement challenges that would make them impossible. Situational Judgment Tests (SJTs) are an effort to approximate such a simulation in a way that is manageable, scalable, and cost-effective. Applicants are asked to read vignettes or view (in video or animated form) scenarios. They are then asked how they would respond to each scenario. Usually, applicants are asked to rate the effectiveness of a set of possible responses or identify the most effective and least effective options. The tests are either scored empirically or scored based on expert ratings of response effectiveness. A sample SJT item is presented in Figure 16.1.

SJTs have been used in operational high-stakes settings for admission and have demonstrated useful levels of predictive power for work (McDaniel et al., 2001) and academic performance (Lievens, Buyse, & Sackett, 2005). In an especially noteworthy study, SJTs for medical school admissions were developed to help predict interpersonal skills that would matter for treating patients (Lievens, Buyse, & Sackett, 2005). Early in medical school, when students were learning in the classroom, SJTs were not related to performance, as expected. Later in training, when students began working with patients, the interpersonal SJTs demonstrated correlations with performance and provided incremental information over other predictors. In college admissions, an SJT was developed that was used in a research setting (not used for decision-making) and it demonstrated significant correlations with outcomes including GPA ($r = .16$), absenteeism ($r = -.27$), and peer ratings of performance ($r = .16$) (Oswald et al., 2004).

16.4.2.1   *Bias Issues*
Research on SJTs has demonstrated moderate subgroup differences by race/ethnicity favoring Whites, but gender differences favoring females (Whetzel, McDaniel, & Nguyen, 2008). Race/ethnic group differences are strongly moderated by focus on judgments related to personality and SJTs reading demands. For example, video-based SJTs demonstrated stronger predictive power for interpersonal performance while also reducing the association with standardized test scores (Lievens & Sackett,

Your term paper for an upper level course is due in less than 2 days and although you have been reading and working on it, you realize that you have no idea how to integrate the material to create a good paper.

Action	Least	**Effectiveness**	Most
Do your best writing a good term paper and turn it in on time.			
Contact the professor, explain the situation, and ask for an extension.			
Discuss the material with classmates so you can figure out how to integrate it.			
Meet with the professor or teaching assistant to discuss your material and ask for help on integrating it.			
Read a book chapter review on the topic and adopt its framework.			

Figure 16.1   A situational judgment test item for a college student

2006). In a multi-school university study, an experimental SJT demonstrated zero to small differences across racial/ethnic subgroups and a large positive effect favoring females (Oswald et al., 2004) and, consistent with this effect, females tended to outperform males across college outcomes measures including grades (d = .11) and peer ratings of a behaviorally anchored rating scale (BARS) for college performance (d = .19).

16.4.2.2   *Practice Recommendations*
SJTs can be developed around any decision. They could be constructed to evaluate a variety of applicant characteristics. In practice, many are developed to evaluate interpersonal skills and ethical behavior. Ideally, an analysis of the performance domain should be conducted in a manner similar to developing a structured interview. In an educational setting,

clear specification of the performance domain and a systematic effort to sample that domain (e.g., a critical incidents study) should produce better results (see Flanagan, 1954).

Interestingly, careful efforts to develop SJTs that measure multiple independent characteristics consistently fail to do so yet still yield a measure that predicts subsequent performance (e.g., Oswald et al., 2004). Instead, the resulting measure captures a general interpersonal knowledge or socialization characteristic. One possible explanation for this finding is that school scenarios are, of themselves, diverse and draw on multiple attributes of the respondent. Another related explanation is that targeting specific characteristics with items that are influenced by many sources of variance would require far more items than are typically written for an SJT. That is, obtaining a "clean" trait signal from complex behavioral observations can require aggregating many independent pieces of information (Kuncel & Sackett, 2014). This suggests that SJTs should sample important behaviors and choices at school to inform admissions but may not lend themselves to highly targeted measurement.

One reasonable concern about SJTs is that they may be fakeable and coachable (Lievens, Buyse, & Sackett, 2005). Results of a study that examined faking directly in an academic setting showed that the predictive power of SJTs diminished but was not eliminated for the faking group (Peeters & Lievens, 2005). Similarly, results from field settings show that SJTs retain their predictive power even in the presence of a coaching industry (Lievens et al., 2012).

Historically, SJTs were written asking applicants what they *would* do, and this demonstrated, in the laboratory, different responses than asking what they *should* do. More recent experimental research in an actual operational setting indicates that participants answer "should do" regardless of the instructions (Lievens, Sackett, & Buyse, 2009). This distinction only seems to be salient in laboratory settings where participants may be less guarded and more authentic.

What seems to be happening in operational settings is that SJTs capture whether or not the applicant knows the appropriate behavior. A high score in SJTs suggests that admitted applicants at least know the appropriate behavior, making it more likely that they will engage in these behaviors when the time comes. From this perspective, test preparation also becomes a reduced threat for criterion-related validity. If applicants spend the time learning ethical, empathetic, and interpersonally effective responses to school relevant situations, so much the better. They will have improved in the areas that are important to schools. To help ensure fairness, we recommend first asking participants to rate the overall effectiveness of each response (should do) instead of asking them what they would do. This eliminates any concerns about whether participants are faking. Second, providing test-preparation materials will help ensure uniform opportunities to prepare for the assessment.

16.5 Biodata

A person's past behavior, background, and accomplishments can provide valuable information about their personality, values, and skills. Measures that compile and score this information are often called biographical data, application blanks, or biodata. Although this type of information is often evaluated judgmentally from résumés, lists of accomplishments, or personal statements, several scholars have created more structured measures with some success. Researchers differ in terms of the information they include in biodata measures, leading to considerable variability in the design of measures. Despite this obstacle, several conclusions can be drawn.

Most research on biodata has focused on predicting subsequent grades and has included high school course information, study habits, and social class, with some attention to personality traits and self-assessments of academic skills (e.g., Cirillo, Smith, & Kiran, 2008; Oswald et al., 2004). Correlations between overall biodata measures and subsequent GPAs is .39 (in a meta-analysis across 15 studies, N =3,896; Zhang & Kuncel, 2018). These correlations, however, may be inflated because the data are obtained in low-stakes settings and a reduction in predictive power occurs when implemented in high-stakes settings, particularly for non-verifiable information such as the number of hours students reported studying.

Interpreting these results for grade outcomes is somewhat difficult. Studies typically include prior grades as an element of the biodata composite, which presents a problem because although it helps boost the measure's predictive power, prior grades are already a fundamental element of nearly every admissions system. In other words, why use scores from self-reported grades if we already have more reliable scores from high school grades? A measure with added incremental information is needed.

A few studies have examined biodata measures that are more focused on personal extracurricular accomplishments. For example, Holland and Nichols (1964) developed the Extracurricular Achievement Record to capture engagement and accomplishments and Mackenzie (1967) demonstrated that it was predictive of actual student leadership and scholarship behaviors. More recently, Oswald et al. (2004) adapted items from several biodata instruments with the goal of creating a measure that evaluates student characteristics on 12 scales that align with a 12-dimensional model of student performance. The biodata scales demonstrated appropriate convergent validity with personality scales such that biodata items for perseverance were most strongly associated with a Conscientiousness scale, art with Openness, leadership and interpersonal with an Extroversion scale, and health with an Emotional Stability scale. Some of the scales demonstrated nontrivial correlations with absenteeism, GPA, and peer ratings of student accomplishments.

Biodata could also be considered as a resource for building a class. To the extent that schools want a student body with a diverse set of life experiences, biodata would provide a method for capturing these experiences. When used in this manner, the goal would be to identify the types of experiences a school wants represented and then ensure that at least some students are admitted each year that have those experiences.

16.5.1   Subgroup Differences

Little is known about subgroup differences in academic biodata measures, although unlike simple reviews of accomplishments biodata measures actually facilitate studying possible effects. In a study of a biodata measure designed to capture multiple student characteristics, subgroup differences by race/ethnicity and gender varied widely from much higher average scores to much lower average scores depending on the dimension and group (Oswald et al., 2004). Biodata measures can raise concerns about access and opportunity. Biodata items can (but do not have to) focus on accomplishments and experiences that may not be available to all students. Expensive international travel is one example. Travel can provide perspective and rich life experiences, which are desirable, but such travel is normally easier for affluent families to undertake. Developers of biodata measures should keep this in mind and investigate the disparate impact by group membership, including socioeconomic-status categories.

16.5.2   Practice Recommendations

Overall, biodata measures represent an effort rigorously and systematically to evaluate prior behaviors, experiences, and accomplishments. This approach has two major advantages over informal reviews of student accomplishments and extracurricular activities. First, it collects the same information from everyone, avoiding incomplete information problems. Second, it provides a record of information that can be used to evaluate and improve the admissions process.

However, attention would need to be given during the development of the measure to the content of the instrument to avoid construct-irrelevant subgroup differences and consider the accessibility, affordability, and opportunity of the experiences and accomplishments it measures. In addition, some effort would need to be put into verification or documentation of experiences to discourage applicants over-claiming experiences. A related concern might be that a biodata measure could be used by students as a checklist and cause them to try to maximize experiences to obtain a higher score. This is not necessarily a bad thing to the extent that the measure reflects important experiences and accomplishments. Nonetheless, it should be recognized that such a measure could drive student behavior. Although these issues are important to consider, such information is already used informally in admissions and this is done without much scrutiny.

Nonetheless, biodata measures (either general or targeted) can help provide supplemental information about key characteristics of applicants. For example, if persistence is a major concern for a school, a biodata measure targeting it could add incremental information alongside an interview and LOR ratings. The combination of three valid indicators of persistence will be more reliable than one used in isolation. However, additional data may increase the complexity of analysis as is elaborated next.

16.6 Data Integration

Admissions officers are faced with trying to maximize multiple goals based on many pieces of information, each with moderate levels of predictive power. Decision feedback is distant, ambiguous, or absent. This is a textbook example of a "wicked" decision-making environment that can result in poor decision quality. Even when the decision-maker is experienced and the information sources are the best available, there is considerable evidence that, although expert judgments (e.g., admissions decisions) do have utility, they tend to be less optimal than what could be obtained combining data using an equation. In other words, admissions and hiring judgments can be improved by simple mechanical or algorithmic aggregation of information (Grove & Meehl, 1996; Kuncel et al., 2013). The underlying problem is that decision-makers are not consistent in how they use and combine information, and this undermines accuracy. Given this reality, we should be just as concerned about how information is used as to the type of information used in the first place.

But we need to be realistic. We doubt that purely algorithmic approaches are going to be widely adopted anytime soon. We need to use methods that improve how consistent decision-makers are when evaluating information while, at the same time, preserving the role and acceptability of human judgment in the decisions. We can make three recommendations. First, the final decision should be based on multiple independent decision-makers. Having multiple independent readers for applicants is valuable but they should not share scores or judgments during the process. Those separate independent judgments should then be combined to form an overall decision. Second, if decision-makers are committed to having discussions, applicants should be presented with aggregated independent scores, all members should be encouraged to participate, and final voting should be anonymous. Third, it is possible to create expert systems that support, but do not force, decision-making.

Creating expert systems sounds more daunting than it is. A simple agreement among decision-makers on what information matters and how much it matters is the foundation. These weighting schemes can be used to produce overall scores for applicants. Presenting overall scores to decision-makers can anchor their judgment and improve accuracy. One approach is to use a tool called an integration grid. These are commonly used in high-level executive assessments. An integration grid compiles, in one place, all of the measures of interest (e.g., tests, interview, grades, and letters) and crosses them with all of the characteristics of interest (e.g., academic skills, persistence, and leadership), resulting in a display of all of the information organized by characteristic (or competency). Competency scores can then be aggregated into an overall recommendation for decision-makers. Figure 16.2 provides an example of a completed integration grid for college admissions.

Recognizing the limitations of human information processing and taking simple steps to support decision-making can yield greater gains than the addition of expensive and elaborate assessments.

16.7   Conclusion

We see two fundamental truths. First, success in higher education is multidimensional. Second, each of these dimensions of success is predicted by not one but many student attributes. Therefore, effective admissions

	Standardized test	Extracurri-cular activities	High School record	Interview	Letters	Totals
Foundational academic skills	4.5		4.00		4.50	4.33
Persistence and drive		3.75	4.25	4.00	4.00	4.00
Intellectual curiosity		2.50		3.00	2.75	2.75
Leadership and social skills		3.50		4.00		3.75
					Overall	3.70

Figure 16.2 A sample integration grid for college admissions

Note. Each assessment is scored or rescored on a 5-point scale. Totals for each competency and the overall score can be differentially weighted depending on admissions values or predictor strength.

will need to obtain multiple assessments of applicants and find effective methods for combining that information. Schools will obtain the best results by identifying success priorities and targeting the relevant student characteristics. To achieve this goal, the current suite of traditional admissions measures that target a student's character and accomplishments needs to be upgraded and complimented with innovative new methods. Paired with thoughtful methods that support effective and unbiased decision-making, we think the future of admissions in higher education is bright.

REFERENCES

Aamodt, M. G., Bryan, D. A., & Whitcomb, A. J. (1993). Predicting perform-ance with letters of recommendation. *Public Personnel Management, 22,* 81–90. https://doi.org/10.1177/009102609302200106.

Al Ansari, A., Al Khalifa, K., Al Azzawi, M., Al Amer, R., Al Sharqi, D., Al-Mansoor, A., & Munshi, F. M. (2015). Cross-cultural challenges for assess-ing medical professionalism among clerkship physicians in a Middle Eastern country (Bahrain): Feasibility and psychometric properties of multisource feedback. *Advances in Medical Education and Practice, 6,* 509. https://doi.org/10.2147/AMEP.S86068.

American Educational Research Association, American Psychological Association, & National Council on Measurement in Education. (1985). *Standards for educational and psychological testing.* Washington, DC: American Psycho-logical Association.

Beach, L. R. (2010). *The psychology of narrative thought*. Bloomington, IN: Xlibris.

Biernat, M., & Eidelman, S. (2007). Translating subjective language in letters of recommendation: The case of the sexist professor. *European Journal of Social Psychology, 37*, 1149–1175. https://doi.org/10.1002/ejsp.432.

Bouton, L. F. (1995). A cross-cultural analysis of the structure and content of letters of reference. *Studies in Second Language Acquisition, 17*, 211–244. https://doi.org/10.1017/S0272263100014169.

Brown, A., & Maydeu-Olivares, A. (2013). How IRT can solve problems of ipsative data in forced-choice questionnaires. *Psychological Methods, 18*, 36–52. https://doi.org/10.1037/a0030641.

Campion, M. A., Palmer, D. K., & Campion, J. E. (1997). A review of structure in the selection interview. *Personnel Psychology, 50*, 655–702. https://doi.org/10.1111/j.1744-6570.1997.tb00709.x.

Cirillo, M., Smith, T., & Kiran, J. (2008). The development of biographical inventory for use in the prediction of first-year college success. *TCNJ Journal of Student Scholarship, 10*, 1–11.

Connelly, B. S., & Ones, D. S. (2010). Another perspective on personality: Meta-analytic integration of observers' accuracy and predictive validity. *Psychological Bulletin, 136*, 1092. https://doi.org/10.1037/a0021212.

Costa, P. T., Jr., Terracciano, A., & McCrae, R. R. (2001). Gender differences in personality traits across cultures: Robust and surprising findings. *Journal of Personality and Social Psychology, 81*, 322–331. https://doi.org/10.1037/0022-3514.81.2.322.

Credé, M., & Kuncel, N. R. (2008). Study habits, study skills, and study attitudes: A meta-analysis of their relationship to academic performance among college students. *Perspectives on Psychological Science, 3*, 425–453. https://doi.org/10.1111/j.1745-6924.2008.00089.x.

Credé, M., Tynan, M. C., & Harms, P. D. (2017). Much ado about grit: A meta-analytic synthesis of the grit literature. *Journal of Personality and Social Psychology, 113*, 492–511. https://doi.org/10.1037/pspp0000102.

Educational Testing Service. (1974). *SIGI: A computer-based system of interactive guidance and information*. Princeton, NJ: Educational Testing Service.

Fajardo, D. M. (1985). Author race, essay quality, and reverse discrimination. *Journal of Applied Social Psychology, 15*, 255–268. https://doi.org/10.1111/j.1559-1816.1985.tb00900.x.

Finegold, A. (1994). Gender differences in personality: A meta-analysis. *Psychological Bulletin, 116*, 429–456. https://doi.org/10.1037/0033-2909.116.3.429.

Flanagan, J. C. (1954). The critical incident technique. *Psychological Bulletin, 51*, 327–358. http://dx.doi.org/10.1037/h0061470.

Foldes, H. J., Duehr, E. E., & Ones, D. S. (2008). Group differences in personality: Meta-analyses comparing five U.S. racial groups. *Personnel Psychology, 61*, 579–616. https://doi.org/10.1111/j.1744-6570.2008.00123.x.

Friedman, R., Fang, C. H., Hasbun, J., Han, H., Mady, L. J., Eloy, J. A., & Kalyoussef, E. (2017). Use of standardized letters of recommendation for otolaryngology head and neck surgery residency and the impact of gender. *Laryngoscope*, *127*(12), 2738–2745. https://doi.org/10.1002/lary.26619.

Gale, J., Ooms, A., Grant, R., Paget, K., & Marks-Maran, D. (2016). Student nurse selection and predictability of academic success: The multiple mini interview project. *Nurse Education Today*, *40*, 123–127. https://doi.org/10.1016/j.nedt.2016.01.031.

Girzadas, D. V., Jr., Harwood, R. C., Dearie, J., & Garrett, S. (1998). A comparison of standardized and narrative letters of recommendation. *Academic Emergency Medicine*, *5*(11), 1101–1104. https://doi.org/10.1111/j.1553-2712.1998.tb02670.x.

Grove, W. M., & Meehl, P. E. (1996). Comparative efficiency of informal (subjective, impressionistic) and formal (mechanical, algorithmic) prediction procedures: The clinical-statistical controversy. *Psychology, Public Policy, and Law*, *2*, 293–323. https://doi.org/10.1037/1076-8971.2.2.293.

Hawkins, D. A., & Lautz, J. (2005). *State of college admission*. Alexandria, VA: National Association for College Admission Counseling.

Henderson, M. C., Kelly, C. J., Griffin, E., Hall, T. R., Jerant, A., Peterson, E. M., Rainwater, J. A., Sousa, F. J., Wofsy, D. & Franks, P. (2018). Medical school applicant characteristics associated with performance in multiple mini-interviews: A multi-institutional study. *Academic Medicine: Journal of the Association of American Medical Colleges*, *93*(7), 1029–1034.

Holland, J. L., & Nichols, R. C. (1964). Prediction of academic and extra-curricular achievement in college. *Journal of Educational Psychology*, *55*, 55. https://doi.org/10.1037/h0047977.

Houser, C., & Lemmons, K. (2017). Implicit bias in letters of recommendation for an undergraduate research internship. *Journal of Further and Higher Education*, *38*, 1–11. https://doi.org/10.1080/0309877X.2017.1301410.

Huber, C. (2017). Faking and the validity of personality tests: Using new faking-resistant measures to study some old questions (Doctoral dissertation). University of Minnesota.

Huffcutt, A. I., & Arthur, W. (1994). Hunter and Hunter (1984) revisited: Interview validity for entry-level jobs. *Journal of Applied Psychology*, *79*(2), 184–190. http://dx.doi.org/10.1037/0021-9010.79.2.184.

Huffcutt, A. I., Conway, J. M., Roth, P. L., & Stone, N. J. (2001). Identification and meta-analytic assessment of psychological constructs measured in employment interviews. *Journal of Applied Psychology*, *86*, 897–913. https://doi.org/10.1037/0021-9010.86.5.897.

Huffcutt, A. I., & Roth, P. L. (1998). Racial group differences in employment interview evaluations. *Journal of Applied Psychology*, *83*, 179–189. https://doi.org/10.1037/0021-9010.83.2.179.

Hurtz, G. M., & Donovan, J. J. (2000). Personality and job performance: The big five revisited. *Journal of Applied Psychology*, *85*, 869–879. https://doi.org/10.1037/0021-9010.85.6.869.

Keiser, H. N., Sackett, P. R., Kuncel, N. R., & Brothen, T. (2016). Why women perform better in college than admission scores would predict: Exploring the roles of conscientiousness and course-taking patterns. *Journal of Applied Psychology, 101,* 569–581. https://doi.org/10.1037/apl0000069.

Kryger, B. R., & Shikiar, R. (1978). Sexual discrimination in the use of letters of recommendation: A case of reverse discrimination. *Journal of Applied Psychology, 63*(3), 309–314. http://dx.doi.org/10.1037/0021-9010.63.3.309.

Kuncel, N. R., Borneman, M., & Kiger, T. (2011). Innovative item response process and Bayesian faking detection methods: More questions than answers. In M. Ziegler, C. Maccann, & R. D. Roberts (Eds.). *New perspectives on faking in personality assessment.* Oxford: Oxford University Press. https://doi.org/10.1093/acprof:oso/9780195387476.003.0036.

Kuncel, N. R., Brenneman, M., Petway, K., & Liu, J. (2018). *Validation of the character skills snapshot (CSS).* Skillman, NJ: Enrollment Management Association.

Kuncel, N. R., & Hezlett, S. A. (2010). Fact and fiction in standardized admissions testing. *Current Directions in Psychological Science, 19,* 339–345. https://doi.org/10.1177/0963721410389459.

Kuncel, N. R., Klieger, D. M., Connelly, B. S., & Ones, D. S. (2013). Mechanical versus clinical data combination in selection and admissions decisions: A meta-analysis. *Journal of Applied Psychology, 98,* 1060–1072. https://doi.org/10.1037/a0034156.

Kuncel, N. R., Kochevar, R. J., & Ones, D. S. (2014). A meta-analysis of letters of recommendation in college and graduate admissions. *Reasons for hope. International Journal of Selection and Assessment, 22,* 101–107. https://doi.org/10.1111/ijsa.12060.

Kuncel, N. R., & Tellegen, A. (2009). The measurement of the social desirability of items: A conceptual and empirical reexamination. *Personnel Psychology, 62,* 201–228. https://doi.org/10.1111/j.1744-6570.2009.01136.x.

Kuncel, N. R., & Sackett, P. R. (2014). Resolving the assessment center construct validity problem (as we know it). *Journal of Applied Psychology, 99*(1), 38. http://dx.doi.org/10.1037/a0034147.

(2018, March 10). The gatekeeper tests. *The Wall Street Journal,* pp. C1–C2.

Lerner, J. S., & Tetlock, P. E. (2003). Bridging individual, interpersonal, and institutional approaches to judgment and decision making: The impact of accountability on cognitive bias. In S. L. Schneider & J. Shanteau (Eds.). *Emerging Perspectives on Judgment and Decision Research* (pp. 431–457). https://doi.org/10.1017/CBO9780511609978.015.

Lievens, F., Buyse, T., & Sackett, P. R. (2005). The operational validity of a video-based situational judgment test for medical college admissions: Illustrating the importance of matching predictor and criterion construct domains. *Journal of Applied Psychology, 90,* 442–452. http://dx.doi.org/10.1037/0021-9010.90.3.442.

Lievens, F., Buyse, T., Sackett, P. R., & Connelly, B. S. (2012). The effects of coaching on situational judgment tests in high-stakes selection. *International Journal of Selection and Assessment, 20,* 272–282. https://doi.org/10.1111/j.1468-2389.2012.00599.x.

Lievens, F., & Sackett, P. R. (2006). Video-based versus written situational judgment tests: A comparison in terms of predictive validity. *Journal of Applied Psychology*, *91*(5), 1181. http://dx.doi.org/10.1037/0021-9010.91.5.1181.

Lievens, F., Sackett, P. R., & Buyse, T. (2009). The effects of response instructions on situational judgment test performance and validity in a high-stakes context. *Journal of Applied Psychology*, 94, 1095–1101. http://dx.doi.org/10.1037/a0014628.

Lumb, A. B., Homer, M., & Miller, A. (2010). Equity in interviews: Do personal characteristics impact on admission interview scores? *Medical Education, 44*, 1077–1083. https://doi.org/10.1111/j.1365-2923.2010.03771.x.

McDaniel, M. A., Morgeson, F. P., Finnegan, E. B., Campion, M. A., & Braverman, E. P. (2001). Predicting job performance using situational judgement tests: A clarification of the literature. *Journal of Applied Psychology*, *86*, 730–740.

Mackenzie, R. S. (1967). Predictive validity of a biographical inventory in higher education. *Journal of Applied Psychology*, *51*, 544–546. https://doi.org/10.1037/h0025108.

Max, B. A., Gelfand, B., Brooks, M. R., Beckerly, R., & Segal, S. (2010). Have personal statements become impersonal? An evaluation of personal statements in anesthesiology residency applications. *Journal of Clinical Anesthesia*, *22*, 346–351. https://doi.org/10.1016/j.jclinane.2009.10.007.

Morgan, W. B., Elder, K. B., & King, E. B. (2013). The emergence and reduction of bias in letters of recommendation. *Journal of Applied Social Psychology*, *43*(11), 2297–2306. https://doi.org/10.1111/jasp.12179.

Murphy, S. R., Klieger, D. M., Borneman, M., & Kuncel, N. R. (2009). The predictive power of personal statements in admissions: A meta-analysis and cautionary tale. *College and University*, *84*(4), 83–88.

Nicklin, J. M., & Roch, S. G. (2008). Biases influencing recommendation letter contents: physical attractiveness and gender. *Journal of Applied Social Psychology*, *38*, 3053–3074. http://dx.doi.org/10.1111/j.1559-1816.2008.00425.x.

Nye, C. D., Su, R., Rounds, J., & Drasgow, F. (2012). Vocational interests and performance: A quantitative summary of over 60 years of research. *Perspectives on Psychological Science*, *7*, 384–403. https://doi.org/10.1177/1745691612449021.

Oliveri, M. E., McCaffrey, D., Ezzo, C., & Holtzman, S. (2017). A multilevel factor analysis of third-party evaluations of noncognitive constructs used in admissions decision making. *Applied Measurement in Education*, *30*, 297–313. https://doi.org/10.1080/08957347.2017.1353989.

Osman, N. Y., Schonhardt-Bailey, C., Walling, J. L., Katz, J. T., & Alexander, E. K. (2015). Textual analysis of internal medicine residency personal statements: Themes and gender differences. *Medical Education*, *49*, 93–102. https://doi.org/10.1111/medu.12487.

Oswald, F. L., Schmitt, N., Kim, B. H., Ramsey, L. J., & Gillespie, M. A. (2004). Developing a biodata measure and situational judgment inventory as predictors of college student performance. *Journal of Applied Psychology*, *89*, 187–207. http://dx.doi.org/10.1037/0021-9010.89.2.187.

The papers of Benjamin Franklin. n.d. Retrieved from http://franklinpapers.org/.

Pau, A., Jeevaratnam, K., Chen, Y. S., Fall, A. A., Khoo, C., & Nadarajah, V. D. (2013). The multiple mini-interview (MMI) for student selection in health professions training: A systematic review. *Medical Teacher, 35*, 1027–1041. https://doi.org/10.3109/0142159X.2013.829912.

Pavlov, G., Maydeu-Olivares, A., & Fairchild, A. J. (2018). Effects of applicant faking on forced-choice and Likert scores. *Organizational Research Methods*, 1–30. https://doi.org/10.1177/1094428117753683.

Peeters, H., & Lievens, P. (2005). Situational judgment tests and their predictiveness of college students' success: The influence of faking. *Educational and Psychological Measurement, 65*, 70–89. https://doi.org/10.1177/0013164404268672.

Poropat, A. E. (2009). A meta-analysis of the five-factor model of personality and academic performance. *Psychological Bulletin, 135*, 322–338. https://doi.org/10.1037/a0014996.

Precht, K. (1998). A cross-cultural comparison of letters of recommendation. *English for Specific Purposes, 17*, 241–265. https://doi.org/10.1016/S0889-4906(97)00012-4.

Roberts, B. W., Kuncel, N. R., Shiner, R., Caspi, A., & Goldberg, L. R. (2007). The comparative predictive validity of personality traits, SES, and cognitive ability. *Perspectives on Psychological Science, 2*, 331–345. https://doi.org/10.1111/j.1745-6916.2007.00047.x.

Salgado, J. F. (1997). The five factor model of personality and job performance in the European community. *Journal of Applied Psychology, 82*, 30–43. https://doi.org/10.1037/0021-9010.82.1.30.

Shahani, C., & Dipboye, R. L. (1993). Attractiveness bias in the interview: Exploring the boundaries of an effect. *Basic and Applied Social Psychology, 14*, 317–328. https://doi.org/10.1207/s15324834basp1403_5.

Sisk, V. F., Burgoyne, A. P., Sun, J., Butler, J. L., & Macnamara, B. N. (2018). To what extent and under what circumstance are growth mind-sets important to academic achievement? Two meta-analyses. *Psychological Science, 29*, 549–571. https://doi.org/10.1177/0956797617739704.

Stark, S., Chernyshenko, O. S., & Drasgow, F. (2005). An IRT approach to constructing and scoring pairwise preference items involving stimuli on different dimensions. *Applied Psychological Measurement, 29*, 184–203. https://doi.org/10.1177/0146621604273988.

Terregino, C. A., McConnell, M., & Reiter, H. I. (2015). The effect of differential weighting of academics, experiences, and competencies measured by multiple mini interview (MMI) on race and ethnicity of cohorts accepted to one medical school. *Academic Medicine: Journal of the Association of American Medical Colleges, 90*, 1651–1657. https://doi.org/10.1097/ACM.0000000000000960.

Watson, C. (1987). Sex-linked differences in letters of recommendation. *Women and Language, 10*(2), 26. Retrieved from http://erepo.usiu.ac.ke/handle/11732/1283?show=full.

Whetzel, D. L., McDaniel, M. A., & Nguyen, N. T. (2008). Subgroup differences in situational judgment test performance: A meta-analysis. *Human Performance, 21*(3), 291-309.

Wright, S. R., & Bradley, P. M. (2010). Has the UK clinical aptitude test improved medical student selection? *Medical Education, 44,* 1069–1076. https://doi.org/10.1111/j.1365-2923.2010.03792.x.

Zhang, C. S. H., & Kuncel, N. R. (2018). Moving beyond the brag sheet: Predicting student outcomes with biodata measures. Unpublished manuscript. University of Minnesota.

.

PART IV

Rethinking Higher Education Admissions

Cathy Wendler

The higher education admissions process is filled with good intentions but fraught with many issues: Should all students have access to higher education? How do we ensure that fairness and diversity are part of the process? What measures should be used or criteria applied as part of admissions that support access, fairness, and diversity? And how do we even define fairness and diversity? As many chapters in this volume point out, answers to these questions often clash in a real-life context. At a country level, societal philosophies drive attitudes toward fairness and access in higher education. But, in reality, the number of study places at colleges and universities, student preparation and opportunities to learn at the secondary level, and the availability of financing often dictate how accessible higher education really is.

Students and their parents across the globe want the best possible education because it is perceived as a way to enhance future occupational and economic opportunities. This results in higher education admissions being a high-stakes enterprise. Countries continuously grapple with issues such as how students are admitted into particular institutions or study programs, what criteria are used, and how higher education is financed. Even countries with well-established higher education systems are not exempt from these issues or from the actions of those who wish to take advantage of the system. For example, in March 2019, the Justice Department of the United States alleged that some wealthy parents had used bribery, cheating, misrepresentation, and other means to increase their children's chances of admissions into what they perceived to be prestigious institutions (see Barrett & Zapotosky, 2019; Korn, Levitz, & Ailworth, 2019; Taylor, 2019). As a number of chapters in this volume point out, this behavior is not an isolated phenomenon, and it is not a problem caused by – nor can it be resolved by – particular admissions models or types of selection criteria. Threats related to fairness, diversity, and access are faced by almost all countries that maintain a higher education system. Perhaps a new approach to higher education admissions is needed.

The three chapters in this section move beyond current concepts of higher education admissions. They present alternatives as to how the admissions process might be conceived and maintained. They propose new frameworks for conceptualizing what the role of higher education should be and methods for rethinking the assessments used as part of admissions.

In their chapter, Burrus, Way, Bobek, Stoeffler, and O'Connor explore the relationship between academic and workforce skills. Their premise is that the ultimate goal of academic preparation should be to prepare individuals to succeed in the workforce, and so more than just academic knowledge is needed. They identify several additional factors that research has shown helps individuals succeed in higher education and in the workforce. These factors are classified into a framework grouped along four independent but highly related domains: core academic skills; cross-cutting capabilities; behavioral skills; and education and career navigation. The authors point to environmental and technological changes that lead them to believe that it is time for higher education institutions to expand beyond the characteristics of prospective students they have traditionally considered.

Academic measures such as test scores, previous grades, and class rank are frequently used as part of the admissions process. The chapter by Zwick proposes the use of a mathematical approach that helps support the access and diversity goals of higher education institutions while still maintaining academic standards. This approach, called "constrained optimization," allows both academic requirements and other factors – race/ethnicity, income level, social status, geographic region, educational background – to be considered during the admissions process. While diversity efforts vary by country and institution, constrained optimization seeks to improve higher education access for particular groups of students. As such, this may be a useful approach for ensuring that the multiple objectives of the admissions process of any country are achieved.

The final chapter, by Oliveri, Mislevy, and Elliot, presents another perspective on changes likely to impact higher education, including shifts in the population served by higher education, changes in the demographic characteristics of students, and evolving requirements for the skill sets needed to produce successful students. As a result, the authors maintain that changes to the types of measures used as part of higher education admissions are needed, and that such measures should not only focus on selection, but also on ensuring that students are successful. They present two frameworks that guide how assessments might be developed and the types of assessments that might be used. The first, a multilevel design model, guides the design and creation of assessments so that information from the assessments is appropriate for various stakeholders (students, institutions, and government). The second, a complementarity model, integrates data from assessments traditionally used for purposes other than higher education admissions in support of student learning and matriculation. The authors assert that the use of such models will better serve the needs of higher education admissions decisions.

REFERENCES

Barrett, D. & Zapotosky, M. (2019, March 12). FBI accuses wealthy parents, including celebrities, in college-entrance bribery scheme. *Washington Post.* Retrieved from www.washingtonpost.com/world/national-security/fbi-accuses-wealthy-parents-including-celebrities-in-college-entrance-bribery-scheme/2019/03/12/d91c9942-44d1-11e9-8aab-95b8d80a1e4f_story.html?noredirect=on&utm_term=.01cd84ecbce3.

Korn, M., Levitz, J., & Ailworth, E. (2019, March 13). Federal prosecutors charge dozens in college admissions cheating scheme. *Wall Street Journal.* Retrieved from www.wsj.com/articles/federal-prosecutors-charge-dozens-in-broad-college-admissions-fraud-scheme-11552403149.

Taylor, K. (2019, March 13). Fallout from college admissions scandal: Arrests, damage control and a scramble for answers. *New York Times.* Retrieved from www.nytimes.com/2019/03/13/us/college-admissions-probe.html.

CHAPTER 17

The ACT Holistic Framework® of Education and Workplace Success

Jeremy Burrus, Jason Way, Becky Bobek,
Kristin Stoeffler, and Ryan O'Connor

In their quest to admit students most likely to succeed, colleges and universities have traditionally weighed grade point averages (GPAs) and standardized test scores heavily in admissions decisions. The *2016 National Association for College Admission Counseling Admissions Trends Survey* (cited in Clinedinst & Koranteng, 2017) found that colleges rate grades, strength of curriculum, and admissions test scores as the most important admissions decision factors, in that order. That postsecondary institutions value these factors makes intuitive sense. The popular maxim that "the best predictor of future performance is past performance" reflects the notion that an effective predictor of college performance should be some indicator of how a student has performed in high school; and the most common indicators of high school performance are GPA and admissions test scores such as the ACT® and SAT®.

This practice is clearly not unfounded. People with greater academic knowledge and skills perform better and persist longer in college. For example, one meta-analysis found that academic knowledge reflected by high school GPA and ACT/SAT scores were associated with both college GPA and retention (Robbins et al., 2004). These skills translate to workforce success, as well. Academic skills as indexed by college GPA predicts job performance (Roth et al., 1996), and those who have strong literacy and numeracy skills are more likely to have higher wages than those with weaker literacy and numeracy skills (Organisation for Economic Co-operation and Development, 2013).

There is increasing awareness, however, that several additional factors help individuals succeed in higher education and the workforce. Numerous surveys suggest that employers increasingly value skills considered to be nonacademic and, often, they value them even more than academic skills. This is true both within the United States (e.g., Hart Research Associates, 2010) and internationally (e.g., Cullinane & Montacute, 2017). For example, a survey asking employers in the United Kingdom about attributes they wanted to see in young people entering the workforce found that life skills such as communication and motivation were considered more important than cognitive skills such as verbal and numeracy skills (Cullinane & Montacute, 2017).

This awareness is reflected in the current movement toward what is known as holistic college admissions. That is, a growing number of colleges and universities in North America are attempting to incorporate nonacademic, or noncognitive, variables into their admissions process (Kalsbeek, Sandlin, & Sedlacek, 2013). One admissions officer recently described their institution's admissions policy in the following way:

> We're far more interested in who you are and what you can bring to our campus community than how you happened to score on a high-pressure, high-stakes standardized test. We look at your high school achievements, your extracurricular activities, your work and life experiences, community service activities, artistic and creative talents, and more. All the unique, personal traits that make you ... you." (Grove, 2018)

In short, colleges and universities are now looking beyond standardized test scores and GPA in selecting the next generations of students for success.

This trend is also occurring in international admissions. For example, the Chinese Ministry of Education published new guidelines in 2014 that were designed to encourage institutions to adopt a more holistic approach toward admissions in higher education; these guidelines included a number of provisions that reinforce the relevance of nonacademic components. One provision in particular provides institutions with greater latitude when considering admissions criteria that go beyond the primary academic admissions exam: the Gaokao (e.g., awards and honors, athletics, teacher recommendations: Gu & Magaziner, 2018).

Importantly, research evidence supports the belief that these additional factors predict success in both higher education and the workforce. But what constitutes success? There is a long tradition in workforce research to expand the definition of success beyond traditionally measured outcomes such as supervisor ratings of job performance (Campbell, 1990). Other factors are deemed as important outcomes, such as task-specific behaviors, non-task-specific behaviors, oral communication, effort, personal discipline, teamwork, and supervisory or leadership and managerial skills. Importantly, nonacademic skills tend to predict less cognitive-determined outcomes such as teamwork (Mount, Barrick, & Stewart, 1998). In these ways, the definition of success at colleges and universities can be expanded accordingly. The most obvious criteria include timely degree attainment, retention, and absenteeism, all of which are well predicted by nonacademic skills (Allen & Robbins, 2010; Robbins et al., 2004; Schmitt et al., 2009).

For both traditional and nontraditional indicators of success, nonacademic factors are among the most powerful predictors. Factors such as conscientiousness (Poropat, 2009) and interest-major congruence (Nye et al., 2012) predict college GPA. The story is similar for performance in the workplace: Conscientiousness, agreeableness, emotional stability, and interest–job congruence predict outcomes such as task performance, organizational citizenship, and persistence on the job (Nye et al., 2012; Sackett & Walmsley, 2014).

Because the preponderance of evidence suggests that success depends on more than simply academic knowledge and skills, we propose that colleges and universities consider expanding the set of characteristics they value in prospective students. Oliveri and Markle (2017) provide a detailed review of skills college graduates need for success in the workforce. Many frameworks were reviewed in the Oliveri and Markle paper, and nonacademic skills were identified as important, including (but not limited to) oral communication, work ethic, critical thinking, teamwork, digital literacy, citizenship, creativity, leadership, adaptability, and cultural awareness. Each of these skills is valued in some way by the workforce, yet it is not always the case that each of them is taught effectively in college. To help students succeed beyond college, as well as to ensure better alignment with twenty-first-century workforce requirements, these skills should become part of the selection criteria for use in admissions and cultivated in higher education coursework.

It is also the case that it is not clear if some of these skills are the same skills or different, and which should be priorities. Thus, a framework that can guide the selection of relevant characteristics used in the admissions process is of the utmost importance. One such framework is the ACT Holistic Framework (Camara et al., 2015). The Holistic Framework details what students should know and be able to do to succeed from kindergarten through to their career and is organized into four broad domains that were developed, "based on a comprehensive review of relevant theory, education and work standards, empirical research, input from experts in the field, and a variety of other sources for each of the four broad domains" (Camara et al., 2015, p. vi). The four domains are as follows:

- core academic skills
- cross-cutting capabilities
- behavioral skills
- education and career navigation

Each framework domain is hierarchical; at the highest level, they include several broad dimensions of the domain and then drill down into more detailed components, subcomponents, and performance-level descriptors (PLDs). The Holistic Framework also includes additional levels of specificity that are developmentally appropriate and aligned to important transitions in education and work. We should note that there are other skills frameworks that have been developed that also outline the knowledge, skills, and abilities students need to succeed in the current workforce environment. For instance, the National Research Council (2013) developed a framework that outlined cognitive competencies (e.g., critical thinking, creativity), intrapersonal competencies (e.g., openness, work ethic), and interpersonal competencies (e.g., teamwork, leadership) as key twenty-first-century skills. Conley (2008) put forth a college readiness framework that includes cognitive strategies (e.g., reasoning), content knowledge, academic behaviors (e.g., self-management), and contextual skills and awareness (e.g., college knowledge). Finally, the Organisation for Economic Co-operation and Development (OECD) has adopted the Big Five personality framework (conscientiousness, agreeableness, emotional stability, openness, and extraversion) as its organizing framework for the assessment of student and adult noncognitive skills. To the best of our knowledge, however, the ACT Holistic Framework is a much more comprehensive and detailed model than any other model previously advanced. Each of the Framework orientations is described below. What follows is a brief description. More detail on the Framework can be found in Camara et al. (2015).

17.1   Core Academic Skills

The core academic skills component of the Holistic Framework identifies, describes, and organizes the cognitive knowledge and skills in key foundational areas. No Child Left Behind (2002) and the Common Core State Standards (2010) have focused exclusively on core academic indicators, specifically in mathematics and English language arts (ELA). While readiness in numeracy and literacy are critical prerequisites for success in education and workplace settings, this focus maintains a narrow view of college and career success that is primarily designed to serve accountability needs rather than student needs (Mattern et al., 2014). A holistic model of education and work success should not be restricted to just core academic subjects in K–12 education; rather, it should build upon what we know about how people learn and provide greater insights on not simply what they have learned, but the potential of each individual learner. To that end, the core academic skills framework aims to identify the cognitive learning outcomes required for success at critical education and work transitions and provides a detailed articulation of their development from kindergarten through to a career.

17.1.1 Core Academic Skills Predict Important Outcomes for Postsecondary Students

Cognitive skills have typically been shown to be strong predictors of academic success (Poropat, 2009). In a comprehensive meta-analysis of predictors of academic performance at all levels of schooling, Poropat found that core academic skills (e.g., ACT/SAT scores) predicted course grades at each educational level. National validity studies have reached the same conclusion with results indicating that ACT and SAT scores predict college GPA throughout the college career (e.g., Mattern & Patterson, 2011).

17.1.2 Core Academic Skills Predict Important Outcomes for Workers

Cognitive predictors are among the strongest predictors of job performance across a variety of job situations. Schmidt and Hunter (1998) conducted a meta-analysis of the validity of 19 selection methods for predicting job performance. Of all the selection methods investigated, the researchers found that tests of cognitive ability were clearly the most predictive of job performance. This finding has been demonstrated across several meta-analyses (Schmidt & Hunter, 2004), and for job training performance in addition to supervisor-rated job performance (Colquitt, LePine, & Noe, 2000). Proficiency in each of these core academic skills greatly facilitates later efforts to develop specialized expertise from major courses and job training experiences (Carter, 2002).

17.1.3 Relevance for International Contexts

Hanushek and Woessmann (2008) looked at the 40-year growth rate of the gross domestic product (GDP) in 50 countries as it related to the average years of schooling in each. They found that each additional year of schooling increased the average GDP growth rate by about 0.37 percent. A replication with average test score performance by country found a 1 percent improvement in GDP growth for every half-standard-deviation increase in international student achievement test scores. Note that in the realm of economic growth, 1 percent is a very large number; GDP growth in the United States is currently hovering around 2.3 percent. Taken together, these results clearly support the value of ensuring that each citizen receives an education that enables participation in the emerging economy.

17.1.4   Specific Dimensions of the Core Academic Skills Domain

The core academic skills framework includes three academic subjects (language arts, mathematics, and science), each of which is organized into a set of academic domains specific to each subject. Importantly, the terminology of strands and substrands is meant to emphasize the connected, progressive nature of their content. In this way, each of these academic domains is then broken down into large strands and more focused substrands. Accordingly, each substrand focuses on a sequence of skills, and these skill progressions are supplemented and supported by a comprehensive database of related knowledge, misconceptions, common errors, and strategies in order to provide a richer picture of student learning.

17.1.4.1   Language Arts and Literacy

ACT has considered both academic and workplace literacy demands in the design of the language arts and literacy framework. Evidence shows that facility with the English language predicts important outcomes at the high school to college transition (Jackson, 2005). One consequence of inadequate literacy proficiency is that students are less prepared to handle the reading tasks required in college, leading to diminished performance (Schoenbach, Greenleaf, & Murphy, 2012).

There are five domains in the language arts and literacy framework, and each are detailed with special attention to the empirical research on developmentally sensitive knowledge, skills, and practices. Because development is integrated across the more specific strands and substrands of language arts and literacy, the framework is organized to show connections to the greatest extent possible.

17.1.4.2   Mathematics

The ACT mathematics framework proposes an interconnected and progression-based approach to ensure that the concepts against which students are assessed are necessary for education and work success. To succeed in majors and careers that are even moderately demanding mathematically, students must have a level of fluency that allows them to spare attention and working memory to adapt to unfamiliar situations.

Additionally, a firm conceptual understanding is critical to leveraging technology to solve real-world problems. The organization of the mathematics framework attends to these foundational and practical considerations.

17.1.4.3 Science

ACT has long employed an expanded model of college and career readiness that incorporates scientific skills and knowledge. In addition, ACT assessments have long included science as an academic domain because skills and interest in science are not totally subsumed by mathematics or ELA. With the increased demand for STEM (science, technology, engineering, and mathematics) skills, measures of science are critically important to prepare students, and use of mathematics or ELA as proxies introduces construct irrelevance and does not provide a substantive validity argument to support inferences about science skills. The core academic skills framework expands on the current ACT College and Career Readiness Standards (ACT CCRS) by adding STEM and cross-cutting concepts to the current science framework.

The approach to science readiness enumerated in the core academic framework builds on the ACT CCRS by highlighting knowledge and skills that are foundational in science. This should provide students with the foundation necessary to pursue careers in STEM fields while also enabling them to transfer scientific knowledge and skills to a broad range of non-STEM careers. This focus on scientific reasoning and practices is significant because these evidence-based reasoning skills are central to many fields of study and have wide applicability on the job (Jonassen & Kim, 2010).

17.1.5 Potential Applications of the Framework

One potential application of the core academic skills framework is to help nontraditional students achieve academic and career success. Adult students who want to continue to pursue either educational or career advancement can use the framework to understand what knowledge and skills they possess (or lack) in order to set goals for their future development.

Another potential application of the core academic skills framework is to help teachers tailor instruction to individual students based on their needs. Because this framework reaches constructs in much more depth than existing standards, teachers can design formative assessments to diagnose students' strengths and weaknesses and help them achieve academic success in an effective, efficient, and timely manner.

17.1.6   Summary

The core academic skills framework serves as an anchor for the ACT Holistic Framework, which offers an expanded view of education and work success. By identifying and organizing these core academic knowledge and skills, ACT looks to provide a detailed articulation of progress from kindergarten to career that is developmentally sensitive and emphasizes the connected, progressive nature of learning.

17.2   Cross-Cutting Capabilities Framework

ACT's cross-cutting capabilities (CCCs) are transferable skills that extend and enhance learners' abilities to succeed in a global society rich with both information and opportunity. These CCCs are collections of skills that include behaviors, thinking skills, and technology skills. When combined with the core academic knowledge and skills, CCCs can empower learners to fulfill their potential as effective and creative knowledge seekers, communicators, and problem-solvers. ACT currently includes four CCCs in the Holistic Framework:

- information and communication technology
- collaborative problem-solving
- learning skills
- critical thinking

17.2.1   CCCs and Postsecondary Setting

The role of CCCs in the postsecondary setting has been more implicit than explicit. Despite this, the ability of students to succeed in the postsecondary setting is increasingly dependent on CCCs. Critical thinking skills have long been understood to be valuable for success in the postsecondary environment, showing significant correlations with GPA (Facione, 1991). Technology skills are increasingly required to access course materials and complete course assignments. Levels of technology use have also been linked to grades in postsecondary courses (Huffman & Huffman, 2012). Effective interpersonal skills are required to collaborate with peers and professors and improve cognitive learning outcomes (Pace, 1990; Simons & Peterson, 2000). The role of learning skills in the postsecondary environment has taken on new importance with an improved understanding of the role that behaviors central to the learning skills framework play in successful learning outcomes (e.g., Lounsbury et al., 2005; Steel, 2007).

17.2.2 CCCs and the Modern Workforce

The value of CCCs is particularly apparent in the twenty-first-century workforce and economy, which place a premium on skills required for innovation, collaboration, technology, and problem-solving (Autor & Price, 2013; Baller, Dutta, & Lanvin, 2016). This could be considered a reflection of the changing nature of work and an increasingly global economy (Baller, Dutta, & Lanvin, 2016). These new environments are bringing together resources, insights, tools, and fields (e.g., physical, biological, technological) and merging them in ways to create new and groundbreaking insights. Indeed, innovation often requires the coordination of expertise from a range of backgrounds and fields, rather than simply the contributions of an individual expert (Schwab, 2016; World Economic Forum, 2016).

Success in the future workforce will also require that workers have the ability to upskill and reskill as necessary as well as harness the skills necessary to use technology effectively (World Economic Forum, 2016). The number of occupations requiring high levels of thinking skills is predicted to increase, as well as experience an increase in wages (Autor & Price, 2013). Interpersonal and intrapersonal skills that support collaboration and learning skills have also been linked to job satisfaction and performance (e.g., Lindqvist & Vestman, 2011; Roberts et al., 2007).

17.2.3 Relevance for International Contexts

The degree to which tertiary educational institutions take CCCs into account for admissions varies across the globe. While the inclusion for admissions of assessments that measure these skills explicitly is still rare, more common is the inclusion of course requirements that draw upon these skills either explicitly (e.g., computer science) or implicitly (e.g., business) as an indication of the degree to which these skill sets are valued by educational institutions.

The importance of these skills for the workforce has long been a focus for the OECD and the World Economic Forum (WEF). The OECD has focused on these skills specifically through their inclusion as the supplemental constructs for both the Programme for International Student Assessment (PISA) and the Programme for the International Assessment of Adult Competencies (PIAAC) (Organisation for Economic Co-operation and Development, 2013). The WEF has also highlighted a range of CCCs as of critical importance for the current and future workforce (World Economic Forum, 2016).

17.2.4   Organization of the Domain

The ACT CCCs exist within the ecosystem of the ACT Holistic Framework. This dynamic ecosystem allows us to identify and align the knowledge, behaviors, and skills shared between existing constructs, supporting their acquisition and application. Individual CCCs are divided into dimensions supported by components, subcomponents, and performance-level descriptors (PLDs). The PLDs for the Framework are supported by the identification and alignment of knowledge, skills, and behaviors from the behavior and core academic areas of ACT's Holistic Framework. ACT currently includes four CCCs frameworks in the Holistic Framework, and a brief description of each follows.

17.2.4.1   Information and Communication Technology (ICT)
The components in this dimension outline the knowledge and skills required to acquire and apply information using technology. This includes the knowledge and skills necessary to plan an information search using sources accessed using technology; locate, collect, and evaluate information accessed using technology; transform information using technology; and share information using technology. These skills have become an essential component of both academic and work environments. The ACT ICT framework outlines and details the knowledge and skills required to fulfill these highly valuable functions.

17.2.4.2   Collaborative Problem-Solving (CPS)
The CPS dimension is divided into team effectiveness and task effectiveness components. The subcomponents of these components outline the cognitive and behavioral skills required to support an effective team dynamic including inclusiveness, clarity, communication, and commitment. The subcomponents of the task effectiveness component outline the cognitive and behavioral skills necessary for successful task completion including problem space and goal awareness, strategy, execution, and monitoring.

17.2.4.3   Learning Skills
Modern society has expanded our independent access to knowledge and the tools to access that knowledge. The learning skills dimension focuses on the intrapersonal skills and learning strategies that support learners' abilities effectively to access, acquire, and retain knowledge. The framework outlines the cognitive, noncognitive, metacognitive, and technology

skills that empower learners to understand themselves as learners, as well as to outline the strategies and processes that support effective learning.

17.2.4.4   Critical Thinking

Critical thinking has long been in high demand by educators and employers. It is often a key part of the bridge that brings together the K–12 educational system and the workforce. ACT's critical thinking framework contains the fundamental divisions of critical thinking and the skills involved in those divisions. The function of this framework is to provide an outline of the nature of critical thinking and the skills involved in critical thinking. The framework itself is divided into seven subcomponents: argument analysis, basic epistemology, argument development, argument evaluation, advanced epistemology, properties of statements, and argument extension.

17.2.5   Potential Applications of the Framework and Summary

The implication of including these skills for secondary admissions is primarily in their ability to provide a more authentic representation of the skills that will be required for success in college and careers. Researchers continue to support the understanding that cognitive diversity is associated with better performance outcomes (Hong & Page, 2004; Page, 2008) and that diversity, more broadly defined, supports a more effective workforce (Lanvin & Evans, 2018). The inclusion of a diverse set of skills in the admissions process could also serve to allow students with diverse backgrounds and strengths to demonstrate their potential in ways that may not present themselves in traditional academic contexts. A better understanding of students' proficiencies with this expanded range of skills, as well as the role that these skills play in supporting successful outcomes, could serve to improve alignments in recruitment, retention, and completion.

17.3   Behavioral Skills

The third major domain of the ACT Holistic Framework is behavioral skills. This is the first truly noncognitive domain of the Holistic Framework. As a key component of the holistic approach ACT takes to education and work readiness, the behavioral skills domain focuses on interpersonal, self-regulatory, and effortful behaviors related to successful performance in education and workplace settings. Our conceptualization of this domain leverages research from multiple areas of psychology, including educational, developmental, industrial/organizational, and personality, to define what individuals need to know and be able – and willing – to do from a behavioral perspective in order to be successful across a range of settings.

17.3.1   Behavioral Skills Predict Outcomes for Postsecondary Students

When it comes to an individual's performance in postsecondary settings (college and graduate-level programs), research has shown that behavioral skills predict grades above and beyond the effects of admissions tests (ACT or SAT) and high school GPA (e.g., Poropat, 2009). Research also shows that these predictors are related to engagement in academic and interpersonal college environments, such as participating in class discussions, participating in extracurricular activities, and establishing relationships with peers (e.g., Asendorpf & Wilpers, 1998); these are important contributors to higher-quality academic experiences and improved performance in college (e.g., Conley, 2007). In addition, there is a growing literature that shows behavior (measured by checklists, experience sampling, or other ratings) predicts a range of other outcomes in postsecondary settings, including academic dishonesty, time management and procrastination, ability to cope with problems and stressors, satisfaction with the college environment, and health and well-being (e.g., Lounsbury et al., 2005; Steel, 2007).

17.3.2   Behavioral Skills Predict Important Outcomes for Workers

Industrial/organizational (I/O) psychology provides substantial evidence concerning the role of behavioral skills for predicting important workplace outcomes. Specifically, this literature documents the utility of behaviors for predicting a broad range of job performance criteria, including task performance, engaging in appropriate and ethical work conduct, effective use of interpersonal skills (e.g., leadership), and other important outcomes like work satisfaction and perceived work stress (e.g., Lindqvist & Vestman, 2011; Roberts et al., 2007; Schmidt & Hunter, 1998). Specifically, the *sustaining effort* dimension of the behavioral skills domain is also important for people moving into the workforce, has repeatedly been shown to be the strongest predictor of job performance after cognitive ability (e.g., Schmidt & Hunter, 1998), and is consistently considered to be the most important behavior dimension for work whether one is looking at predictors of performance, employer-desired attributes in employees, or skills required on the job (Sackett & Walmsley, 2014).

17.3.3   *Relevance for International Contexts*

Aspects of the behavioral skills domain have been found in studies of personality and individual differences throughout the world (Ashton et al., 2004; Roberts, Martin, & Olaru, 2015), showing that these skills are truly universal expressions of human behavior. International organizations such as the OECD have recognized this, incorporating measures of personality and behavior into their programming and frameworks that lay out the skills students need to be successful in the twenty-first century (Organisation for Economic Co-operation and Development, 2013; 2016).

17.3.4   *Specific Dimensions of the Behavioral Skills Domain*

This section presents research evidence on the validity of some of the specific dimensions within this domain (and their underlying behaviors) for specific outcomes in college and at work. The work was guided by the HEXACO taxonomy (Ashton et al., 2004), a taxonomy that has been replicated across cultures and thus represents a near universal description of human behavioral characteristics. Specifically, an attempt was made to group behavioral skill dimensions within the appropriate HEXACO domains.

17.3.4.1   *Acting Honestly*

Although this dimension is a relatively new addition to the literature, behaviors such as being honest, ethical, and fair have been of interest to educators and organizations for a long time, and research shows that components from this domain relate to measures of integrity (Lee, Ashton, & de Vries, 2005). Behaviors such as acting sincerely, treating others fairly, and being modest are associated with higher GPAs and lower levels of counterproductive behavior in college students (de Vries, de Vries, & Born, 2011), as well as higher levels of other positive outcomes, such as continuous learning, ethics, and leadership (McAbee, Oswald, & Connelly, 2014).

17.3.4.2   *Getting Along Well with Others*

The components in this dimension have to do with the manner in which a person interacts with others, such as being respectful and patient, showing concern when appropriate, and trusting and assisting others. Among college students, they predict higher performance (Okun & Finch, 1998) and are associated with higher levels of study and communication skills, social connections with others, and commitment to college (Peterson, Casillas, & Robbins, 2006).

17.3.4.3   *Keeping an Open Mind*

Traditionally, this dimension, consisting of components such as curiosity, creativity, and flexibility, was not considered to be strongly relevant for performance-related outcomes, but this view is beginning to change. For example, components in this domain have recently been shown to predict achievement in college (Paunonen & Ashton, 2013). High levels of these components also predicted greater levels of continuous learning, appreciation for diversity and the arts, and interpersonal skills (McAbee et al., 2014). In addition, intellectual curiosity was found to be a strong predictor of academic performance independently of intelligence (von Stumm, Hell, & Chamorro-Premuzic, 2011).

17.3.4.4   *Maintaining Composure*

Research on components in this dimension has shown that being effective at tolerating stress, regulating emotion, and having confidence improve one's chances of success. In academic contexts, components in this domain containing behaviors such as effectively managing stress and anxiety and making decisions without being overly reliant on others predict academic achievement and performance in K–12 students (Poropat, 2009) and college students (Robbins et al., 2004).

17.3.4.5   *Socializing with Others*

Research has found that components of this dimension, including sociability, assertiveness, and optimism, consistently predict positive outcomes such as higher GPAs in college (Paunonen & Ashton, 2013). In particular, measures of optimism predict higher levels of performance and engagement in employees (Judge et al., 2013) and more continuous learning, adaptability and life skills, and perseverance in college settings (McAbee et al., 2014).

17.3.4.6   *Sustaining Effort*

In all the research on behavior, personality, and their correlates, aspects of this dimension, including being motivated, organized, dependable, and self-controlled, have consistently been found to relate strongly to performance across all age groups. When examining effects in individual studies on academic achievement, it was the only dimension that consistently predicted achievement from elementary school through to college (Poropat, 2009). The persistence component, in particular, which includes overcoming challenges in the face of obstacles, maintaining effort, and focusing on tasks in the presence of distractions, predicts higher GPAs in college students (de Vries et al., 2011) and in medical school students (Lievens, Ones, & Dilchert, 2009).

17.3.5   Potential Applications of the Framework

One potential application of this domain is in the context of postsecondary admissions. Given the relationships between behavioral skills and important postsecondary outcomes cited above, they could be used to supplement information currently collected by postsecondary institutions. This information could then be used to identify those students who may fall just below standard achievement-based criteria such as GPA and standardized test scores, but who have the behavioral skills (e.g., motivation, persistence) that make them more likely to succeed.

Additionally, behavioral skills can be used to inform the assessment of alternative job-related performance outcomes. For example, they have been associated with a range of activities that generally involve more interpersonally relevant tasks, such as working in teams, providing courteous service, managing conflict, and displaying leadership (e.g., Judge, Bono, Ilies, & Gerhardt, 2002; Morgeson, Reider, & Campion, 2005; Organ & Ryan, 1995). Similarly, these interpersonal and self-regulatory behaviors have been associated with inappropriate interpersonal conduct (e.g., Bolton, Becker, & Barber, 2010).

17.3.6   Summary

The behavioral skills domain of the ACT Holistic Framework lays out skills that research has shown to be critical for success in educational and workplace settings.

17.4   Education and Career Navigation

The fourth domain of the ACT Holistic Framework is education and career navigation. It focuses on the knowledge, skills, and other factors needed to negotiate key education and work transitions successfully. The navigation domain emphasizes what individuals know about themselves and their environments, and how they use this information to make informed, personally relevant decisions and build actionable plans as they move along their education and career paths.

17.4.1   Navigation Important for College and Work Success

Research on education and career navigation shows that its components are important contributors to postsecondary educational outcomes. Studies indicate that these components predict academic performance (Lent, Brown, & Gore, 1997), as well as college persistence, major persistence, and degree attainment (Allen & Robbins, 2008). Further, these predictors are related to college student adjustment, college major choice, certainty of career choice, and greater satisfaction with the college experience (Bowman & Denson, 2014; Chen & Yao, 2015).

Research also points to the importance of navigation factors for predicting work outcomes. Regarding job performance, research shows that interests provide incremental validity above and beyond the effects of cognitive ability and personality variables (Van Iddekinge, Putka, & Campbell, 2011), especially when there is good interest-job fit (Nye et al., 2017). Navigation predictors contribute to other outcomes such as organizational commitment, job continuance intentions, and job satisfaction (Kristof-Brown, Zimmerman, & Johnson, 2005; Oh et al., 2014).

17.4.2   Education and Career Navigation Is Relevant for International Contexts

International research and practices have provided insights as to how different countries and cultures facilitate the education and career trajectories of their inhabitants. Components of the navigation domain have been found in cross-cultural comparison studies and non-US studies (Lent et al., 2014; Oh et al., 2014), highlighting that these critical knowledge and skills are being examined across the globe. The OECD also recognizes the importance of navigation, calling for "improving the information available to young people when choosing their field of study," increasing students' familiarity with the labor market, and strengthening "measures that make it generally easier for students to gain work experience" (Organisation for Economic Co-operation and Development, 2014, p. 213).

17.4.3   Dimensions of the Education and Career Navigation Domain

17.4.3.1   Self-Knowledge

For this dimension, research on self-perceptions of abilities/skills, interests, and values components are related to a sense of belonging and subsequent retention in college (Soria & Stubblefield, 2015), measures of job knowledge (Van Iddekinge et al., 2011), and intentions to remain in a STEM major (Perez, Cromley, & Kaplan, 2014), respectively. College and academic self-efficacy (ability to complete tasks and succeed in the college and academic environment) are significant predictors of first to second semester persistence (Wright, Jenkins-Guarnieri, & Murdock, 2013) and retention (Robbins et al., 2004). Research also shows that less discrepancy between student expectations and college experiences predicts retention (Pleitz et al., 2015).

17.4.3.2   Environmental Factors

The components in this dimension consist of education and work knowledge (e.g., types of majors, work settings), experience, as well as the supports and barriers (e.g., financial, family, school resources) that influence education or work progress. Research shows that social supports predict satisfaction with academics among African college students (Lent et al., 2014), and perceived institutional support is predictive of college completion intentions (Thomas, 2014). Participation in experiences (co-op or internship) predicts retention in STEM majors and college (Raelin et al., 2015).

17.4.3.3   Integration

The components in this dimension have to do with exploring and using knowledge about oneself and the environment to evaluate options, and make good fit goals, choices, and action plans. Extensive research evidence on the compatibility between personal and environmental characteristics (i.e., fit) shows it is a meaningful predictor of STEM field choice, major persistence, GPA, and college satisfaction (Allen & Robbins, 2008; Bowman & Denson, 2014; Le, Robbins, & Westrick, 2014). In terms of work outcomes, fit predicts job performance, organizational commitment, turnover intentions, and job satisfaction (Oh et al., 2014; Yu, 2016). Further, choosing a major later during college or changing majors contributes to delays in graduation and degree attainment (Yue & Fu, 2017).

17.4.3.4   *Managing Education and Career Actions*

Research on components in this dimension has shown that being effective at implementing education and career plans and engaging in appropriate search behaviors contributes to success. Among unemployed individuals, focused career plans that include a range of job-search strategies contributed to higher-quality reemployment and job satisfaction (Koen et al., 2010). Research also shows that role clarity in a work context and role balance (work–life balance) is related to job satisfaction (Brough et al., 2014).

17.4.4   *Potential Applications with Education and Career Navigation*

With research showing the importance of navigation components (e.g., goals, fit) for postsecondary success, these components can provide supporting information beyond existing admissions criteria. For example, examining person–environment fit when considering which students to admit to a particular college or program of study provides additional information that may improve the likelihood of entering student persistence to degree. Navigation can also be used to increase postsecondary access to traditionally underserved student populations (e.g., first-generation students). For example, incorporating components (e.g., supports, barriers, experience) that may be particularly salient for these students into admissions interviews provides opportunities for institutions to more fully understand their prospective students, and to consider this information when determining which students may be more likely to succeed.

17.4.5   *Summary*

The research-based navigation domain emphasizes the ongoing process of developing and employing personally relevant knowledge and skills to be successful in education and work contexts.

17.5   Discussion

The time is right to expand the number of characteristics colleges and universities consider in prospective students. Why? The world is changing, and probably faster than most think. Consider how technology has accelerated the pace of change in how we live our everyday lives. After landline telephones were invented, it took 75 years before 50 million people were using them. It took television 13 years to reach 50 million users. Contrast these numbers with what we are seeing today. In merely two years, Twitter reached 50 million users. Even more astonishing, 50 million people were playing the app *Angry Birds* only 35 days after its release (Aeppel, 2015). Imagine how quickly the next "big thing" can infiltrate our lives and imagine the type of person that must have the ability adapt to these changes.

Similarly, technological innovation is changing the way we work, and the skills needed in the workforce. For example, one often cited study found that the share of routine cognitive and routine manual work tasks has fallen sharply since 1960 (Autor & Price, 2013). These are tasks that follow relatively well-defined procedures often taught in school. One example of a routine cognitive task is accounting; and, consistent with this study, a recent analysis from the field of economics predicts a 94 percent probability that computerization will lead to major job losses in that field in the next two decades (Frey & Osborne, 2017). In contrast, nonroutine analytic and nonroutine interpersonal work tasks are on the rise since 1960. Nonroutine tasks are those that cannot be automated through computerization. Many of these tasks require skills such as collaborative problem-solving, critical thinking, and teamwork.

So, where can colleges and universities go for help in identifying the most important characteristics student need to succeed in this changing environment? Our argument is that the ACT Holistic Framework, with its extensive research basis, is currently the most comprehensive framework in existence that outlines the things students should know and be willing and able to do in order to succeed throughout both their education and work lives. The Framework can be used in several ways. Some examples of this are:

- to serve as a guiding framework in the selection and prioritization of measured constructs on student applications,
- to serve also as a guiding framework in the development and revision of outcome measures assessing the effectiveness of college and university education, and
- more specifically, to use PLDs (an empirically derived set of performance-level descriptors developed for the behavioral skills portion of the Framework that provide example behaviors at different levels of effectiveness) as items for assessment content to accurately measure a student's level in several skills (Latino et al., 2017).

However, as it is ultimately used, the ACT Holistic Framework represents a significant advancement in our thinking of what it means to be ready for college and, later, the workforce. In light of our rapidly changing world, it is our contention that such thinking can better serve individuals and society as a whole.

REFERENCES

Aeppel, T. (2015, March 13). It took the telephone 75 years to do what Angry Birds did in 35 days. But what does that mean? [Blog post]. Retrieved from https://blogs.wsj.com/economics/2015/03/13/it-took-the-telephone-75-years-to-do-what-angry-birds-did-in-35-days-but-what-does-that-mean/.

Allen, J., & Robbins, S. B. (2008). Prediction of college major persistence based on vocational interests, academic preparation, and first-year academic performance. *Research in Higher Education, 49*, 62–79. https://doi.org/10.1007/s11162-007-9064-5.

(2010). Effects of interest–major congruence, motivation, and academic performance on timely degree attainment. *Journal of Counseling Psychology, 57*, 23. https://doi.org/10.1037/a0017267.

Asendorpf, J. B., & Wilpers, S. (1998). Personality effects on social relationships. *Journal of Personality and Social Psychology, 74*, 1531–1544. https://doi.org/10.1037/0022-3514.74.6.1531.

Ashton, M. C., Lee, K., Perugini, M., Szarota, P., de Vries, R. E., Di Blas, L., Boies, K., & De Raad, B. (2004). A six-factor structure of personality-descriptive adjectives: Solutions from psycholexical studies in seven languages. *Journal of Personality and Social Psychology, 86*, 356–366. https://doi.org/10.1037/0022-3514.86.2.356.

Autor, D. H. & Price, B. (2013). The changing task composition of the US labor market: An update of Autor, Levy, and Murnane (2003). Retrieved from https://economics.mit.edu/files/11600.

Baller, S., Dutta, S., & Lanvin, B. (Eds.). (2016). The global information technology report 2016. Retrieved from www.weforum.org/reports/the-global-information-technology-report-2016.

Bolton, L. R., Becker. L. K., & Barber, L. K. (2010). Big Five trait predictors of differential counterproductive work behavior dimensions. *Personality and Individual Differences, 49*, 537–541. https://doi.org/10.1016/j.paid.2010.03.047.

Bowman, N. A., & Denson, N. (2014). A missing piece of the departure puzzle: Student-institution fit and intent to persist. *Research in Higher Education, 55*, 123–142. https://doi.org/10.1007/s11162-013-9320-9.

Brough, P., Timms, C., O'Driscoll, M. P., Kalliuth, T., Siu, O-L, Sit, C., & Lo, D. (2014). Work–life balance: A longitudinal evaluation of a new measure across Australia and New Zealand workers. *International Journal of Human Resource Management, 25*, 2724–2744. https://doi.org/10.1080/09585192.2014.899262.

Camara, W., O'Connor, R., Mattern, K., & Hanson, M. A. (2015). *Beyond academics: A holistic framework for enhancing education and workplace success* (ACT Research Report Series 2015 No. 4). Iowa City, IA: ACT Inc.

Campbell, J. P. (1990). Modeling the performance prediction problem in industrial and organizational psychology. In M. D. Dunnette & L. M. Hough (Eds.). *Handbook of Industrial and Organizational Psychology* (pp. 687–732). Palo Alto, CA: Consulting Psychologists Press, Inc.

Carter, S. D. (2002). Matching training methods and factors of cognitive ability: A means to improve training outcomes. *Human Resource Development Quarterly*, 13, 71–88.

Chen, A., & Yao, X. (2015). Socialization tactics, fit perceptions, and college student adjustment. *Journal of Career Assessment*, 23, 615–629. https://doi.org/10.1177/1069072714553082.

Clinedinst, M., & Koranteng, A. (2017). 2017 State of college admission. Retrieved from www.nacacnet.org/globalassets/documents/publications/research/soca17final.pdf.

Colquitt, J. A., LePine, J. A., & Noe, R. A. (2000). Toward an integrative theory of training motivation: A meta-analytic path analysis of 20 years of research. *Journal of Applied Psychology*, 85, 678–707. https://doi.org/10.1037/0021-9010.85.5.678.

Common Core State Standards. (2010). *Common core state standards for English language arts and literacy in history/social studies, science, and technical subjects*. Washington, DC: National Governors Association Center for Best Practices & Council of Chief State School Officers.

Conley, D. T. (2007). *Toward a more comprehensive conception of college readiness*. Eugene, OR: Educational Policy Improvement Center.

(2008). Rethinking college readiness. *New Directions for Higher Education*, 144, 3–13. https://doi.org/10.1002/he.321.

Cullinane, C., & Montacute, R. (2017). *Life lessons: Improving essential life skills for young people*. Retrieved from www.suttontrust.com/research-paper/life-lessons/.

de Vries, A., de Vries, R. E., & Born, M. Ph. (2011). Broad versus narrow traits: Conscientiousness and honesty–humility as predictors of academic criteria. *European Journal of Personality*, 25, 336–348. https://doi.org/10.1002/per.795.

Facione, P. A. (1991). *Using the California critical thinking skills test in research, evaluation, and assessment*. Retrieved from https://files.eric.ed.gov/fulltext/ED337498.pdf

Frey, C. B., & Osborne, M. A. (2017). The future of employment: How susceptible are jobs to computerisation? *Technological Forecasting and Social Change*, 114, 254–280. https://doi.org/10.1016/j.techfore.2016.08.019.

Grove, A. (2018). What are holistic admissions? At selective colleges, admission is based on more than grades and test scores. Retrieved from www.thoughtco.com/what-are-holistic-admissions-788426.

Gu, M., & Magaziner, J. (2018). The Gaokao: History, reform, and rising international significance of China's national college entrance examination. Retrieved from https://wenr.wes.org/2016/05/the-gaokao-history-reform-and-international-significance-of-chinas-national-college-entrance-examination.

Hanushek, E. A., & Woessmann, L. (2008). The role of cognitive skills in economic development. *Journal of Economic Literature*, 46, 607–668.

Hart Research Associates. (2010). Raising the bar: Employers' views on college learning in the wake of the economic downturn. Retrieved from www.aacu .org/sites/default/files/files/LEAP/2009_EmployerSurvey.pdf

Hong, L., & Page, S. E. (2004). Groups of diverse problem solvers can outperform groups of high-ability problem solvers. *Proceedings of the National Academy of Sciences of the United States of America*, *101*(46), 16385–16389. https://doi.org/10.1073/pnas.0403723101.

Huffman, W. H., & Huffman, A. H. (2012). Beyond basic study skills: The use of technology for success in college. *Computers in Human Behavior*, *28*, 583–590. https://doi.org/10.1016/j.chb.2011.11.004.

Jackson, N. E. (2005). Are university students' component reading skills related to their text comprehension and academic achievement? *Learning and Individual Differences*, *15*, 113–139. https://doi.org/10.1016/j.lindif.2004.11.001.

Jonassen, D. H., & Kim, B. (2010). Arguing to learn and learning to argue: Design justifications and guidelines. *Educational Technology Research and Development*, *58*, 439–457. https://doi.org/10.1007/s11423–009-9143-8.

Judge, T. A., Bono, J. E., Ilies, R., & Gerhardt, M. W. (2002). Personality and leadership: a qualitative and quantitative review. *Journal of Applied Psychology*, *87*, 765–780. https://doi.org/10.1037/0021-9010.87.4.765.

Judge, T. A., Rodell, J. B., Klinger, R. L., Simon, L. S., & Crawford, E. R. (2013). Hierarchical representations of the five-factor model of personality in predicting job performance: Integrating three organizing frameworks with two theoretical perspectives. *Journal of Applied Psychology*, *98*, 875–925. https://doi.org/10.1037/a0033901.

Kalsbeek, D., Sandlin, M., & Sedlacek, W. (2013). Employing noncognitive variables to improve admissions, and increase student diversity and retention. *Strategic Enrollment Management Quarterly*, *1*, 132–50. https://doi.org/ 10.1002/sem3.20016.

Koen, J., Klehe, U.-C., Van Vianen, A. E. M., Zikic, J., & Nauta, A. (2010). Job search strategies and reemployment quality: The impact of career adaptability. *Journal of Vocational Behavior*, *77*, 126–139. https://doi.org/10.1016/j .jvb.2010.02.004.

Kristof-Brown, A. L., Zimmerman, R. D., & Johnson, E. C. (2005). Consequences of individuals' fit at work: A meta-analysis of person-job, person-organization, person-group, and person-supervisor fit. *Personnel Psychology*, *58*, 28–342. https://doi.org/10.1111/j.1744-6570.2005.00672.x.

Lanvin, B. & Evans, P. (2018). *The global talent competitiveness index 2018*. Fontainebleau: INSEAD, Adecco, and HCLI.

Latino, C. A., Way, J., Colbow, A., Bouwers, S., Casillas, A., & McKinniss, T. (2017). *The Development of Behavioral Performance Level Descriptors* (ACT Research Report Series 2017 No. 7). Iowa City, IA: ACT Inc.

Le, H., Robbins, S. B., & Westrick, P. (2014). Predicting student enrollment and persistence in college STEM fields using an expanded P-E Fit framework: A large-scale multilevel study. *Journal of Applied Psychology*, *99*, 915–947. https://doi.org/10.1037/a0035998.

Lee, K., Ashton, M. C., & de Vries, R. E. (2005). Predicting workplace delinquency and integrity with the HEXACO and five-factor models of personality structure. *Human Performance, 18*, 179–197. https://doi.org/10.1207/s15327043hup1802_4.

Lent, R. W., Brown, S. D., & Gore, P. A. (1997). Discriminant and predictive validity of academic self-concept, academic self-efficacy, and mathematics-specific self-efficacy. *Journal of Counseling Psychology, 44*, 307–315. https://doi.org/10.1037/0022-0167.44.3.307.

Lent, R. W., Taveira, M., Pinto, J. C., Silva, A. D., Blanco, A., Faria, S., & Goncalves, A. M. (2014). Social cognitive predictors of well-being in African college students. *Journal of Vocational Behavior, 84*, 266–272. https://doi.org/10.1016/j.jvb.2014.01.007.

Lievens, F., Ones, D. S., & Dilchert, S. (2009). Personality scales validities increase throughout medical school. *Journal of Applied Psychology, 94*, 1514–1535. https://doi.org/10.1037/a0016137.

Lindqvist, E., & Vestman, R. (2011). The labor market returns to cognitive and noncognitive ability: Evidence from the Swedish enlistment. *American Economic Journal: Applied Economics, 3*(1), 101–128. https://doi.org/10.1257/app.3.1.101.

Lounsbury, J. W., Saudargas, R. A., Gibson, L. W., & Leong, F. T. (2005). An investigation of broad and narrow personality traits in relation to general and domain-specific life satisfaction of college students. *Research in Higher Education, 46*, 707–729. https://doi.org/10.1007/s11162-004-4140-6.

McAbee, S. T., Oswald, F. L., & Connelly, B. S. (2014). Bifactor models of personality and college student performance: A broad versus narrow view. *European Journal of Personality, 28*, 604–619. https://doi.org/10.1002/per.1975.

Mattern, K. D., Burrus, J., Camara, W. J., O'Connor, R., Gambrell, J., Hanson, M. A., Casillas, A., & Bobek, B. (2014). *Broadening the definition of College and Career Readiness: A Holistic Approach*. Iowa City, IA: ACT, Inc.

Mattern, K. D. & Patterson, B. F. (2011). *The validity of the SAT for predicting fourth-year grades: 2006 SAT validity sample* (College Board Statistical Report 2011-7). New York, NY: The College Board.

Morgeson, F. P., Reider, M. H., & Campion, M. A. (2005). Selecting individuals in team settings: The importance of social skills, personality characteristics, and teamwork knowledge. *Personnel Psychology, 58*, 583–611. https://doi.org/10.1111/j.1744-6570.2005.655.x.

Mount, M. K., Barrick, M. R., & Stewart, G. L. (1998). Five-factor model of personality and performance in jobs involving interpersonal interactions. *Human Performance, 11*, 145–165. https://doi.org/10.1080/08959285.1998.9668029.

National Research Council. (2013). *Education for life and work: Developing transferable knowledge and skills in the 21st century*. Washington, DC: National Academies Press.

No Child Left Behind Act of 2001. (2002). P.L. 107-110, 20 U.S.C. § 6319.

Nye, C. D., Su, R., Rounds, J., & Drasgow, F. (2012). Vocational interests and performance a quantitative summary of over 60 years of research. *Perspectives on Psychological Science*, *7*, 384–403. https://doi.org/10.1177/1745691612449021.

(2017). Interest congruence and performance: Revisiting recent meta-analytic findings. *Journal of Vocational Behavior*, *98*, 138–151. https://doi.org/10.1016/j.jvb.2016.11.002.

Oh, I.-S., Guay, R. P., Kim, K., Harold, C. M., Lee, J.-H., Heo, C.-G., & Shin, K.-H. (2014). Fit happens globally: A meta-analytic comparison of the relationships of person-environment fit dimensions with work attitudes and performance across East Asia, Europe, and North America. *Personnel Psychology*, *67*, 99–52. https://doi.org/10.1111/peps.12026.

Okun, M. A., & Finch, J. F. (1998). The big five personality dimensions and the process of institutional departure. *Contemporary Educational Psychology*, *23*, 233–256. https://doi.org/10.1006/ceps.1996.0974.

Oliveri, M. E., & Markle, R. (2017*). Continuing a culture of evidence: Expanding skills in higher education.* (Research Report No. RR-17-09). Princeton, NJ: Educational Testing Service. https://doi.org/10.1002/ets2.12137.

Organ, D. W., & Ryan, K. (1995). A meta-analytic review of attitudinal and dispositional predictors of organizational citizenship behavior. *Personnel Psychology*, *48*, 775–802.

Organisation for Economic Co-operation and Development (2013). OECD skills outlook 2013: First results from the survey of adult skills. Retrieved from www.oecd-ilibrary.org/education/oecd-skills-outlook-2013_9789264204256-en

(2014). *OECD employment outlook.* https://doi.org/10.1787/empl_outlook-2014-en.

(2016). *Global competency for an inclusive world.* Retrieved from http://reposi torio.minedu.gob.pe/handle/123456789/4561.

Pace, R. C. (1990). Personalized and depersonalized conflict in small group discussions: An examination of differentiation. *Small Group Research*, *21*, 79–96. https://doi.org/10.1177/1046496490211006.

Page, S. E. (2008). *The difference: How the power of diversity creates better groups, firms, schools, and societies.* Princeton, NJ: Princeton University Press.

Paunonen, S. V., & Ashton, M. C. (2013). On the prediction of academic performance with personality traits: A replication study. *Journal of Research in Personality*, *47*, 778–781. https://doi.org/10.1016/j.jrp.2013.08.003.

Perez, T., Cromley, J. G., & Kaplan, A. (2014). The role of identity development, values, and costs in college STEM retention. *Journal of Educational Psychology*, *106*, 315–329. https://doi.org/10.1037/a0034027.

Peterson, C. H., Casillas, A., & Robbins, S. B. (2006). The student readiness inventory and the Big Five: Examining social desirability and college academic performance. *Personality and Individual Differences*, *41*, 663–673. https://doi.org/10.1016/j.paid.2006.03.006.

Pleitz, J. D., MacDougall, A. E., Terry, R. A., Buckley, M. R., & Campbell, N. J. (2015). Discrepancy between expectations and experiences on college student retention. *Journal of College Student Retention: Research, Theory & Practice, 17*, 88–104. https://doi.org/10.1177/1521025115571252.

Poropat, A. E. (2009). A meta-analysis of the five-factor model of personality and academic performance. *Psychological Bulletin, 135*, 322–338. https://doi.org/10.1037/a0014996.

Raelin, J. A., Bailey, M. B., Hamann, J., Pendleton, L. K., Reisberg, R., & Whitman, D. L. (2015). The role of work experience and self-efficacy in STEM student retention. *Journal on Excellence in College Teaching, 26*(4), 29–50.

Robbins, S. B., Lauver, K., Le, H., Davis, D., Langley, R., & Carlstrom, A. (2004). Do psychosocial and study skill factors predict college outcomes? A meta-analysis. *Psychological Bulletin, 130*, 261–288. https://doi.org/10.1037/0033-2909.130.2.261.

Roberts, B. W., Kuncel, N. R., Shiner, R., Caspi, A., & Goldberg, L. R. (2007). The power of personality: The comparative validity of personality traits, socioeconomic status, and cognitive ability for predicting important life outcomes. *Perspectives on Psychological Science, 2*, 313–345. https://doi.org/10.1111/j.1745-6916.2007.00047.x.

Roberts, R. D., Martin, J. E., & Olaru, G. (2015). A Rosetta Stone for non-cognitive skills: Understanding, assessing, and enhancing noncognitive skills in primary and secondary education. Retrieved from www.proexam.org/images/resources/A_Rosetta_Stone_for_Noncognitive_Skills.pdf

Roth, P. L., BeVier, C. A., Switzer, F. S., III, & Schippmann, J. S. (1996). Meta-analyzing the relationship between grades and job performance. *Journal of Applied Psychology, 81*, 548–556. https://doi.org/10.1037/0021-9010.81.5.548.

Sackett, P. R., & Walmsley, P. T. (2014). Which personality attributes are most important in the workplace? *Perspectives on Psychological Science, 9*, 538–551. https://doi.org/10.1177/1745691614543972.

Schmidt, F. L., & Hunter, J. E. (1998). The validity and utility of selection methods in personnel psychology: Practical and theoretical implications of 85 years of research findings. *Psychological Bulletin, 124*, 262–274. https://doi.org/10.1037/0033-2909.124.2.262.

(2004). General mental ability in the world of work: Occupational attainment and job performance. *Journal of Personality and Social Psychology, 86*, 162–173. https://doi.org/10.1037/0022-3514.86.1.162.

Schmitt, N., Keeney, J., Oswald, F. L., Pleskac, T. J., Billington, A. Q., Sinha, R., & Zorzie, M. (2009). Prediction of 4-year college student performance using cognitive and noncognitive predictors and the impact on demographic status of admitted students. *Journal of Applied Psychology, 94*, 1479–1497. https://doi.org/10.1037/a0016810.

Schoenbach, R., Greenleaf, C., & Murphy, L. (2012). *Reading for understanding: How reading apprenticeship improves disciplinary learning in secondary and college classrooms* (2nd ed.). San Francisco, CA: Jossey-Bass.

Schwab, K. (2016). *The Fourth Industrial Revolution*. New York, NY: Crown Business.

Simons, T., & Peterson, R. (2000). Task conflict and relationship conflict in top management teams: The pivotal role of intragroup trust. *Journal of Applied Psychology, 85,* 102–111. https://doi.org/10.1037/0021-9010.85.1.102.

Soria, K. M., & Stubblefield, R. (2015). Knowing me, knowing you: Building strengths awareness, belonging, and persistence in higher education. *Journal of College Student Retention: Research, Theory & Practice, 17,* 351–372. https://doi.org/10.1177/1521025115575914.

Steel, P. (2007). The nature of procrastination: A meta-analytic and theoretical review of quintessential self-regulatory failure. *Psychological Bulletin, 133,* 65–94. https://doi.org/10.1037/0033-2909.133.1.65.

Thomas, D. (2014). Factors that influence college completion intention of undergraduate students. *Asia-Pacific Educational Research, 23,* 225–235. https://doi.org/10.1007/s40299-013-0099-4.

Van Iddekinge, C. H., Putka, D. J., & Campbell, J. P. (2011). Reconsidering vocational interests for personnel selection: The validity of an interest-based selection test in relation to job knowledge, job performance, and continuance intentions. *Journal of Applied Psychology, 9,* 13–33. https://doi.org/10.1037/a0021193.

von Stumm, S., Hell, B., & Chamorro-Premuzic, T. (2011). The hungry mind: Intellectual curiosity is the third pillar of academic performance. *Perspectives on Psychological Science, 6,* 574–588. https://doi.org/10.1177/1745691611421204.

World Economic Forum (2016). *The future of jobs: Employment, skills and workforce strategy for the fourth industrial revolution.* Retrieved from www3.weforum.org/docs/WEF_Future_of_Jobs.pdf.

Wright, S. L., Jenkins-Guarnieri, M. A., & Murdock, J. L. (2013). Career development among first-year college students: College self-efficacy, student persistence, and academic success. *Journal of Career Development, 40,* 292–310.

Yu, K. Y. T. (2016). Inter-relationships among different types of person–environment fit and job satisfaction. *Applied Psychology: An International Review, 65,* 38–65. https://doi.org/10.1111/apps.12035.

Yue, H. & Fu, X. (2017). Rethinking graduation and time to degree: A fresh perspective. *Research in Higher Education, 58,* 184–213. https://doi.org/10.1007/s11162-016-9420-4.

CHAPTER 18

Using Mathematical Models to Improve Access to Postsecondary Education

Rebecca Zwick[*]

Access to higher education is a major concern in many parts of the world. In the United States, for example, the under-representation of Black, Latino, and Native American students, as well as students from low-income families, is a significant problem. Many other nations have initiated efforts to boost the college admission rates of certain demographic groups. These programs include attempts to increase the representation of members of certain castes in India (Overland, 2004), residents of particular provinces in China (Zhang, 2010), socioeconomically disadvantaged students in Chile (Koljatic & Silva, 2013; Koljatic & Silva, in this volume), public high school graduates and Black and mixed-race students in Brazil (Lloyd, 2004; Somers et al., 2013), women in parts of sub-Saharan Africa (McMurtrie, 2004; Oanda, in this volume), ethnic Malays in Malaysia (Cohen, 2004), and students from remote and mountainous areas in Vietnam (Pham & Sai, in this volume). These attempts to improve access, some of which have been highly controversial, have included the enforcement of quotas, the use of less stringent admissions criteria for members of under-represented groups, and the establishment of preference systems. The institutions implementing these programs are, of course, committed to maintaining academic standards while pursuing improvements in the accessibility of higher education.

Constrained optimization (CO), a mathematical technique borrowed from the operations research field, allows incorporation of both academic requirements and diversity goals in college admissions. In CO, the user can optimize a quantity of interest while simultaneously placing certain constraints on the solution. A classic problem in the CO literature is the

[*] I am grateful to Lei Ye and Steven Isham for conducting data analyses and to Teresa Jackson for performing a review of the literature on student yield. This work was supported in part by the ETS Challenge project, *Towards a Better Understanding of Educational Admissions Decisions*. The opinions and recommendations expressed here are those of the author and not necessarily those of Educational Testing Service.

knapsack problem, in which a hiker must choose which items to carry in her knapsack, subject to an overall weight constraint – say, 40 pounds. If the candidate items can be rated in terms of their importance (rain gear is absolutely necessary; a coffeemaker is not), the hiker can use CO to maximize the importance value of the items she chooses while ensuring that the overall weight does not exceed 40 pounds. This problem is similar in form to an admissions situation, albeit a very simple one: An optimal class must be selected, subject to a limit on the number of available seats.

In applications of CO in the admissions setting, we are typically interested in maximizing an academic measure, such as the previous grades or test scores of the entering students. In addition, there is a limit on the number of students that can be admitted, as well as other constraints, possibly including those intended to ensure the diversity of the student body. In many of the studies described here, the diversity-related constraints take a particularly simple form: It is required that a certain number of the admitted students be from a particular category such as low-income students or students from a particular ethnic group. Constraints of the same form could be applied to encourage the representation of various disadvantaged groups, as defined by social status, geographical region, or educational background. In theory, constraints of this type could be used to address the accessibility goals now being pursued in other countries; for example, to increase the representation of women in Tanzania (see Oanda, in this volume) or of particular castes in India.

In other applications of CO, scores on a particular measure are constrained in some way. For example, this chapter includes a description of analyses in which the average score of the admitted class on a measure of disadvantage is constrained to exceed a minimum value. More-complex constraints can be applied as well, and multiple constraints can be imposed simultaneously. The type of constrained optimization needed to solve admissions problems is called integer linear programming (see Kolman & Beck, 1995). Free software for conducting this type of analysis is readily available.[1]

In this chapter, I review research in this area and describe possible future applications. In the following section, I describe previous applications of CO in the admissions context. Next, I discuss some limitations of the

---

[1] All the analyses conducted by my research team used an R routine called lp_solve (Berkelaar, 2014; lp_solve reference guide, n.d.). Methodological details appear in Zwick et al., 2018 and Zwick, Ye, & Isham, 2019.

approach. Finally, I describe extensions that we are now developing and present some conclusions about the potential for using CO in admissions.

18.1 Previous Applications of Constrained Optimization to Admissions Problems

Durán and Wolf-Yadlin (2011) described what is apparently the only documented use of CO in an actual admissions process. In 2007, 2008, and 2009, the Department of Industrial Engineering at the University of Chile used CO to select classes for a master's degree program in globalization management. After imposing rigorous screening procedures to reduce the applicant pools, Durán and Wolf-Yadlin used a CO approach to optimize the credentials of the admitted students, while incorporating constraints intended to encourage the participation of women, students of low socioeconomic status (SES), and those from outside the Santiago region. An additional constraint was included in 2009 to improve the representation of non-engineers. Program administrators applauded the CO method for its transparency and for producing high-quality admissions decisions that would have been almost impossible to achieve otherwise because of the number of requirements that needed to be met (Durán & Wolf-Yadlin, 2011).

The remaining applications of CO in the admissions setting were conducted for research purposes only; they were not used to make actual admissions decisions. Pashley and Thornton (1999), researchers at the Law School Admission Council, conducted the first of these studies. Using data from applicants to an unidentified law school, they tried to reproduce the results that had been obtained through the actual admissions process without incorporating information about the applicant's race. More specifically, they aimed to maximize an index that combined undergraduate grades and Law School Admission Test scores and to achieve ethnic diversity through the use of constraints based on the percentage of minorities at the applicant's undergraduate school and in the applicant's area of residency. The researchers also imposed other constraints involving the applicant's community, undergraduate institution, age, and in-state status. The overlap between the applicants selected via CO and those who had actually been admitted to the law school was about 75 percent, and the ethnic composition of the two overlapping groups was similar. Pashley, Thornton, and Duffy (2005) noted that they had successfully applied this approach to data from many other law schools.

Kreiter and his colleagues evaluated the use of CO in medical school admissions, seeking to develop admissions models that would promote diversity while maintaining academic quality. To illustrate the approach, Kreiter (2002) applied CO to a small artificial dataset. The goal was to select ten students from a pool of 25 applicants, maximizing the average Medical College Admission Test (MCAT®) score while applying constraints on class composition in terms of a diversity rating (hypothetically assigned by faculty), undergraduate grade point average (GPA), and type of community (suburban, urban, or rural). Kreiter concluded that CO "provides a method for the accurate translation of class composition goals while also optimizing applicant attributes" (Kreiter, 2002, p. 151).

Kreiter et al. (2003) used CO methods to select 80 students from a pool of 409 medical-school applicants. They sought to maximize the average MCAT score of the selected class and to admit "a representative number of minority applicants" by using information on economic disadvantage rather than race. The number of disadvantaged students in the admitted class was constrained to be at least 15. The resulting class included 12 ethnic minorities and had a fairly high MCAT average (Kreiter et al., 2003, p. 121). Although a simple problem like this one might lend itself to a more straightforward solution method, real-life admissions problems tend to be much more complex and the potential gain from applying CO correspondingly greater.

In what we believe to be the first research application of CO for purposes of increasing diversity in undergraduate admissions (Zwick, Ye, & Isham, 2016), my colleagues and I implemented the technique using data from the Education Longitudinal Study (ELS) (Ingels, Planty, & Bozick, 2005), a survey conducted by the National Center for Education Statistics. The ELS database includes information on more than 13,000 students who graduated from high schools in the United States in 2004. We studied a portion of these seniors – the 2,190 students who applied to at least one institution that was categorized in 2004 as "most competitive" or "highly competitive" in the Barron's rating system (Schmitt, 2009).

The overriding goal of our analyses was to maximize the academic performance of the admitted class, while imposing diversity requirements. These CO analyses were among 16 admissions models investigated in a larger study (Zwick, 2017). Our performance measure was an equally weighted composite of high school GPA and admissions test scores. For students who took the SAT®, the score was the sum of the verbal and math scores, ranging from 400 to 1600. For ACT® test-takers, the ACT composite score had been transformed to a 400–1600 scale in the ELS database.

In each CO analysis, we admitted a class from among the 2,190 applicants in such a way as to maximize the GPA–test score composite.

In the analyses described in this chapter, we constrained the number of admitted students to be 970 – exactly the same as the number of ELS participants who actually enrolled in the colleges in the top two Barron's categories.[2] This requirement served to facilitate comparisons between the CO class and these enrollees. In our first application, we also constrained the percentage of under-represented minorities (URMs) – American Indian, Black, or Hispanic students – to be at least as large as the actual percentage of URMs among the enrollees in the selective schools (12.6 percent). In our more ambitious second analysis, we required that at least 20 percent of the selected class be URMs and that at least 20 percent be from the lower half of the SES distribution for the high school class of 2004.

Our approach was quite effective in increasing diversity while optimizing academic performance. One of our main findings, which emerged from the analysis that matched the percentage of URMs to the percentage among the enrollees, is illustrated in Table 18.1. The average high school GPA, admissions test score, college GPA, and college graduation rate for the class selected via CO were superior to those of the enrollees and were almost identical to those obtained by simply selecting the 970 applicants with the highest values on the GPA–test score composite. The constraints, then, had little impact on the academic performance of the admitted class. As intended, the CO class was substantially more diverse than the class obtained via simple ranking, with 12.6 percent URMs (vs. 7.5 percent URMs for the ranking approach) and 13.4 percent in the lower half of the SES distribution (vs. 12.5 percent).

Some caution is warranted in interpreting the findings of these analyses. In particular, we treated the 2,190 applicants to competitive colleges as though they had applied to a single school. In reality, the applicants applied to a total of 170 colleges, and the enrollees attended 160 of these colleges. Similarly, the classes selected using the two admissions methods in Table 18.1 obtained their college grades and degrees at a variety of schools, some of which may have been less selective than those attended by the enrollees. In addition, it is important to note that the characteristics of the enrolled students reflect not only the outcome of admissions decisions, but also the accepted candidates' own decisions about whether to attend.

A further limitation involves the generalizability of the results. ELS data typically must be weighted in order to generalize the results to the target

---

[2] To comply with Institute of Education Sciences data security requirements, all sample sizes are rounded to the nearest 10 in our description of the ELS analysis.

Table 18.1 *Results for enrollees and two admissions models*

	Enrollees in competitive schools	CO	Ranking on GPA–test score composite
Percent in lower half of SES distribution	13.5	13.4	12.5
Percent URMs	12.6	12.6	7.5
Percent women	55.1	57.2	56.7
High school GPA			
Average	3.5	3.7	3.7
Standard deviation	0.4	0.3	0.3
Admissions test score			
Average	1250	1307	1310
Standard deviation	153	116	112
College first-year GPA			
Average	3.2	3.4	3.4
Standard deviation	0.6	0.5	0.5
College graduation rate (6-year)	84.2	85.6	85.4

Source: Zwick, Ye, and Isham (2016).
Note. CO = constrained optimization; GPA = grade point average, SES = socioeconomic status, URM = under-represented minorities.
The number of applicants was 2,190, and the number of enrollees was 970. In both admissions methods, 970 students were selected. In the CO procedure, the percentage of URMs was constrained to match that of the enrollees. Because this table is based on unweighted data, the percentages cannot be generalized to the target population for the Education Longitudinal Study.

population. The CO approach, however, becomes unwieldy if sampling weights are included in the analysis.[3] Because this technical complication would never occur in an actual admissions situation, we chose simply to omit the weights in our analyses. Although the results serve as an illustration of the feasibility of using CO in the admissions setting, they cannot be generalized to high school seniors of 2004.

    In a subsequent study, we used data from a large public university to illustrate the use of CO to boost the proportion of admitted students who come from low-income neighborhoods (Zwick, Ye, & Isham, 2019). Our analysis sample consisted of 3,894 students who entered the university in 2007. We treated this sample as if it was an applicant pool and then implemented four admissions processes – one CO approach and three

---

[3] Further details appear in the technical appendix to Zwick, 2017, which can be found at www.hup.harvard.edu/supplementary/who-gets-in/who-gets-in-technical-appendix.pdf.

methods that simply ranked applicants and picked the top students on the basis of SAT scores, high school GPA, or a composite of the two. We used a selection rate of 25 percent for all four admissions methods. In the CO analysis, we maximized the admitted class's average on a GPA–SAT score composite, subject to the constraint that at least a quarter of the admitted students be from low-income neighborhoods. Although our dataset included no income information, we were able to use students' zip codes to obtain the median income in their neighborhoods. We considered neighborhoods to be low-income if their median income was below the 2007 median income in the US region in which the university was located. According to this definition, only 16.4 percent of our applicants came from low-income neighborhoods.

The CO analysis yielded an admitted class that was more socioeconomically diverse than the classes produced by the three competing admissions methods. A quarter of the students were from low-income neighborhoods, as required, whereas, in the classes produced by the other models, the percentages were 12.0 percent or lower. The CO class and the class selected by ranking on high school GPA had the highest percentages of URMs (11.6 percent and 12.5 percent, respectively). Although the CO class did not have the highest average SAT scores or high school GPA among the competing admissions models, its average first-year college GPA (3.3) was identical to the average college GPA for the class selected by ranking students on the GPA–SAT composite and higher than the average college GPA for the other two ranking methods. Highlights of our results are shown in Table 18.2.

In our most recent research (Zwick et al., 2018), we showed how a strategy that combines CO with a measure of disadvantage can facilitate the admission of a diverse class. Our CO analyses incorporated the Admissions Obstacles Index (AOI), developed by Blatter and Glynn (2016), which is a measure of the impediments encountered by the candidate, such as low family income, a low counselor-to-student ratio in high school, or the absence of Advanced Placement or International Baccalaureate courses in high school. The original version of the AOI (previously called the Distance Traveled Index) is a count of these obstacles, ranging from zero to 10. It does not take into account the student's race. We also experimented with a revised version, the AOI-R, which added a point to the scores of students who were URMs.

Like our earlier study (Zwick, Ye, & Isham, 2016), this research was based on the 2,190 applicants to selective schools from the ELS database, and the same limitations apply. As in the previous study, we sought to

Table 18.2 *Results for applicants and two admissions models*

	Applicant pool	CO	Ranking on GPA–SAT score composite
Percent low income	16.4	25.0	7.2
Percent URMs	21.4	11.6	6.8
Percent women	51.0	49.0	48.3
High school GPA			
Average	3.6	3.9	3.9
Standard deviation	0.4	0.2	0.1
Admissions test score			
Average	1157	1299	1319
Standard deviation	143	119	92
College first-year GPA			
Average	2.9	3.3	3.3
Standard deviation	0.6	0.6	0.6

Source: Zwick, Ye, & Isham (2019).
Note. CO = constrained optimization; GPA = grade point average, URM = underrepresented minorities.
For both admissions methods, 974 students were selected from a pool of 3,894. In the CO procedure, the percentage of low-income students (as defined in the text) was constrained to be at least 25 percent.

admit 970 students, to facilitate comparison with the actual enrollees in the selective schools. In our CO analyses, we again maximized a GPA–test score composite. However, in this study, we applied constraints to the AOI (or AOI-R) scores of the admitted class. In one set of analyses, we required that 20 percent of the admitted students have an AOI (AOI-R) score of at least 4. In another set, we constrained the mean AOI (AOI-R) score for the admitted class to be above a threshold. We used 2.4, the average AOI value for the ELS high school seniors of 2004, as the cutoff.

Characteristics of the admitted classes obtained by constraining the mean AOI and the mean AOI-R are summarized in Table 18.3. For comparison, the results for the enrollees in the competitive schools are included, along with results obtained by ranking students on the basis of their GPA–test score composite values and then selecting the top 970. As shown in the first row of data, the CO methods yielded a class with a much higher percentage of students from the lower half of the SES distribution (roughly 21 percent to 23 percent) than the enrollees (13.5 percent) or the class produced by the ranking method (12.5 percent). Both CO methods also yielded classes with a higher percentage of URMs (12.7 percent for

Table 18.3 *Results for enrollees and three admissions models*

	Enrollees in competitive schools	CO: Mean AOI	CO: Mean AOI-R	Ranking on GPA–test score composite
Percent in lower half of SES distribution	13.5	22.8	21.1	12.5
Percent URMs	12.6	12.7	14.7	7.5
Percent women	55.1	56.5	55.9	56.7
High school GPA				
Average	3.5	3.6	3.7	3.7
Standard deviation	0.4	0.3	0.3	0.3
Admissions test score				
Average	1250	1271	1282	1310
Standard deviation	153	154	145	112
College first-year GPA				
Average	3.2	3.3	3.3	3.4
Standard deviation	0.6	0.6	0.6	0.5
College graduation rate (6-year)	84.2	81.8	82.8	85.4

Source: Zwick et al. (2018).
Note. AOI = Admissions Obstacles Index; CO = constrained optimization; GPA = grade point average, SES = socioeconomic status, URM = under-represented minorities.
The number of applicants was 2,190 and the number of enrollees was 970. In all three admissions methods, 970 students were selected. The CO methods required that the mean AOI or AOI-R for selected students be at least 2.4. Because this table is based on unweighted data, the percentages cannot be generalized to the target population for the Education Longitudinal Study.

AOI and 14.7 percent for AOI-R) than the enrollees or the class produced by the ranking method, despite the fact that the AOI did not explicitly take race into consideration. The percentage of women was very similar for the enrollees and the three admissions methods, ranging from roughly 55 percent to 57 percent. Average high school GPAs were higher for all three admissions methods than for the enrollees. Average admissions test scores, however, were highest for the ranking method, followed by the two CO methods, and the same pattern held for first-year college GPA. Six-year graduation rates were higher for the ranking method and for the enrollees than for the two CO methods, although differences were relatively small. In general, we concluded that the CO methods based on the AOI and AOI-R led to the admission of ethnically and socioeconomically diverse classes that performed well academically.

18.2   Limitations of the Constrained Optimization Approach in the Admissions Setting

A drawback of the research that has been conducted on the use of CO in admissions is that, with the exception of the real-life application of Durán and Wolf-Yadlin (2011), the admissions procedures that have been modeled are very simple. Only a small number of applicant characteristics have been considered and many aspects of the admissions process have been ignored. For example, these studies have not considered exceptions for special talents or veterans; continuous admissions; or financial aid packages. Another limitation is that past researchers have not explicitly considered the distinction between admissions and enrollment. The collection of students who ultimately enroll may have characteristics that differ substantially from the admitted class. However, models that are much more complex than those used in these illustrative studies can be accommodated within the constrained-optimization framework. In particular, extensions that accommodate waiting lists, rolling admissions, and student yield have been considered (Durán & Wolf-Yadlin, 2011; Kreiter et al., 2003; Pashley, Thornton, & Duffy, 2005). In the next section, I describe some elaborations of the CO approach.

In addition to the need for more-complex models that are better suited to the admissions setting, there are some general technical issues to consider when using CO. In particular, it is not always possible to find a solution that satisfies all constraints. In this situation, it may be possible to reach a solution by gradually relaxing constraints. CO can also produce multiple solutions if two or more students have identical data, possibly creating a need for tie-breaking mechanisms.

Yet another category of limitations involves public perceptions and political considerations. CO is an unfamiliar mathematical method that could be seen as undermining what should be a deliberative and perhaps collaborative process. However, even if this kind of algorithmic technique were applied in making actual admissions decisions, human judgment would continue to play a central role. Admissions policies would still need to be developed and applications would still need to be read. Ratings of various applicant characteristics and accomplishments could still be incorporated into the selection process, just as they are in typical admissions decisions, and, of course, admissions personnel could review and modify the initial selections emerging from the CO algorithm. Alternatively, a CO analysis could be conducted in parallel with an institution's usual admissions procedure and could help to identify candidates for admission who might otherwise have been ignored.

Although it may appear to be a "black box," CO is extremely transparent in that it allows for a clear and direct translation of admissions policies. This, however, can be a weakness as well as a selling point. This is particularly true in applications of CO that involve the implementation of quotas. In fact, the analysis of ELS data in which we imposed a minimum on the number of URMs admitted (see Table 18.1) is an example of an admissions approach that would not pass legal muster in the United States. The Supreme Court ruled that if race-neutral polices are unavailable, "narrowly tailored" policies to promote racial diversity can be implemented. Fixed quotas, however, are not permitted (see Zwick, 2017). But, even when quotas are not illegal, they are often controversial. In Malaysia, the policy requiring that a certain number of spaces in public universities be reserved for ethnic Malays "became the subject of a volcanic national debate" in 2001 (Cohen, 2004) and was subsequently abandoned. Similarly, the quota system in Brazil has provoked hundreds of lawsuits (McMurtrie, 2004), and the quota systems in China and India have been contentious as well. It is important, then, to keep in mind that applications of CO need not involve the imposition of quotas. I discuss this point further in the next section. Also, while racial quotas tend to be controversial, other types of quotas – for example, a requirement that a certain number of in-state applicants be admitted – tend to be well accepted.

18.3 Directions for Future Research

Although some of the applications presented in this chapter involve constraints on the number of admitted students who fall into some demographic category (and thus take the form of quotas), many other types of analyses are possible within the CO framework. For example, constraints can be imposed on the average score of the entering class on some measure. An example is the study, described earlier, in which my colleagues and I required the average number of admissions obstacles encountered by the selected students to exceed a criterion value, while simultaneously maximizing their performance on a composite of high school GPA and admissions test score (Zwick et al., 2018). The idea of constraining a mean value can be extended in such a way as to maximize an outcome variable. For example, in one dataset we analyzed, a measure of sociability had been found to predict the likelihood of students' participation in student government, once admitted. By constraining the mean on the sociability measure to exceed a cutoff, while simultaneously maximizing the academic credentials of the selected class, we could increase the proportion of the class who ultimately participated in student government. In practice, a predictive analysis would first be performed on data for students who had already enrolled (so that student government participation would be known) and results would then be applied to a fresh set of applicants. Yet another type of constraint involves a requirement that the difference between the admissions rates for two groups (e.g., men and women) fall below a certain level.

We are now elaborating on our CO approach by incorporating information on expected yield – the percentage of accepted students who are expected to attend. In this way, the composition of the expected entering class, rather than the pool of admitted students, can be shaped to be consistent with the institution's mission. This modification requires consideration of the fact that the rate at which students enroll (given that they are admitted) varies across student groups. In an illustrative example I constructed, the applicant pool consisted of 100 individuals, some of whom had low income. Yield rates were assumed to be lower for low-income students than for other applicants. The goal of the CO analysis was to maximize the average test score of the expected class while achieving an expected class size of 20, including at least four low-income students. Results showed that 36 students, including 10 low-income applicants, had to be admitted in order to meet the requirements.

Research has shown that yield rates depend on a number of factors, such as test scores, grades, family income, geographical region, and the availability of financial aid (see Sarafraz et al., 2015; Walczak & Sincich, 1999). We have developed a two-stage process in which student enrollment probabilities are first modeled using a logistic regression analysis incorporating these key predictors. This regression is based on admitted applicants from an earlier cohort for whom enrollment status is known. The obtained logistic regression equation can then be used to estimate the probabilities of enrollment, given admission, for a new set of applicants. These estimated probabilities can then be fed into our CO program so that we can shape the properties of the expected class. We have successfully applied this approach to the ELS data.

18.4 Conclusion

One of the challenges faced by university admissions personnel around the world is the integration of diversity goals with academic standards.

Diversity efforts vary by country and institution, but often involve improving college access for particular ethnic or socioeconomic groups. Constrained optimization has the potential to be a useful tool for integrating the multiple objectives of the admissions process by optimizing academic performance while simultaneously imposing requirements on class composition. The CO approach forces admissions policymakers to formalize both the academic and nonacademic aims of the admissions process, thus making admissions policies much more transparent. Although this level of openness might be resisted by many institutions, it would serve to increase both fairness to applicants and accountability to the public.

REFERENCES

Berkelaar, M. (2014). Package "lpSolve." Retrieved from https://cran.r-project .org/web/packages/lpSolve/lpSolve.pdf.

Blatter, A., & Glynn, J. (2016, November). Recognizing distance traveled in selective college admissions. Presented at the annual meeting of the Association for the Study of Higher Education, Columbus, Ohio.

Cohen, D. (2004, February 13). In Malaysia, the end of quotas. *Chronicle of Higher Education.* Retrieved from www.chronicle.com/article/In-Malaysia-the-End-of-Quotas/10391.

Durán, G., & Wolf-Yadlin, R. (2011). A mathematical programming approach to applicant selection for a degree program based on affirmative action. *Interfaces, 41,* 278–288. https://doi.org/10.1287/inte.1100.0542.

Ingels, S., Planty, M., & Bozick, R. (2005). *A profile of the American high school senior in 2004: A first look-initial results from the first follow-up of the education longitudinal study of 2002* (NCES 2006-348). Washington, DC: US Department of Education, NCES.

Koljatic, M., & Silva, M. (2013). Opening a side-gate: Engaging the excluded in Chilean higher education through test-blind admission. *Studies in Higher Education, 38,* 1427–1441. https://doi.org/10.1080/03075079.2011.623299.

Kolman, B., & Beck, R. E. (1995). *Elementary linear programming with applications* (2nd ed.). San Diego, CA: Academic Press.

Kreiter, C. D. (2002). The use of constrained optimization to facilitate admission decisions. *Academic Medicine, 77,* 148–151. https://doi.org/10.1097/00001888-200202000-00011.

Kreiter, C. D., Stansfield, B., James, P. A., & Solow, C. (2003). A model for diversity in admissions: A review of issues and methods and an experimental approach. *Teaching and Learning in Medicine: An International Journal, 15,* 116–122. https://doi.org/10.1207/S15328015TLM1502_08.

Lloyd, M. (2004, February 13). In Brazil, a new debate over color. *Chronicle of Higher Education.* Retrieved from www.chronicle.com/article/In-Brazil-a-New-Debate-Over/4343.

lp_solve reference guide. (n.d.). Retrieved from http://web.mit.edu/lpsolve/doc/.

McMurtrie, B. (2004, February 13). The quota quandary. *Chronicle of Higher Education*. Retrieved from www.chronicle.com/article/The-Quota-Quandary/35480.

Overland, M. A. (2004, February 13). In India, almost everyone wants to be special. *Chronicle of Higher Education*. Retrieved from www.chronicle.com/article/In-India-Almost-Everyone/3612.

Pashley, P. J., & Thornton, A. E. (1999). *Crafting an Incoming law school class: Preliminary results* (LSAC Research Report 99-01). Newtown, PA: Law School Admission Council.

Pashley, P. J., Thornton, A. E., & Duffy, J. R. (2005). Access and diversity in law school admissions. In W. J. Camara & E. W. Kimmel (Eds.). *Choosing students: Higher education admissions tools for the 21st century* (pp. 231–249). Mahwah, NJ: Erlbaum.

Sarafraz, Z., Sarafraz, H., Sayeh, M., & Nicklow, J. (2015). Student yield maximization using genetic algorithm on a predictive enrollment neural network model. *Procedia Computer Science, 61,* 341–348. https://doi.org/10.1016/j.procs.2015.09.154.

Schmitt, C. M. (2009). *Documentation for the restricted-use NCES-Barron's admissions competiveness index data files* (NCES 2010-330). Washington, DC: NCES.

Somers, P., Morosini, M., Pan, M., & Cofer, J. E. (2013). Brazil's radical approach to expanding access for underrepresented college students. In H.-D. Meyer, E. P. St. John, M. Chankseliani, & L. Uribe (Eds.). *Fairness in access to higher education in a global perspective*, pp. 203–221. Rotterdam: Sense. https://doi.org/10.1007/978-94-6209-230-3_12.

Walczak, S., & Sincich, T. (1999). A comparative analysis of regression and neural networks for university admissions. *Information Sciences, 119,* 1–20. https://doi.org/10.1016/S0020-0255(99)00057-2.

Zhang, R. (2010). Media, litigation, and regional discrimination in college admission in China. *Chinese Education and Society, 43*(4), 60–74. https://doi.org/10.2753/CED1061-1932430406

Zwick, R. (2017). *Who gets in? Strategies for fair and effective college admissions.* Cambridge, MA: Harvard University Press. https://doi.org/10.4159/9780674977648

Zwick, R., Blatter, A., Ye, L., & Isham, S. (2018). Using constrained optimization with an index of admission obstacles to increase the diversity of college classes. Manuscript submitted for publication.

Zwick, R., Ye, L., & Isham, S. (2016). Crafting a college class using constrained optimization. Paper presented at the annual meeting of the Association for the Study of Higher Education, Columbus, Ohio.

(2019). Using constrained optimization to increase the representation of students from low-income neighborhoods. *Applied Measurement in Education,* 281–297, https://doi.org/10.1080/08957347.2019.1660346.

CHAPTER 19

After Admissions: What Comes Next in Higher Education?

María Elena Oliveri, Robert J. Mislevy, and Norbert Elliot

The chapters in this volume provide an international perspective on multiple areas of concern to higher education. Chapters focus on expanding the skill sets and constructs measured as part of college admissions (see Niessen & Meijer, in this volume; Kuncel, Tran, & Zhang, in this volume) and approaches to developing assessments that are sensitive to sociocognitive and sociocultural differences of the populations taking them (see Wikström & Wikström, in this volume). Efforts in these two areas aim to reduce sources of construct-irrelevant variance in assessments administered to students from diverse backgrounds in support of fair access to higher education institutions and to provide students with opportunities to develop a comprehensive (cognitive and noncognitive) skill set necessary for college success. In this chapter, we build on these areas and extend them to include a discussion about ways to better support students after admitting them to higher education institutions. The goal is to provide evidentiary data to help improve learning, decrease the percentage of remedial courses students take, and increase graduation rates.

A focus on enrollment and graduation is especially warranted as information on remedial-course enrollment and graduation rates of undergraduate students in the United States reveals challenges to remedial-course enrollment and the graduation of students from diverse ethnic groups in 2- and 4-year public institutions. As Figure 19.1 illustrates, enrollment in remedial courses is widespread and differs among subgroups. While 68 percent of Asian and 64 percent of White students were enrolled in remedial courses at public 2-year institutions, higher rates were reported among Black (78 percent) and Hispanic students (75 percent). Similar group differences are observed in 4-year institutions: While only about one-third of White (36 percent) and Asian (30 percent) students

The opinions and recommendations expressed here are those of the authors and not necessarily those of Educational Testing Service.

participated in remedial courses, a greater percentage of Black (66 percent) and Hispanic (53 percent) students were enrolled in such courses (Chen, 2016).

In terms of graduation rates, as Figure 19.2 reveals, these also differ by subgroup, with 35 percent of Asian and 29 percent of White students graduating from 2-year institutions within three years completion time and lower rates among Black (24 percent) and Hispanic (34 percent) students. Similarly, in 4-year institutions a higher percentage of Asian (73 percent) and White (64 percent) students graduated from 4-year institutions within six years completion time, with lower rates reported among Black (40 percent) and Hispanic (54 percent) students (Snyder, deBrey, & Dillow, 2019).

A comparison of Figures 19.1 and 19.2 shows that subgroups enrolled in a higher percentage of remedial courses had lower percentages of graduating students. For instance, Black and Hispanic students partici-pated in a higher percentage of remedial courses (78 percent and 75 percent, respectively) in 2-year institutions and had the lowest graduation

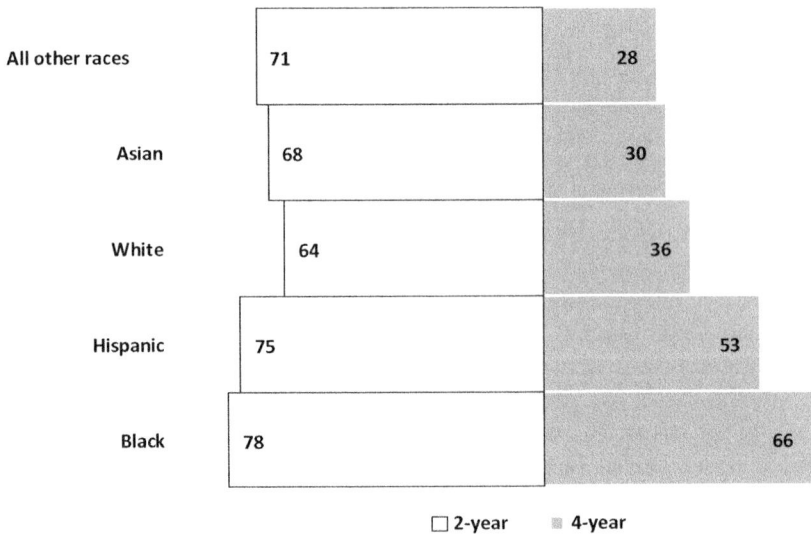

Figure 19.1   2003–2004 Remedial course enrollment in higher education institutions in the United States by race/ethnicity subgroup
Note. Numbers indicate the percentage of students among 2003–2004 beginning postsecondary students who first enrolled in 2- and 4-year higher education institutions who took remedial courses in any field by ethnic subgroup.
Source. Adapted from Chen (2016).

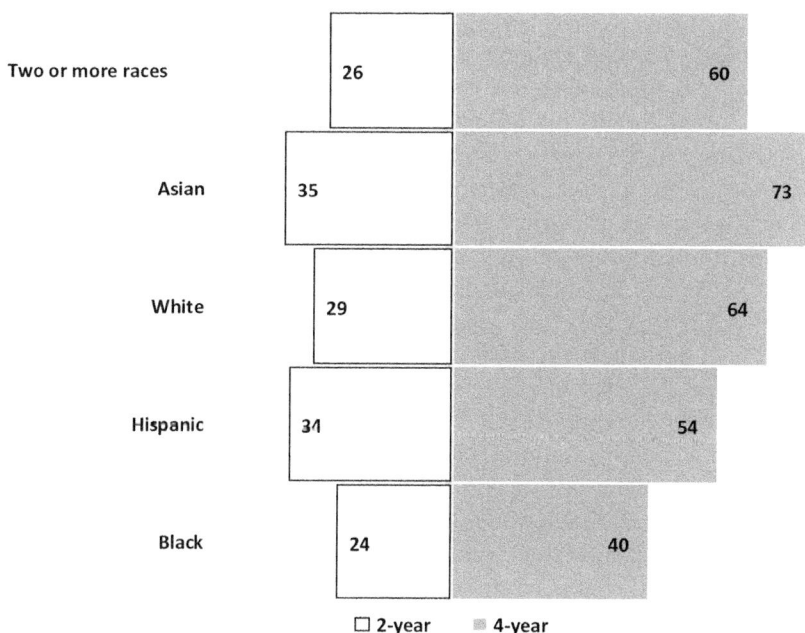

Figure 19.2 Graduation rates by higher education institution in the United States and race/ethnicity

Note. Cohort years are 2000–2013 for 2-year higher education institutions and 1996–2010 for 4-year higher education institutions. Numbers indicate the percentage of students who completed their 2-year degree within 150 percent (3-years) and 4-year degree within 150 percent (6-years) completion time. The table does not include race/ethnicity unknown or nonresident aliens.

Source. Adapted from Snyder, de Brey, & Dillow (2019).

rates (24 percent and 34 percent, respectively). Comparatively, in both 2- and 4-year institutions, White and Asian students participated in fewer remedial courses and had higher graduation rates. It appears that remediation is not having the desired effect on graduation rates. As discussed by Chen (2016), relationships between remedial coursework taken by students and their college outcomes vary by a student's level of academic preparedness. To elaborate, weakly prepared students who successfully completed all remedial courses in English/reading or mathematics may have experienced better postsecondary outcomes than did their counterparts who were weakly prepared but did not enroll in remedial courses. These same patterns did not hold for those students with moderate/strong preparation who were enrolled, perhaps incorrectly, in remedial courses.

The key, therefore, may not rest in single solutions such as remediation but, rather, in understanding obstacles comprehensively and designing strategies to overcome them in more exact ways.

Instead, alternative strategies are needed. We propose that assessment for learning is an important option to explore. Consequently, we discuss the need for new assessment frameworks. While our examples are drawn from assessments primarily within the United States, we believe that the lessons learned, proposed models, and future directions we identify have value for an international audience.

As such, we provide two models: the multilevel design model (MDM) and the complementarity model (CM). When taken together, the models aim to better support diverse students' learning by improving the connection between assessments and instruction once students are admitted to higher education institutions. Thus, we suggest that students benefit when admissions, retention, and graduation processes are considered within unified frameworks rather than as unconnected atomistic events.

The goal of MDM is to minimize the unintended effects of test use when scores are employed primarily (or uniquely) to inform admissions decisions. Such effects may include the disjuncture between assessment and instruction, the use of assessments that do not provide data to inform student learning, or potential biases that may disadvantage subgroups of students identified by race, ethnicity, gender, or other discrete or intersectional categories when scores are used to inform decisions in isolation from other data sources. In such cases, assessment use may result in unintended consequences on stakeholders such as decision-makers, instructors, and students. Therefore, MDM considers both consequences of test use and the meaning of score-based interpretations together to help reduce sources of construct-irrelevant variance and support valid score-based inferences. As discussed later, these issues gain importance with shifts in the higher education climate that occur due to rising demands to assess an expanded skill set and an increasingly diverse student population.

CM aims to expand the uses and purposes of assessments from their current focus on summative uses (i.e., assessments used to evaluate student learning and skill acquisition at the end of an instructional period, such as a study unit or course) to include formative and embedded assessments. Formative assessments are used to monitor progress and provide ongoing feedback for instructors to improve their teaching and help students improve their learning. Embedded assessments are administered more frequently than formative assessments as course assignments, activities, or exercises as evidence of progress toward achieving a particular learning outcome. Expanding the use of assessments to more frequent administrations during the course of the higher education program may also involve complementing the use of distributed assessments (assessments that are standardized for administration across settings) with locally based assessments (assessments used within specific institutions). We conjecture that expanding the types of assessments used optimizes evidentiary data and better supports student learning, retention, and graduation.

In this chapter, we further describe the MDM and CM models and discuss their use to increase retention and graduation. To situate the models, we first describe shifts in higher education related to expanding the skill set, identifying the complexities of assessing culturally and linguistically diverse students, and increasing the uses of assessments. We believe if assessments are designed and used in ways that are more closely connected to institutions' contexts and purposes, they have the potential to support student retention and graduation.

19.1 Shifts in the Higher Education Environment

19.1.1 Implications of an Expanded Skill Set

Changes in higher education's landscape have implications for expanding the skill set that needs to be assessed. This expansion means that not only do the cognitive and academic skills needed for college success need to be assessed but that noncognitive skills must also be evaluated. Examples of noncognitive skills are collaboration (in the interpersonal domain) and persistence (in the intrapersonal domain). Both types of skills are important for degree completion and college success (National Research Council, 2012).

The skill set needs expanding because of an "increasingly global economy, elevated use of technology, and shifts in the types of economies and industries dominating the national and global economies" (Oliveri & Markle, 2017, p. 1). An expanded skill set is also needed, in light of research on classroom learning, student diversity, and the skills required for earning credit. For instance, teamwork may be necessary to complete classroom assignments and group projects or to summarize a particular student's contribution to projects (Oliveri, Lawless, & Molloy, 2017). The same is true of self-efficacy as a way to examine the independent and interactive effects of race and social class when evaluating interventions to close science, technology, engineering, and mathematics achievement gaps (Harackiewicz et al., 2016).

In broader terms, Hesse et al. (2015) note that higher education institutions do not tend formally to teach or assess collaborative skills. Results from employer surveys suggest that recent graduates are poorly prepared to meet workplace demands due to a lack of relevant noncognitive skills (Hart Research Associates, 2010). Coley, Goodman, and Sands (2015) warn that reacting too slowly in expanding students' skill sets may adversely affect a nation's ability to respond to increasing international demands, with negative effects on employability and economic prosperity.

Assessing this expanded skill set, important to both academic and workplace settings, presents challenges to testing organizations. The challenges include the need to develop new assessment frameworks and tasks that better integrate cognitive and noncognitive constructs to meet shifting demands of the twenty-first century (Bereiter & Scardamalia, 2012).

19.1.2   Implications of Population Changes

Additional changes to assessments are needed due to the increased diversity of the student body attending higher education institutions. Mislevy (2018) argues for a sociocognitive approach to assessment design when assessing diverse populations to reduce sources of construct-irrelevant variance in assessments and obtain accurate score-based inferences. A sociocognitive approach to educational assessment and measurement views capabilities as emerging from the interplay of cognitive processes within persons and social and cultural processes across persons in a complex adaptive system. A sociocognitive approach to test development and score-based interpretations describes ways to remain attentive to key elements of task design and construct representation and the type of resources and knowledge culturally and linguistically diverse populations might bring to the assessment (O'Sullivan & Weir, 2011; Weir, 2005). To allow for valid and fair score-based interpretations when assessing populations from diverse backgrounds, the purpose of this approach is to guide decisions (e.g., the types of vocabulary, items, or situations) that can be included in an assessment without creating unnecessary complexity in the assessment (construct-irrelevant variance) or adapting tasks in accordance with test-takers' supporting capabilities.

A sociocognitive approach to testing is called for given the projected demographic shifts in the United States and internationally. Hussar and Bailey (2017) foresee an increasing number of students from various racial and ethnic backgrounds enrolling in higher education over the next 40 years. Internationally, Altbach, Reisberg, and Rumbley (2009) and Kelly,

Moores, and Moogan (2012) describe that increasing numbers of specific subgroups are attending higher education institutions, such as Asian international students.

Shifts in the demographic composition of potential students have implications for assessment design, conceptualization, and fairness (Dorans & Cook, 2016). One set of implications includes increased problems with the standardization of content or language and calls for developing tests that are more sensitive to the diverse backgrounds of test-takers. Consequently, professional organizations highlight the need for fairness considerations in assessment design and conceptualization. For example, the *Standards for Educational and Psychological Testing* include fairness as part of the section on foundational measurement, signaling a growing need "to support appropriate testing experiences for all individuals" (American Educational Research Association, American Psychological Association, & National Council on Measurement in Education, 2014, p. 5).

The International Test Commission (2018) proposes that considerations for fairly assessing culturally and linguistically diverse learners span an assessment's lifecycle, starting from conceptualization and design and extending to uses and score interpretation. For instance, administering the same test to diverse individuals may lead to incorrect inferences about individuals if tests contain language, item formats, or tasks that are differentially familiar to test-takers. Validity threats may emerge from the use of so-called exported assessments, those developed for domestic use and then administered in other countries in the same or a different language (Oliveri & Lawless, 2018). As the use of exported higher education assessments increases, attention to design principles from a sociocognitive perspective are necessary for identifying ways to minimize irrelevant sources of score variance that may emerge due to differences in the opportunity to learn, curricular exposure, or familiarity with cultural references used, which may all present additional validity threats for these assessments.

19.1.3 Uses of Higher Education Assessment Scores

Changes in the skill set measured by assessments and demographic shifts also have implications on how information gleaned from tests is used to monitor student learning or placement decisions regarding which courses students are ready to pursue. In *Who Gets In? Strategies for Fair and Effective College Admissions*, Zwick (2017) described admissions policies as more than a set of rules, and proposed principles for informing decisions. These principles include acknowledging that there is no universal definition of merit. Therefore, the selection of which students to admit may vary, depending on the predictors evaluated. Such evaluation may expand to using high school grades to measure noncognitive constructs (e.g., tenacity and commitment), being transparent in the use of admissions rules to increase fairness and access to colleges for diverse student groups, or using a combination of criteria to inform admissions.

A non-universal definition of merit is particularly relevant in the assessment of diverse populations because candidates may have different backgrounds or educational and life experiences. Such differences challenge the paradigm of comparing individuals on a set of common criteria and using a ranking system to inform admissions decisions in which only some individuals are admitted. We believe that while the principles described by Zwick (2017) are important to admissions, similar principles may be applied to students with diverse backgrounds throughout their higher education studies to improve retention and graduation rates, as we elaborate later. Concomitant with the expansion of uses of assessments is a growing need for arguments and evidence to support score interpretations, from which implications for assessment design, construction, and the interpretation of claims are derived. Many assessment models focus on psychometrics and technical accuracy and do not explicitly include approaches using assessment data to inform score-based decisions affecting stakeholders.

Now situated with reference to shifts in higher education related to expanding skill sets and addressing the needs of culturally and linguistically diverse students, we turn to applying an MDM model for designing and using assessments to guide decisions and efforts in a structured manner.

19.2 A Multilevel Design Model
for Assessment Development and Use

We start our description of the MDM by providing a taxonomy of assessment purposes, institution type, and stakeholders (see Figure 19.3). The face of the cube lists test purposes we described earlier (e.g., informing classroom instruction), which go beyond the use of tests to inform admissions decisions to the use of tests to also provide information that is useful to inform decisions throughout students' higher education studies in support of student retention and graduation. The cube also displays the stakeholders, which may require information at different grain sizes. For instance, policymakers may require information at a coarser level to make high-level policy decisions that offer meaningful strategies for monitoring

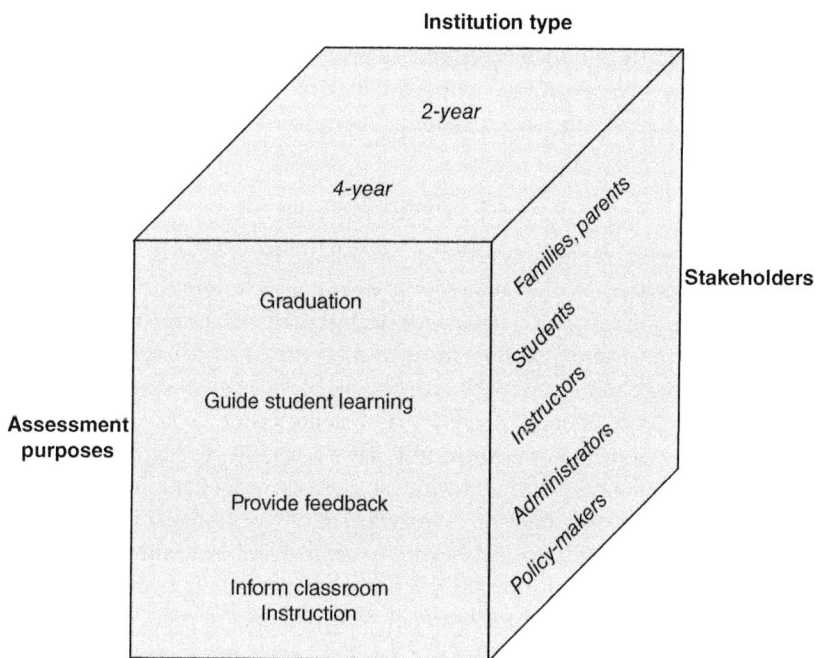

Figure 19.3   Taxonomy of assessment purposes, institution types, and stakeholders

educational improvements and outcomes for the performance of higher education institutions (Haertel & Herman, 2005). Administrators may require student-level data to inform decisions and institution-specific data to enable them to monitor student learning and progress within fields and programs within their institution. Individual students and instructors also require different types and levels of data (Oliveri & Wendler, 2017).

The diversity of assessment aims, institutional types, and stakeholders' needs presents additional challenges to developers to provide meaningful results. In this fluid environment, one challenge is the need to collaborate across multidisciplinary teams to design assessments. Evidence-centered design (ECD) (Riconscente, Mislevy, & Corrigan, 2016) can play a central role in guiding multidisciplinary teams of experts (i.e., assessment developers, cognitive psychologists, scientists, statisticians) and stakeholders (i.e., policymakers, administrators, instructors) to jointly identify and meet the goals of assessment use. This framework may involve developing a common language, mental models, artifacts, and best practice to capture the connected thinking underlying test design. ECD tools and concepts are not sufficient, however, as they can capture design elements and rationales, but do not encompass the social system in which an assessment will function. The resources, constraints, purposes, and stakeholder perspectives composing the social system also need to be considered.

19.2.1   Model Overview

The MDM goals are to understand the following aspects of assessments: (a) the social system within which they operate, including the viable space they have for design and related constraints; (b) the purposes and constraints they must satisfy in operation; and (c) the effects that score use will have on the stakeholders. Explicit articulation of the goals and system within which assessments operate is needed to support the development of the more complex assessments attuned to today's economy; to help mitigate the negative consequences associated with the primary uses of summative assessments and the measurement of a narrower set of traditional constructs; and improve the use, meaning, and impact of score-based assessments.

Figure 19.4 illustrates the MDM for assessment design, development, and use. The MDM has three layers of components: (a) consequences, (b) logic, and (c) construction. The consequences layer articulates key properties and objectives with an eye toward possible unintended effects that may reduce an assessment's utility. The logic layer is where the assessment design is conceptualized in relation to the desired Theory of Action (ToA) specified in the consequences layer. The construction layer specifies the machinery used in assessment development. The goals are to operationalize the argument specified in the logic layer and the ToA specified in the consequences layer. We use double-sided arrows to indicate the interactive nature across layers.

19.2.1.1   Consequences

The consequences layer is located at the top of the model. We discuss consequences in relation to the ToA. Bennett's (2010) application of ToAs to assessment highlights the importance of explicitly identifying the assessment components, the claims that will be made from the results, the action mechanisms designed to lead to the desired effects, and the identification of potential unintended negative consequences and what will be done to mitigate them. Bennett suggests that a ToA is needed when assessments are viewed as instruments of change, so that designers do not focus only on the instruments' technical adequacy but also consider consequences of using assessments.

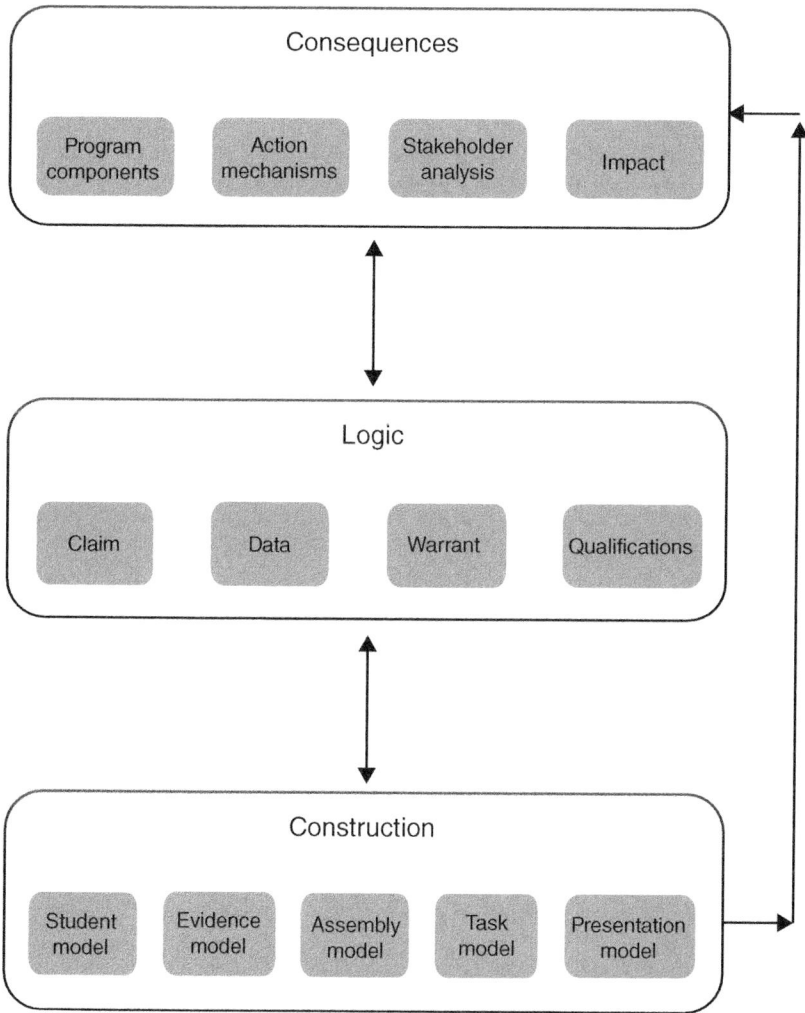

Figure 19.4 A multilevel design model for assessment development and use

Consistent with the ToA, we suggest that explicitly articulating beliefs underlying consequences involves identifying the components of an assessment, action mechanisms, stakeholder analysis, and impact. The program components include the items and scores obtained from the assessment, services designed for test-takers, and services designed for score users. The action mechanisms capture the types of decisions, behaviors, and solutions expected from different stakeholders using scores for decision-making. Stakeholder analysis components include anticipating interpretation and use of scores by varied populations, from policymakers to parents. Finally, impact includes intended and unintended direct and indirect consequences of the assessment (Oliveri, Rutkowski, & Rutkowski, 2018). To help minimize short- and long-term unintended effects of decisions informed by scores, we suggest the use of various types of data sources, as well as considerations that include the degree to which the assessments cover the appropriate constructs and acknowledge test-taker diversity in interpretive arguments. Otherwise, potential unintended effects may occur, including over remediation (see Figure 19.1), as well as retaining and graduating a particular student subgroup of students more frequently than another (see Figure 19.2).

19.2.1.2 Logic

The next layer in the model is logic, which Toulmin (2003) describes as a claim, data, warrant, and qualification. With modification, Toulmin's model is useful for constructing validity arguments (Bachman & Palmer, 2010; Kane, 2006). An example of an assessment-use claim may be the use of scores from a writing test to inform higher education decisions, such as readiness to take courses that are more advanced. The data may involve providing evidence, which may range from a test score to the use of additional variables beyond test scores to inform inferences on students' readiness to pursue more advanced college courses.

The warrant supporting the claim may be that "the test" is designed to assess written proficiency, which might be measured using proficiency indicators such rhetorical knowledge, critical thinking, writing processes, and knowledge of conventions (Council of Writing Program Administrators, National Council of Teachers of English, & National Writing Project, 2011). The test may be designed to resemble the types of written compositions students need to carry out in the more advanced college courses. The qualifications (or qualifiers) may range from weak to strong. Qualifiers are strong, and call for more caution in interpretation, if there is more distance between the evidence (e.g., writing assessed through multiple-choice questions focusing on knowledge of conventions) and the skills students need (e.g., rhetorical knowledge) to have to complete their courses. Conversely warrants are stronger when the skills assessed are closely connected to course content (e.g., writing assessed by demonstrating proficiency in the use of rhetorical structures in various academic and workplace genres across a more representative construct domain).

Rebuttals to claims may arise when test-takers are tested using tasks that are unfamiliar, or irrelevant to the construct or domain assessed. Their use introduces inferential errors for construct-irrelevant reasons. Considering these issues during assessment design is important to identify validity and fairness issues early on and develop more-appropriate interpretive inferences and validity arguments for all students (International Test Commission, 2018; Mislevy, 2018; Oliveri & Lawless, 2018). To identify the types of intended and unintended consequences that might arise when developing assessments, it is important to work through the consequences and logic layers of the MDM prior to test construction. Examples of unintended consequences potentially leading to unintended outcomes may include: (a) under-representing the constructs needed for college success by only assessing cognitive constructs and leaving out noncognitive constructs, (b) emphasizing elements of the writing construct that focus solely on easily capturable features such as conventions that, in turn, suggest narrow views of writing, (c) failing to identify tasks that authentically align with the assessment's language-use domain, and (d) developing test items that use technology that is unfamiliar to test-takers.

19.2.1.3 *Construction*

Construction is the final layer of the model. As indicated, there is an interactive connection between the consequences and logic layers. This connection reflects the necessary linkage between the key elements of the construction and the other two layers, such as the inferential limits of data use and considerations for the populations that comprise the test-taker population. The five elements that belong to the construction layer are consistent with an ECD model and include conceptual models that describe technical specifications of the assessment and considerations relative to the student, evidence, assembly, task, and presentation components of the assessment. The student model identifies variables for the knowledge, skills, or other attributes of the construct measured by the assessment. The evidence model provides information about how the student model variables should be updated given student performance, as captured in the form of work products. The assembly model describes how the student, evidence, and task models work together to form the assessment. The task model describes how to structure the kinds of situations that allow evidence to be obtained for analysis. The presentation model describes how the tasks appear in various settings, thus providing a test specification for organizing the material to be presented and captured (Mislevy, Almond, & Lukas, 2004; Mislevy & Haertel, 2006).

19.2.1.4   Reflection on the MDM

The MDM includes useful considerations for the design, development, and uses of tests appropriate in higher education and are particularly needed when developing assessments for complex constructs (e.g., critical thinking, collaboration, or interactive communication). To maximize the desired, intended consequences from their use and to minimize undesirable and unintended consequences, developing assessments requires collaborations across stakeholder groups to design constructed-response tasks and link them to the assessment-based claims. Moreover, effective assessment development may involve the construction of a variety of linked tools and tests to produce a comprehensive assessment system capable of providing multiple and varied forms of evidence to support higher education decisions. Such considerations would apply to construct conceptualization, task development, and interpretive materials to guide the decision-maker. As we explain next, some of these types of assessments already exist.

19.3   A Complementarity Design Model for Assessment Development and Use

Breland et al. (2002) suggest that a single assessment may be insufficient to address all stakeholders' needs, particularly as the assessment purposes increase due to the desire to assess an expanded skill set for more diverse populations. The complementarity model we are about to describe is best seen as within the family of integrated assessment systems (IAS). An IAS may enable a more meaningful alignment of data from higher education assessments that serve different purposes and share common goals. An IAS's goal is to provide additional information about students in local contexts (e.g., within higher education institutions) to support learning by providing students and instructors with ongoing feedback. An IAS may include familiar, large-scale assessments (e.g., ACT®, SAT®, SweSAT, TOEFL®) used by multiple institutions to provide information across locations, users, and populations and compare individuals from different backgrounds on common items to inform higher education decisions. An IAS may also include locally administered assessments, such as intelligent tutoring systems or curriculum-based, computer-delivered tasks.

An IAS differs from a classic selection paradigm that uses an outcome (e.g., first-year grade point average) and predictor variables (e.g., admissions test scores) assumed to be linearly related in the full population of applicants based on an instructional program. In the United States, the classic selection paradigm was a starting point for many institutions, as it provided the foundation for the use of admissions tests. An IAS also differs from a placement paradigm, which allows multiple treatments (e.g., grades from different courses) to seek optimal placement of individuals (Cleary, 1968; Novick & Petersen, 1976). Instead, an IAS uses data from different assessments to evaluate students' course-taking patterns to provide them with feedback within and across courses. Such feedback may be used to evaluate students' performances more frequently to better inform their course placement decisions, such as which courses to take next, based on how others with similar course and covariate backgrounds fared.

Bayesian inference networks may be used to link data from different assessments. They may be built around an institution's population and data (Braun & Jones, 1984). The goal is to analyze how students with different data patterns fare under various placement decisions through time while allowing for potentially missing data as students may not have available information on all variables.

Making decisions more rapidly, with the student as decision-maker (to increase students' involvement and agency in the decisions made), are perhaps best when interwoven through courses. With shorter feedback cycles, the traditional notions of placement and instruction through a course become blurred. The notion of placement blends into the notion of supported, individualized, instruction – made possible by learning frameworks of modules/experiences that can be tailored to individuals in relation to content, timing, and intensity. The idea of individualized feedback based on localized assessment is not new. The Individually Prescribed Instruction project, grounded in behavioral psychology and using criterion-referenced tests, was implemented in schools in the Pittsburgh, Pennsylvania area of the United States in the 1960s and 1970s (Glaser & Nitko, 1970). More recently, Pane et al. (2017) examined pedagogies based on personalized learning in 40 institutions dedicated to personalized learning-based instruction and concluded that there is evidence that implementation of personalized learning practices may have positive effects on achievement. As we illustrate through examples of CMs, such systems may incorporate and balance the strengths of formal and informal assessments by capitalizing on an array of conceptual, methodological, and technological developments.

In addition, these papers challenge the testing industry to develop assessment systems that can capture evidence of student learning at multiple time points, from different sources (i.e., inside and outside of school settings) and different types (i.e., quantitative and qualitative), and that allow for resonance with the teaching, learning, and assessment processes.

19.3.1 Model Overview

In agreement with the statement of Breland et al. (2002) that a single test is insufficient to meet all stakeholders' goals, the CM to which we now turn provides an expanded space for assessment uses to support not only admissions decisions but also student retention and graduation. Figure 19.5 shows the CM. Four types of assessments fill the figure's quadrants. The selected assessments are administered either by colleges or in high school for college credit. The assessments are independent of each other and do not act as a system; the aim of Figure 19.5 is to identify elements of complementarity in order to achieve an IAS. In the figure, summative and formative assessments are on the y-axis; distributed and local assessments are on the x-axis. In the figure's center is "complementarity" to show that the assessments can serve various purposes through their balance of local utility, portability, formative, and summative types of score uses. The assessments were selected for their desirable features to meet stakeholders' needs, such as providing interactive experiences that more closely align with skills students need in their future careers and expanding opportunities for students to learn in more meaningful and contextualized learning situations.

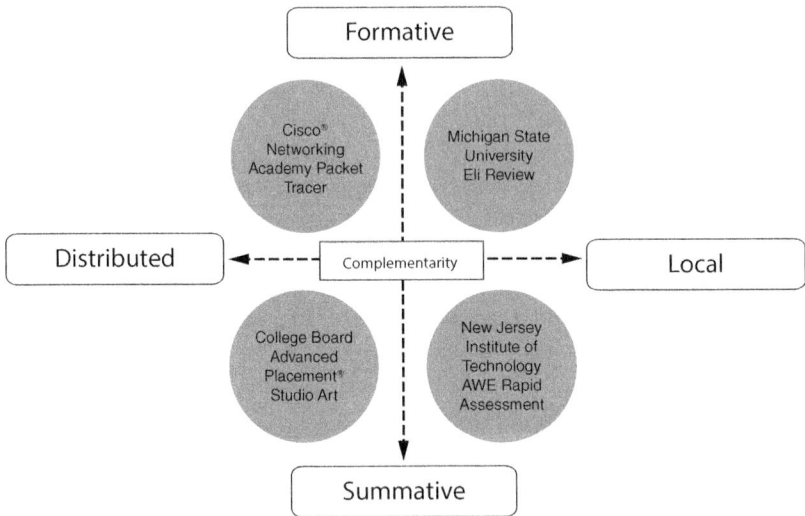

Figure 19.5   A complementarity model for assessment development and use
Note. AWE = automated writing evaluation.

19.3.1.1   Cisco® Networking Academy (CNA)

The CNA illustrated in the upper-left quadrant shows the complementary relationship between formative and distributed assessments with its use of a simulation tool called Packet Tracer software (Cisco Systems Inc., 2010). The CNA, designed to help students develop skills in beginning network engineering, emphasizes both formative and distributed aspects of assessment: It provides learning materials, assessment tools, and a social network connecting local CNA classrooms globally (Frezzo, Behrens, & Mislevy, 2009). The software's environment enables students and teachers to construct, configure, troubleshoot, and share computer network simulations. Web-based-delivered exercises and embedded assessments provide students with unlimited opportunities to engage in the interactive experiences central to learning how to think and act like network engineers.

Packet Tracer tasks are open-ended in operation but standardized with respect to interfaces, standards, and evaluation methods; thus, the use of Packet Tracer is distributed throughout the CNA community. Students can engage with the tasks individually, at times and places that the instructors or the students themselves determine; this use is local and formative. Extended tasks are used in course assessments and for learning (often by students working collaboratively, again locally and formatively, but as applied with distributed substance and standards). Shorter facsimiles of Packet Tracer-like tasks appear in the Cisco Certified Network Associate (CCNA) Exam that many CNA students take; a use that is distributed and summative but retains the environment, substance, and standards of the formative use of Packet Tracer in learning environments. CNA leverages technology and elements of standardization to create assessments that advance learning, allow for considerable local adaptation, and provide evidence of a common set of valued skills for subsequent college or career decisions. Successful completion of the sequence of four CNA courses, for example, provides admissions officers, placement counselors, and employers with information about a student's networking experience. A CCNA certificate provides even stronger evidence of proficiency, whether it was developed in a CNA course or otherwise, due to the layering of standardized and monitored testing conditions on top of the evidence gathering in the common networking domain.

19.3.1.2   Advanced Placement® Studio Art

First introduced in 1955, the College Board's Advanced Placement (AP®) examinations emphasize distributed and summative elements (see the lower-left quadrant of Figure 19.5). Although AP assessments are not administered in higher education, we include them in this chapter because they have implications in higher education as AP scores are used to award course credit or to allow students to place out of certain college requirements and thus allow them to take more advanced courses earlier in their college career (College Board, n.d.).

In most AP subject areas, students prepare for a common end-of-course examination based on a course-specific syllabus and other curriculum requirements. Thus, these examinations are both distributed and summative. Most students participate in AP as part of local high school classes, although the examinations are open to all. Instructional methods, curricula, and local assessments are customizable for local and formative uses within the boundaries set by the College Board. Scores from the examinations provide valid and credible information to college admissions officers and departmental counselors about students' capabilities in particular subjects (College Board, n.d.).

AP Studio Art courses differ from other AP subject assessments because they represent more localized approaches. If AP Studio Art appeared separately in the CM, it would be closer to the "local" quadrant than would the other subjects. There is no culminating written examination for Studio Art courses. Instead, students submit portfolios of works they created throughout the school year for central evaluation. AP Studio Art offers locally situated experiences for students that require them to produce a certain number and type of artifacts evaluated using a centralized rating. These aspects make central evaluation possible in support of their high-stakes distributed use. The course design balances support for localized student learning and provides information that helps college personnel evaluate students' accomplishments (Myford & Mislevy, 1995).

19.3.1.3   *Eli Review*

Construct-specific digital ecologies are now being used to improve students' writing (Hart-Davidson & Meeks, forthcoming). Within a web-based environment, instructors and students provide specific and explicit feedback on student writing using rubrics tailored to assignments they create individually or shared within or across institutions. In turn, this feedback leads to improved instructor and peer reviews enabling writing program administrators to make evidence-based curricular changes by assessing student learning at the class, student, and program levels. It also enables the identification and subsequent support of students at risk, to improve retention and graduation rates. Platforms such as Eli Review, created at Michigan State University, as well as Peerceptiv, and Peergrade.io, are examples of such systems that focus on student feedback.

These systems exemplify formative and local uses of higher education assessments. They also illustrate distributed uses, as they are part of a family of other web-based assessments. They illustrate the complementarity between local and distributed views that can occur when information is gathered across sites within a digital environment. While assignments and course grades are within the domain of summative–instructor judgment, formative feedback is associated with both curricular change and positive outcomes for students. As such, resonance is established between summative grading and formative feedback to better support admitted students' learning.

19.3.1.4   Criterion®

The use of automated writing evaluation (AWE) technologies has led to a comprehensive body of knowledge associated with both summative judgment and local, formative feedback in various educational settings (Shermis & Burstein, 2013; Shermis et al., 2016). An example is Criterion (see the lower-right quadrant of Figure 19.5), which is an online writing evaluation service and a machine-scored, web-based writing tool that helps students plan, write, and revise their writing (Burstein, Chodorow, & Leacock, 2004). It represents local and distributed uses and can be useful in providing a rapid assessment of students placed in remediation classes to reduce unwarranted remediation by identifying students in need of additional instructional support.

The use of AWE in rapid assessment (i.e., to collect information about students' knowledge or skills prior to designing an intervention) reveals how local adaptation can be linked to scores often associated with summative assessments in a formative way. The results of a study with undergraduate students ($N = 1,482$) at the New Jersey Institute of Technology (NJIT), a public technological research university in the United States, indicates that Criterion offered a defined writing construct congruent with established models (Klobucar et al., 2013). It achieved acceptance among students and instructors and showed no statistically significant differences between ethnic and racial groups of sufficient sample size. It also correlated at acceptable levels with other writing measures, performed in a stable fashion, and enabled instructors to identify at-risk students to increase their course success. NJIT utilized the automated system to gain real-time information about student writing performance and aligned its local efforts with trends calling for decreased remediation of qualified students in basic skill areas of English. Rather than use scores to remediate students, the institution adopted the philosophy that an admitted student was a qualified student and used the AWE technology to leverage resources to students enrolled in credit-bearing courses. This novel AWE use demonstrates how a system that was designed to be distributed can be tailored to a local setting in valid, reliable, and fair ways.

Although it would have been impossible to have read hundreds of essays twice in the first week of class to produce evidence of inter-rater reliability without exhausting the instructional staff, the AWE produced scores in real-time. Because maintaining diversity is key to the mission of the institution, the scores could be examined before use to ensure that group differential impact was not evident. Therefore, while AWE rapid assessment is depicted in the lower-right quadrant of Figure 19.5, it is important to see how summative scores can be used formatively. It is equally important to see how assessments that are designed to be distributed can, with attention paid to categories of evidence, be used locally to advance opportunities for students by removing barriers and increasing opportunity to learn.

We highlight that Burstein et al. (2018) modified the AWE scoring engine within Criterion to develop the Writing Mentor™ application. Writing Mentor is a Google Docs add-on designed to help students improve their writing by obtaining real-time, formative feedback. It provides feedback using natural-language processing approaches and linguistic resources according to a defined model of the writing construct that includes the use of sources, claims, and evidence; coherence; and knowledge of English conventions. Because this new technology provides individual feedback in relation to content, timing, and intensity, Writing Mentor may be described as a form of personalized-learning experience.

19.3.2   Reflection on the CM

The above examples illustrated how assessments can be used to meet various purposes, expand the construct being measured, and leverage additional data sources to inform varied decisions, such as course placement, remediation, and support for student learning with ongoing feedback. Kane and Mislevy (2017) also suggest augmenting information from summative tests because although they provide much-needed information about achievement, they provide limited information in terms of how test-takers perform various tasks. Therefore, summative assessments are of limited value to inform instructional planning or support student learning. They propose the use of intelligent tutoring systems or formative assessments that use a cognitive diagnosis model connected to curricular outcomes and instructional units as an optimal way to select instructional options and design curricula. Ercikan and Pellegrino (2017) also describe the possibilities associated with integrating process-model interpretations (e.g., understanding test-taking behavior such as eye movements, mouse clicks, and time on task) to draw additional inferences about student learning that are extractable from digital assessments. Currently, such information is only starting to be used for test validation, but its use in formative assessments and digital-learning environments – both lower-stakes applications – is a topic of interest in the learning analytics community. These approaches may help minimize the types of unintended consequences of using summative assessments, which may provide decontextualized information about students or may not comprehensively measure the constructs needed for college success.

19.4 Looking Forward

According to Holland (2008) in "The First Four Generations of Test Theory," the first three generations of testing involve acquiring increasingly sophisticated understandings and methods in the field of applied statistics. The fourth generation, now emerging, broadens its understandings to assessment as integrated into social systems, in many forms and roles to create and use assessments in a complex world of test-takers, teachers, policymakers, and institutions. The models we provided are our attempt to contribute to the use and score-based interpretations of assessments used for diverse purposes beyond admissions to placement, course grading, and providing formative feedback to students to support learning. We draw on: (a) a sociocognitive perspective for learning and the reconceived roles assessment can play (Mislevy, 2018); (b) a sociocultural perspective on learning and assessment in increasingly diverse populations (Oliveri, Lawless, & Mislevy, 2019); (c) a sociopolitical perspective on educational systems (Feuer, 2013); and (d) a philosophical position of assessment design and use as applied ethics (Elliot, 2016; Mislevy & Elliot, forthcoming). We used these integrative perspectives to bring out the deeply interrelated nature of forms of assessment and the consequential basis of our actions. We suggested how we might do more than design assessments for sequestered selection problems; as well, we have demonstrated how coordinated assessment practices that encompass selection, placement, and within-course guidance can be used together to optimize both students' and higher education's educational goals.

We ask how institutions and sponsors of assessments would behave differently if they used an alternative (formative assessment) paradigm in which assessments are used to inform student learning in lower stakes environments, as our proposed models suggest. It is clear that changes are already occurring in the United States. For instance, the Idaho State Board of Education (2015) began working with Compete College America, a nonprofit organization whose mission is to eliminate achievement gaps by providing an equality of opportunity for college completion. Since 2014, institutions have provided for-credit options for underprepared students in various ways, ranging from offering co-requisite models (concurrently delivered remedial instruction) to emporium models (computer-lab-delivered instruction). Idaho's example illustrates a range of responses when admissions and placement are considered as complementary processes. In some cases, however, budgets are cut to reduce remediation without equal commitment to providing instruction for students in need. And, in other cases, necessary instruction is provided without the benefit of distributed assessments, which would allow precise information on student ability to be provided to administrators and teachers.

Across these cases, we suggest that the use of the MDM would yield benefits for varied stakeholders, from students to assessment sponsors. The model highlights the need to account for consequences and fairness in the initial stages of assessment design, without forfeiting the emphasis on the logic of the interpretation and use-arguments and the evidential basis for test construction. Similarly, the CM offers value by bridging diverse types of assessments under a common goal. In the proposed expanded assessment space, measurement innovation is more likely to be realized in a way that better suits local needs by augmenting the available data-based information to enrich connections between high school and higher education institutions to better support instructional guidance.

For assessment developers, the future would be based on designing, validating, and using varied forms of assessments and providing information that could result in both selection and subsequent success. For students, the educational environment could be structured to provide a continuum of actionable pedagogies aligned to academic and workplace demands (see Burrus, Way, Bobek, Stoeffler, & O'Connor, in this volume). We also envision the possibility of eradicating the term "remedial," as new forms of assessment with rapid feedback cycles would help students know in detail which skills and what level of complexity are needed for success. Even if the proposed benefits of the models are conjecture, we believe there is reason to think that change is possible. We close by providing three innovations that may expand higher education assessments to better meet stakeholders' needs.

19.4.1 Progress in Measuring Noncognitive Skills

Currently, educational measurement has advanced in several ways that will continue to influence higher education assessments. One example is the inclusion of noncognitive skills (e.g., intrapersonal and interpersonal domains) into assessments, which would be relevant to higher education admissions (see Niessen & Meijer, in this volume) as well as workplace success (see Burrus, Way, Bobek, Stoeffler, & O'Connor, in this volume). Although the quality of current measures and their use in consequential decisions have been open to doubt, new advances in how to better assess these types of skills in lower-stakes situations continue (Kuncel, Tran, & Zhang, in this volume; Oliveri, McCaffrey, Ezzo, & Holtzman, 2017).

19.4.2 Innovation in Task Design

Another example of innovation is task design. Oliveri (2018) describes the development of assessment prototypes using scenario-based tasks of twenty-first-century (e.g., communication and collaboration) skills. The research prototype is designed formatively to assess students' ability to communicate and collaborate in workplace-relevant contexts. Because the prototype was developed to be aligned with the Occupational Network's content model (Occupational Information Network Resource Center, 2017), its tasks align with workplace activities (Oliveri & McCulla, forthcoming). The tasks also align with college curricula potentially to inform classroom instruction in support of student learning. This example illustrates the complementary relationship between formative assessment and the use of culminating tasks and summative grades that may be integrated within an IAS.

19.4.3 Technological Advancements

Technological advances also open up possibilities for assessments by using tasks that are adaptive, immersive, interactive, and customizable to students' backgrounds and capabilities, and that can be delivered in test centers, online, or integrated into learning systems. Such tasks have a potential to enhance the skills measured by distributed assessments, used locally by higher education institutions, and embedded in learning environments for shorter feedback cycles. The assessment of writing using AWE systems exemplifies these innovations, as they provide rapid feedback to students and instructors to help them identify what kinds of supports are needed. Such computer-assisted feedback allows instructors and their students to make decisions more frequently and provide learning experiences that more closely match students' needs, thus supporting retention.

Advances in data science, such as using optimization algorithms from operations research, allow institutions to choose from a range of predictor variables and specify a targeted balance across a range of desirable, and often competing, outcomes (see Zwick, in this volume). Moreover, statistical models such as Bayesian modeling may "borrow strength" across institutions to improve score-based decisions, which can enable smaller institutions to build admissions and placement models tailored to their populations and decision environments while leveraging information from empirical patterns in other institutions. The creation of shared databases across institutions may allow for improving higher education decisions by rendering innovative methodologies feasible.

19.4.4   Reflection on Beginning Again

We began this chapter with an overview of changes in the higher education environment, as to the constructs assessed and the composition of test-taker populations. In response, we offered an MDM to guide assessment design, development, and use that provides data at various levels (student, institutional, and state) to meet stakeholders' needs. We also described a CM that integrates data from assessments used for various purposes to improve uses of data from assessments in ways that support admitted students' learning. We described existing assessments that illustrate a complementary relationship across assessment uses. We also suggested that a similar design approach, combined with our evidence model, could be used to inform future assessment design and development efforts for use in informing higher education score-based decisions. We hope that our models will prove useful in the national and international assessment contexts described in this volume.

REFERENCES

Altbach, P. G., Reisberg, L., & Rumbley, L. E. (2009). *Trends in global higher education: Tracking an academic revolution. Report prepared for the UNESCO 2009 World Conference on Higher Education*. Paris: United Nations Educational, Scientific and Culture Organization. Retrieved from http://unesdoc .unesco.org/images/0018/001831/183168e.pdf.
American Educational Research Association, American Psychological Association, & National Council on Measurement in Education. (2014). *Standards for*

educational and psychological testing. Washington, DC: American Educational Research Association.

Bachman, L. F., & Palmer, A. S. (2010). *Language assessment in practice: Developing language assessments and justifying their use the real world*. Oxford: Oxford University Press.

Bennett, R. E. (2010). Cognitively based assessment of, for, and as learning: A preliminary theory of action for summative and formative assessment. *Measurement: Interdisciplinary Research and Perspectives*, 8, 70–91. https://doi.org/10.1080/15366367.2010.508686.

Bereiter, C., & Scardamalia, M. (2012). *What will it mean to be an educated person in mid-21st century?* Princeton, NJ: The Gordon Commission on the Future of Assessment in Education. Retrieved from https://gordoncommissionblog.wordpress.com/commissioned-papers/what-will-it-mean-to-be-an-educated-person-in-mid-21st-century/.

Braun, H. I., & Jones, D. H. (1984). *Use of empirical Bayes methods in the study of the validity of academic predictors of graduate school performance* (ETS RR-84-48). Princeton, NJ: Educational Testing Service. https://doi.org/10.1002/j.2330-8516.1984.tb00074.x.

Breland, H. M., Maxey, J., Gernand, R., Cumming, T., & Trapani, C. (2002). *Trends in college admission 2000: A report of a national survey of undergraduate admissions policies, practices, and procedures*. Princeton, NJ: ACT, Inc.; Association for Institutional Research; The College Board; Educational Testing Service; and National Association for College Admission Counseling. Retrieved from www.ets.org/research/policy_research_reports/publications/report/2002/cnrr.

Burstein, J., Chodorow, M., & Leacock, C. (2004). Automated essay evaluation: The Criterion Online service. *AI Magazine*, 25(3), 27–36.

Burstein, J., Elliot, N., Beigman Klebanov, B., Madnani, M., Napolitano, D., Schwartz, M., Houghton, P., & Molloy, H. (2018). Writing Mentor™: Writing progress using self-regulated writing support. *Journal of Writing Analytics*, 2, 285–313. Retrieved from https://wac.colostate.edu/docs/jwa/vol2/bursteinetal.pdf.

Chen, X. (2016). *Remedial coursetaking at U.S. public 2- and 4-year institutions: Scope, experiences, and outcomes* (NCES Report No. 2016-405). Washington, DC: National Center for Education Statistics. Retrieved from https://nces.ed.gov/pubsearch/pubsinfo.asp?pubid=2016405.

Cisco Systems Inc. (2010). Cisco packet tracer data sheet. Retrieved from www.cisco.com/c/dam/en_us/training-events/netacad/course_catalog/docs/Cisco_PacketTracer_DS.pdf.

Cleary, T. A. (1968). Test bias: Prediction of grades of Negro and White students in integrated colleges. *Journal of Educational Measurement*, 5, 115–124. https://doi.org/10.1111/j.1745-3984.1968.tb00613.x.

Coley, R. J., Goodman, M. J., & Sands, A. M. (2015). *America's skills challenge: Millennials and the future*. Princeton, NJ: Educational Testing Service. Retrieved from www.ets.org/s/research/30079/asc-millennials-and-the-future.pdf.

College Board. (n.d.). AP central. Retrieved from https://apcentral.collegeboard
.org/.

Council of Writing Program Administrators, National Council of Teachers of
English, & National Writing Project. (2011). Framework for success in
postsecondary writing. Retrieved from www.nwp.org/img/resources/frame
work_for_success.pdf.

Dorans, N. J., & Cook, L. L. (Eds.). (2016). *Fairness in educational assessment and
measurement*. New York, NY: Routledge. https://doi.org/10.4324/
9781315774527.

Elliot, N. (2016). A theory of ethics for writing assessment. *Journal of Writing
Assessment*, 9(1). Retrieved from http://journalofwritingassessment.org/art
icle.php?article=98.

Ercikan, K., & Pellegrino, J. W. (Eds.). (2017). *Validation of score meaning for the
next generation of assessments: The use of response processes*. New York, NY:
Taylor & Francis. https://doi.org/10.4324/9781315708591.

Feuer, M. (2013). Validity issues in international large-scale assessments: "Truth"
and "consequences." In M. Chatterji (Ed.). *Validity and test use: An international dialogue on educational assessment, accountability and equity* (pp.
197–216). Bingley: Emerald Group.

Frezzo, D. C., Behrens, J. T., & Mislevy, R. J. (2009). Design patterns for
learning and assessment: Facilitating the introduction of a complex
simulation-based learning environment into a community of instructors.
Journal of Science Education and Technology, 19, 105–114. https://doi.org/
10.1007/s10956-009-9192-0.

Glaser, R., & Nitko, A. (1970). *Measurement in learning and instruction*. Pittsburgh, PA: Learning Research and Development Center, University of
Pittsburgh.

Haertel, E. H., & Herman, J. L. (2005). A historical perspective on validity
arguments for accountability testing. In J. L. Herman & E. H. Haertel
(Eds.). *Uses and misuses of data for educational accountability and improvement. The 104th Yearbook of the National Society for the Study of Education,
Part II* (pp. 1–34). Malden, MA: Blackwell. https://doi.org/10.1111/j.1744-
7984.2005.00023.x.

Harackiewicz, J. M., Canning, E. A., Tibbetts, Y., Priniski, S. J., & Hyde, J. S.
(2016). Closing achievement gaps with a utility-value intervention: Disentangling race and social class. *Journal of Personality and Social Psychology*, 111,
745-765. http://dx.doi.org/10.1037/pspp0000075.

Hart Research Associates. (2010). *Raising the bar: Employers' views on college
learning in the wake of the economic downturn*. Washington, DC: Association
of American Colleges and Universities. Retrieved from www.aacu.org/sites/
default/files/files/LEAP/2009_EmployerSurvey.pdf.

Hart-Davidson, B., & Meeks, R. (forthcoming). Behavioral indicators of writing
improvement: Feedback analytics for peer learning. In D. Kelly-Riley and N.
Elliot (Eds.). *Improving outcomes: Disciplinary Writing, local assessment, and
the aim of fairness*. New York, NY: Modern Language Association.

Hesse, F., Care, E., Buder, J., Sassenberg, K., & Griffin, P. (2015). A framework for teachable collaborative problem solving skills. In P. Griffin & E. Care (Eds.). *Assessment and teaching of 21st century skills: Methods and approach.* Dordrecht: Springer.

Holland, P. W. (2008, March). The first four generations of test theory. Paper presented at the Association of Test Publishers on Innovations in Testing, Dallas, Texas.

Hussar, W. J., & Bailey, T. M. (2017). *Projections of education statistics to 2025* (NCES Report No. 2017-019). Washington, DC: U.S. Department of Education, National Center for Education Statistics. Retrieved from https://files.eric.ed.gov/fulltext/ED576296.pdf.

Idaho State Board of Education. (2015). Governing policies and procedures: Section III: postsecondary affairs, subsection S: Remedial education. Retrieved from https://boardofed.idaho.gov/board-policies-rules/board-pol icies/higher-education-affairs-section-iii/iii-s-development-and-remedial-edu cation/.

International Test Commission. (2018). ITC guidelines for the large-scale assess-ment of linguistically and culturally diverse populations. Retrieved from www.intestcom.org/files/guideline_diverse_populations.pdf.

Kane, M. T. (2006). Validation. In R. J. Brennan (Ed.). *Educational measurement* (4th ed.) (pp. 18–64). Westport, CT: Praeger.

Kane, M. T., & Mislevy, R. J. (2017). Validating score interpretation based on response processes. In K. Ercikan & J. W. Pellegrino (Eds.). *Validation of score meaning for the next generation of assessments: The use of response processes* (pp. 11–24). New York, NY: Routledge. https://doi.org/10.4324/9781315708591-2.

Kelly, P., Moores, J., & Moogan, Y. (2012). Culture shock and higher education performance: Implications for teaching. *Higher Education Quarterly*, 66, 24–46. https://doi.org/10.1111/j.1468-2273.2011.00505.x.

Klobucar, A., Elliot, N., Deess, P., Rudniy, O., & Joshi, K. (2013). Automated scoring in context: Rapid assessment for placed students. *Assessing Writing*, 18(1), 62–84. https://doi.org/10.1016/j.asw.2012.10.001.

Mislevy, R. J. (2018). *Sociocognitive foundations of educational measurement.* London: Routledge. https://doi.org/10.4324/9781315871691.

Mislevy, R. J., Almond, R. G., & Lukas, J. (2004). *A brief introduction to evidence-centered design* (CSE Technical Report No. 632). Los Angeles, CA: The National Center for Research on Evaluation, Standards, and Student Testing (CRESST), Center for Studies in Education, UCLA.

Mislevy, R. J., & Elliot, N. (forthcoming). Ethics, psychometrics, and writing assessment: A conceptual model. In J. Duffy & L. P. Agnew (Eds.). *Rewrit-ing Plato's legacy: Ethics, rhetoric, and writing studies.* Logan, UT: Utah State University Press.

Mislevy, R. J., & Haertel, G. D. (2006). Implications of evidence-centered design for educational testing. *Educational Measurement: Issues and Practice*, 25(4), 6–20. https://doi.org/10.1111/j.1745-3992.2006.00075.x.

Myford, C. M., & Mislevy, R. J. (1995). *Monitoring and improving a portfolio assessment system* (CSE Technical Report No. 402). Los Angeles, CA: The National Center for Research on Evaluation, Standards, and Student Testing (CRESST), Center for Studies in Education, UCLA.

National Research Council. 2012. *Education for life and work: Developing transferable knowledge and skills in the 21st century.* Washington, DC: The National Academies Press. https://doi.org/10.17226/13398.

Novick, M. R., & Petersen, N. S. (1976). Towards equalizing educational and employment opportunity. *Journal of Educational Measurement*, 13, 77–88. https://doi.org/10.1111/j.1745-3984.1976.tb00183.x.

The Occupational Information Network Resource Center. (2017). *O*NET 22.2 Database* [Data file and code book]. Retrieved from www.onetcenter.org/database.html.

Oliveri, M. E. (2018, April). Kitchen Design: A research prototype to assess communication at work. In O. Troitschanskaia (Chair), *Assessing student learning outcomes in higher education*. Symposium conducted at the meeting of the American Educational Research Association, New York, NY.

Oliveri, M. E., & Lawless, R. R. (2018). *The validity of inferences from locally developed assessments administered globally.* (ETS RR-18-35). Princeton, NJ: Educational Testing Service. https://doi.org/10.1002/ets2.12221.

Oliveri, M. E., Lawless, R. R., & Mislevy, R. J. (2019). Using evidence-centered design to support the development of culturally and linguistically sensitive collaborative problem-solving assessments. *International Journal of Testing*, 19(1), 1–31. https://doi: 10.1080/15305058.2018.1543308.

Oliveri, M. E., Lawless, R. R., Molloy, H. (2017). *A literature review of collaborative problem solving for college and workforce readiness.* (ETS RR-17-06; ETS GRE RR-17-03). Princeton, NJ: Educational Testing Service. https://doi.org/10.1002/ets2.12133.

Oliveri, M. E., & Markle, R. (2017). *Continuing a culture of evidence: Expanding skills in higher education* (ETS RR-17-09). Princeton, NJ: Educational Testing Service. https://onlinelibrary.wiley.com/doi/pdf/10.1002/ets2.12137.

Oliveri, M. E., McCaffrey, D., Ezzo, C., & Holtzman, S. (2017). A multilevel factor analysis of third-party evaluations of noncognitive constructs used in admissions decision-making. *Applied Measurement in Education*, 30, 297–313. http://dx.doi.org/10.1080/08957347.2017.1353989.

Oliveri, M. E., & McCulla, L. (forthcoming). *Using the occupational network database to assess and improve English language communication for the workplace* (Research Report Series). Princeton, NJ: Educational Testing Service.

Oliveri, M. E., Rutkowski, D., & Rutkowski, L. (2018). *Bridging validity and evaluation to match international large-scale assessment claims and country aims* (ETS RR-18-27). Princeton, NJ: Educational Testing Service. https://doi.org/10.1002/ets2.12214.

Oliveri, M. E. & Wendler, C. (2017, April). Enhancing the validity argument of assessments: Identifying, understanding, and mitigating unintended consequences of test use. Professional development workshop presented at American Educational Research Association, San Antonio, Texas.

O'Sullivan, B., & Weir, C. J. (2011). Test development and validation. In B. O'Sullivan (Ed.). *Language testing: Theories and practices* (pp. 13–32). Basingstoke: Palgrave Macmillan.

Pane, J. F., Steiner, E. D., Baird, M. D., Hamilton, L. S., & Pane, J. D. (2017). *Informing progress: Insights on personalized learning implementation and effects.* Santa Monica, CA: RAND Corporation. Retrieved from http://rand.org/t/ RR2042.

Riconscente, M. M., Mislevy, R. J., & Corrigan, S. (2016). Evidence-centered design. In S. Lane, M. R. Raymond, & T. M. Haladyna (Eds.). *Handbook of test development* (2nd ed.) (pp. 40–63). New York, NY: Routledge.

Shermis, M. D., & Burstein, J. (Eds.). (2013). *Handbook of automated essay evaluation: Current applications and new directions.* New York, NY: Routledge. https://doi.org/10.4324/9780203122761.

Shermis, M. D., Burstein, J., Elliot, N., Miel, S., & Foltz, P. W. (2016). Automated writing evaluation: An expanding body of knowledge. In C. A. McArthur, S. Graham, & J. Fitzgerald (Eds.). *Handbook of writing research* (2nd ed.) (pp. 395–409). New York, NY: Guilford.

Snyder, T. D., de Brey, C., & Dillow, S. A. (2019). *Digest of education statistics 2017* (NCES 2018-070). Washington, DC: National Center for Education Statistics, Institute of Education Sciences, US Department of Education. Retrieved from https://nces.ed.gov/pubsearch/pubsinfo.asp?pubid=2018070.

Toulmin, S. E. (2003). *The uses of argument.* Cambridge: Cambridge University Press. (Original work published 1958). Retrieved from https://doi.org/ 10.1017/CBO9780511840005.

Weir, C. (2005). *Language testing and validation: An evidence-based approach.* Basingstoke: Palgrave Macmillan. https://doi.org/10.1057/9780230514577.

Zwick, R. (2017). *Who gets in? Strategies for fair and effective college admissions.* Cambridge, MA: Harvard University Press. https://doi.org/10.4159/ 9780674977648.

Index